Aristotle on Human Nature

Also available from Bloomsbury:

Aristotle and the Ethics of Difference, Friendship, and Equality, by Zoli Filotas
Aristotle's Syllogism and the Creation of Modern Logic, edited by Lukas M. Verburgt and Matteo Cosci
Ethics and Time in the Philosophy of History, edited by Bennett Gilbert and Natan Elgabsi
Nietzsche's Renewal of Ancient Ethics, by Neil Durrant
Virtue Ethics and Contemporary Aristotelianism, edited by Andrius Bielskis, Eleni Leontsini, Kelvin Knight

Aristotle on Human Nature

The Animal with Logos

Edited by
Gregory Kirk and Joseph Arel

BLOOMSBURY ACADEMIC
LONDON • NEW YORK • OXFORD • NEW DELHI • SYDNEY

BLOOMSBURY ACADEMIC
Bloomsbury Publishing Plc
50 Bedford Square, London, WC1B 3DP, UK
1385 Broadway, New York, NY 10018, USA
29 Earlsfort Terrace, Dublin 2, Ireland

BLOOMSBURY, BLOOMSBURY ACADEMIC and the Diana logo are trademarks of
Bloomsbury Publishing Plc

First published in Great Britain 2023
This paperback edition published 2024

Copyright © Gregory Kirk, Joseph Arel and Contributors, 2023

Gregory Kirk and Joseph Arel have asserted their right under the Copyright, Designs and Patents Act, 1988, to be identified as Editors of this work.

For legal purposes the Acknowledgements on p. vii constitute an extension of this copyright page.

Cover image: Aristotle, 384–322 BC, Greek philosopher, youth, while studying, wood engraving, 19th century. (© INTERFOTO / Alamy Stock Photo)

All rights reserved. No part of this publication may be reproduced or transmitted in any form or by any means, electronic or mechanical, including photocopying, recording, or any information storage or retrieval system, without prior permission in writing from the publishers.

Bloomsbury Publishing Plc does not have any control over, or responsibility for, any third-party websites referred to or in this book. All internet addresses given in this book were correct at the time of going to press. The author and publisher regret any inconvenience caused if addresses have changed or sites have ceased to exist, but can accept no responsibility for any such changes.

A catalogue record for this book is available from the British Library.

A catalog record for this book is available from the Library of Congress.

Library of Congress Control Number: 2023939548.

ISBN: HB: 978-1-3503-4831-8
PB: 978-1-3503-4835-6
ePDF: 978-1-3503-4832-5
eBook: 978-1-3503-4833-2

Typeset by Deanta Global Publishing Services, Chennai, India

To find out more about our authors and books visit www.bloomsbury.com and sign up for our newsletters.

Contents

Acknowledgments	vii
List of Abbreviations of Works by Aristotle	viii

Introduction *Gregory Kirk and Joseph Arel* 1

Part I The *Logos* of *Logos*

1 Language, Logic, and Metaphysics: The Being with *Logos* and the *Logos* of Being *John Russon and Ömer Aygün* 11

Part II The *Logos* of *Phusis*

2 "For There Are Gods Here Too": Embodied Essence, Two-Footedness, and the Animal with *Logos* *Eli Diamond* 21
3 The Significance of Self-Nourishment: Aristotle's *De Anima* II.4 *Greg Recco* 39
4 Flesh as *Logos* *Rebecca Steiner Goldner* 54
5 Perception, Thought, and Error in Aristotle's *De Anima* *Whitney Howell* 68
6 "Actuality in the First Sense" and the Question of Human Nature in Aristotle *John Russon* 81

Part III The *Logos* of *Ethos*

7 Wishful Thinking in Aristotle *Ömer Aygün* 95
8 The Dissociative Power of *Logos* in Taking Account of Oneself *Gregory Kirk* 109
9 Aristotle on the Rationality of Virtue *Eve Rabinoff* 122
10 Learning How to Be at Leisure through Musical Education *Jacob Singer* 137

Part IV The *Logos* of the *Polis*

11 The Vicissitudes of *Logos*: On Nature, Character, and Time-of-Life *Robert Metcalf* 149
12 Practical *Logos* in Aristotle's Ethics, Rhetoric, and Politics *Fred Guerin* 163
13 The Movement of Political Animals *Joseph Arel* 179

| 14 | Aristotle: The Politics of Life and the Life of Politics *Walter Brogan* | 189 |
| 15 | *Logos* and the *Polis* in the *Poetics* *Patricia Fagan* | 201 |

Bibliography 211
Notes on Contributors 221
Index 223

Acknowledgments

This volume came about in part through a conference on Aristotle at Northern Arizona University in 2014. We would like to thank the Philosophy Department at NAU for their support in making it happen, and specifically the Wood Fund for providing the financial support, Julie Piering for facilitating making that funding available, and Chris Griffin and Jason Matteson for the various ways in which they supported us.

We would like to thank John Russon for his help in the process of making this volume come to be and for his years of mentorship.

Finally, we would like to thank our contributors.

Abbreviations of Works by Aristotle

Cat.	*Categories*
De Int.	*On Interpretation*
An. Pr.	*Prior Analytics*
An. Post.	*Posterior Analytics*
Phys.	*Physics*
GC	*On Generation and Corruption*
De Cael.	*On the Heavens*
Meteor.	*Meteorology*
DA	*On the Soul/De Anima*
Sens.	*On Sense and Sensibilia*
Juv.	*On Youth and Old Age*
HA	*History of Animals*
PA	*On the Parts of Animals*
MA	*On the Movement of Animals*
GA	*On the Generation of Animals*
Metaph.	*Metaphysics*
EN	*Nicomachean Ethics*
EE	*Eudemian Ethics*
Pol.	*Politics*
Rhet.	*Rhetoric*
Poet.	*Poetics*
Top.	*Topics*

Introduction

Gregory Kirk and Joseph Arel

In passages in both the *Nicomachean Ethics* and the *Politics*, Aristotle characterizes the human being as the animal with the distinctive character of having *logos*.[1] In Book I, Chapter 7, of the *Nicomachean Ethics* in particular, he arrives at this account through an analysis and identification of the distinctive function (*ergon*) of human beings. Throughout Aristotle's writings, human beings are also characterized as "political animals," "two-footed animals," the "animal that laughs," and the "animal with buttocks."[2] Aristotle has many ways of characterizing human nature. However, when he identifies human beings as animals having *logos*, he presents most precisely the kind of nature that human beings have. A human life is most properly understood by taking into consideration its characteristic function, *logos*.

But how are we to understand this interpretation of human nature properly? The ancient Greek word *logos* is rich in meaning and can be used in diverse ways. As Patricia Fagan writes (Chapter 15), "*Logos* . . . covers a great deal of ground: it is language and rationality; it is proportion and accounting for; it is story and word." If we apply this word specifically to ourselves, we see this also has diverse senses for us. *Logos* is that capacity by which we are distinguished as human beings, by which we found the laws governing political life, by which we articulate human excellence and the education through which we hope to accomplish it, and by which we can present to ourselves and each other the laws of thought through which scientific knowledge can be accomplished. There is, accordingly, no simple way to translate this conceptually rich word and its varied meaning for human beings. To understand what it means to be the animal having *logos* one must not make the mistake of thinking one could rely on merely one of its senses; rather, in order to appreciate what this word means for Aristotle, one must aim to reflect the complexity and richness of the term. It is in the spirit of testifying to such complexity, and of showing how the range of significant meanings of *logos* informs human nature—in the constitution of reason, of the body, of reality, of poetry—that this volume has been assembled.

The contributions in this volume take up the diverse senses of *logos* in its application to the human animal. Aristotle, as the reader will see, does not intend our "having *logos*" to be simply an additional feature of our otherwise animal nature. Instead, we can see *logos* in human thinking, in the organizing principles of our bodies, in our perception of the world, in our social and political life, and in our productive arts. That is, *logos* is not one feature among others but rather the feature that organizes all others, from the most "animal" to the most "spiritual." Our contributors present *logos* in the various ways in which it is made manifest, with the result that we, the readers, are given a complex account of the diversity of human nature as that which is informed by *logos*. Before outlining the structure of the volume, let us reflect briefly on the diverse manifestations of *logos*.

An initial approach to the notion that *logos* organizes and informs human nature is found in the study of our most immediate nature, and of the various attributes of our soul, as well as in the very fact that we engage in such study. As beings characterized by *logos*, we can understand the organization of our bodies, the nature of our flesh, even our perception, in terms of *logos*. On the one hand, this is to say that the actual operations of nature are articulated for us—are made comprehensible by and to us—according to *logos*. On the other hand, this is to say that we are put into contact with the natural world *through* the *logos* we share in common with the world, in the sense that we possess the capacity to receive that world as something comprehensible, proportioned and organized. We are, in this specific sense, *connected to* the world by *logos*; our grasp of the world occurs by virtue of the *logos* that we find in it.

As human beings, we are capable of inquiring into the processes of nature (*phusis*), which is to say the processes by which natural things bring forth (*phusousin*) their own growth and development in accordance with their own internal principles of motion and rest. Indeed, we are also able to inquire into these processes as they occur within ourselves. As a result of our ability to account for the transformations that natural things (including ourselves) undergo, we are able to experience the world as something comprehensible and predictable: the world "makes sense." In accounting for the motions natural to living organisms and simple bodies (i.e., nonliving things beholden to the organizing principle of the cosmos as a whole—specifically, earth, air, fire, and water), we can understand the motions of our immediate environment as operating in accordance with nature.[3] To be connected to the world by *logos* in this sense is to recognize that the growth and development, the motion, of things accord with what we know the nature of those things to be. To identify some organism's motion as "natural" in this sense is to identify that that organism will move and change in a manner in accord with its own principle. In apprehending the patterns of naturally occurring things, we experience the world as knowable.

Though *logos* connects us to the world, it is also in another of its manifestations the very thing that *disconnects* us from the world.[4] Indeed, we are disconnected from the world by our own nature. It is in Aristotle's ethical and political writings that this aspect of being the animal with *logos* is powerfully articulated. While it is the case that we, like other organisms in our world, have a principle of motion and rest within us that determines a predictable trajectory for our growth and development, the distinctive presence of *logos* within us makes it the case that we must play an active role in the full accomplishment, the excellence or virtue (*aretē*), of our natures. Put differently, other natural living organisms have the accomplishment of their virtue built into their natures; by contrast, we must actively participate in the process of striving for virtue to fully realize our nature. The forms that this takes for us include the following: first, we experience our judgments to be at odds with our habituated impulses (to indulge this or that desire for pleasure, to allow ourselves to express our anger vehemently and whenever it occurs to us, to take flight from things that threaten to cause us pain, etc.) and consequently to be compelled to call into question the goodness of those habituated impulses; second, to have our existing conceptions of truth challenged through dialectic and to be compelled to strive for more perspicuous concepts. These are the processes by which we strive for moral and intellectual virtue, respectively.[5] In both cases, our immediate intuitions, bodily and intellectual, are sites of disconnection. Let us briefly consider each in turn.

In giving shape to ourselves, to our characters, we must put into question the immediate unfolding of the current trajectory of our character; we must identify ourselves in distinction from what we might conventionally describe as our "natural inclinations" but which should more accurately be called the specific, immediate determinacies of our bodies. Our nature unfolds in such a manner that the complete accomplishment of that nature, its virtue, requires certain kinds of cultivated action not guaranteed by nature. This means that, in contrast with the natures of the other organisms that we encounter and account for, *logos* can separate us from being rooted in the immediacy of the contingent determinacies of our bodies and therefore puts us at odds with the natural world, by requiring of us that we reflect upon our actions and ask essential questions like "How should I live?" This capacity makes it possible to imagine being otherwise, to plan out a way of transforming oneself, to accomplish this transformation and equally—and crucially—to ignore essential questions or potentially to fail to accomplish such a transformation.

In contrast to moral virtue, intellectual virtue is concerned with, in Aristotle's formulation, "ways in which the soul attains the truth" (*EN* VI.3 1139b15),[6] the highest of which—wisdom (*sophia*)—is concerned with what is necessary. The subject matter of the intellectual virtue of wisdom is stable; it is our *conception* of what is true that is initially unstable and that we must strive, through learning and reasoning, to stabilize. In the domain of intellectual virtue, it is through error on our part that we find ourselves to be disconnected from the world. Over the course of living, we accumulate notions of the truth, both passively and through reflection. Throughout our experience, if our ideas are false, we ought to feel compelled to reflect further and consequently to cultivate a more accurate set of ideas about reality. The process of inquiry results, in other words, from a breakdown between our ideas and the world.

Note that in both cases—in the cultivation of moral virtue and in the cultivation of intellectual virtue—the standpoint that leads to an *improvement* of our relation to the world results from applying *logos* in a way that disconnects us from that world. We live well when *logos* puts us at odds with the nature with which we otherwise experience ourselves as connected.

This obligation that we participate actively in the full accomplishment of our nature, according to Aristotle, cannot be realized by individual human beings alone but must be accomplished within the political realm. *Logos*, as we have said, separates us from ourselves and makes our excellence a project to be completed. In the political realm, *logos* is made manifest in our practice of speaking and being spoken to, of communicating and deliberating with others regarding what is best, as a means to support and enable our flourishing.

We see that *logos*, at one and the same time, puts us into intimate contact with the natural world and places us at odds with it. In accordance with the diverse ways in which *logos* must be understood as it is applied to our nature, this volume is divided into four main parts. Part I, "The *Logos* of *Logos*," examines the fundamentally discursive nature of human beings. Part II, "The *Logos* of *Phusis*," examines nature as such as well as the nature of the soul, to understand the way in which *logos* permeates the human animal. In Part III, "The *Logos* of *Ethos*," we look to ethical life, specifically at ways in which *logos* complicates and makes possible human excellence. Finally, in Part IV, "The *Logos* of the *Polis*," we turn to the political realm, where we see the way in which *logos* allows for communication between citizens with an aim to making possible a life where *logos* is fully able to inform our nature.

In Part I, we begin with the study of *logos* itself, which is to say that which allows for the production of this volume, Aristotle's own writings, and any articulated speech of any kind. Put differently still, we examine the feature by which all study is opened and made available to us.

John Russon and Ömer Aygün begin the volume with "Language, Logic, and Metaphysics: The Being with *Logos* and the *Logos* of Being." Focusing on the relationship between human nature and the projects of logic and metaphysics, they show the relationship between Aristotle's identification of the human being as "the being with *logos*" and his discourses on logic and metaphysics as "the *logos* of being." Russon and Aygün present language as the fundamental sense of *logos* and, consequently, of logic as well. *Logos* as language allows us to give an account of things, ourselves included, and to give an account of the being of *logos*. They argue that Aristotle's logic is the account of how one gives an account, which involves abstracting what can be separated in *logos* but not in being. In this way, we can experience things in the world as such through reasoning; consequently, animals with *logos*, being those who can give an account of things, have an experience both of their individual perspective and of what is "absolute."

In Part II, "The *Logos* of *Phusis*," our study continues with an examination of the respects in which nature (*phusis*) exists as a *logos* and is comprehensible according to *logos*.

In Chapter 2, "'For There Are Gods Here Too': Embodied Essence, Two-Footedness, and the Animal with *Logos*," Eli Diamond presents Aristotle's rigorous analysis of the material parts of the bodies of living organisms. Diamond argues that Aristotle does so, not in the spirit of turning away from Platonic universal intelligibility and toward particular material things (as Aristotle is commonly characterized to be doing) but, on the contrary, in the spirit of intensification of the Platonic account of what *is* in terms of mind (*nous*) made manifest through its material potentiality.[7] Diamond argues that Aristotle finds evidence of mind in the material elements of reality which one might prima facie regard to be the most remote from intelligibility, thereby showing the operations of *logos* within the bodies themselves.

In Chapter 3, "The Significance of Self-Nourishment: Aristotle's *De Anima* II.4," Gregory Recco continues the treatment of *phusis* as testifying to *logos* by studying Aristotle's account of nourishment and the notion that the living organism exists as a ratio (*logos*). Both the living being and the nutritive faculty that maintains the life of that being are ratios, and those ratios and that soul generally are the cause of both the body's being and its maintenance.

In Chapter 4, "Flesh as *Logos*," Rebecca Steiner Goldner takes up this sense of logos as ratio and applies it to the embodied capacity to perceive which distinguishes animals

Introduction 5

from plants, specifically, to the sense of touch. Goldner explores the relationship between the *logos* of flesh and touch, through Aristotle's account of touch from *De Anima* II.11, as well as in *Parts of Animals* and *Generation of Animals*. Goldner notes that touch—along with its organ, flesh—is found to be first among the senses because it is the as-yet-undifferentiated unity of body and sense upon which the difference of body and sense depends, concluding that touch is body-as-*logos*.

In Chapter 5, "Perception, Thought, and Error in Aristotle's *De Anima*," Whitney Howell continues to develop our study of the place of *logos* in the human soul, through a comparison of the powers of perception and intellect. The very character of intellect as a power requiring active cultivation demonstrates the sense in which being an organism naturally endowed with intellect makes one in a certain sense experience oneself as alien to one's world, and further, makes one experience oneself as required by nature to strive to make oneself at home in the world. This characteristic of human nature, Howell argues, informs not just intellect but perception as well.

In Chapter 6, "'Actuality in the First Sense' and the Question of Human Nature in Aristotle," John Russon presents an analysis of Aristotle's discussion of "first actuality" (*entelecheia hē prōtē*), arguing that Aristotle's distinction between what a given substance *is* and what that substance *does* at any particular moment is evidence of the fact that a living being's first actuality is something never exhaustible and never completely present at any given moment in time. Russon goes on to show, though, that the distinctive character of human beings—that we cultivate ourselves through habit (*hexis*) or "second nature"—demonstrates that, *for human beings*, the relationship between first actuality—what we are—and "second actuality"—how we manifest what we are in particular moments of action—is in a specific respect reversed; because we have natural capacities whose realization is only to be determined through action, what we *do* has primacy in giving shape to what we *are*. This metaphysical fact about the relationship between first actuality and habituation, Russon argues, opens up the reality of what we call ethics.

In Part III, "The *Logos* of *Ethos*," and with this characteristic of our nature—that we find ourselves required to cultivate our natural capacities through habit—in mind, we turn to the practical significance of *logos*.

In Chapter 7, "Wishful Thinking in Aristotle," Ömer Aygün investigates Aristotle's account of the "wishful attitude." Beginning with remarks from *On Interpretation* 4 claiming that *eukhē* ("prayer," "vow," "curse," etc.) is a kind of *logos* that is neither true nor false, Aygün shows that *eukhē* is a kind of desire, *boulēsis* ("wish"), but a desire that has no necessary relationship to choice and therefore one which is fundamentally detached from action. As such, the "wishful attitude" implies an interpretation of the world as governed by the concept of "chance" (*tukhē*).

In Chapter 8, "The Dissociative Power of *Logos* in Taking Account of Oneself," Gregory Kirk discusses the way in which being an animal with *logos* permits human beings to relate to our actions at different registers of dissociation. Kirk argues that the ability of human beings to reflect upon their own activity provides them with two possibilities of dissociation. First, reflection provides them with the potential to liberate themselves from acting primarily in response to immediate emotional states, and therefore to respond to objects themselves, rather than to their own dispositions toward those objects. Second, reflection provides them with the ability to reflect on possible future states of character that will be generated by engaging in this or that particular action and thus committing that kind of action to habitual disposition. This ability to dissociate is something that human beings must do in order to live a life informed by moral virtue (*ēthikē aretē*) and practical wisdom (*phronēsis*).

In Chapter 9, "Aristotle on the Rationality of Virtue," Eve Rabinoff presents Aristotle's distinction between the rational and the nonrational parts of the soul in human beings, in which he explicitly claims that the seat of "the appetites and of desire in general" (*epithumētikon kai holōs orektikon*) is nonrational (though in a sense it participates in reason), while the intellect is rational. Prima facie, this suggests that the rational part is subordinate to the emotions once the emotions are properly cultivated to dispose one toward the right actions, which is to say, once moral virtues are accomplished. If this is so, it seems reason is not ultimately essential to human excellence, an assertion that contradicts Aristotle's explicit claims to the contrary. Rabinoff addresses the interpretive problem that appears to arise when Aristotle claims the virtues of character line up the correct target while the intellectual virtue of practical wisdom determines how the target is to be achieved (*EN* VI.12 1144a7-9) through a reconsideration of the relationship between rational (*logon*) and nonrational (*alogon*) parts of the soul. Rabinoff argues that rather than conceiving of virtues of character and the activity of practical wisdom as separate from each other, we should understand them as two components of one activity.

In Chapter 10, "Learning How to Be at Leisure through Musical Education," Jacob Singer provides an account of the process by which human beings develop into mature beings capable of choosing our actions freely. Singer focuses on Aristotle's distinction between three ways in which people make use of their leisure (*scholē*)—in pleasure for its own sake, in relaxation for continued virtuous activity, and in contemplation (*theōria*). Singer argues that the distinctive character of the life of contemplation is that its leisure is attentive to and conscious of the conditions under which it is made possible and valuable for its own sake. Singer argues that musical education is an essential part of shaping a person to become capable of devoting her leisure time to the high levels of satisfaction to be found in contemplation and that learning how to listen to music provides a pleasant and stimulating venue for the establishment of *logos* in the character of the youth, thereby preparing the youth for committing their leisure activity to contemplation.

In Part IV, "The *Logos* of the *Polis*," our attention shifts to *logos* in political life.

In Chapter 11, "The Vicissitudes of *Logos*: On Nature, Character, and Time-of-Life," Robert Metcalf discusses what it means to be the animal with *logos* in different times of life. Metcalf specifically looks at Martin Heidegger's study of Aristotle's *Rhetoric*, focusing on the accounts of being-in-the-world in youth and old age, to argue that on Aristotle's account, we are "having *logos*" not merely in the more familiar sense of being capable of rational thought but also in a more basic and fundamental sense of being open to discourse. This "being open to discourse" allows us to understand the human condition as one confined by what Metcalf calls the "vicissitudes of *logos*," that is, of moving from the rashness and impulsiveness of youth to the withdrawn calculations of old age. Metcalf presents Aristotle's discourse in the *Rhetoric* as attentive to the complexity and variety of the different times of life, as well as to the natural rhythms that inform what it is to be the animal with *logos*.

In Chapter 12, "Practical *Logos* in Aristotle's Ethics, Rhetoric, and Politics," Fred Guerin uses an analysis of Aristotle's *Rhetoric* to show that in human life, *logos* is enacted in the social and political domain, and that it is consequently inextricable in practice from *pathos* and *ethos*. The proper application of *logos* in this shared social and political domain is thus enabled by practical wisdom (*phronēsis*) and intellect (*nous*). Guerin claims that Aristotle identified rhetoric as an inextricable aspect of the human domain, and thus that the true orator (*rhētōr*) would likewise be the *phronimos* or the person with practical wisdom. Thus, rhetoric should not be seen as belonging only to those who use it to manipulate others according only to their own agenda. On the contrary, Guerin argues, insight into the various tools of persuasion would belong to those who have insight into the ways of the human soul, coupled with a sense of what is good.

In Chapter 13, "The Movement of Political Animals," Joseph Arel examines the movement of animals with *logos*, focusing primarily on *Movement of Animals* and *On the Soul*. Arel argues that to find the ultimate origin of movement for animals with *logos*, one must look to the *polis*. This connection is found through Aristotle's "practical syllogism," wherein movement follows the "logic" of major and minor premises, and conclusion. The major premise of this "practical" syllogism is the general claim of what is good, and, consequently, organizes what is to be pursued and how we are to conceive things in light of our aims. For the animal with *logos*, this "major premise" is something shaped through law, education, and rhetoric. Thus, human movements ultimately refer to the polis. Aristotle's syllogistic style of explanation with respect to movement shows that our movements are necessarily evidence that we have chosen a view of what is good and, further, are indications of what this view is.

In Chapter 14, "Aristotle: The Politics of Life and the Life of Politics," Walter Brogan performs a careful study of Book One of Aristotle's *Politics*. There, Aristotle distinguishes between the purpose of the family and the small village, which is to provide the necessities for life, and the purpose of the *polis*—the "city" or "state"— which is to provide the necessities for the good life. Brogan analyzes the ambiguous place *within* the *polis* for those aspects of life limited to concern with its maintenance, particularly insofar as these are provided by those who are—to varying degrees— typically excluded from full participation in the good life available to the animal with *logos*, such as slaves, moneymakers, and women. Brogan finds two important tensions in Aristotle's *Politics*: first, within the exclusion or partial exclusion from political life of those who make political life possible, and second, in the fact that, despite these exclusions, Aristotle makes fundamental to the properly functioning *polis* that its members rule and are ruled in turn.

In Chapter 15, "*Logos* and the *Polis* in the *Poetics*," Patricia Fagan provides an account of one of the most cultivated spheres of *logos*, namely, tragic poetry. Fagan presents the historical origins of tragedy and its profound connection to the political developments that led Athens away from the traditional primacy of the family—and particularly the transfer of political power within powerful families—toward the primacy of citizens and thus toward the democratic reforms of Cleisthenes *c*. 508/7 BC. Fagan argues that the political character of the central themes of Aristotle's analysis of tragedy in the *Poetics*, namely, *mimēsis*, or reenactment, and *katharsis*, or purging, serve essentially political ends. Fagan places high importance on the fact that people experience the emotional purification of primordial human crimes through their ritualization and, crucially, ritualization *among fellow community members*. Thus, in participating in the ritual experience of tragedy as a political community, the Athenians would have a strengthened sense of themselves *as* Athenians and would have a sense of their humanity upheld and supported by their fellows.

Together, the chapters provide a rich and detailed account of ways in which the human being is a being that must be understood from the standpoint of *logos*, one that produces a synoptic vision of the animal with *logos* drawing from diverse texts of Aristotle and using diverse approaches to analysis of his corpus. Aristotle's philosophical works are comprehensive in scope, and his definition of the human being finds a wide variety of articulations and resonances throughout these works. In moving from the basic motion of the human body through the increasingly complex layers of soul to the interpersonal and political relations between human beings, and, ultimately, to reflection on the highest forms of cultural activity, we see in what diverse respects human nature is informed by having *logos*.

Notes

1 Note that Aristotle never explicitly defines human beings as "the animal with *logos*"; however, this is the relevant meaning of several passages in the corpus. Versions of this claim occur at *Politics* (*Pol.*) I.2 1253a10 "*logon de monon anthropos echei tōn zōiōn*," *Pol.* VII.13 1332b4 "*anthropos de kai monon gar echei logon*," and *Nicomachean Ethics* (*EN*) I.7 1098a3 "*leipetai dē praktikē tis tou logon echontos*." It is in the latter that this characterization is most richly developed.
2 See *Pol.* I.2 1253a2, *Posterior Analytics* (*An. Post.*) I.14 79a28, *Parts of Animals* (*PA*) III.10 673a5, and *History of Animals* (*HA*) II.1 499b1, respectively.
3 At *Physics* (*Phys.*) II.1, Aristotle defines the nature of an organism as an internal principle of motion and rest. For Aristotle's account of the natural motion of the simple bodies, see *On the Heavens* II.3.
4 Note that we are here referring to the way *logos* functions in distinctively human nature. Different but analogous relationships of connection and disconnection could be discerned in the functioning of *logos* at the animal level and the vegetal level.
5 Aristotle makes the relevant distinction between the two at *EN* VI.2 1139a21-31.
6 Translation by Bartlett and Collins (Chicago: University of Chicago Press, 2011).
7 See Plato, *Phaedo* 97b-102a.

Part I

The *Logos* of *Logos*

1

Language, Logic, and Metaphysics

The Being with *Logos* and the *Logos* of Being

John Russon and Ömer Aygün

Introduction

Using his standard method of identifying genus and specific difference, Aristotle defines the human being as "the animal having *logos*."[1] We humans are a naturally occurring species of sensing, desiring, locally moving organisms (i.e., a member of the genus "animal"), but we are uniquely differentiated from all other animals by "*logos*." Though the meaning of *logos* in this context is rich and complex, what is ultimately most definitive of it is its relationship to our ability to "make sense" of reality, an ability dependent upon our constitutive involvements in the domains of logic and metaphysics. Our goal here is to unpack this basic relationship between "the being with *logos*," which we uniquely are, and "the *logos* of being," to which we uniquely have access. We will do this in three steps. First, we will outline Aristotle's basic philosophical method and its relationship to this definition of the human being. Second, we will outline the basic projects of logic and metaphysics as they relate to the human being thus defined. Third and finally, we will reflect on the distinctive nature of our human experience and its constitutive relationship to the basic principles of logic and metaphysics.

I. Aristotle's Method and Human Nature

We typically refer to Aristotle as a "philosopher," and surely this is correct. At the same time, however, it is important to remember that what we nowadays typically associate with the name "philosopher"—middle-class university professors writing journal articles—bears little resemblance to Aristotle and his practice. Aristotle's social position already distinguishes him quite dramatically from this contemporary picture, but he is even more importantly different in his basic philosophical practice. More than anything else, Aristotle is an observational biologist. He does, of course, have comprehensive writings on the whole of the physical universe, on the full range of human affairs, and especially on the distinctively "philosophical" topic of "being as such"—"metaphysics"—but the root of all of these studies is found in his fundamental empiricist naturalism: his commitment to the ontological primacy of living organisms and the epistemological primacy of describing them.[2]

Aristotle's understanding of the nature of a living being is of a piece with his observational method: when one observes living organisms, they reveal their nature. Natural beings just are their processes of living, and, for that reason, in existing, they precisely put their reality on display.[3] When one, for example, spends time with horses or with dogs, one learns what horses or dogs are like, which means one comes to grasp their characteristic patterns of behavior and development, their needs, and their pleasures. And, just as one can learn the nature of a horse through caringly observing it, so can one learn the nature of human beings through the careful and intelligent observation of their behavior.

To *know* what one encounters, though, it is not enough that one have a unity of experiential familiarity (*empeiria*) with the life-form in question:[4] beyond this practical familiarity, which is typically rooted in instrumental concerns of pleasure and pain, one must intelligently reflect upon those familiar appearances to grasp theoretically the principle of that unity.[5] Across the diversity of many specific life-forms, for example, one can recognize that one is encountering so many variant forms of the unitary process of self-nutrition, growth, and reproduction, the principle of that distinct domain of organisms we call "plants"; or, again, across the diversity of many specific life-forms, one can recognize that one is encountering so many variant forms of the unitary process of self-locomotive, desiring perception, the principle of that distinct domain of organisms we call "animals." Aristotle's method thus requires both the empirical familiarity that gives one the basic "phenomenon" to be understood and the intellectual insight that allows one to recognize the unity of that phenomenon.[6]

It is this method that gives rise to Aristotle's definition of the human being. We are, of course, broadly familiar with the distinctive behaviors of human beings: beyond our immediate practical perspective, which leads us to choose others as allies or enemies, we can more disinterestedly notice that, in addition to the self-nutrifying that we share with plants and animals and the desiring, perception, and locomotion that we share with the rest of the animal world, we also make political committees, write tragedies, cultivate our characters, argue, investigate the world scientifically, and so on. When Aristotle reflects intelligently upon the unity of these observable phenomena of human being, he identifies the human as a species of animal but an animal characterized by the distinctive (and unique) ability to *take account* of things—hence his (descriptive) definition of the human being as "the animal having *logos*."

Our "taking account" happens at every level of our behavior, from the meaningful way we interrogate the world with our touch, seeing, and hearing, through the way we regulate our emotional responses in our practical engagement with our daily affairs, to the way we grapple with the understanding of causes in our scientific investigations and our persuasive speaking.[7] In all of these activities, the basic principles of "taking account" are operative, and the recognition of these basic principles is itself a distinctive form of "taking account." Aristotle's "logical" writings (the so-called organon) and his writings about being as such (the so-called metaphysics) are this taking-account of "taking-account," this *logos* of *logos*.[8]

Now, as Hans-Georg Gadamer notes, at a basic level, to say that we have *logos* is to say that we are language users and, when we think of "taking account," we are, more than anything else, thinking of *speaking*.⁹ Aristotle's definition of the human being as "the animal having *logos*" would thus more properly be translated as "the animal with language" or "the animal who speaks" than as the traditional "rational animal."¹⁰ When we investigate "logic" in the Aristotelian sense, we are thus at root investigating the phenomenon of speaking, and "rationality" is the "logic," so to speak, of language, a rationality that exists in and as discourse. Aristotle's study of "rationality," then, is first and foremost an observation of our distinctive practice of speaking.

II. Logic and Metaphysics

Aristotle observes what goes on when we engage with the world and with each other in our *logos*-capacity. First, our speaking, he notices, is not about the sounds we make but about the meanings we communicate.¹¹ Other animals communicate too, of course, but Aristotle notices that our communication goes qualitatively beyond what other species do:¹² beyond the communication of practical imperatives, for example, we adopt the theoretically absolute perspective that affirms fact (affirmations "*hoti*") and cause (affirmations "*dioti*"), and we affirm *with necessity*.¹³ Finally, he further notices that within this meaningful exchange, sometimes our attempt to take account works and sometimes it does not. His logical writings give an account of the principles of this "working or not."

Aristotle's logical works are not "making rules" for how we should think. Rather, in making articulate the terms of this "working or not" of our affirming, these works report on what people do, namely, we put ideas together and affirm the results of so doing, results with which others find themselves compelled to agree (or not). Aristotle gives an account, in short, of what is involved in adequately giving an account. His logic, then, is giving a description of fact, but it is the fact of how recognizable and specifiable norms are operative in our meaningful discourse. In this account of the normativity in the context of meaning, his logic is thus analogous to a work of geography in the sense that he is giving expression to a determinate structure, the parameters of which we find imposed upon us rather than inventing, like those of a newly discovered land.

There are two observations within this study of our meaningful discourse—the phenomenon that is simultaneously and inseparably our thinking and our speaking—that are particularly relevant to our understanding of "first philosophy," that is, to our understanding of the ultimate principles of our "accounting." The first pertains to Aristotle's account of how our grasp of the relationships between things in the world is rendered in meaningful discourse or his "logic." The second pertains to Aristotle's study of our ability to ask about the ultimate causes—the ultimate nature of reality that accounts for things being the way that they are—or his "metaphysics."

First, our "rationality" is fundamentally an answering to the nature of things, and, inasmuch as things naturally are individual members of species, our conceptuality primarily depends upon the relation of species and genus (and thus the notion of "subsumption"). Our rationality first and foremost is a rendering manifest of the sense ("*logos*") immanent in the things themselves. This sense is rendered manifest first in the assertions (the *apophanseis* or "showings forth") that express in the relation of subject (*hupokeimenon*) and predicate (*katēgoroumenon*), the relations of ontological dependence between the species and the genus it belongs to, or the functional property and the organism it belongs to. This rationality is completed in the syllogisms that spontaneously display the compelling bonds immanent to this sense of things.[14] It is because of the nature of "rationality" as "the sense of things" that our "logic" must take the form that it does—the form of the subsumption of a particular (*to kath'hekaston*) under a universal (*to katholou*)—and this "geography" of the self-occurring world of reality (*phusis*) is a logic of genus and species.[15]

The reason we are able to engage in "logic"—in reasoning—is that in dealing with things, we are able to "abstract," that is, we are able to recognize what can be separated "in *logos*" even if it cannot be separated in being. Confronted with a single natural individual, for example, we can differentiate its unique individuality from its species, its properties, its substance, and so on, though it is only the living individual that is capable of independent existence.[16] To say that we are animals with *logos* is precisely to say that we can relate to things "*qua*," that is, we can distinguish (onto)logical aspects within things. This ability to "abstract" and deal with things "*qua*" also means that we can deal with those aspects of things "as such," that is, we can, for example, "abstract" the quantity of things (when we count them), and we can also investigate quantity as such (in the study of mathematics).[17] In particular, this ability to "abstract"—to grasp things *qua*—and to approach the *qua* not just in relation to its actual instantiations but absolutely or "as such" allows us to ask about "is"—the notion implicitly or explicitly operative in all of our discourse—and, in particular, to ask about "is" as such.[18] This ability to ask about "being *qua* being" opens up for us the domain of metaphysics which, like the organon, reveals to us a new kind of "geography."

When Aristotle undertakes his study of being as such, his key observation is that *being is not a genus*, that is, though it is a kind of "universal" in relationship to all the particular instances of being, it does not function normally according to the kinds of relations we have come to expect from our other analysis of logic: the relationship of being to beings is not one of subsumption.[19] There are two fundamental reasons for this inability to conceptualize being according to the normal categories of "logic." The first, negative reason why "being" cannot be comprehended by the logic of genus and specific difference is that each of "genus," "species," and "difference" must, in some sense, *be*; hence, being must already be presupposed in those terms—it is the more primitive term that will ultimately explain those terms, not they that will supply the more fundamental meaning to make sense of being.[20] The second, positive reason why "being" cannot relate to "beings" as their genus is that inasmuch as "being" names the very *reality* of each and every one of those beings, they each *enact* being in their own unique way: they *are* what being *is*. "Being" is thus not the univocal name for something common shared by all beings but is rather that which is uniquely realized in and as those beings, such that what it is "to be" is something said of all beings only analogically.[21] "Actuality," "potentiality," "substance," "quantity," "accident," and so on are not simply the diversely different "species" of being in a subsumptive sense, like dogs and whales are different "species" of mammalians. These aspects of being are rather the irreducibly unique forms in which being is articulated: they are *how* being is in fact *realized*. Being is not one "kind" of thing actualized diversely in different instances, so a science of being is different from other sciences: it is, again, a singular kind of "geography," responding to the singular complexity of the forms of being.

III. *Nous* and Intellectual Virtue

What is ultimately most distinctive of the "animal with *logos*" is that we are, indeed, a "logical" being and, indeed, a "philosophical" being, that is, we are that animal that is oriented in its being to taking account of the ultimate principles of meaning and the ultimate forms of being.[22] "All human beings," Aristotle writes at the beginning of the *Metaphysics*, "by nature strive toward knowing":[23] it is precisely definitive of our nature—our "species"—that we ascertain the nature of reality as such.

If we turn to our experience, we can describe this discovery of the "logical" parameters of being. These—being as such, the relation of genus and species, number, the principle of noncontradiction—are the principles (*archai*) presupposed in but not exhausted by the existence of any thing, and we have the experience that within the domains of both "logic" and "metaphysics," these realities "as such" impress themselves upon us with the force of necessity:[24] these *archai* impress themselves upon us in a way that we are not capable of denying because they are constitutive of the very acts of denying, affirming, and demonstrating to begin with. Indeed, in experiencing any such reality "as such," we experience a force that exceeds the particular experiences within which we encounter it and we experience a force that governs, rather than being governed by, the finite things of our experience.[25] It is characteristic and, indeed, precisely definitive of our (human) experience that we apprehend a sense that exceeds our perspective, both subjectively (in the sense that we can make an affirmation that has compelling force beyond the limits of our individual experience) and objectively (in the sense that we can make an affirmation that goes beyond the limits of the specific objects through which we encountered this sense). Aristotle describes this miraculous process:

> We conclude that these states of knowledge are neither innate in a determinate form, nor developed from higher states of knowledge, but from sense-perception. It is like a rout in battle stopped by first one man making a stand and then another, until the *archē* has been restored. The soul is so constituted as to be capable of this process.[26]

The most striking thing, then, about our reality as "the animal with *logos*" is that our experience, though necessarily limited in the sense that our experience will always be both the perspective of an individual body and the perspective of a particular species, can also be absolute.

And, again, inasmuch as these realities exceed our finite experience, we precisely *discover* them, that is, our apprehension of the *archai* is precisely something we *receive* as a compelling intuition. This is what Aristotle calls "*noēsis*" (insight), the activity of *nous* (mind).²⁷ The mind is not a faculty or function we *possess*; it is, rather, a reality to which we *find ourselves* open *by nature*. We are answerable to its summons and we receive its gift, but it is never "ours" in the sense that intellectual apprehension is never our own *doing*.²⁸

This, then, is the experience of mind: we *find ourselves* subject to the apprehension of compelling realities "as such," an apprehension that illuminates the fundamental nature of the world of which we are perceptually aware. Subsequent to this event of illumination, we can think (*dianoein, logizesthai*) *with* the insights we have received, an ability we cultivate and refine in the "intellectual virtues" of *technē, epistēmē*, or *phronēsis*.²⁹ We thus do experience an activity of thinking, but this discursive practice of "making sense"—precisely of "taking account"—is subsequent, both logically and temporally, to the passive experience of insight in which we find ourselves to be the recipients of the illuminative grasp of being. Indeed, it is the revelation of the "*logos*" of being that precisely enables us to be the being "with *logos*," that is, it is by virtue of our constitutive openness to mind that we are the being who can take account.

Conclusion

The relationship between human nature on the one hand and the projects of logic and metaphysics on the other is by no means an accidental one. On the contrary, our identity as "the being with *logos*" precisely requires that we be constitutively oriented toward the *logos* of being, and it is precisely the revelation of the *logos* of being that allows us to be the being with *logos*.

Notes

1 *Politics*, Book I, Chapter 2, 1253a9-10; the meaning of this definition is most fully explored in *Nicomachean Ethics* Book I, Chapter 7. Aristotle does not explicitly present this as a definition of the human and, indeed, in other contexts he commonly (critically) considers "two-footed animal" as a definition; see, for example, *Categories* 5 3a9-15, *Posterior Analytics* I.14 79a29 and II.4 91a28, *Physics* I.3 186b25-30, and *Metaphysics* VII (Z).12 1037b12. On the sense in which "animal having *logos*" is an appropriate definition of the human, see Christian Kietzmann, "Aristotle on the Definition of What It Is to Be Human," in *Aristotle's Anthropology*, ed. Keil and Kreft (Cambridge: Cambridge University Press, 2019), 25–43, who emphasizes the difference between defining the human in natural and theological contexts, and Eli Diamond, "'For There Are Gods Here Too': Embodied Essence, Two-Footedness, and the Animal with *Logos*," Chapter 2 of this volume, who emphasizes the insufficiency of bodily determinations to express the distinctive human function (*ergon*).

2 For Aristotle's most powerful methodological statement, see *Physics* II.1 193a3-4: "What nature is has been stated. That nature is it would be absurd to try to prove." For a discussion, compare Michael Frede, "Aristotle's Rationalism," in *Rationality in Greek Thought*, ed. Frede and Striker (Oxford: Oxford University Press, 1996), and Robert Bolton, "Scepticisme et véracité dans le *De Anima* et *La Métaphysique* d'Aristote," in

Corps et âme: Sur le De Anima d'Aristote: Sur le De Anima d'Aristote, ed. Romeyer-Dherbey and Viano (VRIN, 1996); for the primacy of living beings and especially animals, see James G. Lennox, "Aristotle's Biology and Aristotle's Philosophy," in *A Companion to Ancient Philosophy*, ed. Gill and Pellegrin (Blackwell Publishing, 2006).

3 This point is made by Francis Sparshott, *Taking Life Seriously: A Study of the Arguments of the Nicomachean Ethics* (Toronto: University of Toronto Press, 1996), p. 45.

4 Compare Aristotle, *De Anima* I.1 402b22-25: "When we are able to give an account conformable to experience [*kata tēn phantasian*] . . . we will have the most beautiful things to say [*hexomen legein kallista*]." For a discussion of Aristotle's method in *De Anima*, see John Russon, "Self-Consciousness and the Tradition in Aristotle's Psychology," *Laval Théologique et Philosophique* 52, no. 5 (1996): 777–803.

5 *Metaphysics* I (A).1.

6 In *De Caelo* I.3 and *Metaphysics* XII (Λ).8, Aristotle emphasizes that knowledge must "account for the what appears" (*apodōsein ta phainomena*); see also *Metaphysics* I (A).5 986b31 on being "forced to follow the phenomena." Compare *Topics* I.1-2 on the need for dialectic to move from *endoxa* to *archai*. These texts are discussed in Russon, "To Account for the Appearances: Phenomenology and Existential Change in Aristotle and Plato," *Journal of the British Society for Phenomenology* 52 (2021): 155–68.

7 For a comprehensive study of the use of the term "*logos*" in Aristotle's philosophy, see Ömer Aygün, *The Middle Included: Logos in Aristotle's Philosophy* (Evanston, IL: Northwestern University Press, 2017).

8 The names "organon" and "metaphysics" are both later interpretations of Aristotle's writings and not his own designations. The grouping together of the so-called logical works as the "organon" or "instrument" reflects an interpretive decision to differentiate logic as the development of a preparatory skill for study rather than as an integral part of philosophical study. The grouping together of various treatises as the "metaphysics" reflects an interpretive decision to identify the study of being as such as a separate study from the study of *phusis*. It is important to recognize that while there are grounds within Aristotle's writings to justify these interpretations, other interpretations of how these works should be organized are also possible.

9 On this point, see Hans-Georg Gadamer, "Man and Language," in *Philosophical Hermeneutics*, trans. Linge (Berkeley, CA: University of California Press, 1976).

10 In the context of an analysis that otherwise emphasizes the richness of the distinctively human forms of meaning, Eve Rabinoff, in "Aristotle on the Rationality of Virtue," Chapter 9 of this volume, translates *logos* as "reason," a translation that seems to us to inappropriately limit the sense of the Greek term; this criticism notwithstanding, our analysis here of our distinctive capacity to engage with "the *logos* of being" shows the sense in which the translation as *logos* as "reason" can be appropriate.

11 *On Interpretation* I.1-2.

12 Aristotle clearly recognizes that many other animals indeed communicate in a meaningful way; see *Politics* I.2 and *On the Soul* II.8, especially the definition of voice at 420b5-22. See also Ömer Aygün, "Wishful Thinking in Aristotle," 95–8. What specifies human communication is not just that it is meaningful but that it involves meaningful units articulated out of meaningless ones, that it is both meaningful *and* conventional.

13 *Posterior Analytics* I.4, I.13.

14 Aristotle defines what he means by syllogism: "A syllogism is speech [*logos*] in which, certain things having been posited, something different from those posited results

of necessity [*ex anagkēs sumbainein*] because of their being so" (*Prior Analytics* 1.2 24b18-20). That the syllogism is not simply a subjective structure of reasoning but is in fact the structure of sense within things is especially made clear through Aristotle's analysis of the syllogistic structure of action. See especially *De Motu Animalium* (*MA*), ch. 7; for discussion, see Martha Nussbaum, "Essay 4," in *Aristotle's De Motu Animalium* (Princeton, NJ: Princeton University Press, 1978), and Brad Inwood, *Ethics and Human Action in Early Stoicism* (Clarendon Press, 1995), Chapter 1.
15 These two concepts are indispensable since they are called for in any task of description and even of speaking. But we should refrain from imagining Aristotle's metaphysics as an attempt to set up a Porphyrean Tree, and his biology as a taxonomy, comparable to Linnaeus', mapping out all the intricacies of the animal kingdom. On the contrary, Aristotle uses "genus" and "species" not as a fixed nomenclature but as functional concepts that enable and support his descriptions on all levels of generality, in all categories, and for all animals.
16 *Categories*, ch. 5, 2a11-14.
17 Compare Plato, *Philebus* 56d; see also *Theaetetus* 195e-196a, and *Republic* VII.525c. On the theme of the "as such" (*auto kath'hauto*) in general, see Plato, *Phaedo* 75d, 78d. Like Diamond, "For There Are Gods Here Too," we are generally critical of the simplistic and oppositional ways in which Plato's and Aristotle's philosophies are commonly portrayed.
18 Compare Plato, *Phaedo* 78d, and *Theaetetus* 185a.
19 See *Metaphysics* III (B).3, XI (K).1, especially 1059b31, and *Posterior Analytics* II.7 92b14. See also Thomas Aquinas, *Summa Contra Gentiles*, trans. Pegis as *On the Truth of the Catholic Faith* (Garden City, NY: Doubleday, 1955), 127, Book I, Chapter 25, paragraph 6: "there can be nothing that can be outside that which is understood by being."
20 See Enrico Berti, "Multiplicity and Unity of Being in Aristotle," *Proceedings of the Aristotelian Society New Series* 101 (2001).
21 For a comprehensive and masterful discussion of the "concrete" character of Aristotle's notion of "being," see Aryeh Kosman, *The Activity of Being: An Essay on Aristotle's Ontology* (Cambridge, MA: Harvard University Press, 2013).
22 See Rabinoff, "Aristotle on the Rationality of Virtue," for the importance of this idea for the interpretation of Aristotle's *Nicomachean Ethics*.
23 *Metaphysics* I (A).1, 980a21.
24 Compare especially Plato, *Theaetetus* 185a-b, and the related list in *Sophist* 237c-d.
25 For the exceeding of our particular perspective, see *On the Soul*, Chapter 4, and the argument that *nous* cannot have a bodily organ. For the exceeding of the objects of our experience, compare Socrates' argument about equality in the *Phaedo* 74a-75b. Compare Aristotle's remark at *Metaphysics* I (A).3, 984a18-19 and 984b9-10, that thinkers are forced by the fact itself (*auto to pragma*) or by truth itself (*hup' autēs tēs alētheias*).
26 *Posterior Analytics* II.19 100a9-13.
27 *Posterior Analytics* II.19 100b5-16. For an interpretation of this text, see John Russon, "Aristotle's Animative Epistemology," *Idealistic Studies* 25, no. 3 (1995). See also Eli Diamond, *Mortal Imitations of Divine Life: The Nature of the Soul in Aristotle's De Anima* (Evanston, IL: Northwestern University Press, 2015), Chapter 4.
28 *On the Soul* III.5.
29 For Aristotle's analysis of the "virtues of thinking" (*hai aretai dianoētikai*), see *Nicomachean Ethics* Book VI.

Part II

The *Logos* of *Phusis*

2

"For There Are Gods Here Too"

Embodied Essence, Two-Footedness, and the Animal with *Logos*[1]

Eli Diamond

Introduction

One of the greatest impediments to a proper understanding of either Platonic or Aristotelian thought is the popular opposition of Plato the idealist, polemically uninterested in sensation, embodiment, and particularity, and Aristotle the empiricist, endlessly devoted to these aspects of existence. While we are growing increasingly aware of how thinking of Plato as dividing reality into two separate worlds and rejecting the sensible in favor of the intelligible is a monumental distortion of his thought, I think we are less sensitive to the ways in which understanding Aristotle as a fierce opponent of Platonic thought who offers a radically opposed philosophy founded on distinct premises hides from view the true character of Aristotelian philosophy. Like any picture that holds on so tenaciously to our philosophical imagination, the oppositional picture of Platonic and Aristotelian philosophy must have a grain of truth that makes it so difficult to break its spell on us. Yet I think it is when we are able to see how Aristotle is at every point revising Plato's principles not in order to reject the Platonic philosophical project but rather in order to realize it more completely that a true picture of Aristotle's own grand project can emerge.[2]

In this chapter, I want to reflect on Aristotle's identification of the human being as the animal having *logos* by comparing that formulation with the far more prevalent definitory formula for human being that Aristotle uses throughout his writings, two-footed animal.[3] The difference I want to examine here is between defining a being through reference to a more formal, psychological feature, such as having *logos*, and defining that same being with reference to something distinctive about the structure of its body parts, such as having two feet.

In order to think about each of these approaches to expressing the nature of the human being and what the connection between these two orders of explanation might be, I shall consider one of the biological treatises that can appear most opposed to the spirit of Platonic philosophy, his *Parts of Animals*. The introductory book of Aristotle's treatise acknowledges that, at least on the surface, there is something very different going on in this new inquiry into animal bodies and their parts than what was typically happening within the walls of the Academy. Aristotle is at pains in these passages to show his Platonically educated audience that when they think in detail about all the animal bodies there are to be studied, they are not turning away from the proper work of philosophy as it has been defined by their teacher. Plato understands the proper object of philosophical thinking to be form, or essence, the unchanging cause of the changing. Toward the end of the first chapter of his introduction to the work, by way of explaining the materialist deficiency of the Pre-Socratic approach of the *phusikoi* in their explanation for why bodies are the way they are, Aristotle writes: "the reason why our predecessors failed to hit on this method of treatment was, that they were not in possession of the notion of essence (*to ti ēn einai*), nor of any definition of substance (*ousia*)" (*Parts of Animals* I.1 642a24-27).[4] It is always worth remembering while Aristotle's term for essence, *to ti ēn einai*, is a neologism, the word usually translated substance, *ousia*, is not at all new in philosophical discussion; in fact, it is a standard word Plato uses for essence. What Aristotle is introducing here is not some new concept but rather a new way of understanding essence. And while Plato is not mentioned in his criticism—since, after all, if Plato has no concern for *ousia*, who does?—I nonetheless want to argue that the difference between Plato's approach to the study of the sensible world and Aristotle's philosophical approach to understanding animal bodies and their articulation into parts does not arise out of a turning away from intelligible essence toward sensible bodies but rather out of a new understanding of the relation of essence to matter, exemplified by the Aristotelian interpretation of *ousia*. Through a comparison between the *Parts of Animals* and a short passage from Plato's *Parmenides* that I think Aristotle must have had on his desk as he wrote his work, I want to indicate the extent to which Aristotle's empiricism and his endless interest in every last detail about the natural world and the animal bodies in it does not involve a turn away from Platonic idealism, but rather an *intensification* of this idealism, one which seeks to realize the deepest ambitions of Plato's thinking, a realization made possible by Aristotle's novel grasp of how essence or form expresses itself in and through the body. Then, after considering the Platonic roots of Aristotle's interest in studying the details of the embodiment of the living being, I want to think about what light Aristotle's new understanding of form and matter might shed on the question of the essence of the human animal and the sense in which nearly everything[5] distinctive about the human being in its embodiment can be brought back to its formally defining feature of possessing *logos*. I will look to some key passages about the human being in *Parts of Animals* in order to reveal the connection between these two determinations of the human—the *zōion echon logon* and the *zōion dipoun*.

I. Platonic Philosophy, *Parmenides*, and *Parts of Animals*

Consider the wonderfully telling and pertinent exchange between Parmenides and the young Socrates, just as Parmenides is about to mercilessly pick apart participation as an adequate way of thinking about the connection between form and its sensible appearances (*Parmenides* 130b-e). Parmenides innocuously asks Socrates—What kinds of things have forms? His answer and Parmenides' reply serve as an illuminating connection between Platonic thinking and Aristotle's project in *Parts of Animals*. Socrates initially replies positively to the fact that extremely universal, logical forms exist separately unambiguously: likeness and unlikeness, for example. The same can be said for ethical and aesthetic absolutes, such as justice, beauty, goodness—the very subjects of most of our Platonic dialogues. But Socrates hesitates as we move into the natural world of sensible individuals. Parmenides asks:

> "What about the form of human being, separate from us and all those like us? Is there a form itself of human being, or fire, or water?"
>
> Socrates said, "Parmenides, I've often found myself in doubt whether I should talk about those in the same way as the others or differently." (Plato, *Parmenides* 130c1-4)[6]

We are here moving away from universals more deeply into particulars. Is there a form of human that exists separately from humans? Or simply the individual soul as the formal aspect of the human being? Is there a form of earth that sensible earth only imperfectly realizes? The particularity and materiality of what it is to be each of these makes the separation at the very least problematic. Parmenides goes on:

> And what about these Socrates? Things that might seem absurd, like *hair and mud and dirt*, or anything else totally undignified and worthless? Are you doubtful whether or not you should say that a form is separate for each of these too, which in turn is other than anything we touch with our hands?
>
> "Not at all," Socrates answered. "On the contrary, these things are in fact just what we see. Surely it's too outlandish to think there is a form for them. Not that the thought that the same thing might hold in all cases hasn't troubled me from time to time. Then, when I get bogged down in that, I hurry away, afraid that I may fall into some pit of nonsense and come to harm; but when I arrive back in the vicinity of the things we agreed a moment ago have forms, I linger and occupy myself with them." (*Parmenides* 130d-e, emphasis added)

On the one hand, Socrates here feels the demand that there should be a unified explanation of all being, but the sheer particularity of these parts of sensible wholes, themselves simply mixtures of more primary elements, leads him to think that they are what they are independent of the causal activity of form. There is eventually, on this view, a sphere of independent brute material particularity which, through its independence from the causal activity of forms, falls below the interest of philosophy. There is the causal power of form and then there is just stuff that is what it is. As endless particularity, parts of parts, mixtures of elements, these things are repugnant to his philosophical sensibilities. Plato makes sure that this attitude is corrected by the elder Parmenides.

> "That's because you are still young, Socrates," said Parmenides, "and philosophy has not gripped you as, in my opinion, it will in the future, once you begin to

consider none of the cases beneath your notice. Now, though, you still care about what people think, because of your youth." (*Parmenides* 130e)

Philosophy has not gripped you yet because of your youth—thought has not had a chance to penetrate into the totality of being, and as a result, there is an unexplained, nonideal residue at the core of what exists, a fundamental irrationality and unintelligibility present in every sensible body.

Compare this to the way Aristotle in *Parts of Animals* frames the difference between essential form and material parts.[7] In his investigations he identifies two chief causes—the final cause, which is just the form or essence of the being considered as the end. The matter, on the other hand, is understood according to what Aristotle calls hypothetical necessity. *If* this form as final end is to be realized, then this needs to exist, and if that is going to exist, then this needs to exist, and these conditions lead one back to the realization of the finality of the form: as he states relative to an understanding of the human, "because the human is an animal with such and such characters, therefore the process of his development must be like this, [and his various parts must be like this]" (*Parts of Animals* I.1 640a34-36.) Understanding any sensible body in nature takes on a necessarily circular character—we need to think through the parts in order to come to the essence of the whole, though the being of the parts will only be fully understood in light of the whole—we need to look at the development of the thing and see its parts unfold chronologically in order to understand the being in its complete reality—but only once we understand it in its full development actively living out its form can we properly understand the stages of its development. The circle is not vicious because of Aristotle's ontology. The form and the matter are two sides of the same activity, and to say that matter is the potentiality of the complete activity of form is to say that it is the extrinsic side of the inner identity. Matter is simply the expression and externalization of exactly what will be required for the being to live out the activities specified in its form. In other words, there is nothing ultimate except for the activity of form; of course, matter as potentiality has the potential to be other than form in the sense of not quite realizing everything that belongs to form, but this lack is nothing in itself, there is not an opposed element in the structure of the natural world intrinsically opposed to form. A natural thing, ultimately, is form all the way down and so no matter what is being studied, there is rationality and goodness and ideality present—studying bees and grubs and digestion and blood and the heart is not a flight from speculative philosophy but a demonstration that everything is explained by the causal activity of form in matter. While, as potential, things can be endlessly moving away from or back toward their essence, nothing ever escapes or falls outside the operation of form which is the horizon of all being.

Parmenides' words to Socrates are almost exactly echoed in Aristotle's justification for turning to the study of the details of animal bodies:

> we proceed to treat of animals, without omitting, to the best of our ability, any member of the kingdom, however ignoble. For if some have no graces to charm the sense, yet nature, which fashioned them (*hē dēmiourgēsasa phusis*), gives amazing pleasure in their study to all who can trace links of causation, and are inclined to

philosophy.... We therefore must not recoil with *childish aversion* (*duschepainein paidikōs*) from the examination of humbler animals. Every realm of nature is a wonder. (*Parts of Animals* I.5 645a6-11, 15-17)

Nature's demiurgic fashioning is nothing other than the activity of form as making all the parts what they are and as the controlling force of the development of the being into its form. To be philosophical and not childish, just as Parmenides said Socrates would eventually become, is to have the patience and attentiveness to detect form in potentiality, in its embodied expression. This is the sense in which I mean that the empirical interest of Aristotle's biology is an intensification of Plato's idealism—it is the carrying out of the idea that Mind or the Good and the formal structure of the world are absolutely comprehensive causes of what exists, an idea already contained in Plato's idea of the Good or Mind as a first principle beyond the distinction of intelligible and sensible and comprehensive of them both. Is this impulse not exactly why in the *Phaedo*, Socrates is let down by the promise of Anaxagoras' philosophical insight: "I never thought that Anaxagoras, who said those things were directed by Mind, would bring in any other cause for them that that it was best for them to be as they are" (*Phaedo* 98a-b). While we might make appeal to *sunaitiai*—complementary causes—which must be in place for the form to realize itself, these do not fall outside the causality of form.

I will conclude this preliminary reflection on the motivation of Aristotle's biological empiricism with the beautiful anecdote he tells of Heraclitus, from which I draw the title of this chapter:

and as Heraclitus, when the strangers who came to visit him found him warming himself at the furnace in the kitchen and hesitated to go in, is reported to have bidden them not to be afraid to enter, as even in that kitchen divinities were present, so we should venture on the study of every kind of animal without distaste: for each will reveal to us something natural and something beautiful. (*Parts of Animals* I.5 645a19-23)

The foreigners came to speak with the most profound of speculative philosophers—the thinker of the one *logos* of all things. Yet when they arrived at his house, there he was, involved in the most mundane and bodily of pursuits, warming himself by the fire, doing something altogether unphilosophical, they thought, and so they stopped, perhaps out of embarrassment. But Heraclitus' *logos*, recall, is fiery—this *archē*, this grand *logos*, is everywhere, and where more so than in the stove on his hearth? If the explanatory principles are truly comprehensive and universal, there is not a department of philosophically interesting phenomena and a department of philosophically uninteresting phenomena. One should be able to turn to the careful study of the bodies of living beings as a way of discovering the forms of these beings, and having done so, to turn back to these bodily differences and explain them with reference to this form as simply external expressions of the inner nature of each being.

II. Essence and Embodiment—The Question of the Human

Consider now this Aristotelian intensification of Platonic idealism relative to the question of *human* essence and *human* embodiment.

In *De Anima* II.1, Aristotle arrives at a preliminary common definition of all soul as "the first *entelecheia* of an instrumental natural body" (*De Anima* II.1 412b5-6).[8] Reading this definition and the development leading up to it, it is difficult not to be amazed at the boldness of the conclusion Aristotle quite nonchalantly draws from this formulation:

> That is why we can dismiss as unnecessary the question whether the soul and the body are one: it is as though we were to ask whether wax and its shape are one, or generally the matter of a thing and that of which it is the matter. Unity has many senses (as many as "is" has), but the proper one is that of actuality (*entelecheia*). (*De Anima* II.1 412b6-9)

The key to understanding why this definition diffuses the question of how soul and body are connected is first to recognize that it has both a formal component (first *entelecheia*) and a material component (natural instrumental body) but that built into each side is the presence of the other side. To call a body *organikon* or instrumental is to refer to its potential for realizing the activity which is specified by the form— "instrumental," like potential, is a relative term. Similarly, by specifying the *first* active realization of the body, we make a reference within the form to the barest activity of bodily self-maintenance. While all the other higher capacities are latent in it, it is this *first* activity which keeps the body alive. Form and matter, body and soul, are here being redefined not as items to be united but as two sides of one activity, potencies relative to each other, a dynamic whole prior to the division of form and matter.

Of course, in thinking of the *essence* of living beings, we do not focus only on this first actuality but on the full realization of the powers latent in that first actuality, because it is only there where we see the distinctive essence of a being displayed. In this way, when thinking about the soul and body of the human being, the formulation "*zōion echon logon*" makes good sense. It is through this distinctive or proper function of the human as the activity of the distinguishing power of its soul that we understand both what the animal in question is and why its body is structured as it is. We can see how the animality in the formula points to the most common characteristics we share with all animals—nutrition, sensation, desire, locomotion—while our having *logos* articulates the more rare and distinguishing feature proper to humans which sets us apart from the genus—our capacity to think.[9] This distinctive and essential characteristic, the proper end of the being in question, will be that which is responsible for all the distinctive aspects of the human body, while many aspects more related to characteristics shared with other animals will be common except insofar as they are taken up and transformed by the higher context of this thinking capacity.

But there is a wrinkle in this tidy view which I do not find commentators have really appreciated. I want to turn briefly to that holy grail of opaque philosophical texts, Book Z of *Metaphysics*, perhaps the most dialectical and as a consequence difficult to follow of all Aristotle's writings. There we have one of Aristotle's most extended reflections on the relation between essence or form and definition as the formula of the essence of a substance. One of this book's most amazing claims is the following:

> Since a definition is a formula, and every formula has parts, and as the formula is to the thing, so is the part of the formula to the part of the thing, the question is already being asked whether the formula of the parts must be present in the formula of the whole or not. (*Metaphysics* VII.10 1034b20-24)[10]

The formula is to the composite object as the parts of the formula are to the parts of the composite object. Aristotle seems to want to argue that the structure of our knowing corresponds to the structure of being—our thinking of *ousia* has the same structure as the *ousia* it thinks. The way this works out in the argument is that a definition of an *eidos* consists of a genus and a differentiating characteristic, while the structure of a sensible substance consists in the material parts and the essence. What is the relation between the material elements of a sensible substance and its form, and how are they one? What is the relation between the genus and its differentiating characteristic, and how are they one? Why are the parts of the body one thing and not a heap, and why are the parts of the definition one thought and not a heap? Should material parts play a role in determining the formula of the essence?

It is the example Aristotle uses in working out this family of questions that I want to explore. He decides to use the example of the definition of human—and he uses not the formula which is the subject of this volume—*zōion echon logon*—but rather *zōion dipoun*, two-footed animal. The differentiating characteristic here, in a way that *should* surprise us despite the fact that Aristotle uses it so frequently as his stock example for a definition, is simply a determination about body parts.[11] This is especially striking given that the very question of how the parts of the being relate to the parts of the definition is precisely one of the questions under investigation in these passages. Yet in this definition of the human there is no reference to soul, no reference to thinking, no reference to having *logos*. Granted, when Aristotle proposes the example which will occupy him for the subsequent chapters, there is something provisional about it: "*esto gar houtos autou logos*: let this be the logos of the human." But why this formula?[12] Should the body parts really be included in the differentiating characteristic which gives specificity to the genus?

So what is the source of unity of the terms in this definition? Aristotle spends a lot of time thinking about what the genus is, what the difference is, what form is, and what matter is, and beyond this, why they come together into one thing, but reaches impasse after impasse as to how to find a satisfying answer. The problem, I suggest, is that throughout, he is thinking through the way previous philosophers have thought about these, as elements which exist as independent and are subsequently combined or united. The parallel that Aristotle exploits in this argument is that a genus, like matter, is not an independently existing thing but a potential to be determined into a thing. The form, like the differentiating characteristic of the genus, is not an independent thing but an activity which acts upon the indeterminate potential of the genus or the matter to yield either the formula of the substance in the one case or the sensible substance in the other. Without the difference, the genus does not yet exist, and vice versa. Without the form, the matter does not yet exist, and, shockingly, in sensible substances, vice versa. Form and matter as well as difference and genus are relative terms. Importantly, Aristotle wants to move us away from thinking about the genus or its difference as universals, complete in themselves. He says that like matter in a sensible substance, the genus does not exist except for as indeterminate potential, like matter, the capacity for determination into something. The difference, here two-footed, acts on the genus and makes the species. Notice his way of expressing this here, it *acts on* the genus, it *makes* the species. Without the genus it is nothing, without the genus the difference is nothing—we are being led to the view that the difference is the activity and realization of the genus' potentiality in the way the form is the activity and realization of the matter. The key to the solution Aristotle will eventually lay out is that "a substance cannot consist of substances present in it in complete reality; for things that are thus in complete reality two are never in complete reality one, though if they are *potentially* two, they can be one" (*Metaphysics* VII.13 1039a2-6). Yet in the whole aporetic discussion of Zeta, it is not until its final chapter that we get a glimmer of light shined on the relation of form and matter, and the formula that could capture them. He says, let us start again, understanding substance as a *principle* and a *cause*.

What we need to seek, he says, is the cause, that is, the form, by reason of which the matter is some definite thing. Already implied here, I suggest, is the consequence that the sample definition of human being as the two-footed animal is deeply problematic, insofar as it sought the determining activity of the genus through the parts of the body. The problem here is that we are trying to explain the essence and definition of the human being with exactly those terms which need to be explained—the two-footed structure of the body. The determining form is not to be considered one of the elements that has to be unified in the matter, but rather as a principle, a cause, not a separate thing but the active cause of the unity and of the being of all the material parts in a sensible substance. As he says, the question when trying to understand the form or essence as cause or activity of the matter is not "why is that thing what it is" but rather "why man is an animal of such and such a nature," or more generally, "why is the matter some definite thing," why does *this* body having *this* shape, the shape of a human? So the answer to the question "what is the human?" will not be determined through the parts of the human body—two feet—but through the form, the soul, as cause of these parts being the way they are.

Contrasting two-footed here with the example of artifacts Aristotle uses to speak of differentiating form is helpful (*Metaphysics* VIII.2). The cause of the unity of a book and of its being a book is the activity of gluing and being glued, the cause of honey-water being what it is is the stirring and the being stirred. The cause of a casket being one thing and being a casket is its being nailed. The cause we are looking for is an activity which makes the thing what it is and makes it one, unifying the parts. The form or essence is now understood not as a thing or an element but as an activity which causes the matter to be what it is and to be unified. And if form is to be understood in the human as the soul, that is, the form of the potentially living body, as the actuality of the matter's potential; and if the formal activity in the definition is the differentiating characteristic which acts on the genus to yield the *eidos*, there was something self-consciously wrong about the two-footed animal we found to be so suspiciously inadequate as a formula of the essence of the human. The soul as form is exactly what needs to explain why a two-footed animal is two-footed. Two-footed animal is simply not an adequate formula of the essence of a human. It is by looking to the soul that we should be able to understand our two-footedness along with the other details of our bodily structure. And so here, having *logos* seems to be a far more promising path toward this destination.

Before we turn to the question of how our bodily structure (to which our two-footedness belongs) might be related to the human soul or form, in particular its distinctively developed rational power, we must make a brief digression on human thinking. It is important not to think too simply about human thinking. Throughout Aristotle's corpus, he identifies three especially important and distinct modes of human thinking. Within the part of the soul having *logos*, there is a basic division: on the one hand, our thinking of beings whose *archai* or principles cannot be any different, necessary beings which are what they are irrespective of what we do—these are grasped by a theoretical thinking; and our thinking of beings whose *archai* can be otherwise, in particular, because they are up to us, we choose to bring them about or not. This is our practical thinking about things that exist in the sphere of free human activity. This difference in objects as always for Aristotle indicates a difference within human thinking, and so our theoretical thinking capacity (*epistemonikon*) differs from our practical thinking capacity (*logistikon*). And within the sphere of things which can be otherwise and so are left up to us, a final distinction emerges between *nous praktikos*, thinking about what we *do*, and *nous poietikos*,[13] thinking about what we *make*. Human *logos* is threefold: it can be theoretical (contemplating), practical (doing) or productive (making).[14] These distinctions are important to keep in mind for what follows, for if we are thinking about why the body is the way it is based on the active causation of a soul defined by thinking, these distinctions in our thinking might very well be reflected in our bodily structure.

So let us now move back to the idea of connecting the material and inadequate definition of the human—two-footed animal—with the more formal formulation of the essence—the animal with *logos*. How are these not simply two distinct orders of explanation? What could possibly be the link between our two-footedness and our capacity for thinking? How might this two-footedness be an embodied expression of the distinctive activity of our human form, that is, our soul as characterized by its thinking capacity? If our distinctive essence were simply locomotive,[15] one could see how this activity might be expressed through this distinctive bodily form. Yet our locomotion on legs and feet is common to other land animals. The reason for our two-footedness as distinct from the pervasive four-footedness and many footedness remains unexplained through appeal to the shared characteristic of locomotion.

I would like to suggest that implied by the two-footed difference within the genus of animals is a whole Aristotelian reflection on the way in which our soul's distinctive nature—its thinking capacity—is embodied. This more intrinsically and essentially distinguishing feature of the human being, which lies behind our two-footedness, is our upright posture, our being straight (*orthon*), as Aristotle puts it. This is where the causal link between our walking on two feet and our having *logos* emerges.[16] Aristotle writes in the *Parts of Animals*:

> For of all animals the human alone stands erect, in accordance with his divine nature and substance (*ousian*). For it is the action of the most divine to contemplate and to think (*to noein kai phronein*).[17] (*Parts of Animals* IV.10 686a25-29)

There is a good deal of Aristotelian physiology at work in this idea—that finer, less earthy, less material, and more formal matter is required for the bodily parts involved in cognition—the sense organs, their center in the heart as the seat of our general awareness and of the internalized images used in our practical and theoretical thinking; that consequently our upper halves are considerably lighter than our weighed-down and less intellectual quadruped counterparts; that is, at least once we develop out of our intellectually primitive and correspondingly top-heavier infancy. Recall further that weight for Aristotle is primarily determined by a cosmological directionality of something's constituent elements—our thinking nature, due to the material requirement of intellectual activity, is upwardly directed.[18]

The property of being two-footed in this formula of the human essence—the two-footed animal—is thus primarily a negative, privative definition—we are unlike the other four-footed animals in our lack of front feet. But there is a more positive side to this definition which follows directly from it. Because we are two-footed we remain upright, and so our front legs are liberated from their locomotive duties, for freer expressions of our *logos*-possessing essence. The corresponding positive expression then, which follows from our two-footed upright posture, is another distinctive bodily mark of the human, our hands:

> Standing thus upright, the human has no need of legs in front, and in their stead has been endowed by nature with arms and hands. (*Parts of Animals* IV.10 687a6-8)

Aristotle, against Anaxagoras, wants to explain the distinctive trait of the hand in and through our thinking nature or form—the actuality of this form precedes the potentiality of the body and its parts. Putting aside this argument about evolutionary origins, I would like to focus on Aristotle's analysis of the human hand. This analysis of the hand provides a wonderful example of how human thinking, which, while it uses images that are bodily affects is not itself bodily, can nonetheless be materially expressed and sensibly manifest in the structure of our bodies.

The first feature of the hand to which Aristotle points is how supremely versatile it is: as an instrument used for making other instruments, it has no fixed and determinate use—it is, in Aristotle's well-known phrase, an instrument for instruments (*organon pro organon*):

> For the most intelligent of animals is the one who would put the most organs to good use, and the hand is not to be looked on as one organ but as many; for it is, as it were, an instrument for further instruments. (*Parts of Animals* IV.10 687a18)

In fact the hand is explicitly associated with our capacity for the *technai* or productive arts—"we are the ones with the capacity for acquiring the most *technai*" (687a22). It might seem that our lack of any fixed, determinate, actualized bodily tools would put us at a great disadvantage in the natural world, and we can easily appear to be the most defenseless and vulnerable of all animals against the harsh variation in our environment and against far better-equipped animals.[19] On the contrary, it is this lack of any fixed weapons or tools in our hands as the embodiment of our productive thinking that the hand contains every possible defense and tool within itself as potential. Aristotle's wonderful analysis is worth citing at length:

> Much in error, then, are they who say that the construction of man is not only faulty, but inferior to that of all other animals; seeing that he is, as they point out, bare-footed, naked, and without weapon of which to avail himself. For other animals have each but one mode of defence, and this they can never change; so that they must perform all the offices of life and even, so to speak, sleep with sandals on, never laying aside whatever serves as a protection to their bodies, nor changing such single weapon as they may chance to possess. But to man numerous modes of defence are open, and these, moreover, he may change at will; as also he may adopt such weapon as he pleases, and at such times as suit him. For the hand is talon, hoof, and horn, at will. So too it is spear, and sword, and whatsoever other weapon or instrument you please; for all these can it be from its power of grasping and holding them all. (*Parts of Animals* IV.10 687a23-b6)

This flexibility in our hand, that all the needs we might have lie potentially within its embodied thinking activity (it can make and then use any tool), means that our whole body has this flexibility to adapt itself to an indefinite number of situations, environments, climates, no matter how different and opposed they may be. We can make ourselves through the work of our hands at home in both peace and war, in Stagira, Athens, Nova Scotia, or the glorious Arizona desert.

I would argue that we are encountering in our hands, in our embodiment, a fundamental feature of all mind on Aristotle's account, whether theoretical, practical, or productive. This is the mind's total indeterminacy, which is the condition for its unlimited capacity for thinking the widest possible range of determinations. This defining characteristic of mind comes out most clearly in the analysis of the receptivity of theoretical mind in *De Anima* III.4. In the background of this argument is a comparison of the mind's awareness to the awareness of our sense organs, which, although they are bodily and so do have a certain determinate character which limits the scope of their receptivity, are made up of the most indeterminate matter possible relative to the range of object they would receive: the eye is made from colorless transparent water, the ear contains a soundless air, and so on. Each organ is constituted as a mean between extremes so it can become perceptually aware of a certain range of object. This limitation is lifted in the transition from sensation to thinking, through an argument strikingly similar to the one in *Timaeus* for the characterless space or *chōra* as recipient of all sensible determinations:

> The thinking part of the soul must therefore be, while impassible (*apathes*), capable of receiving the form of an object; that is, must be potentially identical in character

with its object without being the object. Mind must be related to what is thinkable, as sense is to what is sensible. Therefore, since everything is a possible object of thought, mind in order, as Anaxagoras says, to rule, that is, to know, must be pure from all admixture (*amigē*). (*De Anima* III.4 429a18-20)

Referring here to Anaxagoras' political image of ruling, it is this lack of determinacy, this fact of not just being another one of the determinate objects in the world, which allowed mind to receive them all as they are, without the interference of its own intrinsic characteristics and without needing to exclude whatever objects would be opposed to its own fixed character. The king should not take just another particular, factional perspective opposed to other factions within the community, and so too the mind which will think the determinate being or essence of all things cannot be any one of these beings or have any essence beyond its own receptivity.

If seeing the hand as the physical embodiment of this thinking power seems like a stretch, the comparison is one Aristotle himself makes later on in *De Anima*:

It follows that the soul is analogous to the hand; for as the hand is a tool of tools, so the mind is the form of forms and sense the form of sensible things. (*De Anima* III.8 432a1-3)

Just as the hand is the instrument of instruments, sensation is the sensible form of all sensible forms and mind is the form of all intelligible form or essence (the language here cannot help but recall the Platonic characterization of the Good as the form of the forms). But the difference that emerges in this passage is also instructive—while all bodily parts may be instruments, the hand is in its essence a tool—its instrumental nature for making instruments means that it is especially connected to the mind in its productive mode. This mode of thinking is *intrinsically* instrumental, it is about securing means toward ends. Aristotle writes of our productive rationality in the *Ethics* that "every one who makes makes for an end, and that which is made is not an end in the unqualified sense (but only relative to something, i.e. of something)" (*Nicomachean Ethics* VI.4 1140b2-4).[20] This distinguishes production from praxis, making from doing, since action is an end in itself while it also strives to attain some goal beyond itself and from our theoretical thinking, an activity which produces no further consequences. In this way, the hand is the embodied existence of the power of our thinking and its productive, poietic mode. As much as we might be two-footed animals, we could be just as well defined as the animal having hands. But properly speaking, since the cause of our hand being a hand is its instrumental service to the productive thinking of the human, we could also say we are the *zōion echon logon technikon*.

As we saw, however, our thinking is not simply technical, productive, and purely instrumental. We make things, after all, so that they can be used, so that they can be taken up into our practical activities—practical actions where the goal is the action and not a product beyond its own activity. *Poiēsis* is chiefly about means, and it is *praxis*—ethics and politics—which give production its ends.

At this point we move back more directly to the formula at issue in this book—the human as the animal which has *logos*, in Aristotle's wondrously ambiguous phrase.

Does *logos* in this formulation mean primarily reasoning and thinking—rationality—or our use of language? It does not take great insight to imagine that these might not be mutually exclusive options—it is an outward expression of our rationality that we are able to communicate through articulate language, and our use of language itself is indispensable for the development of our rational capacities. Yet thinking through these two interpretative possibilities can be helpful for understanding the relation between our linguistic and rational animality.

Here too, in our practical and linguistic activity, the upward stance of our two-footed bodies is subtly at play in an embodied expression of our practical thinking. It is a fairly common trope in the older philosophical tradition to notice how our upright posture allows us to look up from the ground and our everyday practical concerns and move our gaze uselessly up to the stars.[21] Aristotle would agree with this, but he also notes a way in which this upright posture fundamentally changes our practical, political, and social existence:

> In the human, however, the part which lies between the head and the neck is called the face (*prosōpon*), this name being, it would seem, derived from the function of the part. For as the human is the only animal that stands upright, he is also the only one that looks directly in front (*prosōthen opōpe*) and the only one whose voice is emitted in that direction. (*Parts of Animals* III.1 662b18-22)

Thus our upright posture allows us to face each other, to stand face-to-face. In facing one another, we address each other, send out words to the one in front of us, and in turn hear their words directed toward us. These meaningful sounds, rather than the sounds made indeterminately as expressions of our own inner experience, are the basis of our social and linguistic nature.

Much of our body, Aristotle points out, is organized for the purpose of making our articulation of complex articulated speech to one another possible. While we need our respiratory system, neck, throat, and mouth for those activities that maintain the survival of the organism, our teeth, for example, are the way they are above all, Aristotle says, *pros tēn dialekton*, for speaking (*Parts of Animals* III.1 661b14-15). Our tongue is likewise, Aristotle notes, characterized in this bodily way by the flexible and indeterminate way of being: "The human," he writes, "has the freest, broadest and supplest tongue." Beyond all of the other things that it does for us, the softness of human lips is the way that it is "on account of the good—*dia to eu*" (659b33). This goodness which points beyond necessity is the good and bad, just and unjust, that appears in our serious conversations. Language allows the practical good to appear to us.[22]

It is this linguistic interpretation of the *zoion echon logon* that is emphasized in the *Politics*. On the one hand this is perhaps unsurprising, given the topic of the treatise—human associations or *koinoniai*. It is to show how the human is the *zōion politikon* that we point to the human possession of *logos* as language. Here, I suggest, our bodily structure as the possibility for articulated language stands in the same relation to our practical thinking—*nous praktikos*—that we saw with the hand as the indeterminate possibility for making tools as the expression of our productive thinking. Language too shares this free, indeterminate character—the views, arguments, poetry, and prose that can be articulated through the language we utter are endless and indeterminate. Both the bodily apparatus required for language and the words themselves are the sensible expression of mind responsible for thinking through what to do and how to do it. The perfection of our practical thinking in *phronēsis* involves both a grasp of the principles or goals and how to realize them, that is, an excellent grasp (through our character) of the right ends to pursue and the ability to deliberate on the best way to achieve these ends in particular situations. It is precisely these two sides of practical thinking that language embodies and makes possible:

> And whereas mere voice is but an indication of pleasure and pain, and is therefore found in other animals (for their nature attains to the perception of pleasure and pain and the intimation of them to one another, and no further), the power of speech is intended to set forth the expedient and inexpedient, and therefore likewise the just and the unjust. And it is a characteristic of man that he alone has any sense of good and evil, of just and unjust, and the like, and the association of living beings who have this sense makes a family and a state (*Politics* I.2 1253a10-18).

Like the hand, language is a dynamic and differentiated unity with independent parts of speech that come together for one purpose—meaning. And while one aspect of our language, like one aspect of our political thinking, is used for instrumental purposes—the reflection on means through the useful or expedient, our language moves beyond this instrumental capacity in order to articulate through debate and collective deliberation the ultimate ends of action—what is good, what is just. While these ultimate ends often lie in the background of our deliberations rather than forming the subject matter of them, we often do collectively debate and attempt to persuade one another about what is good and what is just. This ability to be able to listen to alternate views and be persuaded by them through discussion in the medium of language is the embodiment of our practical reflection. What I am suggesting is that the way our hand and its power to make any number of tools is the physical manifestation of our productive thinking, that our mouths and their ability to address through articulate language our fellow citizens and family members through education, debate, and political deliberation are the physical embodiment of *nous praktikos*.

The answer to how we should think of *logos* in our famous formula—whether *logos* as our defining feature is reason or language—is typically Aristotelian—in one way reason, in another way language. Language is the embodied expression of the formal activity of soul we call *praktike dianoia*. To say this is certainly to subordinate language in a way—it is what is necessary in order for our practical thinking to be itself, but our practical thinking is the form of our linguistic activity, just as productive thinking is the form of the activity of our hands as its matter. This is not to deny that practical thinking cannot emerge without language as its precondition, just as productive thinking can't emerge without the work of our hands as its precondition. But it is to say that *logos* as language does not for Aristotle have independent being from our thinking. But this should not be surprising—to say that it does would be to put Aristotle on the side of

Gorgias, for whom *logos* as language is the ultimate *archē* of all things—to say that *logos* as language is the embodied expression of *logos* as *phronēsis* or *praktikos nous* is to say that it has an intrinsic directionality toward political and practical truth, and that the independence of language from our practical thinking and of rhetoric from political life is something to be avoided.[23]

As for the third mode of human thinking, theoretical contemplation, in one sense this simply cannot be embodied. This thinking cannot itself be material, Aristotle argues in the *De Anima*, but must be wholly unmixed with any determinate bodily characteristic so that it can think *all* things (*De Anima* III.4 429a17-27). But in another sense, since, for humans, theoretical contemplation only emerges in and through learning by means of the essentially embodied activities of sensation and imagination, if theoretical mind is to be the ultimate *telos* of our other cognitive capacities, our bodies will reflect the need to be able to, as much as possible, perceive the world not as it is in relation to our own needs and projects but as it is in itself, apart from our interests. In this way what is required are not extremely powerful sense organs but rather sense powers which can perceive objects apart from an awareness of the pleasure and pain attached to them in relation to us. Aristotle clearly does connect bodily differences with the capacity for theoretical thinking.[24] While in general many animals have keener, more powerful senses than humans, this is largely because of practical requirements of their survival in the environments in which they live. The one exception, Aristotle claims, is the sense of touch, the baseline sense most connected with our general perceptual awareness (the "common sense"). Humans have touch, he argues, in a far more accurate and discriminating way, and as a result, humans are the most thinking (*phronimōtaton*) of animals.[25] What the human perceptual body is especially suitable for is the discrimination of differences (the many differences which our senses show us and which we love experiencing even apart from any usefulness[26])—and it is out of the memory and synthesis of these differences that the complex images which become the matter for theoretical thinking emerge.

Expressing the nature of a living being will involve reflecting on the differentiation of its various bodily parts, many of which will be causally interrelated with one another, with the environment in which the being lives and operates, and with the activities and functions which define it, above all with the most particularly distinguishing and defining activities that make that being what it is. What Furth refers to as the causal systematic interrelatedness of the differentiae, in the case of the human, will involve two-footedness, uprightness, having hands with highly differentiated and opposable fingers, having a face which faces forward toward other faces, a mouth with teeth and tongue suited for articulated language, and sense organs well-suited for the true discrimination of different sensible characteristics.[27] These characteristics are, as we have seen, causally related to one another (there are, for example, no hands without two-footedness and uprightness), but they are also importantly all causally related to the *telos* of the human being, its developed powers of thinking, in its productive, practical, and theoretical modes. If our capacity to think and our possession of *logos* define our nature most fully, we understand our bodily structure in general and each body part specifically once we understand how it is the very embodiment of that *logos*, without which our productive, practical, and theoretical powers could never be activated. Form as the divine good of each being is completely present through all its parts—and the philosophical demand for a detailed study of embodiment comes from the very confidence encouraged by Parmenides in conversation with young Socrates that all being is ultimately caused by the activity of mind, form, and goodness. We are the two-footed animals because we are the animals who have *logos*.

Notes

1 I am grateful to my student assistants, Jacob Glover and Aaron Higgins-Brake, for helping me track down references which were indispensable for writing this chapter, as well as to David Bronstein for his suggestions on an earlier draft.
2 The best treatment of this point in my view is D. K. House's "Did Aristotle Understand Plato?" *Dionysius* 17 (1999): 7–25.
3 The definition of the human as two-footed animal (*zōion dipoun*), sometimes appearing as the two-footed walking animal (*zōion pezon dipoun*) in Aristotle's texts, appears throughout the corpus as a standard example for the components of a definition especially in the *Prior and Posterior Analytics*, *Topics*, and *On Interpretation*. This gives some credence to the majority of interpreters who take the import of Aristotle's example to be merely logical and not substantial with respect to its actual content. In this chapter, I will be trying to show that in the central books of the *Metaphysics*, this formulation is not simply a sample definition indifferent to its particular content, since at issue in the *Metaphysics* discussion is precisely the way the parts of a being and the parts of the definition are unified in the being and in the definition. Two-footed animal is both superficially true and self-consciously problematic as a formulation of the human essence, precisely because of the nature of two-footed (*dipoun*) as a differentiation of the genus.
4 Translations from Aristotle's *Parts of Animals* are taken from W. Ogle's translation in Aristotle, *The Complete Works Aristotle* (Princeton, NJ: Princeton University Press, 1984), but have been occasionally slightly modified.
5 In *Parts of Animals* Aristotle's discovery of certain parts which serve no purpose indicates that there are nonetheless occasional limits to formal explanation in biology—see, for instance, the useless horns in *Parts of Animals* III.2. I am grateful to David Bronstein for this qualification.
6 Translations from Plato's *Parmenides* are taken from Mary Louise Gill and Paul Ryan's translation in Plato, *Complete Works*, ed. John Cooper (Indianapolis, IN: Hackett, 1997), 359–97.
7 The place to look for Plato's own articulation of the parts of the body as expressions of the essence or soul of the human being is *Timaeus*, especially its concluding section (69b ff.) which considers the way in which the tripartite soul of the human being is embodied.
8 Translations from Aristotle's *De Anima* are taken from J. A. Smith's translation in Aristotle, *The Complete Works Aristotle* (Princeton, NJ: Princeton University Press, 1984), but have been occasionally slightly modified.
9 This is merely a preliminary determination—we cannot simply consider as settled the question of what exactly *logos* means in the formulation. I will treat some of the possibilities in the conclusion of this chapter.

10 Translations from Aristotle's *Metaphysics* are taken from Ross' translation in Aristotle, *The Complete Works Aristotle* (Princeton, NJ: Princeton University Press, 1984), but have been occasionally slightly modified.
11 That Aristotle uses a definition of the human which defines the animal through bodily structure rather than some defining characteristic of its formal principle does not seem to have troubled commentators. Almost everyone treats the definition merely as an example whose only philosophically relevant characteristics is that it brings together a genus (animal) with a differentiating characteristic (two-footed). Yet this does not account for the fact that the relation of the parts of the definition to the parts of the being under investigation is an explicit question for Aristotle, and that in his own positive solution, he reformulates the question of the unity of the parts as "*why* the matter is some definite thing" (1041b5) and illustrates this with the question "why is this body having this form a man?" (1041b6-7).
12 Let us put aside the question of why this is even a genuinely differentiating characteristic, given how the human is not the only two-footed animal, a fact which Aristotle readily recognizes in his biological writings.
13 This is not the theoretical mind from *De Anima* III.5 sometimes designated by this name, but rather the productive mind from *Nicomachean Ethics* VI.4 which thinks about how to make things.
14 The threefold distinction between theoretical, practical, and productive thinking, though most explicitly delineated in *Nicomachean Ethics*, Book VI, is structurally crucial to the whole of Aristotle's ethical and political philosophy.
15 Owens, implicitly favoring his formulating *zōion pezon dipoun* over *zōion dipoun*, actually takes "two-footed" to refer to the activity of walking and translates the formula as such, walking animal. The inadequacy of this formulation as a definition for Owens is that walking and human are not essentially linked. Among other problems with this reading of the formulation, I am arguing that one cannot lose from view that "two-footed" is a determination about the parts of the body, and how these are held together and connected to form is one of the problems at hand in these passages. See Joseph Owens, *The Doctrine of Being in Aristotelian Metaphysics: A Study in the Greek Background of Mediaeval Thought* (Toronto: PIMS, 1978), 224–5.
16 Pavel Gregorić, "Plato and Aristotle's Explanation of Human Posture," *Rhizai: Journal for Ancient Philosophy and Science* 2, no. 1–2 (2005): 183–96, treats Aristotle's attempt "to establish some connection between erect posture of human beings and their cognitive abilities," 184.
17 How to distinguish these two words for thinking in this passage is tricky. Does Aristotle mean to distinguish theoretical thinking (*noein*) from practical thinking (*phronein*, the root of *phronēsis*)? This would make good sense, but his identification of *phronein* with practical thinking is by no means consistent.
18 See *Parts of Animals* II.10 656a7 ff. for the claim that up and down for the human conforms to up and down for the cosmos as a whole. Rémi Brague, *Aristote et la question du monde: essai sur le contexte cosmologique et anthropologique de l'ontologie* (Paris: Presses Universitaires de France, 1988), brings out how for Aristotle, the directionality of the universe as a whole is most completely manifest in the human being: "La station droite est, de la sorte, prise dans, et comprise à partir de, la relation particulière de l'homme au Tout," 238.
19 See Plato, *Protagoras* 321c ff. In his Prometheus myth, this is how Protagoras describes the human being prior to the gift of *technē* from Prometheus. See on this point John

Russon "Actuality in the First Sense," in this volume, for an excellent treatment of the hand as the "tool of tools."
20 Translations from Aristotle's *Nicomachean Ethics* are taken from W. D. Ross' translation in Aristotle, *The Complete Works Aristotle* (Princeton, NJ: Princeton University Press, 1984).
21 On this point in relation to both Xenophon's *Memorabilia* and Plato's *Timaeus*, see Pavel Gregorić, "Plato and Aristotle's Explanation of Human Posture." For a more complete statement of the difference between Plato and Aristotle on upright posture, see Brague, *Aristote et la question du monde*, 237 ff.
22 See *De Anima* II.8 420b24-27 for a causal association of our standing up on feet and our ability to speak language, through the *heat* required for both. The entire passage on voice in *De Anima* II.8 (420b6 ff.) is important for thinking about the physiological requirements of our linguistic nature.
23 Recall Aristotle's famous subordination of language to thinking and being at the opening of *On Interpretation*. The teleological view of the relation between language and politics in this section is very indebted to Barbara Cassin's views on the matter. See, for example, Cassin, "Logos et Politique: Politique, rhétorique et sophistique chez Aristote," in *Aristote politique, études sur la Politique d'Aristote*, ed. Pierre Aubenque (Paris: Presses Universitaires de France, 1993), 367-98.
24 See *De Anima* II.9 421a10-27 and *De Sensu* 441a1-4.
25 This is one of the most puzzling passages in Aristotle. To strengthen the correlation of sensitive touch and intelligence, Aristotle claims that soft-skinned people are more naturally endowed with thinking or *dianoia* than hard-skinned people. One sense of this is that the softness of flesh indicates a purity of the blood out of which flesh is constituted, and this less earthy blood is better suited as a material vehicle for discriminating sensations. The essential role played by blood in sensation and the closeness of the sense of touch to the common sense could mean that more sensitive touch indicates greater sensitivity in general. The most sense I have seen made of this important but puzzling passage is Brague, *Aristote et la question du monde*, 258-60.
26 See the opening lines of the *Metaphysics*, where revealing many differences is equated with or at least closely associated with causing knowing.
27 Referring to D. M. Balme's various examples in his article "Aristotle's Use of Differentiae in Biology," in *Articles on Aristotle I. Science*, ed. Barnes, Schofield and Sorabji (Duckworth, 1975), 183-93, Montgomery Furth, *Substance, Form and Psyche: An Aristotelean Metaphysics* (Cambridge: Cambridge University Press, 1988), 101, gives his own rough example of how such a causal nexus would work: "a certain (species of) animal (i) lives in a habitat that offers food of such a kind, (ii) his dentition is adapted to masticate such food, (iii) his dentition as a consequence of (ii) is unsuited for defense, (iv) he has horns for defense, (v) the food of such and such a kind is difficult to digest, (vi) he has two stomachs and is thus adapted to digest such food, (vii) as a consequence of (vi) he is bulky and slow, (viii) his feet, broad and flat, will support a heavy body weight, etc., etc."

3

The Significance of Self-Nourishment

Aristotle's *De Anima* II.4

Greg Recco

Introduction

For mortals, to live first means to feed. To study mortals, then, means at least to study their characteristic activity of feeding, and this is the project of Book II, Chapter 4, of Aristotle's *De Anima*. Feeding might seem to be a process of accretion. But when he first introduces the notion of nutrition or feeding (*trophē*) at the beginning of his positive account of soul (in *De Anima* II.1), Aristotle adds a crucial explanatory qualification that is to be understood as implied in later occurrences: "of natural bodies, some have life and some do not, and by 'life,' we mean *self*-nutrition [*tēn di' hautou trophēn*], as well as growth and decay" (*DA* II.1 412a12-15).[1] In other words, the mark of life is not mere increase in size but being the responsible agent, means, and object of nourishment: it is, we could also translate, "nourishment through (or, 'because of') oneself."

In a sense, this is merely an extension of Aristotle's basic approach to the study of nature: natural beings are those that have a source of motion and rest within themselves (*Phys.* II.1 192b13-15). The simple body that is fire moves (or "is carried") upward, and earth moves downward, both toward their natural places, where they come to rest. The study of nature, then, must involve this kind of study of internal principles of motion and rest. And this is precisely what we see in *De Anima* II.2, where Aristotle notes that growth is among the natural (self-)movements of living beings: "[plants] plainly have *within themselves* a power and source of this sort, through which they grow and decay toward contrary places" (413a26-28), that is, both upward and downward. By "within themselves," though, we are not primarily to understand "located within their spatial boundaries." The source of the motion of living beings is to be sought within *what* they are.

In other words, the kind of motion the principle of which we are seeking is motion that both proceeds from and is relevant to what the living thing is and does. A nonnatural (and thus inanimate) body, such as an ax, has a principle of motion and rest "within itself" in only a derivative sense of "within." Released in mid-air, it will indeed fall—in the terms of Aristotle's physics, it will undergo motion as earth does, in virtue of being "earthen," but its downward motion and subsequent rest have nothing to do with its *being an axe*. It does not fall *as* an axe but as something that happens to be earthen. It is in this sense that while a principle of motion and rest is evidently at work "within" the axe, an axe is not a living being and does not exemplify the requisite kind of self-motion. This is the lesson Aristotle draws from the example: "soul is not the essence or *logos* of *that* sort of body, but of a natural body of such a sort as to have within itself the power of motion and rest" (*DA* II.1 412b15-17). The difference that makes it have the right kind of power for motion and rest "within itself" is thus the difference between two kinds of body. Having the right kind of body is requisite for life, and the right kind of body is the sort that enables the sorts of activities relevant to the form, the sort that allows activity at the level of form, that is, an "organic" body.[2]

In what follows, we will hew closely to the order of Aristotle's text, which defines life in terms of its most common manifestation, the activity of self-nourishment.[3] This takes place in three stages: (1) a brief reflection on the unity of self-nourishment and reproduction, (2) an investigation of the soul as cause, especially of motion and growth, and (3) the precise definition of food, we might say, as potential substance.

The text is somewhat elliptical and requires some interpretive labor to understand. The phenomena, too, are both widespread and difficult to articulate adequately. But what comes of the study of Aristotle's text in light of the phenomena it is struggling to account for is worthwhile: an understanding of what the mere existence of living beings brings to the world through their metaphysically fraught project of being capable bodies that feed. While the existence of the higher powers of perception and thought are also suggestive realities, the focused investigation of self-nourishment brings to light the living being's redefinition of what might appear—especially from a more or less materialist viewpoint such as that of Empedocles—to be the most fundamental aspects of reality: matter and space.

I. Self-Nourishment and Reproduction

In defining kinds of soul as powers, Aristotle begins, one must first say what the corresponding activities are (for the activities are capabilities to engage in those very activities). In order to define the activities, one has to say what these activities' "objects" are, the meaning of which Aristotle indicates with the examples of food, the sensible, and the intelligible. They are what is "set against" (*antikeimena*) the various powers (*DA* II.4 415a16-22), what can be eaten, what can be sensed, what can be thought. When Aristotle finally defines food near the end of the chapter, this essentially relative character comes to the fore. What it is to be food is to be *for* a living being. Like the other two examples of "objects," then, its definition is of the form "that which can be *x*-ed," and implicitly "by a being of the appropriate kind," that is, one that can engage in that activity.

Aristotle next announces, apparently a second time, the order of investigation: the first thing that must be discussed is nutrition and, he adds, reproduction. He explains in a preliminary way the connection between these powers that might seem to us to be distinct, after briefly explaining why this compound faculty must be considered before those of perception and thought. The reason it must be discussed first is that its activities ("reproduction and the use of food" [*DA* II.4 415a26]) underlie all other activities of living beings. It is the most general or common, being "that soul through which life inheres in all" (II.4 415a25). The particular discussion of reproduction that follows seems to go toward explaining this primacy. Aristotle continues: "this is because the most natural thing" for a creature who is adult and not otherwise unable[4] is to produce another that is *like* itself, where the kind of "likeness" (*hoion*—of the same sort) is illustrated by the relation between "animal and animal" or "plant and plant," surely with the implicit notion that offspring are of the same species being understood (II.4 415a26-29). In the first place, this activity can be called "most natural" because of its obviousness: the world teems with living beings that come in kinds and reproduce within their own kinds, which would be difficult to ignore.[5] More importantly, however, this activity of generating another like oneself is "most natural" in the sense that it best exhibits the structure of nature: nature always acts for an end. This reason is less obvious and requires further explanation, for as Aristotle goes on to suggest, living beings' activity of reproduction reveals a kind of ambiguity inherent in being directed toward an end, one that is not obvious in the case of the motion of simple bodies like earth or fire, and this activity is directed at something quite elevated and sublime.

Living beings produce others like themselves, Aristotle says, "in order that they may participate in the eternal and divine [*tou aei kai tou theiou*] in the way in which they are able [*hēi dunantai*]" (II.4 415a29-b1). "Eternal and divine" are not two objects but two names for a good that is in some way both inexpressible and impossible.[6] But the phrase "in the way in which they are able" is ambiguous, for on the one hand, it means living beings cannot achieve immortality, and on the other, it means they can, though only in their own way, namely, through reproduction. Some kind of continuance through reproduction is the ultimate "that for the sake of which." But "for the sake of which," Aristotle continues, has two senses: "for what" (in the sense of the purpose to be attained) and "for whom" (in the sense of the beneficiary). Typically, when we encounter this kind of reflection on Aristotle's part, we next find him telling which of the various senses is at issue in the present discussion, whether it be a primary or focal sense, some kind of derivative sense, or simply one among several options. Not so here. He goes on to explain reproduction on the basis of the mortality of the individual living being:

> Since it is incapable of sharing in the eternal and divine *continuously* [*tēi sunecheiai*], because it is not possible for any mortal thing to remain the same and one in number, each one shares in this continuity in the manner in which it is able to participate, by remaining not itself but *like* itself, one not in number but in kind. (II.4 415b3-7)

The ambiguity of the "for the sake of which," then, seems to explain the necessity and goal of reproduction. There is a divergence between what is to be preserved and who is. Or is it the difference between "in number" and "in kind" that explains both reproduction and the difference between two senses of "end"? Is it in fact the difference between "this"-being and "what"-being that is primary? The text by itself does not seem to settle these questions. If anything, it highlights the undecidability of the question about the relations among Aristotle's physics, biology, and metaphysics.[7] I will return to the question in the final section, where reproduction is mentioned again and studied further.

II. Soul as Cause of the Living Body

The longest section of the chapter concerns the soul as cause of the living body, as its substance, its end, and the source of its motions, in descending order of obviousness. That the soul is substance is "obvious [*dēlon*]" (II.4 415b12). Substance is responsible for the being of everything; for living beings, "to be" means (or "is") "to live"; the soul is the cause or source of living; so, soul is (cause or source in the sense of) substance (II.4 415b12-14).

That the soul is also cause in the sense of "that for the sake of which" is "plain" (II.4 415b15-17). Here, Aristotle spells out what the relation consists in: it is the "instrumental" relation between body and soul: "All natural bodies are organs of the soul" (II.4 415b18-19). To say bodies are organs of the soul is to say they are as they are in order to make possible the activity of living. Whoever says "natural body," then, means "that which makes living possible." Since he is speaking of the "for the sake of which," Aristotle here reiterates the ambiguity he mentioned earlier. This would mean, then, that body means "that which serves the one possessing it, and subserves its being what (kind of being) it is."

While the other two types (II.4 415b10) of the soul's causality were obvious or plain, its being the other kind of moving cause is introduced as needing more explanation: "but the soul is indeed also [*alla mēn kai*] that from which motion . . . first arises" (II.4 415b21-22). Nearly half the chapter is devoted to discussing this, which is one indication that it is in fact less than obvious. In what follows, I will trace out the progress of Aristotle's explanation, with the goal of bringing out those of its features that distinguish "merely physical" interactions from those characteristic of life: we will find that living beings have a distinctive relation to space or "place" that defines its directionality and proportion as inanimate beings do not.

Aristotle relies here on two of his general claims about motion: it has three varieties corresponding to the three categories (other than substance) in terms of which something may change (place, quality, and quantity); and, of these, change in place is in some sense primary (*Phys*. VIII.7). This explains why Aristotle both (1) begins as though "locomotion" were the general sphere in which the third kind of causality works, and then (2) immediately contrasts with it the other species of motion, which are more generally present in the soul. Hence, he writes:

> But the soul is indeed also [cause in the sense of] that from which motion relative to place first arises, though *this* [form of the] power [to cause motion] does not inhere in all living things, for change of quality and change of quantity, too, are both due to the soul. Perception is held to be a change in quality, and nothing

that does not share in soul perceives. The same holds of the changes in quantity involved in growth and decay; nothing grows or decays naturally that does not feed itself, and nothing feeds itself that does not share in life. (*DA* II.4 415b21-27)

Aristotle here maintains these distinctions among the three kinds of motion in nature, but the *De Anima*'s focus on living beings gives the whole schema a particular inflection. In a sense, we might say that the study of life reveals possibilities inherent to these forms of change that could not have been foreseen from within the perspective that looks to nature in general, nor from within that which looks to being as being. We might have thought that the differences among change of place, change of quality, and change of magnitude could serve as a template for explaining the difference between plants and animals. Plants, we might think, have the power of growth only in that they can get bigger by taking in nourishment, while animals' distinctive powers are to be understood as forms of alteration (in the case of perception) and, in most animals, locomotion.[8] What we will find, however, is that nutrition is not adequately defined in terms of mere change in size, just as perception will in a later chapter (II.12) be shown to be something other than mere alteration. That said, for a significant amount of time, Aristotle will focus on this obvious phenomenon of living: the soul as cause of motion in the sense of *growth*. Still, he insists throughout on the double phrase "nutrition and growth" or "being nourished and growing," and he does this for what we will see are essential reasons. For one thing, the change in size and correlative change (in the size) of place have distinctive marks not found in nonliving nature: living beings through their activity of living, even in its basic form of self-nourishment, *define* place. This, we will see, is what Empedocles, and materialist accounts of living faculties in general, get wrong.

Aristotle begins: "Empedocles was not correct to posit this in addition [*prostitheis*], that the growth that occurs in plants extending their roots downward occurs because of earth's natural movement downward and that their upward movement is due to fire's like natural movement" (*DA* II.4 415b28-416a2). The first question we should ask is to what Empedocles is supposed to be adding. The rest of the sentence along with its context provides the answer: Aristotle is apparently responding to Empedocles' account of how living things move, since Empedocles is explaining the motion of plants and Aristotle himself is still in the process of explaining how soul is to be understood as cause in the sense of the source of motion. Empedocles' explanation of the distinctive movement of growing things makes appeal to the distinctive movements of their ultimate material constituents, inferring the presence of those elements from the observed locomotive tendencies. Since plants move downward and what moves downward is earth, plants move downward because of the earth in them; since they also move upward and fire is what moves upward, they move upward because of the fire in them. In sum, then, plants in growing move both upward and downward because of the presence in them of both fire and earth.

We might expect Aristotle's opposition to this account to draw centrally from his own articulation of the multilayered character of the material constitution of living bodies found in *Parts of Animals*; in other words, we might expect Aristotle to criticize Empedocles for misunderstanding *matter*. It is therefore something of a surprise to find Aristotle saying that what Empedocles does not understand is *place*. Aristotle says Empedocles explains growth incorrectly "because he does not grasp 'up' and 'down' correctly, for 'up' and 'down' are not the same for each being as they are for all; rather, as the head is for animals, the roots are for plants, if we are to say that organs are the same or different in virtue of their functions" (II.4 416a2-5).

One might think to accuse Aristotle of irrelevance here. There may well be a functional analogy between plants' roots and animals' mouths, but it is not clear what bearing that might have on their respective orientations, the one downward and the other upward. Aristotle seems merely to be stipulating an uncommon use of the words for these opposed directions, one we find more fully explained in another text:

> the part [of the body] by which food enters we call "upward," looking to the part itself and not to the surrounding whole [. . .]. For plants, which are stationary and take their nourishment from out of the earth, it is necessary for this part to be always pointing downward, for there is an analogy between roots in plants and what is called the mouth in animals. (*Juv.* 468a1-2, 8-12)

If Aristotle wishes to say these common terms have a special sense when they are applied to plants, the inverse of their usual and plain sense, one might still wonder how this is supposed to show how Empedocles' account of plants' upward and downward motion is wrong. In fact, in his initial description of the characteristics of life, Aristotle himself refers to the same phenomenon that Empedocles is explaining: "[plants] do not grow only upward and not downward, but alike in both and all directions" (*DA* II.2 413a28-29).

I propose that we take seriously Aristotle's charge that Empedocles does not know up from down or at least does not define them correctly. The reason is simple to state but not fully explained in the present text. The reason that Empedocles' account of plants' motion fails is neither that his materialism has too few kinds of matter with too few kinds of motion (in accord with the account of bodies' composition in *Parts of Animals*), nor that Aristotle has arbitrarily pulled the plain meanings of "up" and "down" out from under him by a kind of stipulative refutation, but that the directionality of living beings' motion is understood correctly (that is, *is explained*) only in terms of the functional organization of their bodies: plants send their roots "downward" *because* that is whence they are nourished. We can call the direction in which plants move "downward" only if we ignore their essential and defining activity of self-nourishment. If, by contrast, we acknowledge that a plant has something like a point of view on its own activity, we acknowledge also that its motion has to be interpreted in light of that perspective or orientation. Plants, understood on their own terms, deploy their roots neither upward nor downward but "foodward."[9]

In the next few lines, Aristotle adds a further observation that is intended as a criticism of the Empedoclean theory of plants' growth. "Besides, what is it that holds together fire and earth, which move in opposite directions? For they will be torn apart if nothing is there that will prevent it [*ei mē ti estai to kōluon*]. If there is something, soul will be this that prevents as well as what is responsible for growing and being nourished" (II.4 416a6-9). The emphasis here is on the need for some additional "entity" that will function as a source of motion (for, after all, staying together, too, is a kind of motion). Empedocles only half explains the phenomenon of plants' growth and this in the wrong way. Bodily integrity, too, must be explained.

If one dimension or sphere in which living beings try to achieve "continuity" or "holding together" (*sunecheia*: cf. II.4 415b3-4) is time, another, no less essential, is place. They have at a minimum to be together with themselves (not to mention "together [*hama*]" with their food—[*GC* I.5 322a13]) if they are to be something. The Empedoclean explanation is in one sense sufficient—in that it provides a mechanistic explanation of two movements that happen to be co-present in the phenomenon to be explained—but in another sense insufficient, in that its account on its own terms both demands and cannot produce a countervailing force that achieves "continuity." If different kinds of matter display or undergo the influence of forces that are essentially indifferent to one another, then nothing can prevent eventual, final, and total separation of such elements (cf. *Metaph* I.4 985a20-28). The necessity for bodily integrity demands that one think of place not in absolute terms but in terms relevant to the living being's project of living. The study of life suggests that a prime category of place in terms of which living motion is to be explained is "the middle" (see *Juv.* 2.468a16 on the organization of the body around a middle and 3.468b16-19 on growth as beginning from the middle).

Aristotle next considers another account of living beings' nourishment and growth, one that relies on observation of the apparent activity of just one of the elements: "Some hold that the nature of fire alone [*hē tou puros phusis haplōs*] is the cause of nourishment and growth, for it alone of the [simple] bodies appears to nourish itself and grow; this is why someone might take it to be what is at work in plants and animals" (II.4 416a9-13). Given that fire and earth together failed to explain growth, it initially seems unlikely that one of these elements alone will be sufficient. But here, we are not concerned with fire either merely as a kind of stuff or merely as undergoing movement in a certain direction, a fact that Aristotle signals with the compound phrase "the *nature* of fire." Rather, this nature of fire that some hold to be the cause of nutrition and growth is its power to catch and spread itself through whatever is combustible.[10] Fire appears to feed on what it burns, increasing in intensity and extent. Like the living body, then, it appears to engage in self-nourishment; like a soul, it appears to be the origin of motion relevant to what it itself is and to be the end for the sake of which that motion is caused.[11]

This phenomenon, too, as was already stated, will prove insufficient to account for the growth of living things, but it will not be easily dispatched, for reasons that go beyond what can be expressed in this section on the soul as cause. Aristotle merely alludes to what he will discuss at the very end of the chapter: "[fire] is in some sense a concurrent cause [*sunaition*]" (13*f.*). In other occurrences of this word, Aristotle means by a "concurrent cause" one that is active but secondary to a more important or essential explanation (e.g., *GA* V.3 782a26, V.3 783b21; *HA* X.1 634a17; *SS* 4.441a29; in three out of these four cases, what is at issue is some basic quality, like the hot or the moist, which is the sense in which fire, too, will be a contributing cause to nutrition, i.e., in virtue of the heat that is "proper" to it [*SS* 4.441b11].) Here, however, he is concerned to show that even this apparent case of elemental self-nourishment is insufficient to account for growth: "while the growth of fire continues limitlessly so long as there is something combustible, in the case of everything that is naturally constituted [*phusei sunistamenon*] there is a limit and ratio [*logos*] of magnitude and increase, and limit and ratio belong to soul, not fire, to definition [*logos*] rather than matter" (*DA* II.4 416a15-18). In a sense, this is merely another version of the counterargument Aristotle already opposed to the Empedoclean theory that the natural motions of fire and earth explain the simultaneously upward and downward motion of growing plants: without something to *check* the increase, it will go on indefinitely, thus tearing the living being apart. But here, an additional feature of vital growth is presupposed: not only is it *limited*, but it occurs in accordance with a *ratio*.

It is not merely the increase in bulk of something that is indifferent to its own composition, at least that, I think, is what the mention of what is *phusei sunistamenon* is intended to convey. It is not merely "what *occurs* naturally" but whatever is naturally "constituted" or even "composed," and this means having significant (and significantly located and sized) parts relevant to the project of life. While *auxēsis* in a way expresses both, in English we could say, "*growth* (of the organic bodies of living beings) is not mere *increase* (of their bulk alone)." The living being is finite *not* because it fails to master outside forces and push beyond their limit.[12] Rather, it is the source of its own limit because of its maintenance of ratio and proportion in the growth of parts of its body. And it maintains ratio and proportion in two senses, simultaneous growth and what we might call "vital scale." Growth must take place simultaneously in all parts of what is growing (*GC* I.5 321a2-3); the nonuniform parts, however, grow not as such but through the proportionate expansion of the uniform parts.[13] Furthermore, the proportions that are maintained are not merely "numerical" but preserve vital significance. A bone, for example, takes its measure from the activity it is to subtend and the weight, strength, and other properties of the being that is to be capable of that activity. It is not solely the "microphysical" properties of the various kinds of composite matter involved in life (e.g., porous, rough, smooth, greasy, buoyant) that are causally significant but also, and even primarily, the way that life *uses* these properties for its projects. This explains Aristotle's double use of the word *logos* above (II.4 416a15-18), when he says that limit and *logos* in the sense of ratio belong to *logos* in the sense of definition: in living beings, the relation of magnitudes depends on the essence. That is, living beings define place not only in terms of the gross and global features of direction but also in terms of scale: the *logos* of a living being is not merely "the capacity for such-and-such activity embedded in matter suitably *composed* for that purpose," meaning "in the right ratios of basic forms of stuff," but bears essential (not secondary and incidental) reference to limit, ratio, proportion, and in a word, scale. Since these characteristics are nowhere to be found in the action of fire, the nature of fire cannot be the explanation of growth.

This concludes Aristotle's discussion of soul as cause of the living body. He takes it as obvious that it is cause as form and end, but goes to greater length to discuss soul as cause of the distinctive movement that is growth. By examining alternative explanations of growth—one in terms of the natural motions of supposedly basic types of matter, another in terms of the combustive power of fire—Aristotle shows how living beings as living define place in their directionality and scale, aspects of place that make up no part of the more general "physical" account of it that does not distinguish between what has and what has not soul and life.

III. Food: The Soul's External Means of Self-Nourishment

The final part of Aristotle's account of the first form of soul is focused on the "object" of the nutritive faculty, its *antikeimenon*, literally, what is "set against" it. "It is necessary first to define food" (*DA* II.4 416a20), he finally writes, after having established this necessity near the very beginning of the chapter (II.4 415a20). As in the section on soul as a source of motion, here too he develops his own account against the background of others. In fact, there is a reappearance (and elaboration) of something like the same theory we just considered, one that looks to the activity of fire's "proper" quality of heat (*SS* 4, 441b), and in his final words, Aristotle will suggest that the presence of such heat is a necessity for all living things. Before that, we must investigate questions concerning the contrariety or likeness of nutriment to the being it nourishes, the action of the soul upon nutriment (namely, digestion), the difference between growth and self-nourishment, and the identity of nourishment and reproduction.

Aristotle begins by reporting a simple account of what food is—it "is held [*dokei*] to be a contrary for a contrary" (II.4 416a21-22)—and builds his own account largely by refining it. The initial account is plausible. When a living being eats, something that was *not* it *becomes* it; it transforms the food that was formerly not it into what it is. Aristotle adds two qualifications to this. In the first place, not every change from one contrary to another takes place as an *increase*, since "not every contrary is a quantum, for example, someone healthy comes to be out of someone who is sick" (II.4 416a24-25), where the designations "the healthy one" and "the sick one" plainly do not name quanta. A first additional requirement for something's being food, then, is that it must be capable of yielding increase in that to which it is contrary. In the second place, even when one contrary both comes to be and comes to be larger out of another, "they are plainly not food to one another in the same way, for water is food to fire, but fire does not feed water" (II.4 416a25-27). The wording is puzzling unless we take Aristotle's "water" to include oil, liquid which serves as fuel for fire. That the example is somewhat special he is quick to point out: "indeed, among simple bodies, these most of all are held [*dokei*] to be 'food' and 'what is fed' [*to men trophē to de trephomenon*]" (II.4 416a27-29). The self-enacted increase out of a contrary that fire exhibits makes it almost impossible for Aristotle not to call this process self-nourishment, but he will not, as is indicated by *dokei* and the "scare quotes" that *to men trophē* suggest.[14]

However we are to take the case of fire, "there is a difficulty here," Aristotle adds: "some say that *like* is fed, as well as increased, by like" (II.4 416a29-31), while others, as we have seen, hold feeding to be a relation between contraries. Aristotle notes the strong arguments of the "contrarian" side: they think contrary feeds contrary "since like is unaffected by like, while food changes (that is, is digested) [*tēn trophēn <dein> metaballein kai pettesthai*], but change is in every case toward the contrary or the middle" (II.4 416a32-34). I'm omitting Ross' insertion of *dein* ("must"). The argument is not that food *must* change to be digested, but that it *is*, and that since digestion is a form of a change, and change is away from a contrary, food is a contrary to what it feeds. If food were merely like, the living being would be food to itself, and if feeding were a kind of change, like would have to change like, which it does not. The reality and not the necessity of digestion is the focus.

In the next sentence, it is not immediately clear whether Aristotle is merely reporting a further argument in favor of the view that food is a contrary or whether he is adding his own consideration: "furthermore, food is somewhat affected [*paschei ti*] by the one fed, and the latter not at all by food, just as the carpenter is not affected by wood, but wood by him; the carpenter 'changes' only from inactivity to activity" (II.4 416a34-b3). The imbalance between action and passion is, of course, fatal for the theory that food is just like to like, so this sentence might be read simply as a further report of the contrarians' counterarguments. But the analogy of the carpenter, with its emphasis on the change from inactivity to activity, seems better to represent Aristotle's own view of the process of self-nourishment, which is that the categories of like and contrary are insufficient to explain nutrition and must be supplemented by the ontology of potency and actuality. With that in mind, it is not surprising to find that Aristotle's solution of the *aporia* does not revert to the view that contrary feeds contrary.

Instead, he writes:

> It makes a difference whether "food" means what is final and added on or what is first. If it means both—that is, undigested and digested—then it is permissible to talk about food in both ways, for as undigested, contrary feeds contrary [*to enantion tōi enantiōi trephetai*],[15] and as digested, like feeds like. (II.4 416b3-7)

In other words, raising the point about the need for digestion does not really help the thesis of the contrarians; it shows it up as limited. Digestion is the process *by which* contrary becomes like; so food, as that upon which digestion does its work, has to be defined as both contrary to and like what is fed. Aristotle's point about the activity of the carpenter, therefore, was not made in service of the contrarian position; like the sense organ that must maintain a *logos* of contraries, the nutritive faculty must hold *within itself* the difference between "alien" matter and "my" flesh. It "changes" only in the sense that it goes from potentiality to activity. The nutritive faculty is not the same as the fire that takes its increase and coming to be out of its *contrary*; it comes to be and increases out of what is *both it and not it*. The nutritive soul maintains (and defines) the difference between itself and not itself in a way that cannot be adequately defined in terms of mere contrariety or likeness.

In the next few lines, Aristotle extends the results of this discussion of food in terms of contrariety and its difference from the action of fire, concluding that the category of "increase," too, is insufficient for describing the process of self-nourishment. A first key claim is that feeding relates essentially to life: "Since nothing is fed that does not participate in life, the body that is fed would be the living body [*to empsuchon an eiē sōma to trephomenon*] *as living*" (II.4 416b9-10). It is preferable, I think, to translate *empsuchon* as "living" rather than as "ensouled," first, because Aristotle often uses the word in a quite ordinary way in contrast to what is inanimate, and second, since "ensouled" makes it easier to think of "soul" and "body" as names for independent *entities* that might on some occasions happen to be related, instead of as *ways of being* that are inherently related.[16] Elsewhere, Aristotle uses the word in just this way. The question is what makes something a part of something, and the example is one he repeats in several other places: "It is not just 'hand in general' that is part of the human being, but the one capable of carrying out its function, so that it is alive: if it is not alive, it is not a part [*mē empsuchos de ou meros*]" (*Metaph.* VII.11 1036b32-4). My point in laying such stress on the term for what is living or animate is that this is crucial for understanding what food is—and hence what self-nourishment and ultimately soul are. Food addresses, we might say, what is alive *as alive*, that is to say, in terms of its capacity to carry out its function, in short, in terms of its being.

But the primary being of something living is really *substance-being*, not size. "A further result [of the fact that what is fed is the living body] is that food exists relative to the animate, and this not accidentally" (*DA* II.4 416b10-11). In keeping with what we already said about the difference between distinct entities and distinct ways of being, Aristotle resorts to a quasi-adverbial dative construction, which we might render somewhat clumsily as follows: "What it is *for food* [*trophēi*] to be is different from what it is *for something growth-producing* [*auxētikōi*] to be," or more simply, "being food is different from being growth-producing" (II.4 416b11-12). This is what the "as living" clause, discussed earlier, implied, as Aristotle explains: "something is growth-producing for the living as a 'how much,' but something is food for the living as a 'this' or a substance (for it preserves the substance, and that continues to be what it is so long as the process of feeding continues)" (II.4 416b12-15). It is not just that growth reaches a kind of limit; rather, the living being's activity of nourishing itself was *never* directed at it merely as something of a certain size. In fact, its being something of a certain size, a "how much," *depended* on its being a "this." That is one result of what we could call the essential relativity of food; food *is for* the living being, and it is for this being *as what it essentially is*.

Given what Aristotle wrote right at the beginning of the chapter about the supreme naturalness of reproduction, and given his analysis of how the soul as substance has something like a double destination (the "for what" and the "for whom"), it is not surprising that he would follow this discussion of food as directed at substance-being with some consideration of reproduction, for after all, that is just as much the activity of the animate as such: "[food is also] the agent of generation, not of the one that is fed, but of one like the one that is fed, for the substance of this one already is, and nothing by itself gives birth to itself, but preserves itself" (II.4 416b15-17). Even without the detailed physiological analyses (in *GC*) that link semen and *katamenia* to food (and the "finished food" that in animals is blood),[17] or those (in *Juv.*) that describe how the localized nutritive faculty in plants may somehow be split in two, we can see here in the more abstract analysis of *De Anima* how Aristotle conceives the fundamental connection between self-nourishment and reproduction: both aim at preservation, and through it, at the "eternal and divine." Food, as it has been defined, is the unique object of this single faculty, which Aristotle here claims ought to be named "reproductive" rather than "nutritive," for the reason that "this principle of the soul is a power of such a sort as to preserve what has it as this sort of thing [*toiouton*], and food helps it do its work" (II.4 416b17-19). This recalls the theme of alienation I raised near the beginning and gives it a new shape: in eating, I am preserving myself, but "only" as the specific *sort* of being that I am. In other words, what I eat is "human" food, sustaining (my) human life. There is no need to wait for some moment of actual generation of offspring (or actual death, for that matter) in order to experience a kind of alienation: all "my" trophic activity is in the service of ends with which I (as this one, here, now, with this body) form something like an accidental unity. In this connection, we might read the *dia* of *hē di' hautou trophē* ("self-nourishment," II.4 412a15) as referring not to the self-directedness of the process of eating but to the fact that it occurs *through* me, and thus from beyond me and in the direction of what exceeds me.

And yet, the possibility of this very identity between an "I" (or an "itself") and the "sort" of being it is is precisely what is provided for by something very close to the lowest "level" of being, not even one of the basic elements but one of the qualities that hovers between two of them, namely heat. The significance of the closing reference to heat rests on a distinction made in the course of a summary of the factors involved in nutrition. In addition to the soul and the living body, there is "that through which it is fed [*hōi de trephetai*]" (II.4 416b22-23), namely, the food. Aristotle recalls the duality of food that was recently established, but here interprets that very distinction in terms of activity and passivity: "[the expression] 'that through which one feeds' is ambiguous, just as 'that through which one steers [a boat]' is both the hand and the rudder, the one moving and moved, the other merely moved. It is necessary that all food be digested, and what effects [*ergazetai*] digestion is heat; this is why everything animate possesses heat" (II.4 416b25-29). Heat, then, would be something that the soul sets in motion in some portion of (or throughout) its body and preserves so long as it lives, but which in being moved also moves food (namely, from being undigested to being digested, and let us recall the claim that food does not move what is fed). Heat—which "lives" in no one kind of matter, which indeed spans contrary kinds of matter, stretching even across that form of contrariety that the nutritive maintains with respect to food—is for life something like a "concurrent cause," the term which Aristotle used earlier (II.4 416a13) in the discussion of fire as a model for self-nutrition and which we might here connect with his use of the term in his discussion of the contrary-spanning power of what is called in Plato's *Timaeus* by the name of *chōra*: "The nature that remains (underlying) is a concurrent cause along with the form of the things that come to be, like a mother" (*Phys.* I.9 192a13f.).[18] The miracle or providence that it is difficult, with Aristotle's vocabulary echoing in one's ear, to call by any other name than "transubstantiation" is at least a partial redemption of the inescapable alienation involved in feeding. Heat seems to be involved essentially in the dual nature of flesh: the same plasticity and even mutability of form that opens us to decay and death—for, after all, the first soul or nutritive/reproductive faculty is the responsible agent, as Aristotle says over and over, in growth *and decay*—may also be what provides materially for the possibility of mortal life, along with everything good that might come of it.[19]

Notes

1 I follow Ross' text throughout (*Aristotle: De Anima*, ed. with introduction and commentary by Ross [Oxford: Oxford University Press, 1961]), except for one minor change noted further. All translations are my own.
2 Kosman, "Animals and Other Beings in Aristotle," in *Philosophical Issues in Aristotle's Biology*, ed. Gotthelf and Lennox (Cambridge: Cambridge University Press, 1987), 361–7 and *passim*, helpfully distinguishes among different senses of matter in Aristotle, linking the notion of "organic" body to matter understood not in terms of its being a constituent *ex quo* but in terms of its providing powers to one capable of using them—we could even say "body as possibilizing." He writes (385): "the force of such a description [of organic bodies] derives from the light that an understanding of animals and their bodies sheds on the general structure of form and matter in other entities. It is in recognizing an animal's matter not simply as that of which the animal *consists*, but as a complex structure of *instrumental potentiality* by virtue of which it is enabled to enact its life and formal being, that we are able to think in general of the matter of active being in terms of instrumental potentiality." Eli Diamond, "'For There Are Gods Here Too': Embodied Essence, Two-Footedness, and the Animal with *Logos*," 33–9, in this volume, develops this theme further.
3 For an excellent exposition of the question of whether the project of *De Anima* is to produce a "universal" definition of life that applies to all living beings, see Chapters 1 and 2 of Eli Diamond, *Mortal Imitations of Divine Life: The Nature of Soul in Aristotle's De Anima* (Evanston, IL: Northwestern University Press, 2015), who powerfully argues that the "focal" meaning of soul is to found in its highest manifestation, the god, and not in its most common. In this essay, I do not examine the nutritive-reproductive soul in light of how it falls short of this ideal but aim to bring out its positive elements in their specificity.
4 Aristotle refers (*DA* II.4 415a27) to two possible impediments to reproductive viability: the creature must not be "mutilated," which usually means in their reproductive capacities (e.g., a mule), or "spontaneously generated," another exceptional case of the absence of reproductive viability.
5 Cf. *Physics* II.1 193a3–8 on the "ludicrousness" of trying to prove that nature *is* and the lack of knowledge that such attempt at demonstration itself demonstrates.
6 Cf. *Generation of Animals* II.1: "soul is better than body, the animate than the inanimate (because of soul), being better than not being, living than not living. These are the reasons for the reproduction of animals" (731b28–31).
7 In addition to Kosman, whose claim about the relation between Aristotle's metaphysics and his biology we saw earlier (n. 2), I should mention Montgomery Furth, *Substance, Form and Psyche: An Aristotelean Metaphysics* (Cambridge: Cambridge University Press, 1988), whose work first suggested this approach. See also John Russon's ontological and biological development of this theme in the first section (123–9) of "'Actuality in the First Sense' and the Question of Human Nature in Aristotle," in this volume.
8 Of course, this story would already be complicated by the fact that increase is itself a form of change of place, though the most limited kind and very much imperfect in comparison with continuous circular motion. Growth and decay, in the sense of

changes in magnitude, must involve change of "place" inasmuch as a thing's becoming larger or smaller is coextensive with a becoming-different of its "place."

9 The next few lines of *De Juv.* illuminate the meaning of this functional redefinition of place, in that they define another pair of relative directions in terms of living capacities: "we call 'forward' the direction from which sensation comes and 'behind' the opposite" (468a27–31).

10 Cf. *Meteorology* IV.9 387a19–388a9 for discussion of combustible and inflammable bodies.

11 I. Kupreeva, "Aristotle on Growth: A Study of the Argument of On Generation and Corruption I 5," *Apeiron* 38 no. 3 (2005), states well what is attractive (or maybe even catching) about the analogy: "Just as the increase of fire involves the increase of intensity, so biological growth is the increase primarily not in bulk but in a special kind of intensity, biological, which preserves the dynamic and functional unity of a living thing as living" (132).

12 However, we should note that Aristotle does rely on the image of "blocked" or "collapsed" irrigation channels (e.g., *PA* II.1 647b2) as an analogy for describing what we might think of as a "mechanical" limit on living beings' size. Kupreeva's discussion (141–6) of the applicability of this analogy to Aristotle's difficult terminology of "duct" (*GC* I.5 322a29), which is supposed to solve all the aporias of potential magnitude and potential flesh, is perhaps as clear as one could wish. Her conclusion strikes a compelling blow against crude Empedoclean mechanism: "the form of a uniform part is not just a formula of an elemental combination [. . .] but also a sensible qualitative structure [with an] ontological status of its own. This lower-order form depends on the form of the whole living being, but possesses its own phenomenological regularity which allows it to act as a continuant and contribute to the functional unity of the whole thing in the process of growth" (147).

13 See Kupreeva 119–21 for discussion of the proportionality of growth "in any part" and 121–5 for the disagreements among Alexander, Andronicus, Philoponus, and Galen on how to interpret the identity of what grows and what exercises alteration on the "incoming" matter.

14 Of course, the neuter could also simply refer to sōma, hence "the one (body), food, the other (body), what is fed."

15 The change from middle-passive to active was necessary, since the appositive tends to be read in English as referring to the subject. This has the side effect of obscuring Aristotle's use of the dative here ("contrary is fed *through contrary*"), which will become the subject of his analysis in the final section of the chapter.

16 In a slightly different context, Kosman, "Animals and Other Beings in Aristotle," puts the point well, noting that in our usual, non-Aristotelian modes of expression, we speak "as though substance were a category of *entity* rather than a category of the *being* of entities" (369).

17 For discussion of the historical background to Aristotle's ideas about reproduction, see Andrew Coles, "Biomedical Models of Reproduction in the Fifth Century BC and Aristotle's *Generation of Animals*," *Phronesis* 40, no. 1 (1995): 48–88.

18 See also *Parts of Animals* 646a14ff.: "Perhaps it is better to say (that the first composition [of flesh] is made up of) the powers [of hot, cold, wet, and dry]." Cited (459) in Friedrich Solmsen, "Tissues and the Soul: Philosophical Contributions to Physiology," *Philosophical Review* 59, no. 4 (1950): 435–68.

19 Gad Freudenthal, in an ambitious work, strives to construct (or reconstruct) a systematic account of Aristotle's views on heat dispersed throughout his works and alleges that in an important sense, heat for Aristotle is responsible for the good (*Aristotle's Theory of Material Substance: Heat and Pneuma, Form and Soul* [Oxford: Oxford University Press, 1995]). Evidence that Aristotle saw a "cosmic" significance for what we may not even call the matter of generation was already explored by Friedrich Solmsen in "The Vital Heat, the Inborn Pneuma and the Aether," *Journal of Hellenic Studies* 77, no. 1 (1957): 119–23.

4

Flesh as *Logos*

Rebecca Steiner Goldner

Introduction

In *De Anima*, Aristotle differentiates between plants and animals in multiple ways. Animal life is identified through sensation and necessarily includes, at a minimum, a capacity for touch. Plants, on the other hand, have (merely) nutritive souls and are capable (only) of nutrition and reproduction, but they lack locomotion, desire, sensation, and thought. Yet plants and animals, including humans, are comprised of the same material components insofar as they all consist of some ratio of the four basic elements: earth, water, air, and fire. At *De Anima* II.12, Aristotle suggests that the difference between plants and animals concerns sensing, which takes place "according to *logos* (*kata ton logon*)." Furthermore, he notes that since plants "have no mean (*mesotēta*)" and hence "no principle (*archēn*) in them capable of taking on the forms of sensible objects, they are affected together with their matter" (424b1-4).[1] This means the principle whereby animals can be affected without their matter and the *logos* according to which sensing takes place point toward a fundamental ability which animals possess and plants lack. Animals can sense things so long as the sensible remains within a certain range: things which are too bright or too dark render us blind, for example, and things which are too hot or too cold destroy our ability to touch them. The *logos* according to which sensation can happen is a principle of rudimentary discrimination; to be able to sense is both to have narrowed the field (to those things within the range) and to be able to respond to those things in entirely new ways. The *logos* of sense establishes the animal along the path between plants, whose *logos* is purely quantitative and related to growth, and animals possessing *logos* as a rational capacity, that is, the human being. To have the sensitive *logos* entails the possession of only one sense, that of touch, and it is identifiable by one particular component of touch: flesh. Aristotle suggests, then, a relationship between animal life, this *logos*, touch, and flesh; this chapter is an attempt to explore that relationship.[2]

Aristotle's description of the sense of touch at *De Anima* II.11 is, by his own admission, highly aporetic. Of concern is both the unity of touch as a single sense and whether touch can maintain a structural analogy to the senses explicated in the four preceding chapters of the same text. It is a problem, Aristotle tells us, whether flesh is the organ or the medium for touch, and much of the work of *De Anima* II.11

sets about trying to resolve this problem. Nevertheless, by the end of the chapter, ambiguity remains concerning whether flesh is the organ and/or the medium for touch. I will examine Aristotle's notion of flesh not only within *De Anima* but also in *Parts of Animals* and *Generation of Animals* to try to address the doubts lingering within *De Anima*. Tracing Aristotle's account of flesh through the biological works and examining its highly functional and determinative role in the animal body will both suggest some resolutions to the problems presented at *De Anima* II.11 and allow us to explore flesh as the incarnate manifestation of the *logos* that differentiates plants from animals. Aristotle has often been accused of contributing toward a philosophical tradition of scopophilia—of favoring sight as the primary domain of sense and incipient knowledge. Hans Jonas, for example, citing the opening of the *Metaphysics*, takes it as an unquestionable starting point that Aristotle belongs to a tradition of Greek philosophy in which "sight has been recognized as the most excellent of the senses."[3] Contrary to such a reading, it is my claim that Aristotle's accounts of touch and of flesh point to an embodied and primary principle of discrimination—a *logos*—always present, often overlooked, at work in the human being. My claim is that touch is primary in the human being, as in all animals, because touch requires flesh, the site of active maintenance of the living ratio that keeps us from slipping into merely nutritive or physical forms of life. Flesh is the place where *logos* and body meet so that an animal can begin: flesh is body-as-*logos*.

I. Flesh as Body

Though *De Anima* considers flesh in its relationship to sensation, *Parts of Animals* II.8 has perhaps the most prolonged reflection on the nature of flesh in the animal, which Aristotle describes as "a principle (*archē*) and a body in itself of the living being" and the primary organ of sensibility in general.[4] As the necessary organ for a new way of being, that is, an animal, flesh is the bodily element of a radically new kind of soul: a soul with a capacity to sense. I begin by exploring the role of flesh in touch and I expand from there to a broader examination of flesh as a generated and generative principle in the animal, a principle both *for the sake of which* and *by which* sensation becomes possible.

De Anima chapters II.7-11 take up each of the five senses in turn, beginning with sight (II.7) and ending with touch (II.11). Already, a question presents itself: given that touch is the most basic—and only necessary—form of sense for animal life, why is it the last capacity Aristotle examines?[5] The answer to this question suggests the tension between the complexity of touch and Aristotle's belief that touch is a single sense that functions like the other senses. Aristotle establishes the operative paradigm through his accounts of sight, hearing, smell, and, to a lesser degree, taste, and then applies that structure to touch. Senses are capacities of the soul housed in bodily organs (sight, for example, in the eyes); each particular sense is directed at a particular kind of object (sight is directed at color)[6] and the activity occurs through a medium found between the sensing body and the sensible object (for sight, the medium is what is transparent—namely, air or water). The sense, as potency, is brought into activity by the presence of the proper object, and sensing itself is a change of quality (an alteration) in the sensing subject. Though Aristotle's account of the three distal senses is not entirely without *aporia*, it nevertheless effectively establishes the structural framework according to which senses operate; a sense is an ensouled capacity that has a bodily organ separated from and aimed at a proper object through an appropriate medium.

Aristotle has not yet sufficiently accounted for what exactly occurs when sensing takes place. At II.5 416b33 he determines that "sensation depends, as we have said, on a process of movement or affection from without, for it is held to be some sort of change of quality" but he does not adequately elucidate what sort of change of quality it is, merely that it is "some sort (*tis*)," of change—an indefinite reference to what sort of change it might be. Typical changes of quality occur between opposite states and the change is then perceptible—the water that was hot becomes cold; the white wool is dyed red. Yet, in the sensing subject, there is no clear change of quality in like manner: when I see the red wool no part of me, or my eye, becomes red or wooly. Nor is the medium—the air between me and the wool—affected in a typical way; someone observing me from afar would not see the air between us grow red as I observe the red wool. At II.12 424a18, Aristotle famously says that the sense has the power of receiving into itself the sensible form without the material. What he means by this, however, has been the source of much debate.[7] My contention is that in spite of his apparent difficulties explaining the sense of touch, this perplexing notion of sense's receptivity and alteration can, in fact, best be understood with reference to the sense of touch and the nature of flesh.

The problems Aristotle lists pertaining to touch concern the medium (that it is embodied), the organ (that it is essentially the same as the medium), and the proper objects (that they are multiple). All of these problems gesture toward flesh as being that medium. Compositionally, flesh is of the same material as the objects in the world that are tangible.[8] Moreover, Aristotle suggests that flesh might be the organ for touch as well as the medium. We will begin with the question of flesh as medium before turning to the question of flesh as organ.

If flesh is the medium for touch, it certainly does not have a clear analogue with other media, which are external to the body and unaffected entirely by the reception of the sensible form. If all media were like the transparent, a medium ought to lack entirely that quality to which it is receptive, as the transparent is that which lacks color. Flesh fails on this account—it itself has the very qualities that the sensible body has; the medium of touch is hard/soft and moist/dry, and so on, and not merely receptive to these qualities. Regarding the other senses, the organ echoes the medium in the absence of those qualities to which it is receptive. Because the transparent, the quiet, the unscented, and the moist lack color, sound, odor, and flavor altogether, there is a sense in which they are not receptive to these things—at least not receptive in the way of something that can *be* red, loud, perfumed, or sweet. The substances that can take on these qualities in a standard alteration are the underlying subjects of the contraries to which these qualities properly belong. Insofar as the medium and the organ are subjects of change, they are subjects not of the change between black and white or sweet and sour but of a higher order of change: visible and invisible or flavored and not flavored. Thus, when these subjects (the medium and the organ) undergo an alteration, it is not from blue to green but from being void of anything visible to reception of something visible. For change to take place, some contrary must be involved, even if it is not the obvious sort of contrary as seen in examples from *Generation and Corruption* I.7:

> Whiteness could not be affected in any way by a line nor a line by whiteness—except perhaps accidentally, viz. if the line happened to be white or black; for unless two things either are, or are composed of, contraries, neither drives the other out of its natural condition. But since only those things which either involve a contrariety or are contraries—and not any things selected at random—are such as to suffer action and to act, agent and patient must be like (i.e. identical) in kind (*tōi genei men homoion*) and yet unlike (i.e. contrary) in species (*tōi d' eidei anomoion*). (323b25-324a5)

I suggest here that the object with the sensible quality belongs to one genus of receptivity or affectivity, the medium and organ to another. The object, or more properly, its sensible qualities are affective or receptible, the medium and the organ are affectable or receptive.[9] The object, medium, and organ are not alike in kind (*genē* here) regarding the sensible quality—they do not receive it in the same way.[10] The object *is* or *has* the sensible quality, the medium *moves* or *holds* the quality, and the organ *senses* it.

Thus, in sight, we really have two *genē* at work; the color itself belongs to the genus of light and dark things and is a material quality of substance.[11] The medium (the water insofar as it is transparent) and the organ (insofar as it is also transparent) belong to the genus of visible-invisible, the transparent is visible (when colored, thus, when seeing takes place) and invisible (when not colored, when no seeing takes place). The organ and medium of touch (if both are flesh) are never void of tangible qualities—there is no body that lacks tangible qualities[12]—thus there is nothing between touch and its object, void of tangible qualities, that mediates the qualities by receiving them according to a different genus. As both organ and medium, flesh is not void of these qualities but must maintain some ratio of them within itself, lest the organ be destroyed. Flesh that gets too hard, too cold, too hot is simply no longer flesh and the animal is destroyed.

While the organ for sight is relatively simple, because sight is receptive of a single genus of quality, the organ for touch, like the tangible object(s), defies singular qualification. That the organ is necessary has been established in the preceding chapters that cover the other sensitive capacities; that it needs to be materially related to that for which its capacity is receptive is also clear. The object of sight, color, requires the transparent, and the transparent is found in water or air; thus, there must be water or air in the organ for sight.[13] The objects of touch are a multiplicity of sets—cold and hot, moist and dry, hard and soft. Accordingly, the organ in which they will inhere is also of more than one element. Yet the organ of touch, like the other sense organs, is called homogenous (here, this is *homoiomeros*, as opposed to the word for simple, *haplos*) in spite of the fact that touch is "correlated to several distinct kinds of objects" (*PA* II.1 647a17) and, as a result, "not made of earth (alone) nor any other one of the elements alone" (*DA* III.13 435b2). In *PA* II.1, Aristotle tells us that the heterogeneous, instrumental parts are more substantial and the other parts in some way "exist for the sake of" the more complex, such as hands, nostrils, eyes, faces, fingers.[14] The complexity of these body parts results from the need for them to perform a multiplicity of functions: nostrils don't merely smell, they help us breath, expel mucus, and protect us from allergens, for example. The more functions an organ has, the more complex it will be, such that the simplicity of the part of the eye that receives color is in contrast to the relative complexity of the organ that receives tangible qualities, since there is more than one genus of tangibles. "Accordingly," Aristotle writes, "the organ which deals with these varied objects is of all the sense-organs the most corporeal, being either the flesh or the substance which in some animals takes the place of flesh" (II.1 647a20-21). Flesh is consistently called homogenous (*homoiomerous*, which might also be read as "uniform") in spite of its elemental multiplicity—whatever ratio of earth, fire, air, and/or water comprises flesh, all flesh has similar composition, though it is "the least simple of all the sense-organs" (*PA* II.1 647a17).[15] Again, this suggests that outside of certain thresholds, the ratio fails to be maintained and flesh is no longer homogenous, or uniform, and is no longer flesh in the proper sense.

Aristotle avoids suggesting that skin might be the organ for touch and in many places he identifies a difference between flesh (*sarx*) and skin (*derma*).[16] Skin is most often likened to blood, sinews, and other heterogeneous parts that serve the flesh and are designed to protect it. Skin itself is most like a membrane, something we learn by analogy at *DA* II.11 and also at *Generation of Animals* (*GA*) II.6, where he describes skin as the dried and external layer of flesh.[17] That the skin (or exterior flesh) formative of the barrier between the flesh and the external world is of a different quality (being dry rather than moist) seems not to preclude that the flesh is the medium through which touch occurs; actual flesh seems to be just inside the dried layer of skin on the surface, again suggesting there need be a proper ratio (including of dry to moist) in order for it to be considered flesh. While some body parts are more fleshy (bellies) and others have very little flesh (the head), Aristotle suggests that all animal body parts consist of some degree of flesh or its analogue. Flesh (like all sense organs) is made from the purest material (*GA* II.6 744b23-24) and serves a multitude of roles in the physical body: it is soft and stretchy (*PA* II.8 654a15) and forms the encasing for the blood vessels (*GA* IV.1 764b29); body parts that have skin with no flesh under them (eyelids and foreskin) do not heal when cut (*PA* II.13 657b1-4), thus indicating that flesh is a source of health and healing.[18]

Parts of Animals II.8 continues to propose that flesh constitutes the organ of touch, and this chapter serves as a lynchpin to any discussion of the role of flesh in Aristotle's account of the living body. Aristotle here establishes that touch is "the chief (*prōton*) of all the primary sensibility" (II.8 653b23), and he suggests that the central organ of sentience coincides with the organ of touch. "An animal exists," he tells us, "according to its sensory part, that is according to flesh or its analogous organ of touch" (II.6 651b4-5). Aristotle argues here for the importance and necessity of flesh (or its analogue) because it is (a) most corporeal, and thus most substantial of all homogeneous parts (II.8 653b30) and (b) serves as both a principle and a body (*archē kai soma*, II.8 653b21) in itself, meriting its precedence over all other homogenous parts (II.8 653b22). Indeed, he goes so far as to claim that "it is for the sake of this (flesh) that all the other parts exist" (II.8 653b31), parts including bones, skin, sinews, hair, nails (i.e., other homogenous parts). To have the sense of touch is to have flesh or a part that functions as flesh[19]—to have not merely a body but a body with a hierarchical structure, in which parts develop with an increasing level of complexity in order to support increasingly preservative functions. Flesh is not merely a composite, insofar as it is a particular ratio of elements brought together, but it is also functional and essential to being an animal at all. Flesh is most often identified not as matter but by its role and function to the animal, which is why Aristotle can speak of flesh as having an analogue. If flesh were merely a structure made by a particular composition of elements, it would be recognizable as such and not through a function that could be realized in something other than that composition.[20]

Aristotle also points out in II.8 that flesh "is the organ and the medium through which the object acts combined, comparable to the pupil with the whole transparent medium attached to it" (653b25-26). At *De Anima* II.11 423a Aristotle wonders "whether the sense organ [for touch] is within (*entos*) or not, but is the flesh immediately (*eutheos*)." Translated in this way, it appears that flesh is certainly the organ, and the question at stake is whether it is the outer flesh or something inside (taking *entos* and *eutheos* as the opposition of within and without). Whether the outer flesh or an inner organ composed of flesh, there is no real difference, in touch, between the medium and the organ. Indeed, whereas the media and organs of the other senses are discrete, regarding touch "nature was compelled by necessity" to unite them (*PA* II.8 653b27-28). Flesh is not merely an *archē* and a body, it might be an *archē* precisely insofar as it is a body that is at the same time more than body. It is a body with the extraordinary capacity not merely to undergo physical changes but to be receptive to the physical in an entirely different way than mere body, to be a part of and yet different from the rest of those bodies.

II. Flesh as Principle

Related to its role as the organ and medium of touch, flesh acts as a principle of the body with respect to generation and growth. As a principle, we might say that flesh in-forms the new animal as a kind of embodied and concrete potency—as soon as there is some fleshy part, there is a potential animal, and as soon as there is a potential animal there is an organ for touch. Though he does not say this in *De Anima*, at times Aristotle suggests that the heart might play the role of primary sense organ and that the heart is first and foremost the organ of touch.[21] Though I am wary of treating the heart and the flesh as interchangeable, I do think that the fleshiness of the heart contributes to its role as the primary seat of sensation or the internal organ of touch, and, following the model of the other senses, if flesh is the medium of touch, the heart is a limited body of flesh. Since all sensation requires a medium, lest all sense reduce to a form of material contact, it might be that the outer flesh serves as medium and the organ could be the flesh within (*entos*, above). (The argument for the necessity of the medium relies primarily on the phenomenon Aristotle describes whereby an object is not sensed when placed directly on the organ, a claim reiterated in the discussion of smell at II.9 421b16). We must, however, keep in mind that sensation, for Aristotle, falls within the domain of physics, and while it might be a variation on a typical motion, sensation, too, is "a process of movement or affection from without, that is, it is some sort of alteration" (II.5 416b33-34). The medium is the first body moved by the sensible form in this nonstandard alteration, but both because the medium is *apsuchos* and *apeiron*, it fails to register, that is, sense, the object in the way that which has the capacity to sense does. It is possible that the organ is simply a limited, or increasingly limited, form of the medium, and that in the animal capable of a given sense, the organ develops as a limited (i.e., enclosed) version of the air or water that is also affected by the sensible form. The structure and physical limits imposed by the organ allow the sensation to occur in the animal when it could not occur in the unlimited medium: "all bodies are capable of being affected by smells and sounds, but that some on being acted upon, having no boundaries of their own, disintegrate, as in the instance of air, which does become odorous, showing that some effect is produced on it by what is odorous" (II.13 424b14-17).[22]

In other experiences of sense, the medium and the organ share the same material, albeit the former as unlimited and the latter as limited. The medium is the first thing moved by the so-called sensible form, and it is the medium that transports it, which it is able to do on account of material contiguity between the medium and the organ. Typically, the medium is external and the organ internal, but flesh is an exception, being at the threshold of internality and externality. As organ, however, we might decide that flesh has an internal and even more limited—but still fleshy—body part. Since touch is the necessary condition of animal life, we can expect that the organ for touch would be among the first signs that an animal has been generated.

Unsurprisingly, that very fleshy organ—the heart—is the first part of the animal formed in the embryo (*GA* II.4 739b34-740a1, II.5 741b15-20, II.6 743b25).[23] Aristotle identifies the heart as the first principle that brings organization to the body and as the source of the growth and the movement of the other parts. A male and female produce an animal when the male provides the semen to the material, only a potential animal, within the female; the first compound produced is the embryonic heart, which in turn organizes the rest of the body parts and is itself the source of the nutritive and sensitive movements of the animal. The heart is a source of active self-motion and once the most minimal form of animal receives its soul from another like itself, it requires this source of self-motion, so that "there is, then, something which increases it. If this is a single part, this must come into being first. Therefore, if the heart is first made in some animals, and what is analogous to the heart in the others which have no heart, it is from this or its analogue that the first principle of movement would arise" (*GA* II.1 735a21-25). Flesh, as it appears in or around the heart, first distinguishes the living body from mere matter, and it does so because it is not merely matter or body but ensouled body. The heart beats, that is, *moves itself*, and self-motion, another indication of animal life, is deeply connected to sensation, in its discriminatory capacity, as one of the two characterizations of animal life (*DA* II.9). What use would sensation be if the animal could in no way discriminate and then react to what it senses?

Flesh, at least the flesh of the heart, is the first physical manifestation of the animal, but its role extends far beyond organizing and motivating the embryonic animal. Flesh, Aristotle reminds us, bears a disanalogy to the other sense organs because of certain outstanding features, namely, its high degree of corporality and its unity of medium with the organ. In its most rudimentary form, flesh connects us to that which will sustain or destroy us, it informs us as to what to move toward and what to avoid. Flesh is a body, first and foremost, distinguished by its texture, temperature, and solidity, and it remains forever on the threshold of lapsing into those external things to which it is receptive. If it does—if flesh becomes mere body—the animal is destroyed.

The precariousness of flesh is evident in a number of ways, including the way the rest of the body is designed to protect it. Its perilous state is further seen in its role as organ of touch, where it fails to sense that which is too much alike (II.11 424a4) and where too strong a sensation will destroy it (III.13 435b12). As bodily mediator of those external bodies, and operating not by distance, as do the other senses, but by contact, flesh functions as a threshold in maintaining separation and difference from the external world but fails marvelously when the object touched bears either too great a kinship or too strong a difference from it. Flesh can only serve as medium and organ for touch when it can maintain a modicum of difference between itself and the body it touches, a ratio or balance of parts. Flesh must be other than or more than body to be flesh in all its fullness—as medium and organ for touch and as the first physical location of the sentient powers—yet flesh is so very bodily. The animal does not see or touch things because she stands over or against them, but because she is firmly within them and one with them, capable by the merest reversal of being sentient of them rather than merely one among them. At the same time, flesh apart from the living body is no longer truly flesh but only homonymously.[24]

An animate being is twofold unity; it holds itself together but interacts with its environment. Both are necessary conditions of living, and both correspond to the compound nature of animation as in-formed body—as belonging to, yet differentiated from, the rest of the natural world. Animals therefore protect themselves from, yet necessarily engage with, the external world. They must be receptive to that world for their very survival; they must be protected from it for the same reason. These twofold capacities of animation ground the relationship of body and soul but likewise encapsulate the problematic of this structure; the animate being is in and of the world yet constantly at work to preserve itself against that world (in a way that merely natural beings cannot). The body-soul relationship is a hierarchical development of matter-form; it is a noncontingent hylomorphism whereby the substance is not only in-formed from its genesis so that it develops correctly should conditions allow but such that it can take up the conditions and adapt them adequately to better insure its *telos*. The living being is directed outward in order to perfect and complete its own insulated holding-together, but its ability to serve as principle of its own motion in this way reifies the difference between animate and inanimate by creating a distance out of the difference between them.

The language of difference is in some ways misleading; to use the term "difference" invites dualism and encroaches upon an ontological dichotomy; to this, I concede that insofar as for Aristotle degrees and modifications become ontological differences, then there is a real difference between plant and animal. Yet, emphasizing these differences might belie the liminal nature of animal principle—touch—embodied in flesh. Flesh can be this principle, or its material instantiation, because it straddles multiple worlds, animal and natural body. Mere body, when it becomes *passive* flesh in the plant, simply lacks the active principle that enables sensation. Animal flesh fluctuates by "reversal"[25] between active and passive. Insofar as these differences might be a question of degrees, however, the concerns are not reducible to, as Marie McGinn puts it, "an ordering of objects which are nothing more than increasingly complex configurations of basic elements . . . which exhibit no genuinely novel powers, i.e. no powers that are not reducible to the powers of its more basic parts."[26] Rather, an Aristotelian hierarchy of increasing levels of complexity entails "real and increasingly autonomous and integrated objects, each with a distinctive set of capacities, whose role in accounting for what the living thing does is ineliminable."[27] McGinn suggests that there is a two-way interaction between the higher- and lower-order capacities and that the physical is fully integrated into the living, not overcome by it. While both remain natural beings, subject always to physical change and traditional alteration, the animate being distinguishes itself by a capacity to encounter those physical changes in new ways—to take them in and make them like, in nutrition, or to take them in in a nonmaterial way. Altogether, this capacity is the *logos* of living. In the animal, it is the *logos* of flesh.

Plants, though fully animate, do not adequately protect themselves from those physical changes nor do they quite so actively enact their own preservation and perfection so as to present a problem or question of ontological difference. Plants lack *logos* insofar as they have no principle that allows them to seek their own preservation and perfection beyond what is present to them. That they take in nutrients and reproduce makes them different from things which are not alive, things which are *apsuchon*. As Greg Recco shows in his chapter in this volume, all living beings, including plants, grow, and hence take in nutrients, according to a ratio, a *logos*. But these functions do not raise plants to the level of sentient, or active, *logos*. Plants can take in nutrient and make it like in a very limited sense—wholly as material. It is sentience and in particular it is in touch where the reflection or re-action to the world begins to differ from material change. The *logos* that accompanies sentience requires that change take place in a nontypical way and here is where the animal most firmly distinguishes itself from other beings as it discriminates between what will help and what will hinder. The plant merely makes what is other into self or, even when in contact with the other, if the other cannot be food for it, it in no way responds to it. In touching, the animate body both admits its materiality and at once defies it, enabling the living being to desire otherwise, to move elsewhere, to encounter yet endure. Through touch, the animal strives to maintain its composition, its ratio. Flesh is the locus of a principle that belongs not to a soul nor to a body but to a living being, a lived body, and to live actively—to discriminate, to struggle, and to work to stay alive—is to have flesh. Flesh is therefore the principle that first admits of pleasure and pain and discrimination, and it strives for the maintenance of a mean state and thus requires the reception of sensible form without matter. In flesh we find the activity of that form of *logos* which is even more developed in an animal that can produce an image freed from its material conditions in order to allow for thought. Flesh is the first place a ratio is actively held and maintained against external conditions.

Flesh is neither body nor soul, but it is the first and underlying principle of the living body; it is neither matter nor form but informed body. Flesh designates a manner of being first recognized in divergence, as French phenomenologist Maurice Merleau-Ponty puts it, in *écart*. Flesh, in one sense, is physical and compositional, and it comes into being as the intermediate transitions between elements cycling in and out of being, but to be flesh requires ensoulment through generation; flesh helps the living being stay what it is but flesh survives only as long as the soul informs the body. Flesh is thus generated and altogether destructible; as the eye without sight is only an eye homonymously, or in name only (*DA* II.1 412b23), the flesh apart from the living being is mere body, an inanimate part of the physical world.

For Aristotle, some conception of flesh appears in various ways at even the barest forms of life. To take in nutrient is to make flesh out of what is not flesh in order to maintain the composition and ratio of the body, but it involves no active maintaining of a ratio; it is limited by size and scale.[28] Only in animals is there the ability to seek food and that which allows the animal to maintain herself, to resist her own destruction. Reproduction is likewise the process to make more flesh (lest production of waste be a kind of reproduction), and in these ways there is something like flesh as principle present in every living being from generation until destruction. The flesh of the plant, however, is purely passive flesh. Sentience offers flesh a new role, that of medium and organ, the operative threshold between self and other, preserving and protecting the animal life through its work as embodied *logos*—material ratio and underlying principle. Here, we find flesh that is, elementally, just like the flesh of the plant or even inanimate material compositions, and yet, the flesh of the animal is always fundamentally other than what it senses and actively working to stay that way. As sensitive, it recognizes through innate ratio what must be sought out and what must be avoided, but its ability to do so requires a special receptivity to those very things. It is in animal flesh that we find the first place the animal can be receptive of a quality without the matter; here we have a principle that does more than treat the matter to make it like, as in nutrition, but is not yet fully at work as human *logos*.[29] Animals do not merely maintain but seek their own persistence; they *act* in order to preserve themselves in their material and formal elements because they have a *logos*—a principle that is a part of both their composition and their *telos*, one that underlies and enables the living of the animal. The materiality of flesh binds it to the world of the sensible; the ensoulment of flesh makes it not merely sensible but sensitive.

Conclusion

Merleau-Ponty suggests that "If one wants metaphors, it would be better to say that the body sensed and the body sentient are as the obverse and the reverse, or again, as two segments of one sole circular course which goes above them from left to right and below them from right to left, but which is but one sole movement in its two phases" (399).[30] I suggest instead that Aristotle's notion of flesh might be seen by analogy to magnets; the body-subject and the world are like magnets; turned one way they are drawn together and will cleave to one another. However, when turned the other way they push one another away and effect a distance that would lead one, unfamiliar with magnetic polarity, to assume their nature is to be apart, pushing against rather than pulling together. But the true nature of the magnets is demonstrated in dual abilities, in the capacity to fluctuate by the merest reversal between unity and difference. Flesh is the possibility of reversal; it is the reality of being within and yet without but is an always embodied *archē*, animating the living being. Flesh is *logos*, that is, sensation and the capacity for reversal or reflection, for discrimination and preservation, and "flesh is an ultimate notion, that it is not the union or compound of two substances, but thinkable by itself."[31] Flesh, for Aristotle, is the vital *logos* of that which lives by self-determination.

Notes

1 Translations from works of Aristotle are from Barnes, *Complete Works of Aristotle* (1984). I have occasionally modified these translations.
2 The other two forms of *logos*, that of plants and that of the human being, are explored in this volume in chapters by Greg Recco, "Flesh as *Logos*," and Eve Rabinoff, "Aristotle on the Rationality of Virtue," respectively.
3 Hans Jonas, "The Nobility of Sight," *Philosophy and Phenomenological Research* 14, no. 4 (1954): 507–19.
4 *Parts of Animals* (*PA*) II.8.653b21.
5 If he were to follow the embedded hierarchy of the rest of *De Anima*, we would expect Aristotle to treat the broader, more basic, and most necessary capacities before the more specialized and rarer ones. For example, Aristotle treats nutrition and reproduction before sensation because the former capacities are necessary conditions of the latter.
6 "Each sense has one kind of object which it discerns, and never errs in reporting that what is before it is colour (*sic*) or sound (though it may err as to what it is that is coloured (*sic*) or where that is, or what it is that is sounding or where that is). Such objects are what we call the special objects of this or that sense" (II.6 418a14-17).
7 Well-known articulations of rival sides of this debate can be seen from Richard Sorabji and Myles Burnyeat's essays in *Essays on De Anima*, ed. Nussbaum and Rorty (New York: Oxford University Press, 1995). See Burnyeat, "Is an Aristotelian Philosophy of Mind Still Credible?" (15–26), and Sorabji, "Intentionality and Physiological Processes: Aristotle's Theory of Sense-Perception" (195–225).
8 At *De Anima* III.13 435b1-6, Aristotle explains that the organ for touch cannot be made of earth or any other single element. If the organ for touch were simply made of earth, it would only be sensitive to the attributes of earth, and, furthermore, other ensouled body parts made of earth might be sensitive, such as hair or bones, and, even more problematically, plants. The other sense organs, such as the eye, insofar as they contain earth, are also sensitive to touch. Insofar as it is sensitive to what is visible, the eye must contain air or water (II.7 418b28-30).
9 See *Categories* 8 for qualities in general, 9a29-b9 for affective qualities in particular.
10 That is, the sensible objects receive the form materially and perceptibly, the medium and sense organ receive it formally and "according to a *logos*" (II.11 424a24).
11 Though he uses it to suggest a theory from which I depart, Stephen Everson, *Aristotle on Perception* (Oxford: Clarendon Press, 1997), suggests something similar of color and the visible, using *Physics* III.1 as support, "just as colour (*sic*) is not the same as visible thing" (201b3). He then shows that it is clear from *De Anima* II.7 that color

and the visible are not equivalent, because colors are not the only objects of vision when we allow that there is a quality belonging to fish scales, some fungi, horns, and so on (what we now call "phosphorescent"), that belong to the visible but to the genus of color. Thus, vision actually applies primarily to visible and invisible; within the realm of visible we include color and one other thing—phosphorescence (114–15).

12 *DA* II.11 424a15-16: Aristotle says that what is intangible is either tangible to too small or too great a degree but not actually lacking the tangible attributes.

13 I find it to be odd that only in sight can we identify by name that quality of the medium that makes it receptive to the object (color). Transparency is a lack of color. But what is the word for a lack of odor, or sound (Aristotle calls it "empty" at *DA* II.8 420a18) or lack of flavor or tangible qualities. Interestingly, the lack of tangible qualities is the most identifiable—it is no body at all if it lacks tangible qualities, which is likewise why that which is perceptive or receptive of tangible qualities cannot lack those qualities itself (i.e., not be a body).

14 We might not expect to see the eye or the nostril listed among the heterogeneous parts given the claim that follows, that "sensation, then, is confined to the simple or homogenous parts" (*PA* II.1 647a14). This further suggests that the actual organ of sensation is not the eye but some specific part of the eye, such as the pupil or the *kore*. Aristotle proposes that the animal body consists of three levels of composition; the highest level are the heterogeneous parts which determine the forms of those below it, those that are for the sake of the heterogeneous parts. Below the heterogeneous parts are the homogenous parts, but even below these are the elements (and even below these are the elementary forces of wet-dry, hot-cold). Though the heterogeneous are the most substantial and the others exist for the sake of these, the order of development is the inverse, such that the elements form the homogenous parts and these in turn form the heterogeneous.

15 This question remains vexing: Is flesh simple (so that it can be an organ of sense) or is it complex (so that it can be receptive to more than one set of contraries)? The simplicity of the other organs seems related to their being comprised of one and only one element (see *PA* I.2 614a12-13). Perhaps the organ for touch is primarily earth-y (cold and dry) but has bits of the other elements so that it can also be wet and hot. Aristotle says in *de Sensu* (3 438b30) that "the organ of touch consists of earth" though we might contrast this with *De Anima* III.13, where he says that earth cannot constitute an organ of sense (*DA* 435a14) and that touch has to have an organ capable of receiving all tangible qualities, not merely those of earth (*DA* 435a22-23), and, further, that plants can't sense because they consist of earth (*DA* 435b2). T. K. Johansen, *Aristotle on the Sense-Organs*, Cambridge: Cambridge Classical Studies, 1998, argues that flesh is the organ of touch and that the simple (*homoiomerous*) parts are those that are the same in all their parts, even if those parts are themselves not made from a single element (see 193–9).

16 *PA* II.8 653b30.

17 "The skin, again, is formed by the drying of the flesh, like the scum upon boiled substances; it is so formed not only because it is on the outside, but also because what is glutinous, being unable to evaporate, remains on the surface. While in other animals the glutinous is dry, for which reason the covering of the bloodless animals is testaceous or crustaceous, in the sanguinea it is rather of the nature of fat. In all of these which are not of too earthy a nature the fat is collected under the covering of the skin, a fact which points to the skin being formed out of such a glutinous substance, for fat is somewhat glutinous" (*GA* II.6 743b9-15). See also *PA* IV.6 682b21-22.

18 In *Nicomachean Ethics* V.1 firmness of flesh is a sign of health.
19 At *Parts of Animals* II.1 647a20, II.8 653b20, and other sections. Aristotle suggests that some animals have an organ for touch which is not flesh but analogous to flesh. He seems to have certain cephalopods and insects in mind, here. An ensouled being with no flesh (no organ for touch) would be a plant.
20 Flesh is reliant on being some composition of earth and other elements, but this leaves open an incredibly wide range of possible combinations.
21 Even if we grant that the organ of touch is specifically the heart, it is the heart insofar as it is homogenous, simple, and composed of flesh. Aristotle continues in *Parts of Animals* to deduce that the heart must serve as "the primary seat of the principles (*prōton morion tas toiautas archas*)" of the sensitive, motor and nutritive faculties. This does not, however, definitively suggest that the heart is the specific organ for touch, rather that it is an organ for a central sensory power (such as, perhaps, that with which we would sense common sensibles). However, Aristotle here notes that the heart is both heterogeneous and homogeneous, such that it can serve both the affections of body such as nutrition and sensation, but also the "motor and active" (II.1 647a29) faculties of the animal. He writes later, however, that while "the region of the heart (that) constitutes the sensory centre (*sic*)" that "touch and taste are manifestly in immediate connexion (*sic*) with the heart" (II.10 656a30) as opposed to the other senses whose organs locate them in the head. Given that Aristotle does not, within *De Anima*, identify the heart in particular, and that here the heart is purposively described as homogenous and simple in part (in order that it can be a sense organ), that the heart is flesh-y and flesh is the organ of touch, it does not make a great difference whether it is the flesh in general or the heart, as flesh, in particular that serves as organ of touch. The critical point is that in touch alone do the medium and organ coincide.
22 Further, "what has the power of producing sound is what has the power of setting in movement a single mass of air which is continuous up to the organ of hearing. The organ of hearing is physically united with air, and because it is in air, the air inside is moved concurrently with the air outside. Hence animals do not hear with all parts of their bodies, nor do all parts admit of the entrance of air; for even the part that can be moved and can sound has not air everywhere in it. Air in itself is, owing to its friability, quite soundless; only when its dissipation is prevented is its movement sound. The air in the ear is built into a chamber just to prevent this dissipating movement, in order that the animal may accurately apprehend all varieties of the movements of the air outside" (*DA* II.8 420a3-12).
23 The material already exists in the female and can be seen as having soul potentially, but until the semen brings about the principle of movement in this material, its potential is akin to a plant more than an animal (Aristotle deduces this by showing that since a female bird can produce eggs and eggs go bad, the eggs produced by the female alone must have some element of soul). But even a plant is able to perfect its own parts, as Aristotle notes, and yet the potentially ensouled material in the female does not self-perfect or complete because it is not a plant but an animal, and it must therefore have not merely a nutritive but also a sensitive soul, and in this case "the female cannot generate perfectly by herself alone, for then the male would exist in vain, and nature makes nothing in vain" so that "the male perfects the work of generation for he imparts the sensitive soul" (*GA* II.5 741b2-6).
24 Though J. L. Ackrill, "Aristotle's Definitions of PSUCHE," *Proceedings of the Aristotelian Society*, New Series 73 (1972–73): 119–33, has famously identified what

he sees as a fundamental problem in applying the hylomorphic relationship to body and soul, I maintain that Aristotle's principle of homonymy is consistent with a hylomorphic treatment of soul. "Hylomorphism" is the term that traditionally identifies the relationship of form to matter in Aristotle, and I suggest that *flesh* designates that refinement of hylomorphism when it distinguishes the particular relationship of body and soul. Specifically, *flesh* pertains to the work of the living hylomorphic compound (i.e., the living body) or the activity of enacting one's own preservation and perfection.

25 Merleau-Ponty, "The Intertwining—The Chiasm," in *The Merleau-Ponty Reader*, ed. Toadvine and Lawlor (Northwestern University Press Studies in Phenomenology and Existential Philosophy, 2007), 393–413. See pages 396 and 412.
26 Marie McGinn, "Real Things and the Mind Body Problem," *Proceedings of the Aristotelian Society* 100 (2000): 303–17, 311.
27 Ibid.
28 See Recco, "Flesh as *Logos*," 14–15.
29 On this, see Rabinoff, "Aristotle on the Rationality of Virtue," in this volume.
30 Merleau-Ponty, "The Intertwining," 393–413.
31 Ibid., 401. Here, the claim is framed in a question as to whether flesh is an ultimate notion, but I take the question to be rhetorical.

5

Perception, Thought, and Error in Aristotle's *De Anima*

Whitney Howell

Introduction

In Book II, Chapter 3, of *De Anima*, Aristotle contends that in addition to the nutritive powers we share with plants and the appetitive, perceptual, and locomotive powers we share with animals, human beings possess intellect (*nous*), the power of thinking (II.3 414b18). He goes on to argue that even though it is possible to give a general definition of soul that would encompass these diverse powers, such a definition would fail to capture what is distinctive to the specific forms of different living things; thus, he contends, we must examine separately the different forms that life takes in living things with different powers (II.3 414b23-27). This remark, along with his subsequent, more cryptic claim that each successive power of soul contains the preceding powers *potentially* (II.3 414b32), suggests that the distinctively human power of intellect is not an addition to the more fundamental powers, but, rather, that its presence affects their functioning.[1] In other words, the way that human beings experience the world *through* these other powers is different than it is for beings that possess only those powers. This difference has important implications for how we are integrated in the world and what kind of world we are integrated in. Even though, like other animals, we are part of a world that appeals to our perceptual powers and that, as such, incites our desires and movements, we are also capable of standing apart from that world, in reflecting on, describing, explaining, or questioning our immediate perceptual experience. In doing so, we demonstrate our capacity to participate in a world that appeals to the power of intellect.

In Book III of *De Anima*, Aristotle compares and contrasts the perceiving and thinking powers of the human soul, paying special attention to their relationships with their respective objects. He claims that while "thinking, both speculative and practical, is regarded as akin to a form of perceiving" (III.3 427a19-20)—because both powers inform the soul's awareness of, and ability to discriminate among, things in the world (III.3 427a20-21)—it is not analogously accurate.[2] On this point, he writes: "[F]or perception of the special objects of sense is always free from error, and is found in all animals, while it is possible to think falsely as well as truly, and thought is found only where there is discourse of reason as well as sensibility" (III.3 427b11-15). In other words, while a functioning perceptual faculty, in correspondence with the proper objects of perception, ensures the truth of perceptual experience, the intellect, in its relation to the objects of thought, is subject to error. In this chapter, I examine the relationships that perception and intellect have to their respective objects for "animals with *logos*," starting with this basic difference and then proposing what I take to be an important similarity.

I begin by considering how Aristotle's use of the term "*logos*" in his discussion of perception identifies a correspondence between the power of perception and its objects. I show how this correspondence secures the accuracy of perceptual experience, but also requires a kind of activity on the part of the animal in relation to its world. I show further that as a result of the correspondence between the power of perception and its proper objects, the perceiving animal experiences a perceptual world that reflects its powers. Next, in order to account for why, according to Aristotle, thinking is subject to error that is impossible in perception, I consider how, unlike the perceptive potentiality, the intellectual potentiality lacks analogous, native parameters that secure the accuracy of its experience of its proper objects. While Aristotle subsequently claims, in Book III, Chapter 6, that "the thinking of the definition in the sense of the constitutive essence is never in error" (III.6 430b27), and, earlier in the chapter, that "the thinking . . . of the simple objects of thought is found in those cases where falsehood is impossible" (III.6 430a26), I argue that the disanalogy he initially proposes remains because even the apprehension of the simple objects of thought requires development not necessary in perception. More specifically, thinking requires some process of development both in order to experience intelligible objects as such and in order to experience them *truly*, that is, in accordance with what they actually are. I argue that in developing the potentiality of intellect, one becomes capable of thinking objects of thought on the object's terms and, as a result, becomes capable of experiencing a world that, similar to the perceptual world, reflects and reinforces the potential thinker's powers. In the final section of the chapter, I consider how, for human beings, the objects of perception and the objects of intellect are rarely separate, and I propose that the errors we make are indicative of our integration in a perceptual world that also appeals to the power of intellect.

I. The *Logos* of Perception

According to Aristotle's analysis in *De Anima*, to be a living thing in the world is to be subject to the world, integrated in it and affected by it—to be passive, in some sense. But it is equally to be active—to be able to act upon the world, to engage it, change it, or oppose it.[3] Aristotle's development of the distinction between potentiality and actuality in perception emphasizes this ambiguity. As he notes at the beginning of Book II, Chapter 5, for perception to take place, there must be something to perceive; more specifically, there must be something external to the perceiver (II.5 416b35). Thus, one's sensory experience *is* passive insofar as it is dependent on the presence of a sensible object (II.5 417b25). For example, I am affected by the aroma of the roasting vegetables and the heat of the oven when I open the door. However, in order to be affected by sensory objects, the animal must be capable of perception. As Aristotle points out, animals possess this capability, or potentiality, at birth (II.5 417b18), which enables the activity of their sensory powers in the presence of external sense objects (II.5 417b21-22).[4] Thus, while he concedes that "we cannot help using the incorrect terms 'being acted upon or altered'" when describing the transition between potentiality and actuality in perception (II.5 418a3), such terms are incorrect insofar as they conceal the equally necessary activity of the sensory power capable of perception.[5] Exercising this capability *is* a kind of activity, albeit one the perceiver does not initiate. Thus, while the objects of perception do act on the perceiver, their perception requires a corresponding activity on the part of the perceiver, or, more specifically, in the perceptual faculties themselves. For this reason, Aristotle writes that we say that an animal perceives in "two ways"—in its *capacity to see*, for example, and in its *actually seeing* (II.5 417a9-12)—both of which refer to the perceiver's ability to actively correspond with sense objects.

Aristotle develops his analysis of the correspondence between the perceptual faculty and its object in his account of perception in general, in Book II, Chapter 12, and also in the early chapters of Book III, which bring perception into contrast with intellect. In these discussions, he refers to a *logos* of the perceptual qualities of an object *and* of the perceptual faculty itself. He first argues, regarding the object of perception, that it is not *that which essentially defines the object* that is perceived, but rather its *perceivable attributes*, which are perceivable according to a *logos* (II.12 424a22-23).[6] For example, when I see the green cactus, it is not the plant as such that causes me to see it as green, but rather, Aristotle claims, "what *quality* it has, i.e. in what *logos* its constituents are combined" (II.12 424a23). In other words, the perceptual faculty is affected not by the thing as such but by a *logos* embodied in the thing, and the sense organ perceives this *logos* as a particular quality. Correspondingly, in the ensuing discussion Aristotle refers to the *logos* of the perceptual faculty in order to distinguish its power from the organ that is its material condition. He writes that "the sense and its organ are the same in fact, but their essence is not the same. What perceives is, of course, a spatial magnitude, but we must not admit that either the having the power to perceive or the sense itself is a magnitude; what they are is a certain ratio (*logos*) or power (*dunamis*) *in* a magnitude" (II.12 424a26-28).[7] Just as it is not the thing itself that affects the perceptual faculty, but rather the *logos* of its constituent perceivable qualities, it is not the organ *qua* material that enables perception but rather the power the organ embodies. In other words, while the power of perception requires a bodily organ—indeed, the power and the organ "are the same in fact"—it is not reducible to it.

Aristotle's remarks regarding how the organ may be damaged or destroyed by certain objects indicate its effectiveness within an established range of perceptual qualities.[8] These remarks suggest that the *logos* of the perceptual faculty specifies the bounds within which its power may be exercised. Objects that exceed these bounds—such as the hot oven door or the brightness of the midday sun—can damage or even destroy the perceptual faculty (II.12 424a30). This point has two important implications that further support Aristotle's contention that perception involves a kind of activity and, moreover, demonstrate that the animal's relation to its world reinforces its powers of engaging with it. First, because perception can only take place within a delimited range, the perceptual world is always articulated in terms of the animal's perceptual powers.[9] In other words, the sights, sounds, smells, tastes, and textures of its experience are as much expressive of the animal's powers as they are of the richness of the perceptual world. More specifically, in their congruence with the *logos* of the perceptual faculty, the proper objects of perception are expressive of the animal's power to respond to, interact with, and act on its world; they offer the animal various points of further entry into this world, in contrast to an excessively loud sound or bright light, which hinder further interaction with the world. Second, as the examples of destructive objects make apparent, perception is possible only insofar as the power to perceive is preserved in perceiving.[10] Thus, the animal's experience of a perceptual world is premised on the potential for further interaction with this world, its power to pursue a variety of possible paths of involvement and, in turn, to experience an increasingly articulate perceptual world in the actualization of these powers.

Aristotle's attribution of a *logos* to the perceptual faculty indicates the animal's capacity to correspond with the perceptual world, to find its capacities answered in the *logoi* present in the proper objects of perception. That this correspondence involves activity on the part of the animal and, as I have suggested here, encourages the animal's further active engagement with its world points to a way of understanding Aristotle's contention that "perception of the special objects of sense is always free from error" (III.3 427b11). Perception is true because perception is *how* the animal is integrated in its world. Its powers effectively match the proper objects of perception and define the world these objects comprise. Consequently, insofar as perception is possible for the animal, error is impossible.[11] The animal will always be "right" in a world that answers its powers. Moreover, insofar as the world answers the animal's powers, it is increasingly articulate. The animal's truthful perceptual experience ensures the continued exercise of its powers: even within a constant environment, the animal is capable of making new perceptual discoveries and forging further routes of interaction.

In Aristotle's account, the truth of perception follows from the animal's integration in and activity in response to—in short, its correspondence with—the perceptual world. Aristotle's ensuing discussion of intellect draws on this account of perception and, as I will show, illuminates the way in which the human animal—paradoxically, the animal with *logos*—lacks a similar correspondence with the objects of thought.

II. Developing the Power of Intellect

As was shown earlier, the *logos* of the perceptual faculty indicates the range within which perception of its proper objects takes place. Objects that exceed this range destroy the perceptive potentiality, making any future perception impossible. In the more general terms of Aristotle's account of soul, the destruction of the potentiality prevents the living being a particular kind of integration in the world.

In beginning his account of intellect in Book III, Chapter 4, Aristotle contends that though "mind must be related to what is thinkable, as sense is to what is sensible" (III.4

429a17), it lacks "an organ like the sensitive faculty" (III.4 429a27). He goes on to note a further difference between the intellect and the perceptual faculty:

> Observation of the sense-organs and their employment reveals a distinction between the impassibility of the sensitive and that of the intellective faculty. After strong stimulation of a sense we are less able to exercise it than before, as e. g. in the case of a loud sound we cannot hear easily immediately after, or in the case of a bright colour or a powerful odour we cannot see or smell, but in the case of mind, thought about an object that is highly intelligible renders it more and not less able afterwards to think objects that are less intelligible: the reason is that while the faculty of sensation is dependent upon the body, mind is separate from it. (III.4 429a30-429b5)

Interpreting Aristotle's provocative claim that the "mind is separate from [the body]" (which he further elaborates in Book III, Chapter 5) is beyond the ambition of this chapter.[12] Without definitively resolving this difficulty, however, notice that in this passage Aristotle attributes the range of the perceptive potential to the determinacy of the perceiving body.[13] As the site of the animal's perceptual integration in the world, the body—more specifically, the powers embodied in the perceptual organs—establishes the parameters of this integration; objects that fall outside these parameters may damage the potential to perceive or may not be perceived at all. According to the contrast Aristotle is drawing here, the potential of intellect lacks not only an organ but also analogously established parameters that determine its relation to its objects.

Before developing this point of distinction further, let us briefly consider how the potential thinker comes to relate to objects of thought by drawing on Aristotle's discussion in Book II, Chapter 5, of the three different senses in which we speak of a "knower." First, an infant, who "knows" very little, is nevertheless a potential knower insofar as she is the kind of being for whom knowing is an intrinsic possibility. This most basic potential is inherent to the nature of those beings capable of knowing and requires a "change of quality" to become actual; the infant must *learn* how to exercise this potential (II.5 417a30-32). The second kind of knower is that person in whom the potential has been developed but is currently inactive. This potential is present in someone who, for example, knows how to cook but is not currently cooking. The third kind of knower is the person who is engaged in the exercise of knowing, such as when the person who knows how to cook is cooking.

If we now compare the potentialities of perception and intellect, we can see that they differ in an important sense. Whereas we speak of perception in two ways—referring to either the potential to perceive or the act of perception (II.5 417a9-10)—we speak of knowing in three ways, indicating a further division in the intellectual potentiality. This further division is apparent if we consider the difference between how the potentialities of perception and intellect are actualized. As was noted earlier, because animals are born with the perceptive potential at the ready, the potential is actualized by the presence of the perceptual object (II.5 417b18-19). In contrast, though human beings have a similarly native potential of intellect, it is not *automatically* actualized by potential objects of thought. Rather, the intellectual potential requires some course of development (III.4 429b9) in order to encounter objects as knowable, provoking knowing. To draw on the example cited previously, I must first acquire knowledge of how to cook before I am a "knower" in the second sense that Aristotle describes[14]; conversely, my sense of smell does not require an analogous course of development to encounter the cooking food as fragrant.[15] In turn, having knowledge of how to cook, I may choose among a selection of recipes and decide to prepare a meal, but I do not similarly decide to encounter the smells of the cooking food (II.5 417b24).

The further division in the intellectual potentiality and the course of development its actualization requires shed light on Aristotle's claim that intellect incurs error that is impossible in perception (II.5 427b11-15). As noted in Section I, the *logos* of the perceptual faculty indicates the range within which perceivers correspond with a perceptual world. Insofar as it requires some course of development, the native intellectual potentiality lacks an analogously established range of correspondence between the potential thinker and the objects of thought. In other words, the intellectual potentiality differs from the perceptive potentiality not only because it lacks an analogous organ (III.4 429a27) but also because it lacks, at least initially, a *logos* that similarly secures its integration in an intelligible world. Consequently, while there are no objects of thought that could destroy the potential to think, the thinker's relationship to these objects is not guaranteed to be free from error, even once she has developed the power to think.

While it would be a daunting task to account for why and how myriad errors in thought take place,[16] I propose, following the account of perception in Section I, that, in general, error is a failure of the thinker to correspond with the objects of thought. Take, for example, a student in a philosophy course who is a potential knower "in the second sense," insofar as she has developed the power to think. When initially reading Aristotle's text, she may find it simple and uninteresting. However, her impression of the text is a reflection of *her* rather than of the text; it reflects the incorrect terms she is bringing to bear on it in her reading (such as, for example, an incorrect or rudimentary understanding of philosophical ideas, or expectations of the kinds of insight a philosophical text should offer her). Upon further study and instruction, she may come to think *in accordance with* the terms set by the text itself. In this sense, the thinker's power is, like the perceiver's, dependent on the corresponding object, at least initially: thinking takes place in response to the object.[17] Once the student comes to think according to the terms set by the object, however, these terms become *her* power to think; they become part of her orientation toward the text and, perhaps, toward her own experience.[18] As a result, the text itself is richer, subtler, and more complicated, and she is more capable in her reading of and thinking with it.

Thus, in developing the potentiality of intellect, the thinker develops the capacity to correspond with objects of thought. She experiences a more complex and articulate world that is not limited by the initial—and perhaps idiosyncratic—terms she brings to bear on it, but that, rather, offers her the terms according to which it can be understood. As a result, she experiences further avenues of involvement, of inquiry and discovery. This is apparent in the example of the student whose reading of Aristotle extends beyond her undergraduate course, but it is no less the case for the cook who, as a knower in the second sense, experiences the kitchen as the platform for future projects beyond those described in the recipes she followed in initially developing her capacity. Notice that in both examples, the knowers' powers reflect the potential inherent in the worlds they are now integrated in, potential they failed to recognize prior to becoming more capable. Furthermore, because they are more capable, they no longer have to rely on their initial points of entry into the world of thought—in my examples, the text, or a recipe—in order to think in accordance with those points of entry or to access what they make available (II.5 417b20-28).

This last point highlights a contrast between the potentialities of perception and intellect mentioned in the previously cited example of the cook, who decides on her own initiative to exercise her knowledge but does not similarly decide to smell the food. To put this point in more general terms: while the perceiving animal encounters a world that reflects her powers, the knower has the potential to experience a world that reflects her initiative.[19] While this contrast lends apparent support to the characterization of perception as passive (relative to the active initiative of the thinker), we should recall—heeding Aristotle's remark that such characterization is incorrect (II.5 418a3)—that perception of the proper objects reflects and reinforces the perceiver's powers. Similarly, once potential thinkers have developed the power to think, they become capable of experiencing a world that, like the animal's experience of the perceptual world, reflects and reinforces their native powers, which include the power of initiative.

In focusing on the distinction between the potentialities of perception and intellect, I have demonstrated how each enables the living thing a particular kind of integration in the world that reinforces its powers. However, as beings capable of both perception and thought, we do not always exercise these powers separately. Indeed, Aristotle frequently suggests that the objects of perception and intellect are rarely distinct in the experience of beings possessing both potentialities.[20] In particular—and significant to our consideration of error—incidental objects of perception, which Aristotle mentions in Book II, Chapter 6, provide examples of how perception reflects the power of intellect. In Aristotle's discussion, he claims that the perception of the son of Diares is *incidental to* the white patch that is the proper object of the perceptual faculty (II.5 418a20) and thus "in no way as such affects the senses" (II.5 418a22-23).[21] However, even though the son of Diares as such does not affect the functioning of the perceptual faculties *as* perceptual faculties, it nevertheless characterizes the perceptual object for beings possessing intellect. In the final section of the chapter, I turn to a passage in Book III, Chapter 4, to consider how perception reflects the power of intellect—and, in turn, the latter's susceptibility to error—in the experience of beings possessing both potentialities.

III. Human Error

In a difficult passage, Aristotle considers whether the same or different faculties distinguish between a thing and its essence:[22]

> [F]lesh and what it is to be flesh are discriminated either by different faculties, or by the same faculty in two different states . . . . Now it is by means of the sensitive

faculty that we discriminate the hot and the cold, i.e. the factors which combined in a certain ratio (*logos*) constitute flesh: the essential character of flesh is apprehended by something different either wholly separate from the sensitive faculty or related to it as a bent line to the same line when it has been straightened out. Again in the case of abstract objects what is straight is analogous to what is snub-nosed; for it necessarily implies a continuum as its matter: its constitutive essence is different, if we may distinguish between straightness and what is straight: let us take it to be two-ness. It must be apprehended, therefore, by a different power or by the same power in a different state. (III.4 429b13-23)

Aristotle reiterates here that the proper objects of perception are perceptual qualities, that is, "hotness," "coldness," "whiteness." However, as noted earlier, we perceive these qualities *in* particular things, namely, the incidental objects of perception such as the son of Diares. Thus, it would seem that in this passage, the faculty that apprehends flesh (albeit incidentally) is perceptual, whereas the faculty that apprehends the being of flesh is intellect.[23] Aristotle does not directly answer the question of whether or not these are different faculties, but, rather, he considers the relation between them.[24] In an apparent attempt to clarify this relation, he goes on to suggest that it is analogous to the relation intellect has to itself in apprehending two different kinds of objects, "what is straight" (a line, presumably) and "straightness." Other commentators have noted that the analogical move Aristotle proposes here is between levels of abstraction: straightness is an abstraction from what is straight, just as what it is to be flesh is an abstraction from embodied flesh.[25] Such moves between levels of abstraction are distinctive to human beings and indicate our potential involvement in domains that transcend immediate perception, for example, in language, mathematics, and metaphysics.[26] In addition, however, they point to our capacity to engage in these domains *through* perception: I perceive the *logos* of hot and cold in flesh, and, if I have developed my native potential as a thinker, my perception of flesh introduces the question of what flesh *is*. Similarly, it is through the image of the line that I see straightness, and, in doing so, that I may ask further, "What is straightness?" Thus, while Aristotle's inquiry in this passage does not unequivocally resolve which faculty apprehends which objects, it nevertheless illuminates the human capacity to encounter objects of thought in perception, a capacity that he will identify explicitly two chapters later in his claim that "the objects of thought are in the sensible forms, viz. both the abstract objects and all the states and affections of sensible things" (III.8 432a4-5).

It is the power of intellect that makes possible our encountering objects of thought in perception. However, because this power defines us as human beings, it also transforms perception itself. In the more specific terms of Aristotle's account, the ensouled being, rather than isolated faculties, exercises its powers.[27] Aristotle makes this point when he writes early in *De Anima* that "Thinking, loving, and hating are affections not of mind, but of that which has mind, so far as it has it" (I.4 408b26-27). Similarly, we could contend, perceiving, for the human animal, is not merely a function of its perceptual faculties, but rather of that which has perceptual faculties *and* intellect. Consequently, though our integration in a perceptual world is secured by the corresponding activity of our perceptual faculties, it nevertheless involves and will reflect the contributions of intellect.

One such contribution is the susceptibility to error. As Aristotle notes, error is impossible in the relation between the perceptual faculty and its proper objects. However, human perception includes not only the proper objects of perception but also, as noted earlier, incidental objects of perception, which reflect our capacity to perceive objects as being particular ("my friend Peter") or universal ("man") things, beyond their perceptual qualities (shape, color, sound, etc.). Because incidental objects of perception reflect the power of intellect, it follows that errors in human perception would most often pertain to these objects. Consider, for example, the experience of preparing a meal with a skilled chef in her kitchen: the space—the kitchen's dimensions, layout, organization, and so forth—may be unfamiliar to me and, more significant to the purposes of our task, so may the instruments, ingredients, and terminology that the chef has at her regular disposal. If I am inexperienced at baking, for example, her request that I "cream sugar and butter" may confuse me, and her mixer and tools may confront me as alien objects. My confusion reflects my inability to perceive what I am perceiving; more specifically in terms of Aristotle's account, it reflects my inability to perceive incidental objects of perception, which, in this example, include special appliances and tools, but also unfamiliar combinations of otherwise familiar food items. Still more telling, however, are the errors I make in attempting to orient myself: in thinking, for example, that my friend's instructions to mix the sugar and butter in a particular way are a list of ingredients or, even more likely, in mistaking the organizing principles of this foreign kitchen for those of my more modest one—by opening drawers and cabinets where I expect to find the needed items—I am bringing to bear on my experience terms that fail to correspond with it. These terms are furnished by intellect—by the processes of learning and habituation that inform my experience of cooking at home—and distinguish my attempts to correspond with the perceptual world of the kitchen I currently occupy. It is only in corresponding with this world that I can actualize my powers within it—in correctly identifying objects in the kitchen, but also in successfully pursuing other possible projects it offers.

This consideration of error in human perception reinforces the central point that my studies of Aristotle's accounts of perception and intellect revealed: the powers of soul enable the beings possessing them to be integrated in the worlds they make available. It is only as integrated within the world that is proper to it that the ensouled being is powerful. For beings possessing intellect, however, this integration is not secured by the presence of the native power. Consequently, we are potentially less integrated in the world of our experience—a world that, as we have seen, is both intelligible and perceptual—than beings possessing only the lesser powers of soul are integrated in the worlds available to them.

Notes

1 For an excellent analysis of the analogy Aristotle draws in this passage between figure and soul, and an account of how the higher-order powers of soul affect the lower faculties, see Section IV of Eve Rabinoff, "Aristotle on the Intelligibility of Perception,"

The Review of Metaphysics 68, no. 4 (2015): 719–40. Rabinoff's contribution to this volume, "Aristotle on the Rationality of Virtue," also questions the strict separation of the rational and nonrational parts of the soul and discusses the moral implications of their being, as she puts it, "inseparably intertwined." See also Deborah K. Modrak, "The *Nous*-Body Problem in Aristotle," *The Review of Metaphysics* 44, no. 4 (1991): 756–8.

2 All references to Aristotle's *De Anima* will be to J. A. Smith's translation in *The Basic Works of Aristotle*, ed. Richard McKeon (New York: Random House, 1941), 535–603.

3 As Russon points out, even plants, in their metabolic capacities, act upon the world in such a way as to preserve what they are in opposition to other bodies. See John Russon, "Aristotle's Animative Epistemology," *Idealistic Studies* 25, no. 3 (1995): 243.

4 John Russon's contribution to this volume, "'Actuality in the First Sense' and the Question of Human Nature," offers a helpful analysis of the relation between potentiality and actuality in Aristotle's philosophy. Russon's claim, in Section I, that actuality never fully realizes its potentiality—which he seeks to defend with respect to how an individual's actuality relates to its potentiality as a member of a natural species—applies perfectly to sense perception: it is uncontroversial to note that the potentiality to perceive a variety of sights, sounds, textures, tastes, and smells is never fully actualized in any one perceiving animal.

5 See Kosman, "Perceiving that We Perceive: *On the Soul* III. 2," *Philosophical Review* 84 (1975): 507–17, for an excellent discussion of why perception is never simply "being affected" by an external object but always involves an apperceptive awareness that is commensurate with the perceptual life of the animal.

6 Consistent with my reading here, Ward contends that it is the *logos* of particular sensible kinds—for example, color, flavor, sound—that affects the sense organ. See Julie K. Ward, "Perception and *Logos* in Aristotle's ii 12," *Ancient Philosophy* 8 (1988): 218–21.

7 See David Bradshaw, "Aristotle on Perception: The Dual-Logos Theory," *Apeiron* 30, no. 2 (1997): 149–56, for arguments supporting the translation of *logos* as "ratio" in this passage.

8 In the passage I am focusing on here, Aristotle does not indicate that the range is established by the material determinacy of the organ; however, in Book III, Chapter 4, he explicitly refers to sensation as "dependent upon the body" (III.4 429b4), which suggests that the animal's body determines the parameters within which sensation can take place. Other scholars have considered more specifically the way in which the sense organ itself is a *logos* that in turn determines the *logos* of its power to perceive. See, e.g., Bradshaw, "Aristotle on Perception," 149–56; Ward, "Perception and *Logos* in Aristotle's ii 12," 222–5.

9 The enactive approach to perception in contemporary work in phenomenology and the philosophy of mind resonates with Aristotle's emphases on the activity of the animal necessary for perception to take place and the animal body's setting the terms for its engagement with the world. For example, Evan Thompson, *Mind in Life: Biology, Phenomenology, and the Sciences of Mind* (Cambridge, MA: Harvard University Press, 2007), contends that living organisms are self-generating and self-maintaining and that their life processes—nutrition, perception, movement, cognition—cannot be understood apart from the organism's meaningful interaction with its environment (13–14, 37–65). Thompson writes that "no animal is a mere passive respondent; every animal meets the environments on its own sensorimotor terms" (47).

10 This point is consistent with Aristotle's characterization of the nutritive power—the most basic power of any ensouled being—as "that which tends to maintain whatever has this power in it of continuing such as it was" (II.4 416b17-19). A significant implication of Aristotle's analysis of perception is that the possibility of future perception is necessary for the present perceptual experience to take place. This implication resonates strongly with phenomenological accounts of perception that emphasize the way in which possible perceptual futures contextualize the subject's perceptual present. See, e.g., Alva Nöe's contention in *Action in Perception* (Cambridge, MA: MIT Press, 2004) that the meaningful experience of a perceptual object is informed by the body's sensorimotor capabilities for further interaction with that object (59–65). While Nöe's analysis pertains to complex perceptual objects, such as a bottle, and Aristotle's point in this passage is confined to the proper objects of perception, such as color and sound, both contend that any present perceptual experience requires the possibility of future perception.

11 Irving Block, "Truth and Error in Aristotle's Theory of Sense Perception," *The Philosophical Quarterly* 11, no. 42 (1961), claims that perception is true, according to Aristotle, because the natural function of the perceptual faculties—the end toward which they are directed—is perception of their respective proper objects. An advantage of Block's "teleological solution" is that it accounts for why error *is* possible in cases of (1) the common sensibles—that is, because the common sensibles (e.g., shape and motion) are not among the proper objects of the individual perceptual faculties—and (2) injury to the perceptual faculty, which prevents it from fulfilling its natural function (see especially 6–8). I take my argument to be consistent with Block's; however, while his teleological solution emphasizes the design of nature in fitting the organism to the perceptual world, my argument focuses on how this "fit" makes possible the activities that characterize the life of the organism.

12 For such discussion, see, e.g., Modrak, "The *Nous*-Body Problem in Aristotle," esp. 757–67, and Charles H. Kahn, "Aristotle on Thinking," in *Essays on Aristotle's De Anima*, ed. Nussbaum and Rorty (New York: Clarendon, 1995), esp. 360–4 and 375–9.

13 See footnote 8 for a more detailed discussion of this point.

14 In other words, I must develop the habits of a cook. See Section II of Russon's contribution to this volume, "'Actuality in the First Sense' and the Question of Human Nature," for a discussion of the role of habit in the relation between first and second actuality in the case of human beings.

15 Phenomenological accounts emphasize that perception reflects developed capacities. For example, in *Phenomenology of Perception*, trans. Donald A. Landes (New York: Routledge, 2012), Merleau-Ponty demonstrates that our experience of color cannot be separated from our skillful bodily adjustment to a situation that is established in lighting and in the tasks toward which we are directed (318–25). Similarly, Noë argues in *Action in Perception* that we learn how to perceive in tandem with the development of our bodily capabilities for movement, and thus that perception always involves an understanding of the "sensorimotor significance" that makes it possible (103). Thus, Merleau-Ponty and Noë both contend that perceptual capabilities develop as our capabilities to move and engage with the environment develop and improve. Nevertheless, their accounts are not wholly at odds with the claim I am identifying in Aristotle's account, insofar as the potential to perceive is, in an important sense, *ready*, such that these more refined adjustments become possible. This point is perhaps more clearly evident if we consider the effect of culture on perception: that I encounter the food as fragrant is a consequence of the "readiness" of my perceptual faculty; whether

I encounter the fragrance of the food as appetizing or repellent is a consequence of the cultural influence on the development of my perceptual capacity. In contrast to the "readiness" of my perceptual faculty, however, I am not similarly ready to cook until I have developed a capacity beyond my innate power to do so.

16 In further considering the analogy that other thinkers have drawn between perception and thinking, Aristotle remarks that many have failed to account for error, even though "it is more intimately connected with animal existence and the soul continues longer in the state of error than in that of truth" (III.3 427b1-3).

17 Modrak, *Aristotle: The Power of Perception* (Chicago, IL: University of Chicago Press, 1987), 118, similarly notes that thinking and perceiving are passive in relation to their respective objects.

18 Russon, "Aristotle's Animative Epistemology," 247–8, makes this same point with reference to a similar example in his analysis of Aristotle's discussion of *epagōgē* at the end of the *Posterior Analytics*.

19 Aristotle contends that the "man of science" is able "to exercise the power [of intellect] on his own initiative" (III.4 429b6-7).

20 In addition to the incidental objects of perception, which I discuss here as examples of how intellect informs perception, Aristotle also claims, at III.7 431a16 and III.8 432a6-8, that intellect relies on perception in order to learn and as the source of images that are necessary for thinking to take place.

21 Scholars disagree on the extent to which, according to Aristotle's account in *De Anima*, the incidental objects of perception involve intellect. In his reading of this passage, Kahn, "Aristotle on Thinking," 368, argues that "'the son of Diares' is already a *noēton*." In contrast, Modrak, *Aristotle: The Power of Perception*, 70, argues that "The incidental object is an object of perception for Aristotle because the apprehension of the complexes of proper and common objects is sufficient in a particular context for the perception of the incidental object. Moreover, there is no textual evidence for attributing to Aristotle a narrow notion of perception that would exclude interpretation." For her full discussion of this passage in relation to Aristotle's account of the common sense, see Modrak, *Aristotle: The Power of Perception*, 69–71. See also Rabinoff, "Aristotle on the Intelligibility of Perception," section I, for a discussion of arguments in support of the claim that incidental objects require interpretation, and sections II–III for Rabinoff's counter to such arguments in her novel analysis of incidental perception as "apprehend[ing] a thing in its significance to the perceiver's desires, projects, and aims," and her further claim that, for human perceivers, "the incidental perceptible is indeed perceived and . . . , in some cases, . . . informed by intellectual accomplishments" (731).

22 Kahn, "Aristotle on Thinking," fn. 20, 370, notes that this passage evokes Aristotle's claim at 1037b4-5 in *Metaphysics Z* that material things are not the same as their essence.

23 My reading of this passage follows Hicks in *Aristotle: De Anima* (Cambridge: Cambridge University Press, 1907), 487. Modrak, *Aristotle: The Power of Perception*, 119, also contends that it is by the perceptual faculty that we apprehend flesh. More specifically, she suggests that because Aristotle proposes, in *De Anima* and elsewhere, a continuum of objects of thought from concrete particulars through abstract universals, "the line between perception and intellection is difficult to fix." She argues that intellect "might just be the outcome of a special and peculiarly human employment of the perceptual faculty" (119). In other words, what apprehends flesh and the being of flesh is "the same [cognitive] faculty in two different [i.e.,

perceptual and intellectual] states." See Modrak, *Aristotle: The Power of Perception*, esp. 118–19 and fn. 18, 214–25. Drawing on Aristotle's claim that intellect contains the other powers potentially (II.3 414b28-32), Rabinoff, "Aristotle on the Intelligibility of Perception," Section IV, similarly argues that human perception is informed by intellect. In contrast, Kahn, "Aristotle on Thinking," 370–1, argues that the perceptual faculty does not apprehend the *logos* that constitutes flesh, and that it is only insofar as the perceptual faculty is working in conjunction with intellect that it perceives the particular thing. In short, according to Kahn, what apprehends flesh and the being of flesh is intellect.

24 Kahn, "Aristotle on Thinking," 371.
25 See Kahn, "Aristotle on Thinking," 371, and Modrak, *Aristotle: The Power of Perception*, 118–19. As noted in fn. 21, Kahn and Modrak disagree about which faculties apprehend which objects in this analogy.
26 Modrak, *Aristotle: The Power of Perception*, 119, refers to these moves as "cognitive shifts."
27 Hicks, *Aristotle: De Anima*, 487, and Modrak, *Aristotle: The Power of Perception*, 115, and "The *Nous*-Body Problem," 756–7, both note Aristotle's emphasis on the soul as a unified living organism rather than as a collection of distinct powers. See also Rabinoff's discussion of the difference between *parts* of soul and *kinds* of soul in "Aristotle on the Intelligibility of Perception."

6

"Actuality in the First Sense" and the Question of Human Nature in Aristotle

John Russon

Introduction

In Book II, Chapter 1, of *On the Soul*, Aristotle distinguishes two senses of *entelecheia*, "actuality," in order to express his definition of the soul. I will explore some of the logical and ontological parameters of this very powerful distinction. I will first consider how the distinction accords with characteristics of reality with which we are naturally familiar in everyday life. I will then reflect upon the metaphysical complexity inherent to this notion and especially relate this to the life of a natural organism. From here, I will turn to my real interest: the human soul. We will see that when applied to the human being, the distinction takes on a significantly different form. We will ultimately see that it is this metaphysical distinction between the two forms of actuality that gives rise to ethics as a dimension of human life.

I. The Metaphysics of Everyday Life

It is central to Aristotle's method to "account for the phenomenona" (*apodōsein ta phainomena*), that is, to begin from, and to hold his analyses answerable to, what is immediately apparent.[1] In keeping with this methodological commitment, Aristotle argues, in *Physics*, Book II, Chapter 1, that *phusis* is obvious (*dēlon*) and that such obviousness must be the starting point for thought.[2] There is a similar obviousness, it seems to me, that lies behind the definition of soul that Aristotle gives in Book II, Chapter 1, of *On the Soul*.

Aristotle defines soul as "the first actuality [*entelecheia hē prōtē*] of a natural body capable of life."[3] This definition relies on a distinction that Aristotle draws at a number of points between two senses of "actuality," a distinction that makes an important metaphysical point and draws its force from familiar features of everyday life.[4] He writes as follows:

> This [the word actuality] has two senses corresponding respectively to knowledge (*epistēmē*) and the exercise of knowledge (*theōrein*). It is obvious (*phaneron*) [that soul is actuality] in the sense of knowledge (*epistēmē*).[5]

The root idea here is the simple distinction between what something is and what it does. In everyday life, we notice that living things have abiding identities that are not simply summaries of their actions. In other words, their identities explain their actions, rather than their actions explaining their identities. A tomato plant as such, for example, has characteristic ways of behaving, a dog as such has characteristic patterns of action, and so on. The dog, for example, runs to greet you at the door when you come home. Had you not come home at that time, however, the dog would have continued sleeping on the mat or gnawing on the rawhide chew. In either circumstance, it is the same dog, and the action it takes could have been otherwise. We recognize the same dog to be there, day after day, and we would have recognized the same dog, even had the actions been different. The *actions* are something *done by* the dog—*it* is their *source*; the identity of the dog is not just the aggregate of the actions. It is this actuality in the sense of "what the thing is" that Aristotle points to in his definition of soul as "the first actuality," or *enthelecheia* as *echein*.[6]

Aristotle here describes the actuality that defines soul as "first." Though the word "first" as used here in the text could simply mean "the first one listed," in fact the notion of firstness describes well the metaphysical weight implied in the distinction of the two senses of actuality, such that we could properly translate "*entelecheia hē prōtē*" as "the primary reality." "First" actuality is first inasmuch as it is what the thing primarily is.[7] It is the essential "what" of the thing (*to ti esti*) that to which we attach its name (indeed, that by virtue of which we can say "its").[8] In my example earlier, it is "dog." Of course, at the same time, however, that living thing—dog, plant, or person—is always active, always actually doing something. This "doing" is also its actuality, but it is to be explained by the first and thus (though Aristotle does not use this expression), it is a secondary actuality, a derivative reality: *entelecheia* as *energeia*.[9]

We should recognize that like the notion of *phusis*, the obviousness of which Aristotle remarks in *Physics* II.1, this distinction is something that is *manifest in everyday life*. In everyday life, what we thus obviously experience is an important metaphysical distinction, namely, the distinction between substance, on the one hand, and its accidents or properties, on the other.[10] Let us reflect further on this distinction—this *experienced* distinction—and, specifically, let us reflect upon this distinction in relation to the theme of time.[11]

Note, then, first, that the dog *is* a dog *at the same time* that it *acts*. The distinction between the primary and the secondary actuality is not a distinction between a chronological earlier and a chronological later. The dog is always—and totally—acting: it is breathing, twitching, imagining, looking, and so on: there is no part of it that is exempt from this and no time when it is exempt from this. (Indeed, to be exempt from this is to be dead—and here we have an essential difference between the natural and the artificial.[12]) Indeed, the actions themselves are always the actions of the animal as a whole, actions of the living body as a whole, for the animal is a "one," not an assemblage.[13] So *being* a dog (first actuality) and the dog *acting* are simultaneous in that from the point of view of the clock, there is no difference between "when" each is: they are exactly chronologically coextensive.

Nonetheless, the time of the first actuality and the time of the second are not the same. As we saw earlier, the actions of the dog are ever-changing. Yet, precisely through those changes, the being of the dog endures. Even more, those actions could be different and the same being would endure—as we saw earlier, the first actuality is not defined by the second, even though they are "coextensive." This means, then, that what it is to be a dog is not made fully present in any (or even all) of the actions. The *actions* happen now: they belong to the present. The *being* is never realized in the present; it is the very nature of the first actuality that it cannot be realized in a moment. We should recall what Aristotle refers to, in *Categories*, Chapter 5, as the most definitive mark of substance: while remaining self-same, it can endure a change between contrary qualities.[14] The dog, to be a dog, must at some times sleep and at some times be awake, at some times bark and at some times not, at first be a puppy and later be mature. The nature of a dog will not be realized by either one of the contraries in these pairs but must contain both, and, since these contraries can only be present at different times, that nature that contains both by necessity cannot be realized in the present. In the present, the being of the animal can only show a side of itself and never its whole reality. The answer, then, to the question "when?" is different when asked of primary and secondary actuality. In short, unlike the secondary actuality which is precisely the present action, the first actuality endures and, while always present, is never fully present. I will describe this by saying that, though simultaneous, first and second actuality are not synchronous.

Let me also revisit a point made earlier. Though in a certain sense—namely a derivative sense—we can say the second actuality is what the thing "actually" is, it is more fundamentally true that what the thing actually is is never equatable with its second actuality. It is certainly true that in the absence of any second actuality there "is" no first actuality, but although second actuality, both in the moment and over the course of the animal's life, is temporally and spatially coextensive with the first actuality, it is not adequate to that first actuality. It is coextensive but not exhaustive. Let me say a bit more about this non-exhaustion, this non-adequation of one side of the organism's reality to its other side.

To make this idea of non-exhaustion clear, we need to invoke the companion term to actuality: "potentiality." It is the distinction between actuality and potentiality that is, in many ways, the key to Aristotle's philosophy, and it is the distinction that he is drawing upon when he initially draws the distinction between the two sorts of actuality in *On the Soul*, Book II, Chapter 1, (and especially when he revisits it in Book II, Chapter 5).[15] Let us think about the theme of potentiality as it pertains to our discussion.

I said that the dog could have acted otherwise while remaining the same dog. This, really, is the key insight behind the distinction between the first and the second actuality, and from which all my further reflections are drawn. To say the same dog could have acted otherwise is to say that its identity as a dog—its actuality as a dog—is a kind of potentiality. It is the power to act (dog-ly). To actually *be* a dog is *to be able* to act in a multiplicity of ways. We could equally say, then, that the primary reality of the dog is its potentiality—the potential it actually is—and the acts that actualize it are derivative.[16] Every action of the dog, then, is an actualizing of this potential. But neither any individual act nor the sum of all its acts fully realizes that potential.

Now, there might seem to be an Aristotelian objection to what I have just said about whether potential is ever fully realized, in the very notion of natural teleology that characterizes Aristotle's physics. The dog, remember, is a member of a natural species. In respect of this, its species identity, its natural potential, is realized when it is organically mature, that is, when it can reproduce the species-life. In this sense, what it is to be a dog, defined from the point of view of the natural species "dog," *is* adequately realized—is exhausted—in its actions of growth and reproduction. Does this challenge my claim about the non-exhaustion of the thing's potentiality? Yes and no.

Recall that in the *Categories* Aristotle distinguishes between the primary and secondary senses of substance: the natural species dog (which would be the "genus" [*genos*] in Aristotle's vocabulary from the *Categories*) is a substance in only a secondary sense: the primary reality is the *individual* substance.[17] The natural maturation of the dog *qua* species being is accomplished in its reaching adulthood and reproduction. The dog *qua* individual substance, however, has no such adequate completion. The dog will expire, and its potentialities will be gone, but not because all it could have been or all it could have done *as an individual* was accomplished. So exactly what the ultimate import of this non-exhaustibility is depends on whether the "what" of a dog is simply the species identity or whether its "what" is uniquely individual—and this, it seems to me, is a difficult question both for Aristotle's text and for the world of natural organisms.[18] For my purposes, though, we do not need to settle this with respect to the animal, for we will be turning to an area where we will not face this ambiguity.

Regardless, then, of the ultimate significance of the notion of maturation for the natural organism, we can hold on to this basic point about actuality. Something's "actuality" in the sense of the specific way it has actualized itself is non-synchronous and non-exhaustive with respect to its primary reality. And that primary reality—its "first actuality"—is a potentiality, a potentiality never fully realized. The dog—the first actuality—only exists *as* and *insofar as* it is actualized in specific actions, but those specific actions are not equal to its reality. Itself *qua* actualized (second actuality) is never adequate to itself *qua* potential (first actuality).

II. Habit and Human Nature

I want to turn now to look at the human soul. What is particularly interesting here is that the relation of first and second actuality in the case of the human is importantly different from that which I have just been describing in the first section of this chapter. This difference will have important consequences both for our understanding of the human soul and for Aristotle's metaphysics.

The distinction between the two sorts of actuality is invoked by Aristotle in his definition of soul, but this distinction can be applied elsewhere. In addition to outlining the metaphysical parameters essential to life as such, this distinction also outlines the parameters of various things that come up within the context of a life. Aristotle himself gives examples of sleeping and waking, sensory perception and developed cognition.[19] I want to use the distinction to talk about the formation of habits.

To be a smoker is not the same as to be someone who has once smoked a cigarette. Though in a simple logical or grammatical sense, anyone smoking a cigarette is a smoker, in a metaphysical sense it is not true. To be a smoker is to be someone for whom smoking is definitive of one's reality. A smoker is what I *am* only if I have developed that character as a positive state (*hexis*) of myself. Being a smoker is an acquired state, a habit. One swallow, one might say, does not a drinker make.[20] The same thing could be said for singer, teacher, driver, friend, or parent: as identities, these are all states that can be acquired only as habits.[21] In each case, we must distinguish between an activity—of teaching, smoking, being friendly, and so on—and the actuality—of being a teacher, smoker, or friend. This is, again, simply the distinction of first and second actuality.

There are, however, two specially noteworthy features of the distinction of first and second actuality in these cases of habit. First, note that, whereas one must *be* a dog in order to perform a canine action, one need not *be* a teacher, smoker, or friend in order to perform a teacherly, smoking, or friendly act. Second (and the first point is the condition for this second point), it is only *by performing such acts* that one *brings into being* the state of character.[22] In the case of habits, the identity, the first actuality, is acquired through the acts, the second actuality.

Let us note, though, that, when one accomplishes a habitual character, the relation of first and second actuality is as we saw in other natural organisms. When I have truly become a singer or piano player, my acts of singing or piano playing are the non-exhaustive actualizations of a real power that I have. While it is true that it is through acts of playing piano that I became a piano player, my identity as a piano player is not simply a shorthand for referring to the aggregate of those historical acts but is, rather, *a real ability* that I have developed, and, once having developed that identity/ability, my subsequent acts of piano playing are actualizations of it, noticeably different in kind from the acts that went into the developing of the habit. This practical process of developing a habit is analogous to the theoretical process of *epagogē* ("induction") in which one not yet possessing a first principle moves toward its apprehension by a kind of cognitive imitation of it, to the point of its actual apprehension, from which point a qualitatively new kind of knowledge emerges.[23] Habituation is something like this grasp of a principle through a process of imitating acts that express that principle.[24] But it *is* such a grasp, and, when it is accomplished, a habitual identity is a first actuality, then, in the sense that it is a causal ground that is responsible for the novel qualitative character of my action made on its basis. And, further, when a musician dies, one can legitimately say—indeed, we often do say—that his or her musical potential was not exhausted.

So, in habits we see a legitimate relation of first and second actuality, but it is one in which the second actuality chronologically precedes and founds the first actuality. This story of habit, though, is not just an interesting curiosity: it is, rather, of the utmost importance. The reason for this is that human identity itself is realized only through habits. This means, as we shall now see, the relation of first and second actuality in humans cannot be the same as that which holds in other natural organisms.

In *Politics* Book I, Chapter 2, Aristotle remarks that the *polis* is the natural environment for humans—the only environment in which they can accomplish their nature—but the *polis* does not itself exist by nature: it is a historical human accomplishment.[25] He also remarks that the human is the animal having *logos*, but *logos*, at least in its significance as language and discourse, does not occur naturally but again waits upon the historical human accomplishment of bringing language into being.[26] In *Nicomachean Ethics* Book II, Chapter 1, Aristotle further remarks that, within the *polis* and the world of language, the human *ergon*—the definitive "work" of being a human—is accomplished only through the development of moral and intellectual virtue, themselves *habits* realized through personal histories of practices.[27] Aristotle's *Nicomachean Ethics* and *Politics* make it unambiguously clear that human nature can only be fulfilled historically and habitually: history and habit are essential to and definitive of human nature. The question that interests me here is what this shows about the nature of human potentiality, that is, the nature of our first actuality.

The essentiality of history is equally the essentiality of creativity. To say that the fulfillment of our own nature does not naturally occur but requires our agency is the same as saying that *what we are* is something we create. How can it be true to say *both* that we fulfill our nature *and* that we create ourselves? How can it be true to say *both* that our actions realize our nature *and* that our actions do not happen by nature, are not natural? I think these claims can be reconciled only if we are *defined by self-transformation*: if to be human is to go beyond what we are. The potentiality that defines human nature—our first actuality—must be the potentiality to be otherwise, the very potentiality of potentiality. As a being who develops habit, we have *the power to develop powers*. I can become a piano player. This means, I have *the ability to develop the ability* to play piano. "The ability to develop the ability": this structure is what I think is definitive of humanity on Aristotle's account, and it is what I mean by "the potentiality of potentiality."[28]

There is an excellent illustration of this notion in an unrelated discussion by Aristotle. In Book III, Chapter 8, of *On the Soul*, Aristotle refers to the hand as the "tool of tools."[29] This remark fits perfectly, I think, with the (onto)logical structure I am talking about. The hand, as a tool for working on the world, is valuable but comparatively weak. I can grab an orange to eat, I can scratch away at the dirt or the bark, and I can push stones off the surface upon which I wish to lie. These are examples of direct applications of the hand to the world. In this usage of the hand, the human as a natural organism is weak. The hand, however, need not be such a directly applied tool. I can also use the hand to hold a stone that I use to hit something else. Perhaps I use the stone against some wood, to fashion the wood into some more sophisticated tool. Instead of using the hand directly on the world, I can use my hand to turn other existing things into tools for acting on the world and, indeed, into tools for making further tools. Through this practice, I can make tools which are fantastically more effective for operating on the world than my simple hand can be. The power in the hand is not simply the *actual* ability it affords for direct engagement but *the power it has for magnifying power*, the power it has to bring into being powers for engagement with the world that do not preexist its creation of tools. In referring to the hand as the tool of tools, Aristotle is identifying what I called above the potentiality of potentiality: the ability to develop abilities. We can see something similar if we consider the idea that the human is the animal having *logos*.

First, let us think of *logos* as language. One of the examples Aristotle uses for discussing the two senses of actuality is the person with knowledge of *hē grammatikē*.[30] This reference to the one who knows grammar is often interpreted as referring to "the grammarian," but it also might be understood to mean simply "the literate person": not the grammar scientist but simply the person who has learned his or her grammar. I am going to accept that latter interpretation here, because it fits very neatly with my larger interpretation, though it is not at all essential to that larger interpretation that this interpretation be correct. Let us think about the literate person. First, let us think of this in relation to the definition of us as the animal having *logos*.

Language, like the *polis*, is not something with which the individual or the human species as a whole was born. The human species had to invent both. The individual has to learn how to participate in both. So, is the power of language natural to us? Yes, but in the sense that *it is in our power to develop that power*. We do not come pre-equipped with the developed power. So, insofar as *logos* at least in part means "language," Aristotle's very definition of the human as "the animal having *logos*" is already clearly a definition of us as having the ability to develop abilities.

But, second, let us think what this very ability is that one develops with "the knowledge of grammar." Like the possession of the hand, the possession of grammar by itself is small. Knowledge of grammar—or language more broadly: grammar, vocabulary, and so on—is not valuable for itself alone but for *what it makes possible*. Possessing the power of language—"the knowledge of grammar"—makes available to me the thoughts of others and not just immediately present others but the past generations of humankind as well.[31] The importance of language is not its actual *possession*—my "actual" knowledge—but the power it offers to live through what is beyond me. As the hand is the tool of tools, language is the access to other *logoi*, a reality that lets me live in other realities—realities that are not my own. So, not just because our *logos*-nature is only fulfilled through processes of education and habituation but also because of the specific character of *logos* as language, we can see that the first actuality of "the animal having *logos*," the human, is not the potentiality of a specific actualization but the potentiality of potentiality: our definitive ability is the ability to create new abilities for ourselves. Our reality is precisely not to be confined to our actuality. Our nature is not to have a given end, a proper goal, but is rather precisely openness to the new.

III. Happiness and Human Nature

I spoke in the first section about the non-synchronous, non-exhaustive relationship between the temporalities of first and second actualities. I now want to revisit that theme in relation to first and second actuality as they characterize the human being. We saw earlier a reason for asking whether the first actuality of the natural organism was common to every member of the species or unique to the individual. What we have said about the human, though, obviates that question with respect to human nature. In the natural organism, the species identity provides the kind of end that makes talk of "maturation" meaningful. If, though, human nature does not have an actual end but is defined, rather, as openness to the new, then this conflict of species versus individual does not arise, that is, there is no given end that might serve to define completion independently of the history of the individual.

This, it seems to me, is why there is such a thing as ethics in the sense that is given in Book I of the *Nicomachean Ethics*. How will we be happy? The questions Aristotle raises in his discussion of this are not trivial but are the very issues that plague our lives. Should we seek wealth or fame? Should we pursue contemplation? We grapple with these questions throughout our lives.[32] Though of course I cannot address all the issues involved here, I want nonetheless to say something about the overall theme of Aristotle's discussion that will, I hope, illuminate these matters a bit.

What we struggle with in our life is precisely how to think of our own life as a whole and how to make it succeed as a whole. If we came with a settled species-goal, the unity and trajectory of our lives would not be a puzzle.[33] It is precisely because we do not come with this that what our life is to mean—what it is to be or, more properly, who we are to be—is a question for us. Ethics, as Aristotle introduces it in the *Nicomachean Ethics*, is the effort to take our lives seriously, to have a perspective on *our life*. My own life *as a whole* is an issue for me.[34] Taking my life as a whole means looking ahead—it means judging my situation from the perspective of my own future—and that is why it is only for beings like us who have a temporal consciousness that such things can be an issue.[35] But for that very same reason, it seems to me, we can never satisfactorily settle these questions of happiness.[36] Aristotle's own answer in the *Nicomachean Ethics* is that we should become virtuous, that is, we should equip ourselves with such plastic abilities as courage, moderation, and friendship that will allow us to deal well with the situations we do face. Our "function" (*ergon*), then, does not so much define for us a specific *telos* but instead defines our fulfillment in terms of our readiness to deal with a meaningful life, the form of which cannot be predicted in advance[37]: the idea that we can take a perspective on our lives as a whole and ask the question of meaning, the question of happiness, means that *we experience ourselves as beings of possibility*. It is precisely because we know our own actualization has not lived up to our first actuality that we can have our future path as a question that we can have choice. But this also means that nothing we do will ever settle the question. We will always experience ourselves as more (and less) than what we are. We will always be able to see how our potentiality is not fully captured or expressed in any choice we make, in any situation to which we commit ourselves.

We are the kind of being that is unique for having its second actuality be essential to it: our nature is a second nature. This means we are the being whose definitive ability is the ability to develop new abilities. Such a being is a being that is aware of itself as a being of potentiality, which is why the question of happiness is both natural to it and unresolvable. That we can take a perspective on our life as whole, that we can define our lives from the perspective of the future, means that we cannot, *in* our lives, settle the question of the meaning *of* our lives.

Notes

1. For this expression, see *Metaphysics* XII (Λ).8 1074a1; compare *On the Heavens* I.3 270b4-5. I have analyzed this Aristotelian method in "To Account for the Appearances: Phenomenology and Existential Change in Aristotle and Plato," *Journal of the British Society for Phenomenology* 52 (2021); for a discussion of the notion of "saving the phenomena" in relation to Aristotle's method that takes up different themes from those I stress here, see Kosman, "Saving the Phenomena: Realism and Instrumentalism in Aristotle's Theory of Science," in *Virtues of Thought: Essays on Plato and Aristotle* (Cambridge: Oxford University Press, 2014). I have also discussed Aristotle's method in "Self-Consciousness and the Tradition in Aristotle's Psychology," *Laval Théologique et Philosophique* 52, no. 5 (1996). See also Russon, "The Elements of Everyday Life: Three Lessons from Ancient Greece," *Philosophy in the Contemporary World* 13, no. 2 (2006).
2. *Physics* II.1 193a1-7.
3. *On the Soul* II.1 412a27-8. See Diamond, *Mortal Imitations of Divine Life: The Nature of Soul in Aristotle's De Anima* (Evanston, IL: Northwestern University Press, 2015), 44-6, for a helpful discussion of this definition and its philosophical implications. I have also discussed this definition substantially in "Self-Consciousness and the Tradition in Aristotle's Psychology."
4. For different formulations of this distinction, see *On the Soul* II.1 412a10-11, 412a22-8, 412b27-9, II.5 417a9-14, 417a21-417b1, 417b29-418a1, III.4 429b5-9.
5. *On the Soul* II.1 412a22-3.
6. *On the Soul* II.1 412a26. On the nature of definition, see *Metaphysics* VII (Z).12 1037b8-27.
7. My interpretation thus differs from Diamond, "For There Are Gods Here Too," in this volume, who interprets "first actuality" to mean the minimal realization of life in an organism.
8. *to ti esti*—"the what it is"—is one of the four causes (*aitiai*) that Aristotle identifies in *Physics* II.3; it is the so-called formal cause.
9. *On the Soul* II.1 412a26.
10. For the distinction between substance and those realities that depend upon substance, see *Categories*, Chapters 2 and 5, and *Metaphysics* VII (Z), Chapters 1 and 3.
11. Indeed, for such a distinction to be, time is necessary.
12. This distinction is the subject of *Physics* II.1.
13. *On the Soul* II.1 412b6-9.
14. *Categories* 5 4a10-12.
15. *Metaphysics* IX (Θ) offers Aristotle's fullest discussion of actuality and potentiality.
16. For the idea that the primary actuality is a potentiality, see *Metaphysics* IX (Θ) 9 1051a10-17; compare *Metaphysics* IX (Θ), Chapter 2, *passim* and Chapter 5, *passim*.
17. *Categories* 5 2a13-18.
18. As Sparshott says in *Taking Life Seriously: A Study of the Argument of the Nicomachean Ethics* (Toronto: University of Toronto Press, 1996), 15–16: "[T]he 'end' of any animal in Aristotle's teleological biology is not to attain maturity but to live the life of its species." Compare *On the Soul* II.4 415a26-b2. On the relation between individual and species identity, compare also *Metaphysics* Z.1 1028a10-30, Z.6 (*passim*) and Z.11 1037a5-b7. The sense in which the naturally existing individual can be defined by its species is a central theme throughout Derrida, *The Animal that Therefore I Am* (Fordham University Press, 2008). For various contemporary perspectives on the

metaphysical and empirical difficulties in assigning "individuality" within the animal kingdom, see Bouchard and Huneman, *From Groups to Individuals: Evolution and Emerging Individuality* (Cambridge, MA: MIT Press, 2013).
19 See *On the Soul* II.5 417a21-b2, II.5 417b17-19, III.4 429b5-9. See also *Nicomachean Ethics* VII.3 1146b31-4; the distinction between possessing the power (knowledge) and using it is central to the entire analysis of *akrasia* in Book VII.
20 Compare *Nicomachean Ethics* I.7 1098a17-18.
21 Aristotle discusses the fact that being a friend takes time: *Nicomachean Ethics* VIII.4, 1156b25-32, VIII.5 1157b28-9, VIII.6 1158a14-15.
22 *Nicomachean Ethics* II.1 1103a27-b6; see also *Nicomachean Ethics* II.4 *passim*.
23 *Posterior Analytics* II.19. Compare *Metaphysics* A.1. I have discussed this theme in "Aristotle's Animative Epistemology," *Idealistic Studies* 25, no. 3 (1995).
24 Burnyeat compares theoretical cognition and ethical habituation in "Aristotle on Understanding Knowledge," in *Aristotle on Science: "The Posterior Analytics,"* ed. Berti (Cambridge, MA: Harvard University Press, 1981).
25 *Politics* I.2.1252b30-1253a39. Compare *Nicomachean Ethics* I.7 1097b11.
26 For the "animal having *logos*," see Politics I.2 1253a9, and compare *Nicomachean Ethics* I.7, *passim*. Like Diamond, "For There Are Gods Here Too," I here stress the sense of *logos* as "language." See Kietzmann, "Aristotle on the Definition of What It Is to Be Human," and Diamond, "For There Are Gods Here Too," for the sense in which "animal having *logos*," rather than "two-footed animal" (which Aristotle offers in *Metaphysics* VII [Z].12 1037b12 and elsewhere), is an appropriate definition of the human.
27 *Nicomachean Ethics* I.13. On the theme of historical invention, see *Nicomachean Ethics* I.7 1098a20-24, *Metaphysics* A.1 981b13-24. Compare *Politics* Book I, Chapter 2, 1253a32: "human beings are born naturally possessing weapons for *phronēsis* and *aretē*, which are very susceptible for being used for their opposites."
28 Compare *On the Soul* II.5.417b29-418a1. It is this insight that lies behind Dewey's excellent discussion of the "positive state" of immaturity in *Democracy and Education: An Introduction to the Philosophy of Education* (Hardpress Publishing, 2016), Chapter 4.
29 *On the Soul* III.8 432a1-3. Diamond, "For There Are Gods Here Too," similarly links this definition of the human hand (and, likewise, our front-facing character) to the distinctive nature of the animal having *logos*.
30 *On the Soul* II.5 417a22-b1.
31 This is a central theme in Aygün, *The Middle Included: Logos in Aristotle's Philosophy* (Northwestern University Press, 2017), especially Chapter 6.
32 Particularly important is Aristotle's invocation of Solon: count no man happy until he is dead—and even then, we should not forget that the future of his children after his death might still be relevant: *Nicomachean Ethics* I.9-10 1100a3-30. (Solon is also invoked [differently] at *Nicomachean Ethics* X.9 1179a9.) Aristotle answers the question, "should we count no man happy until he is dead?": "He is happy who is active in accordance with complete virtue and is sufficiently equipped with external goods, not for some chance period but throughout a complete life.... We shall call those among *living* men in whom these considerations are, and are to be, fulfilled, happy *men*" (*Nicomachean Ethics* I.10 1101a14-20, my emphasis).
33 Compare Sparshott, *Taking Life Seriously*, 45: "The 'function' of an animal species, we saw, is to live out a characteristic life, coming to maturity generation by generation and realizing piecemeal the physical and psychological potentialities of the animal in

its environment. But an elephant (for example) does not ask itself what an elephant's function is; it *shows* what that function is by living out, in collaboration with its fellow elephants, the range of elephantine existence. We, however, are *asking* ourselves what the function of mankind is, so that we can fulfil it. Being human, it seems, is something that has to be worked at" (emphasis in original).

34 See Sparshott, *Taking Life Seriously*, 6–8, especially, 8: "humans, unlike all other animals, . . . can think of themselves as living 'a life.'" See 48–54 for his excellent discussion of the issue of "taking one's life seriously."

35 Sparshott, *Taking Life Seriously*, 11: "Since our lives are yet to be lived, if we ask what our lives *are*, we can ask what they *will be* for each of us. . . . By the same token, what a human *is* is essentially the life of a being that can ask itself how it is to live its own life."

36 Compare Sparshott, *Taking Life Seriously*, 17.

37 Hence the pertinence of his interesting question in I.7: might we in fact have no characteristic work?

Part III

The *Logos* of *Ethos*

7

Wishful Thinking in Aristotle[1]

Ömer Aygün

Introduction

Aristotle famously determines the human being as the animal having *logos*. Yet there is an often neglected kind of *logos* that seems equally reserved to humans: *eukhē*, "wish" or "prayer." In this chapter, we shall see that the phenomenon of "wish" is both very peculiar and extremely important for making sense of major aspects of human experience: first of all, expressions of "wish" are peculiar in that they do not admit of truth and falsity, verification and falsification, unlike all declarative sentences; second, "wish" is psychologically peculiar in that it is a desire fundamentally divorced from motion and action, unlike all animal motion. After some preliminaries on desire, motion, and voice, I shall first discuss the epistemological question as to what kind of "sentence" (*logos*) an expression of "wish" (or, in this context, "prayer") is; I shall stress that an expression of wish is non-alethic sentence, that is, it is not susceptible of truth and falsity unlike declarative sentences. Then, second, I shall tackle the psychological question as to what kind of desire wish is; I shall claim that wish is a non-kinetic desire, that is, it is a desire that does not move the subject unlike any other kind of desire or "choice." Finally, in the third part, I shall sketch out the ethical and political consequences of these two characteristics of wish. I hope to show that the "wishful attitude" seems to be explanatory of many important aspects of the experience of the "animal having *logos*" we are: from prayer, regret, guilt, and cursing, to fatalism and utopian politics.

I. Three Preliminaries: Desire, Motion, and Voice

Almost all nature is in motion according to Aristotle, *because* it is "dominated" by something—by desire, *orexis*:

> The most natural function, for living beings that are complete and not mutilated or generated spontaneously, is to produce another one like itself, an animal producing an animal, and a plant a plant, so as to partake in the eternal and

the divine as much as possible. Because each strives [*oregetai*] toward this and performs all of its natural functions for the sake of this. (*On the Soul* (*DA*) II.4 415a26-415b2)

This passage does not employ the substantive *orexis* but its telling verbal form *oregesthai*, "to tend," "to reach out," "to stretch out," "to strive." Quite contrary to the Cartesian concept of "extension," *partes extra partes*, here *oregesthai* names an extension whose parts are precisely implicated in one another. Earthly bodies in free fall are less *attracted* by the Earth than they *tend* toward it. Similarly, God does not *exert* an influence on all other beings; it is rather all other beings that *stretch out* toward divine perfection and eternity. As Koyré says succinctly, "motion is the being—the *actus*—of all that which is not God."[2] For Aristotle, the immediately kinetic role of desire in nature is such that it takes part in the definition of nature as "a certain principle, namely, a cause of motion and rest for that to which it belongs immediately in itself and not by accident."[3] Desire manifests itself as the "internal impulse" (*hormē emphytos*, *Phys.* II.1 192b18), which distinguishes nature from art where the change is imposed from without. Roughly then, natural motion implies desire for Aristotle.

Animal motion, however, differs from mere natural motion. Instead of the "vertical" axis on which elements are naturally oriented (top vs. bottom or center vs. periphery), specifically animal motion is stretched on a horizontal axis between front and back. More importantly, while the elements move, so to speak, "universally," in the sense that they do not distinguish the exact time or location of their point of arrival, animals *distinguish* the object of destination. They distinguish, that is, they are capable of sensation (*aisthēsis*).[4] All animals capable of locomotion are endowed with this capacity for discerning the always specific object of their procession.[5] The element engages in a "general" or "universal" motion, for instance, earthy bodies always and only move "downward," in Athens as well as in Alexandria, whereas the animal engages in a "specific" motion, for instance toward the North in spring *or* toward the South in fall, toward the sought object *or* away from the object of flight. Desire manifests itself in animal motion as oriented toward a particular object as a process engaging perception. Then, in the case of animal motion, the faculty of "universal" desire is conjoined with a receptive faculty oriented toward the particular: "this is such and such."[6]

When the particular perceptual datum corresponds to something under universal desire, animal motion follows in the form of flight or pursuit. Animal motion is considered by Aristotle as the conclusion of a *logismos*, of an internal *legein*, between appetite and sensation: "The appetite says 'I must drink,' Sensation, imagination or the intellect says: 'This is drink.' And one drinks immediately."[7] Without entering into the thorny details of the "practical syllogism,"[8] let us simply state that this is less an intellectualist conception of animal motion than the idea that animal motion necessarily engages *two* factors unlike the motion of natural elements: desire *and* discrimination. Animal motion results from the subsumption of the particular premise of perception under the universal premise of desire.

Nevertheless, Aristotle does stress the immediate (*euthus*) character of animal motion.[9] Once the animal receives a particular object well proportioned to its general desire, motion follows immediately. The examples given by Aristotle suggest that these "proportions" or syllogisms may well be nested within larger syllogisms and trigger motions that have more and more complex spatiotemporal structures. For, under the major premise of universal desire, the minor premise providing the particular object may be construed by distant perception, memory, imagination, the "sensation of time,"[10] use of intermediaries, and so on. Hence the great variety of motions that unfold from such syllogisms: migration, hunting, searching, hiding, and so on, all reducible to pushing and pulling, pursuit and flight.[11] If then, as we have seen, all natural motion requires desire, specifically *animal* motion here requires a desire that subsumes a *particular* object of perception, imagination, or memory.

Yet sometimes this "subsumption" does not go smoothly when the animal "interprets" her situation as an impossibility of satisfying her desire, as an aporia, no matter what media, resources, tools, plans, or "syllogisms" she may employ. Here again, desire is the major premise,[12] yet the minor premise is at least perceived by the animal as beyond her reach, if not altogether missing. The object is present to the animal only as an "affection" of her soul[13] in her perception, imagination, or memory. Desire here is no longer "translated" into motion, neither immediately nor in a mediated way through the resources accessible to the individual animal on her own.

This case, that of the frustrated motion, results in vocal emission or "voice" (*phōnē*) in some animals. Leaving aside its physiological aspect for Aristotle,[14] let me remark that the genus of voice is sound (*psophos*) and that its specific difference is that voice is a "meaningful [*sēmantikos*] sound."[15] What does voice mean? "Indeed voice is the sign [*sēmeion*] of the painful and the pleasant."[16] But who is addressed in voice? Another being who may have interest in avoiding pain and pursuing pleasure. Thus, another animal. Voice is then essentially the *invocation* of another animal. The typical examples of vocal emission in animals testify to this: the call of mating, which requires the cooperation of the male and the female,[17] the call for one's babies,[18] the marking of one's territory, the threatening of another animal, or the danger-signal addressed to others—in all these cases, an animal's voice expresses a "particular premise" *to another animal* in order that they may move *together*. Indeed, voice is not intended to move the voice-emitting animal herself; it rather places the other animal in a shared task. Thus, voice emission employs some mediation as in the "practical syllogism," but the emitting animal here seems to make a "sign" to another being which may hear her, understand her, be moved by her, and cooperate with her. Thereby vocal emission implies the significance of the other animal and, to a certain degree, her perspective, her interests, and her evaluation. Voice is no longer marked by the immediacy (*euthus*) of the flight and pursuit of the individual animal as it was the case in the "practical syllogism," since voice is issued to *another* animal as medium. Voice is a demand of "attention" issued from one animal to another. Whereas "sound" is nothing more than the effect of a kind of friction or of the excess of *touch*, thus a "shock,"[19] voice supposes appropriate *contact*, an animal emitting a demand of "attention" destined to another.

Then the major semantic characteristic of voice is that it is a demand, a call, or even a claim (in ancient Greek, *aitēsis*—we shall return to this). In comparison to immediate locomotion, voice appears as a kind of locomotion contained within the body of the animal in order to be translated into the "language" of common interest, an organ which would reorganize the world *with* others and also *for* them.

For Aristotle, it is precisely this common work that characterizes political animals such as humans, wasps, cranes, ants, and bees.[20] In a sense, then, voice proposes an "alliance" or a "coalition." Voice is "tactical." Then, unlike the emission or the reproduction of sound or noise, meaningless and disinterested as such, the "tactical" syllogism of voice functions in an environment of *common* interest or desire with a view to a minimal *community* by which individual animals are not only formed by organs but become parts of an "organization" or of a *taxis* for fleeing a danger or pursuing a pleasant object.[21]

Similarly, hearing voice differs essentially from hearing sound or noise. Unlike the hearing of sound, hearing voice is so provoking that the corresponding ancient Greek verb *akouein* suggests that the "audience" of voice is intimately associated with "obedience."[22] The Homeric examples of the verb *akouein* in this sense denote the obedience of subjects to a king or of people giving heed to a king as if to a god.[23] Unlike the hearing of sound or even the imitation of sound, the cooperation implied by voice is injunctive, imperial, and hegemonic.[24]

To conclude this preliminary section, then, we have seen, first, that roughly all natural motion supposes a *universal* desire according to Aristotle; then that specifically animal motion requires that the reception of a *particular* object be submitted to this universal desire; and finally that some animals, perceiving the impossibility of satisfying their desire on their own, emit voice with a view to a possible cooperation with another animal and this in a subjunctive or even imperative "mood."

Now we shall be able to see how peculiar wish is as a kind of desire, since it does not move the animal at all, and how peculiar wish is as a kind of statement, since it is fundamentally divorced from truth and falsity, verification and falsification.

I. The Epistemology of Wish

Let us now turn to *eukhē*. In ancient Greek, *eukhē* can mean "wish," "vow," "aspiration," "curse,"[25] but also "prayer." In a famous sentence at the beginning of *On Interpretation*, Aristotle says the following:

> Not all sentence [*logos*] is declarative, but that which one can say there is truth and falsity. Yet one cannot say this for all sentences; for instance, a prayer [*eukhē*] is a sentence [*logos*], but it is neither true nor false. (*On Interpretation* (*De Int.*) 4 17a2-4)[26]

Note that it is not the case that "wish" or "prayer" is neither true nor false the way sentences concerning future contingents are, as famously analyzed in Chapter 9. An expression of wish or prayer is *by definition* not susceptible of truth and falsity, regardless of whether it concerns the past, the present, or the future. Thus, Aristotle immediately dismisses the discussion of "wish" or "prayer" from his logical work and relegates it to "rhetoric and the poetics."[27] Thus, one would expect a satisfying account of *eukhē* in the *Rhetoric* and in the *Poetics*.

Yet, in the *Rhetoric*, *eukhē* appears only twice and in the same sentence, and this in its verbal form of *eukhesthai*. Aristotle is discussing the "depreciative metaphor":

> If one wishes to ornament, one should carry the metaphor from that which is better within the same genus; if one wishes to depreciate, from the worse. For instance, to say that the begging man [*ptōkheuonta*] is praying [*eukhesthai*], or that the praying man is begging. Since opposites belong to the same genus. Because both are demands. (*Rhetoric* III.2 1405b14-20)[28]

Although one is honorable and the other dishonorable according to Aristotle, both begging and praying belong to the same genus: demand (*aitēsis*). So the *Rhetoric* provides us not with the promised analysis of *eukhē* but with an example indicating that it is less dishonorable than begging and, more importantly, that its genus is demand. We have seen, however, that animal voice is also a kind of demand. The *Rhetoric* then leaves us at least with the following question: How does *eukhē* differ from the kind of demand we found in animal voice?

Unfortunately, the promised analysis of *eukhē* is not to be found in the *Poetics* either. In the *Poetics*, *eukhē* is briefly mentioned as a form of expression (*skhēma tēs lexeōs*) among others:

> Concerning expression [*lexis*], one aspect to be observed is the forms of expression. For example, what is a command [*entolē*]? What is a prayer [*eukhē*]? and a narration [*diēgēsis*], a threat [*apeilē*], a question [*erōtēsis*], an answer [*apokrisis*], etc. (*Poet.* 19 1456b8-13)

Then *eukhē* is to be distinguished from "narration" and "answer." But also, while probably belonging to the genus "demand," *eukhē* is distinguished from "question." Although both are neither true nor false, the act of questioning may still seem like a "quest," thus a readiness to move and investigate, while *eukhē* lacks these characteristics. Finally, this passage suggests that *eukhē* differs from the kind of demand we saw in our analysis of animal voice: whereas the demand expressed in animal voice took the form of a threat or a promise made to another animal in a "subjunctive" or "hypotactic" mood, this passage clearly distinguishes *eukhē* from "threat" (*apeilē*). Whereas animal voice was "imperative" or "prostactic," Aristotle's list of forms of expression implies that *eukhē* is semantically, if not grammatically, also distinct from "command" (*entolē* or the verbal form *keleusai*).

The same distinction between command and *eukhē* is found in the next lines of the *Poetics*. Here, Aristotle objects to Protagoras' criticism of Homer, which underlines the semantic, if not grammatical, distinction between the imperative and the "precative":

> Why would one agree with Protagoras in criticizing [Homer] who, while supposedly praying [*eukhesthai*] to [the Goddess], commands [*epitattei*] her, saying: "Sing goddess the wrath ..."? (*Poet.* 19 1456b15-17)

This passage suggests that Protagoras criticized Homer for addressing the Goddess in the imperative mood instead of the precative mood, but also that Aristotle finds this criticism irrelevant. For, perhaps, Aristotle might be thinking that poetic license tolerates the use of the imperative for expressing what is clearly a *prayer* to the Goddess.

Let us recapitulate what we have learned so far. *Eukhē* is a *logos* that is not declarative or "indicative" of a present, past, or future state of affairs, as a narration or an answer may be. The *Rhetoric* and the *Poetics*, the two texts referred to in Aristotle's dismissive remark concerning *eukhē* in *On Interpretation*, do not supply us the promised analysis of *eukhē*; yet the *Rhetoric* determines the genus of *eukhē* as "demand" (*aitēsis*), and the *Poetics* distinguishes *eukhē* from other kinds of demands such as "threats" and "questions": *eukhē* differs not only from "question," in that it is *not* a demand for a verbal response, but also from the subjunctive mood of threats and from the imperative mood of command, which both characterized animal voice. In short, *eukhē* does not suggest potential harm or profit as threats and promises do; it does not expect a verbal response as a question does. This is the sense in which *eukhē* is an unaccountable *logos*, a *logos* exempt of truth and falsity, confirmation and falsification: since it does not *indicate* or *propose* an actual or even potential state of affairs, it cannot be held accountable for a commitment it does not make; since it is not a question, it is unanswerable; since it is not a promise, a threat, or a command, it offers nothing to be broken, nothing to be obeyed or disobeyed.

Let us end this section by pointing out that there is an exact mood that corresponds to this kind of *logos* that is neither the indicative, nor the subjunctive, nor even the imperative; the mood of *eukhē* is the optative.[29] The optative mood of prayer is then to be strictly distinguished from the imperative and subjunctive moods of threats, promises, and commands. Yet these grammatical terms may be misleading, for, as we saw in Aristotle's rejection of Protagoras' criticism against Homer, a verb that is grammatically in the imperative mood may well have an optative meaning as when one says "Help me, God!" or even "Good morning!" The latter sentence is certainly distinct from indicative sentences saying that the morning is *already* good, *will be* nice, or *may be* good; it is also obviously different both from the imperative command to *have* a good morning and from the subjunctive or conditional statement (threat or promise) that one will have a good morning provided that this or that happens, under such-and-such conditions. The semantically optative sentence "Good morning!" is not even equivalent to the statement that one *wants* another to have a good morning in the sense that one has committed oneself to making the other's morning a good one. Although *eukhē* or the optative mood in general cannot be exemplified by the statement that *I* desire so and so, perhaps it is simply an expression of the desire itself. Then the question becomes: How is *eukhē* as an expression of desire any different from animal voice, equally an expression of desire?

II. The Psychology of Wish

What exactly does *eukhē* express? Since *On Interpretation*, the *Rhetoric*, and the *Poetics* have nothing more to offer us with respect to *eukhē* and its verbal form *eukhesthai*, we must turn to other texts. Clearly, *eukhē* expresses a kind of desire but what kind? And what would distinguish it from the kind of desire we found in animal voice? We may find a hint in the *Nicomachean Ethics*, III.2, and the parallel text in *Eudemian Ethics*, II.10. In this passage, Aristotle distinguishes "choice" (*proairesis*) from "desire" (*orexis*) by showing that choice corresponds to neither of the three kinds of desire: neither to "appetite" (*epithymia*), nor to "spiritedness" (*thymos*), nor to "wishing" (*boulēsis*). This latter kind of desire is thus analyzed indirectly, in its difference from choice:

> But [choice] is surely not wishing either, even though that appears a close approximation to it, since there can be no choice of impossible things, and if anyone were to claim to choose something impossible, that person would seem to be foolish; but there is wishing even for impossible things, such as deathlessness. And there is also wishing for things that can in no way be done by oneself [*peri ta mēdamōs di' hautou prakhthenta an*], such as for a certain actor to win an award, or for an athlete to win a contest, but no one chooses such things, but only those things one believes could come about by one's own act. Also, wishing is rather for an end [*tou telous*], while choice is of things that are related to the end [*tōn pros to telos*]; for example, we wish to be healthy, but we choose those things by means of which we will become healthy, and we wish to be happy and say so, while it would not fit the meaning to say we choose to be happy, since, universally, choice seems to be concerned with things that are up to us [*peri ta eph' hēmin*]. (*EN* III.2 1111b20-31) (tr. Joe Sachs)

Eukhē seems to express just this state of the human soul: wishing (*boulēsis*).[30] From the verbal expression, we have thus moved to the psychic state. From there we are led to the object of that state. According to the previous passage, wishing is a kind of desire distinguished by its objects: (1) impossible objects (such as immortality) beyond plans for any possible ones, (2) objects that are not realizable or attainable by ourselves (like the victory of a team in a match), and (3) the ultimate objects of our decisions and choices (such as health or happiness). Just as *eukhē* was reserved to human beings as "sentence" (*logos*), here the wishful desire expressed by it may well be an exclusively human desire since Aristotle clearly says in *On the Soul* that "*boulēsis* comes to be in the *logistikē* part [of the soul]."[31] Similarly, in the *Nicomachean Ethics*, Aristotle says that beings deprived of *logos* (*alogoi*) have "appetite" and "passion," but do not partake in "choice"[32] which is a "close approximation" to wish. Hence, according to Aristotle, nonhuman animals and children do not partake in happiness, the paradigmatic object of wish. Just as *eukhē* was an atypical *logos* for not being susceptible of truth and falsity, wishing belongs to the *logistikē* part of the human soul in a problematic way: wish is a unique kind of desire that does not *move* the being that expresses it. But neither does it move the being that is addressed, as does animal voice. For the object of wish is fundamentally severed the actuality or potentiality of its being attained—whether it be by means of the individual animal herself or by means of an alliance with others.

Now let us then bring together the main features of *eukhē* with wishing (*boulēsis*), this atypical, nonmoving kind of desire:

First, the difference between *eukhē* and declarative *logos*: unlike the declarative sentences, *eukhē* is a *logos* that somehow has access beyond past, present, and future states of affairs; it opens up the realm of impossibility that is not susceptible of truth and falsity—note that a wish statement for impossible things is *not* false unlike contradictory declarative statements. The desire behind *eukhē* is susceptible of "extending" or "stretching" into mere unreality, infinitely beyond the actual and even all potentials. Hence wish and prayer are immune to the control of verification and falsification, of corroboration and elenchus, regardless of whether they *happen* to come to pass. For it is not exact to say that a wish *becomes true* in the sense that a bet *turns out to be true*, since that which becomes true is no longer a wish but only a future state of affairs stated in the *content* of wish; yet, as we saw, wish is not reducible to its content since it belongs to a specific mood, the precative or the optative. For instance, when one wishes the execution of Socrates *and* he is executed, what *becomes true* is not the *wish* (the desire) itself but the declarative or indicative proposition: "Socrates will be executed."[33] The optative mood of wishing can operate with regard to the past as much as to the future. Having *logos*, being thus capable of wishing without regard to any limit, reality, and likelihood, human beings are precisely capable of desiring a counterfactual: "If only we had not executed Socrates!" Indeed, in English, the semantically optative "if only" here is to be distinguished from the subjective or imperative phrase "only if" of commands and requirements. Wish is, so to speak, a self-refuting desire. While offering humans access to truth and to correspondence with reality by means of logic and science, *logos* also exposes humans to a specifically human realm of unreality. We may conclude then that having *logos*, human beings are exposed to the human phenomena of regret and bad conscience. Unlike other desires that are geared toward the future, the wishful attitude is particularly important in understanding the human being's relationship to her past.

Second, *eukhē* is distinct from conditionals. In other words, the "optative" is not the "subjunctive." The object of wish is not limited by the realm of reality, of possibility, and of conditions.[34] The wish for Socrates to be executed is modally different from a conditional sentence expressing that he will be executed if he does not stop doing philosophy. In the same way, curses differ from threats, as blessings do from promises. Phrases such as "God willing," "Deo volente," or "Inshallah" cannot be strictly meant *as conditional clauses* if they are to take part in *eukhē*, in the optative or the precative mood. Literally, the sentence "God willing, we shall succeed" is not an *eukhē* if it means: "We shall succeed *if* God wills it"; it is an *eukhē* if it means: "May God will that we succeed." Again, strictly speaking, wishes cannot be expressed with phrases such as "please," "if you will," or "s'il vous plaît." For *eukhē* must be beyond the imperative of "pleasing" and the eventuality of one's willing to please. Oxymoronically, *eukhē* is a disengaged promise. It is not "tactic," "prostactic," or contractual. My wishing somebody a happy birthday in no way binds me at the level of action; in no way am I thereby obligated to make plans and predictions, to take responsibility, and to be prepared to account for my action or nonaction. We have seen that animal voice necessarily implies a threat or a promise made to the other animal; we have come to see why wish is neither. Being unconditional, wish is not subject to conditions, eventualities, justifications, refutations, confirmations, or denials. One then *may* wish an impossibility, beyond actual or even possible experience. One *may* wish that one had not undergone a trauma, that the War of Troy had not happened, that Socrates had not been executed. All kinds and senses of *eukhē* (with the important exception of "vow") are expressions of an *intention* without any regard for its realization and for a trial of its correspondence with reality. So among the forms of *eukhē* and expressions of wish are salutations, best wishes, congratulations, prayers, blessings, swears, and curses.

Third, *eukhē* differs from commands which may appear equally unconditional or categorical. In the *Poetics*, we saw Protagoras criticizing Homer for using an imperative while addressing the Goddess; yet, for Aristotle, this criticism was not valid since it wrongly assumes that semantics is determined by grammatical tense. For a prayer may well be expressed by an imperative without signifying a command, especially when uttered by a poet like Homer. A wish is precisely not a frustrated desire "translated" to another as a call for cooperation by means of animal voice. Wish differs from other kinds of desire in that it does not "immediately" (*euthus*) spill into any action or even into any *call* for action. "Save Socrates!" is a linguistic expression of a desire that would put the subject in motion *had he possessed or perceived the means for satisfying it*. The wish to save Socrates, however, although a desire, is a "universal premise" fundamentally detached from any "particular premise" susceptible of triggering motion. Other desires move the animal, wishing does not. Voice is a call for cooperation and project for action, an expression of wish is not.

This optative mood subtends not only wishful thinking and prayer but also regret, guilt, and even certain kinds of dreams and reveries. The human soul, having *logos*, thus capable of wishing, exposes itself to passions that would seem utterly absurd and irrelevant to other animals, since *eukhē* is a desire that moves nothing. Wish gives access, or supposes access, to a vast domain of detachment and abstraction from facts, possible alliances, and conceivable individual or common projects. Thus, by definition, wish is exempt from invoking others; it remains isolated and absolutely "verbal." Although situated outside the domain of logic, *eukhē* is in a sense *logos par excellence*, since it remains strictly *logikōs*.[35]

III. Ethics and Politics of Wish

One cannot fail to notice that the four exemplary objects of wishing in the earlier passage from the *Nicomachean Ethics* are of utmost importance in human life: immortality, success, health, and happiness. Even the central concept of "choice" in Aristotelian ethics is said to be subsumed under such objects of wish. For Aristotle, then, wish seems to be our psychological relationship to our highest aspirations which exceed our knowledge and planning, and they find their expression in *eukhē*: faring well (*eu prattein*), long life, prosperity, rejoicing (*khaire!*), success, good luck. In short, *eukhē* is a *logos* that acknowledges the vulnerability of *logos* itself at the face of contingency, when things are *not* "up to us." In this respect, the wishful attitude may be seen as a corrective of hubristic claims of rationality for self-sufficiency. In this sense, the wishful attitude maintains a constant reserve for gratitude and for the recognition of our limitations, as well as our constant possibility for hope. So in this respect, for the wishful attitude, the world is fundamentally open, undetermined by history, rational planning, or human understanding.

Hence, there is an important political implication of this wishful attitude. Being the only animal capable of *logos* and thus of the kind of *logos* that *eukhē* is, the human political animal is capable of transcending all *Realpolitik* and of finding refuge in a strictly *logikos* discourse: utopianism. It is not surprising that the word "*eukhē*" occurs regularly in Plato's *Republic*. There it designates the "ideal" city, which, although impossible, is eminently worthy of wish—a city that has no place in reality but can always be envisaged precisely through *logos*, a city constituted in *logos* alone.[36] Similarly, the major Aristotelian text in which *eukhē* most occurs is neither the logical works, nor the *Rhetoric* and the *Poetics*, nor even the psychological works, but the *Politics*, where it appears in the phrase *kat' eukhēn* qualifying a constitution that is most worthy of wish.[37]

Yet, wishing does not imply wishing *well*. And not all prayers are for the *good* of someone. Curses are *eukhai* as well. Thus, the wishful attitude is found not only in the form of gratitude and hope but also in the form of resentment. More profoundly, just as this "precative" aspect of human *logos* implies humility with regard to human powers and accomplishments, by the same token it may turn into misology. For, the wishful attitude interprets not only the future but also the present and the past, in terms of contingency and not, ultimately, in terms of natural necessity and rational human agency. For instance, a strictly wishful attitude reacts to an earthquake that took tens of thousands of lives with the mere "desire" that it had not happened, without taking any action for the causes behind the "tragedy" and for its prevention in the future. This is the misologistic, fatalistic, skeptic, and/or sophistic side of wish and prayer.[38] While enabling us to acknowledge the vulnerability of rationality, the wishful attitude may also turn into an irrefutable denial of responsibility. We saw how the wishful attitude was fundamentally open to that which is *not* "up to us"; here we see that it can obliterate anything that *is* "up to us." For, to assume a wishful attitude is to appeal to the constant possibility of interpreting the world as "happenstance." This attitude, as well as its linguistic expression in the optative or "precative" mood of "prayer," constitutes the everlasting human possibility for viewing being as "precarious" in its etymological sense. It views the past, the present, and the future as coincidental or contingent and not as an always evolving product of prior causes, past decisions, and plans for the future.[39]

> We rightly say that chance is beyond calculation [*paralogon*], for calculation [*logos*] applies either to that which is always [*tōn aei ontōn*] or to that which is for the most part [*tōn hōs epi to polu*], while chance applies in cases beyond these [*para tauta*]. (*Phys*. II.5 197a18-21)

Then chance may be a kind of cause, if not all causality is due to necessity or regularity. Yet again the problem is in *limiting* chance. If I go to the marketplace to buy fish and meet my debtor, that is chance; but so is my buying *this* particular fish, my giving the fisher *this* exact bill, my debtor wearing a tie, and so on. Just as there is no science of accidental attributes in Aristotle's metaphysics, there can be no *logos* of chance events in his physics.

And that is the point: for better or for worse, *logos* as human speech and rationality is capable of interpreting the world and causality as beyond *logos*. Only a being with *logos* is capable of recognizing the *paralogon* and even of appealing to it in her interpretation of the world. The wishful attitude then is not only possible, it is an eternal possibility for animals having *logos*, since by definition it can neither be logically refuted by demonstration nor factually defeated by action. As having *logos*, human beings are uniquely capable of interpreting the world as mere happenstance, of denying their own agency and responsibilities, and of relating to unreality and to contradictions at the risk of claiming to become "similar to a plant."[40]

Conclusion

In this chapter, I tried to offer a brief sketch of the role of "wish" in Aristotle's philosophy. We saw that, according to him, *eukhē* is a kind of sentence in its own right, but that it is neither true nor false; that the "wishing" (*boulēsis*) that subtends expressions of wish is a kind of desire that does not move anything—neither the animal itself, nor another animal as in the example of animal voice; that the objects of wishing are ultimate in human life beyond the possible objects of "choice"; that the wishful attitude can address the world in a specifically "optative" mood and interpret causality as "chance" (*tukhē*). In this chapter, we tried to explore how having *logos* makes us the "wishing" animal, since a statement of wish is a peculiar kind of *logos* in that it is fundamentally divorced from truth and falsity, and since statements of wish express a peculiar kind of desire in that this desire is fundamentally divorced from motion. Being the "precative" or "precarious" animal she is, the human being is thus capable of desiring to do something that is refused even to gods themselves according to Aristotle's quotation of Agathon: namely, "to make undone whatever has been done."[41]

Notes

1 The issues pursued in this chapter concerning *eukhē* stem from *The Middle Included: Logos in Aristotle* (Northwestern University Press, 2017), 170–8. The discussion there was complimented by an analysis of Polyphemus' encounter with Odysseus in the *Odyssey* as well as his "serenade" to Galatea found in Theocritus (194–208). I have further pursued the topic without literary references in "L'être humain, animal précaire. Eukhē chez Aristote," in *Aristote, l'animal politique*, ed. Güremen and Jaulin (Publications de la Sorbonne, 2017), 121–37. This chapter is yet a further, but not last, stage of my work on the same subject. I would like to thank Ayşenur Nuhoğlu for reading the text carefully and making critical comments on it. I would also like to thank the Scientific Research Projects at Galatasaray University for supporting my work on this chapter. All translations from ancient Greek are mine, unless noted otherwise.
2 Alexandre Koyré, "Galilée et Platon," in *Études d'histoire de la pensée scientifique* (Gallimard, 1985), 176.

3. *Physics* II.1 192b22-23. See also *EN* VI.2 1139a35-39.
4. *On the Soul* II.11 424a5-7; II.6 418a15; III.2; III.12 434b3.
5. *On the Soul* III.12 434b25-27.
6. For the "universal premise of desire," see also Martha Craven Nussbaum, *The Therapy of Desire* (Princeton, NJ: Princeton University Press, 2018), 81.
7. *Movement of Animals* 7 701a32-33. See also *On the Soul* III.11 434a17-22; *Nicomachean Ethics* VI.4 1140b3-5.
8. This phrase is not used by Aristotle. See Jean-Louis Labarrière, *Langage, vie politique et mouvements des animaux* (Librarie Philosophique J. Vrin, 2004), 195ff.; Pierre-Marie Morel, *Aristote: une philosophie de l'activité* (Flammarion, 2003), 80–9.
9. Cf. the eight occurrences of *euthus* and its derivatives in *Movement of Animals* 7.
10. *On the Soul* III.10 433b7.
11. *On the Soul* III.10 433b26; III.9 432b29-31.
12. For a discussion, see Labarrière, *Langage, vie politique et mouvements des animaux*, 23–6.
13. *On Interpretation* 1 16a7.
14. For more details on the physiology of phonation, see my article "On Bees and Humans," *Epoche* 17, no. 2 (2013): 337–50. See also, in this volume, Eli Diamond, "'For There Are Gods Here Too': Embodied Essence, Two-Footedness, and the Animal with *Logos*," 52–3.
15. *On the Soul* II.8 420b32-33. See also Diamond, 53.
16. *Politics* I.2 1253a11-12.
17. *Politics* I.1 1252a.
18. See the fourth chapter of Darwin's *The Expression of the Emotions in Man and Animals* (Oxford/New York: Oxford University Press, 1998).
19. *On the Soul* II.8 419b11.
20. *History of Animals* I.1 488a7-10.
21. Since voice invokes the other animal and thus attempts at "subjugating" her within a shared task, voice assumes, so to speak, a "subjunctive mood"—or, to use the Hellenistic grammatical terminology, an *enklisis hypotaktikē*. Cf. Dionysius Thrax, *Art of Grammar* 13, 638b8; Apollonius Dyscolus, *Syntax* 246.15.
22. S.v. *akouein* A.II.2, Liddell, Scott and Jones, *Greek-English Lexicon*, 53–4. In other languages such as French, Latin, Arabic, and Turkish, one again finds the same association between listening and obeying. One striking example of this kind of "imperious" voice is found in Aristotle's remark about elephants fighting with each other. He says that "the one who loses obeys the other and yields to his voice [*tēn tou nikēsantos phōnēn*]" (*History of Animals* IX.1.610a29, 17.)
23. *Odyssey*, VII, 11.
24. Consequently, as much as it belongs to the subjunctive mood (the *enklisis hypotaktikē*), voice belongs to the imperative mood—to the *enklisis prostaktikē*. Dionysius Thrax, *Art of Grammar* 13, 638b7; Apollonius Dyscolus, *Syntax* 31.20. For an insightful analysis of human obedience to reason in the context of child development and human psychology, see, in this volume, Rabinoff, "Aristotle on the Rationality of Virtue," 191–5.
25. Aeschylus, *Seven Against Thebes*, 819–20; Euripides, *Phoenician Women*, 70. See also Bailly, *Dictionnaire Grec-Français*, 863–4; Liddell, Scott and Jones, *Greek-English Lexicon*, 739.
26. Let me add that a treatise by Aristotle entitled *On Prayer* (*Peri Eukhēs*) is found in Diogenes Laertius' catalogue of Aristotle's writings (5.22) and in the *Vita Hesychii*

(Düring, 83). Simplicius refers to it once in fragment 57 (Ross). Jean Pépin, "Aristote: 'De la Prière,'" *Revue Philosophique de la France et de l'Étranger* 157 (1967): 59–70. A larger version of this latter article is reviewed by John M. Rist in "The End of Aristotle's on Prayer," *The American Journal of Philology* 106, no. 1 (Spring, 1985): 110–13.

27 *On Interpretation* 4 17a5-6.
28 In order to compare the Aristotelian conception of *eukhē* with its posterity, let us point out that the *Definitions* of Aquilius put prayer (*eukhē*) under the same genus (namely, *aitēsis*) and define it as a "demand of goods from the Gods" (*aitēsis agathōn para theōn*). Yet, probably dating from the Roman Imperial Period according to Marwan Rashed, this definition bears obviously post-Aristotelian (pseudo-Platonic and Stoic) influences. Most importantly, *eukhē* here is reserved to an address to God or to Gods, whereas it is *not* in the Aristotelian corpus (cf. the mention of *eukhē* as a more honorable kind of demand than begging). Further, in contrast to the Classical Greek usages of the word as in Aeschylus and Euripides, *eukhē* in Aquilius does not contain the sense of imprecation (*ara*) which is defined by Aquilius as *another* kind of demand, namely a "demand of punishment from the Gods" (*timōrias aitēsis para theōn*). Cf. Marwan Rashed, "Les *Définitions* d'Aquilius," in *Ancient Philosophy in Memory of R. W. Sharples* (Oxford: Oxford University Press, 2012), 149–50. See also Rashed's analyses of "vow" (*orkos*) as a "speech act" (150–3). Our analysis of *eukhē* in the following pages are in line with Rashed's remarks. I would like to thank M. Rashed for sharing his erudition and his article with me.
29 Indeed, the *enklisis euktikē* according to Alexandrian grammar. Herbert Weir Smyth, *Greek Grammar* (Cambridge, MA: Harvard University Press, 1920), 107, 406; Dionysius Thrax, *Art Grammatica* (Leipzig: Teubner, 1883), 13, 638b8; Apollonius Dyscolus, *Syntax*, trans. F. W. Householder (Amsterdam: John Benjamins Publishing Company, 1981), 245.27. Dionysius Thrax adds also the infinitive mood (*enklisis aparemphatos*). (13, 638b7; Apollonius Dyscolus, 226.20.) Compare Dionysius' fourfold distinction with Farabi, *Commentary and Short Treatise on Aristotle's De Interpretatione*, trans. F. W. Zimmermann (Oxford: Oxford University Press, 1988). For a comparison between Greek and Latin, which is instructive in that Latin does not have an optative, see Carl Buck, *Comparative Grammar of Greek and Latin* (Chicago, IL: University of Chicago Press, 1933), 299–301; Ralph Westwood Moore, *Comparative Greek and Latin Syntax* (Bristol: Bristol Classical Press, 1934), 98–101.
30 No wonder the word for the optative mood comes from the Latin verb *optare*, which means "to wish." Compare the verb *precare* ("to pray"), the root of the adjective "precative."
31 *On the Soul* III.9 432b5-6.
32 *Nicomachean Ethics* III.2 1111b12-113.
33 Again this is why the semantics of *eukhē* is a fundamentally different question than the famous problem of future contingents in *On Interpretation* 9.
34 "This point should be supplemented by Russon's account of possibility and potentiality in the specifically human context. Cf. In this volume, Russon, "Actuality in the First Sense' and the Question of Human Nature in Aristotle," especially 86 and 88.
35 See, for instance, *Eudemian Ethics* I.8 1217b21.
36 Cf. Plato, *Republic* VI, 499c, but also V, 450d; VII, 540d. All three highlight the impossibility of the city described. Plato employs the same word, *eukhē*, for a child's wish in the *Sophist*, 249d. For a more extensive discussion of the relationship between *logos* and "prayer," see Martha Craven Nussbaum, *The Therapy of Desire*, 50.

37 *Politics* IV.1 1288b23; IV.9 1295a29-30; II.1 1260b28-29; see also the verbal forms of *eukhē* in *Politics* VII.13 1334b22; VII.12 1332a30; VII.10 1330a37.
38 For misology, see Plato, *Phaedo* 89d-e; *Republic* III, 411d.
39 For his attribution of all phenomena to "something divine and most godlike [*daimoniōteron*]," see, for instance, *Physics* II.4 196b6-8.
40 Among the extremely vexing questions to be further explored are the following: How is "wishing" related to the problem of "will" if at all? What is the role of imagination in the wishful attitude? Can one imagine an impossibility wished for? Similarly, does this nonpractical attitude relate to hope, to infinity, and to contemplation? Further, even though prayers and wishes cannot be refuted in the sense in which declarative sentences can be, how can one account for the fact that prayers and wishes can contradict one another?
41 *Nicomachean Ethics* VI, 2, 1139b10-11, tr. Joe Sachs.

8

The Dissociative Power of *Logos* in Taking Account of Oneself

Gregory Kirk

Introduction

To be human is to be capable of being absorbed in one's immediate experiences and also to be capable of holding oneself at a remote distance from those experiences. It is to be immersed in sensuous embodiment and also to be capable of withdrawing to reflect upon one's embodiment. In each case, the latter capability is distinctive to the possession of *logos*. Human beings can account for their immediate experiences and can thereby make those experiences an object of reflection.[1] Possessing such a capacity can liberate one from the dictates of immediate affections, which is to say that it can make one increasingly capable of choice and thus of the full accomplishment of human action.[2] Possessing such a capacity, however, also burdens one with responsibility over one's life, rendering that life simultaneously one's very being and, in a certain respect, one's project.[3] In what follows, I present that burden in the context of Aristotle's account of human nature in the *Nicomachean Ethics*, by presenting two levels at which *logos* allows us to dissociate ourselves from the situations in which we act. I present that burden by emphasizing the existential condition in which one can engage in the practice of dissociation: namely, always and only within the context of the current state of one's character.

In Section I, I present examples of situations calling for one to dissociate from immediate experience. Specifically, I examine situations in which we take ourselves to be responding to those very situations, when we are in fact responding primarily to our own affections. Insofar as one is preoccupied with one's immediate affections, one experiences the given situation in a distorted manner. One must therefore take a critical perspective on one's affections, recognizing the extent to which those affections are preventing one from being capable of choosing how to act according to what the situation itself calls for. In Section II, I claim that Aristotle shows that merely dissociating oneself self-consciously from one's desires for the purpose of criticizing oneself is insufficient to the task of changing one's bad behavior or disposition, due to the habituated character of desires. I demonstrate in what way desires maintain habitual control over how we act by examining the implicit practical syllogisms operative in a person lacking control over their affections. One might be consciously critical of one's affections while also experiencing the immediacy of one's desires in a rationally self-justifying, though recognizably pathological, manner. This is what Aristotle calls lack of self-control (*akrasia*). Such a condition points to the second order of dissociation discussed in Section III, namely, dissociation from one's actions understood as immediate experiences. In such instances of dissociation, one is directed at the future self that is to be generated by the habits shaped by this particular type of action and its repetition. Dissociation from the relevance of one's actions to immediate circumstances allows one to take one's character as a whole as one's concern. I claim that it is a consequence of having engaged in these two orders of dissociation through *logos* that one is made capable of responding to situations as they are, which is to say that one is made better capable of choice.

Operative throughout my discussion is the distinction between the interrelated needs to accomplish practical wisdom (*phronēsis*) and to accomplish moral virtue (*ēthikē aretē*). For Aristotle, practical wisdom consists in part in the ability to deliberate about what particular actions one must perform to live well and to choose as a result of that deliberation (VI.5 1140a24-b30).[4] Moral virtue, by contrast, consists of habits cultivated from experience engaging in good actions that accomplish a mean between two extremes of vice (II.2 1103b7-26; II.6 1106b8-28). Practical wisdom and moral virtue are essential to a good life and bring each other to completion. I show in what way these two essential features of the good life function at different registers—practical wisdom consisting of taking account of situations in a manner that facilitates deliberation about actions chosen for the purpose of accomplishing some good and moral virtue being produced through habits initially *preceding* the ability to choose how to act, though also being shaped in part through choices. These two essential features of living well are consequently realized according to different demands, toward the same end.[5]

I. Affections as Motivations for Action

According to Aristotle, human affections have a share in (*metechousa*) *logos* (I.13 1102b13-14). Though affections themselves are in a sense irrational (*alogon*), they can be made to conform to *logos* and, in that sense, can be said to share in it.[6] An affection sometimes combats and resists (*machetai kai antiteinei*) *logos* (I.13 1102b17-18). At times, says Aristotle, our affections are akin to limbs having been paralyzed (*paralelumena*), where one wishes to direct one's limbs one way, but they move in the other (I.13 1102b18-20).[7] Aristotle notes that unlike paralyzed limbs, in which involuntary movement is visible, the soul's "movements" astray are not visible. A major concern of the *Nicomachean Ethics* is to reflect on the need to cultivate the ability to "see" or have knowledge of what it is in the soul that is moving astray.[8] The project of cultivating this ability is brought about through *logos*.

The reason why there are unnoticed parts of the soul moving us is because we are not constituted by reason alone. Despite our possession of the ability to reflect upon and to take account of ourselves, we are naturally inclined to ignorance concerning what it is that dictates our behavior. Thus, one must become attuned to her own behavior, to those invisible movements of her soul—that is, attuned to her character— to live well. This attunement is an essential component of the kind of person capable of practical wisdom.

To become a person of practical wisdom is to become one who knows which actions are good and who deliberates intelligently about which choices to make to accomplish goods. Good character facilitates practical wisdom by providing the stable comportment that allows one to engage in such deliberations.[9] Becoming a person capable of practical wisdom is the culmination of the project that begins with the cultivation of moral virtues; completing that project, however, inevitably consists in participating consciously in the shaping of one's emotions and appetites such that they allow one to interpret and understand situations well, and therefore such that those emotions *facilitate*, rather than *hinder*, choice. The development of practical wisdom thus becomes a part of the shaping of moral virtues.[10] Broadly, to be practically wise is to be attuned to responding well to the specific demands of practical, unanticipated situations. As Aristotle says, practical wisdom is concerned "not only with universals but with particulars, which become familiar from experience" (VI.8 1142a14-15). What I am concerned with here is the fact that the need to be oriented well to particulars is similarly crucial to the attitude or behavior that is required of one who, within the context of an otherwise healthy character development, has in fact some significant dimension of either vice or lack of self-control. Let us consider what this "concern with particulars" is by examining how we address specific dimensions of vice or lack of self-control within a life broadly informed by moral virtue and practical wisdom, through dissociation from our own actions.

One is sometimes consumed with anger, with desire, or with fear. In such moments, it is not merely the case that one feels these emotions: rather, they compel immediate actions in a manner that commonly discourages deliberation and indeed implies unearned certainty. Aristotle characterizes anger (*thumos*) through various illuminating examples. He first characterizes it as seeming to "listen to argument to some extent, but to mishear (*parakouein*) it" (VII.6 1149a24-26). He compares it to a servant who hears that the master is giving orders and runs out to fulfill them before having heard entirely what the master said. He then compares it to the dog that barks indiscriminately if there is a knock at the door, never checking to see if it is a friend or a foe (VII.6 1149a26-31).[11] The dog who barks when it hears a knock has not deliberated about the likelihood of an intruder. The dog's passions are roused and immediately expressed. Likewise, the servant is roused to perform a task, perhaps driven by a sense of urgency and concern for pleasing the master. The agitation produced by that concern demands release, compelling action prior to having secured a grasp of what release would be most effective. Each of these situations is analogous to the experience of anger in part because it is a reaction to one's affective response to the situation. When we are angry, and to an intensity that exceeds our ability to reflect, the distressed state that we feel demands release. Aristotle characterizes the eventual release of anger as a kind of pleasure that is a release from pain (IV.5 1126a20-22). When we are preoccupied with the need for release, and not to the object with which we are engaged, our attention is diverted from the object.[12]

Consider, for example, an ill-tempered parent who trips over a child's toy lying in an inappropriate place in the home. Such a person might be compelled, foolishly, to kick or to shout at the toy. When they behave in this way, it is not because they momentarily believe the toy to be responsible for their accident. Their attention is not directed at the toy *as* a toy; it is directed, rather, at the affection provoked by having tripped, at the toy *as* catalyst for their affection. Crucially, in such moments, it is not principally the objective situation they react to, but rather their own affective condition. Preoccupation with the affective condition distorts the experience of the circumstances. The person is consumed by anger, then directed by it to their own state and to the pain of unexpressed energy they now possess.[13] The toy becomes the object upon which the anger is unleashed as a site for impotent revenge, causing the simultaneous manifestation of the pleasure of (ineffectual) revenge and the releasing of the pain of frustration. Under such conditions, the person is unable to identify the actual conditions in which they act—they are "blinded by rage," as people say. Under the condition of intense anger that the ill-tempered person feels when she trips over the toy, effectively, she cannot really identify that she is shouting at an inanimate object, because she is absorbed in her affective condition.[14]

Examples related to other affections display this tendency of pathologically developed affections turning in on themselves. If I am excessively inclined to great distress at the site of a spider on my shoulder, for example, I will be so directed to the supposed danger of the experience that I cannot be reasoned with;[15] I will not be adequately swayed if told that what is happening is that a small, nonthreatening animal happens to be on my shoulder and that it is easily removed. Similarly, in moments in which a person is consumed by the desire to indulge excessively in eating unhealthy foods, her attention can be focused so strongly on the expression of that desire that her judgment concerning the state of her health and the effects of the consumption are completely obscured or perhaps experienced as coming from a hostile source.[16]

One of the effects of being directed to respond immediately to one's affective condition is that one is only narrowly engaged by the situation in which one is acting. It is to be deliberately directed at one's affections and only incidentally to the object. The effect of this situation in which one is consumed by the object *qua* object *of* one's anger, fear, or desire is that one fails to identify the *proper* "what" of the object. When a person kicks the toy that she tripped over, she fails to see it *as* a toy. It is only a vehicle for self-relation. Likewise, when a person is put into a state of agitation by the spider, she does not respond by interacting with a spider. She responds by interacting with *this* menace, *this* threat that is suddenly violating her personal space.[17] Though she is in fact addressing her actions to the spider, the ultimate object of her interest is her own agitated state and her desire to alleviate it.

What is missing from this sort of behavior is the recognition that the catalyst of particular affections has its own independent objectivity. While the person interacting with the objects in the examples given earlier experiences those objects as instances of obstruction, in doing so she experiences the object without a sense of the need to recognize it as having its own proper "what" independent of its relation to her. By contrast, the person who interacts wisely with the toy she tripped over, the spider she finds on her shoulder, or the food she desires, relates to the objects of her attention, not only according to the terms of her own experiences but also according to its independent "whatness"; she is thus able to more richly to perceive the *situation*, and her affective responses to that situation are contextualized *by* the situation. Such a person identifies the *kinds* of things that she is dealing with in dealing with these particulars and identifies them as the *right* kinds. Such a person continues to identify the situation as relating to her—indeed, perhaps being initially frustrated by the inconsiderate placement of the toy, startled by the spider, tempted by the food— but she differs from the person *consumed* by her affections in an important way. She experiences her affections as pointing toward a kind of action about which she can choose, rather than experiencing her affections as determining her actions. This ability to choose implies a quasi-independence from situations. Insofar as she experiences her affections as pointing to kinds of action, she can deliberate; she experiences herself as called by her affections to deliberate about how to act. The affections themselves do not exercise on the person well-disposed to the situation the kind of intensity that overwhelms the possibility of choice. Her habits do not impede practical wisdom, which is to say that her character does not present the situation as demanding actions without the possibility of choice. The situation does not demand of her that she act without taking account of that situation. Situations show themselves to such a person as affording choices, whereas the person who is completely consumed by her affections confronts the situations themselves as already determining how she acts.

I have described one person who is consumed by her affections. I have described another whose affections frame situations for her to choose. The first condition consists of acting primarily on the basis of the affections themselves; such a person does not "read" the situation in which she acts but rather attends to her affections. The only way to move beyond such a condition involves reflecting upon her affections. That is, such a person must dissociate herself, in a preliminary way, from her immediate responses to situations of action and act as a critic of herself. As we will see in the following section, though, dissociation of oneself from immediate responses will not be *sufficient* for the accomplishment of the proper conditions for one to act with practical wisdom.

II. Dispositions as Setting the Terms for Action

We have thus far noted the importance of being aware of our affections, which is to say that it is important for us not merely to be absorbed by our affective responses to situations but also to be able to dissociate ourselves from those affections for the purpose of examining them. Dissociating ourselves from immediate experience allows us to consider the role our affections play in how we interpret situations and encourages recognition of the actual character of the situation in which we are inclined to feel intense anger, desire, or fear. A person's mere articulate critical recognition of her character does not itself *change* that character, though, because she is not merely constituted by reason. Our inclinations to act are directed, not merely by immediately conscious thoughts but also by the habitual emotional dispositions that we accumulate over a lifetime of action. These habits form the "backdrop" of our interaction with the world and—to a significant degree—determine whether we will choose intelligently how to act upon the world. This is one reason why Aristotle emphasizes the importance of habituation, claiming that an upbringing that cultivates good habits from the start makes "all the difference" (II.1 1103b23-25).[18]

Aristotle identifies the centrality of habits to cultivating one's character in the context of noting that human beings are naturally neither good nor bad. It is only through living that we become the kinds of people that we do. Just as it is through playing the harp well that one becomes a good harpist and building a house well that one becomes a good house-builder, likewise, it is through acting in a good way that one becomes good. We begin with the capacity to become good but only realize that capacity through action (II.1 1103b6-12). We can consequently say that actions of any kind have a twofold significance—on the one hand they make an impact on the particular situation to which they respond and on the other hand they produce or reinforce the disposition to behave similarly in future situations. By standing firm in the face of a particular fear I might have, I incline myself to face future fearful situations in the same manner, by having fostered confidence that I can face such situations.[19] Similarly, by remaining in control of myself when I experience anger toward a person, I make myself more likely to be capable of doing the same later on (II.1 1103b13-25). It is through habituation from earliest childhood that we develop the affective dispositions that we possess as adults. It is therefore notable that the development of one's affective dispositions thus begins as the responsibility of someone else, namely, one's caregiver(s).[20] Let us further develop this account of the determination of one's affective dispositions.

The affective disposition one has toward one's experiences determines how one interprets a given situation. If one is irascible, one will be more inclined to find slights in the behavior and actions of others. By contrast, if one is gentle, what might otherwise appear as slights are more likely to be ignored or treated calmly. The person not habitually inclined toward irascibility also finds in situations less call for anger (IV.5 1125b33-1126a5). It is similarly the case with fear and desire. For Aristotle, though the true mark of the courageous person is to be found in battle, in the possession of confidence "in the face of noble death" (III.6 1115a25-35), failures with respect to fear include fearing what we should not, fearing as we should not, and fearing when we should not (III.6 1115b15-20). A person lacking courage will tend to find more situations in which to be frightened and will fear in a manner that overwhelms the ability to make intelligent choices about how to act.[21] Correspondingly, the temperate person, for Aristotle, tends not to enjoy the things a self-indulgent person does. As a result of this, such a person is not inclined to feel the pain that accompanies cravings for pleasurable things, instead desiring pleasurable things that are healthy and doing so only moderately (III.11 1119a11-21). In the cases of fear, desire, and anger, a good disposition prevents one from approaching the situation in a manner hampered by preoccupation with one's own condition.

These virtuous dispositions facilitate intelligent choices. It is, at least in part, in this sense that Aristotle identifies virtuous habits with stability (II.4 1105a30-35). Situations, for the virtuous person, typically do not call for undesirable uncontrolled responses. By contrast, the accumulated disposition to be quick to anger, to be dominated by fear, or to indulge one's desires inclines one to amplify the intensity of one's experience of slights, threats, and temptations in various situations one faces.

The cumulative pathologies that result from repeated bad behavior display what should motivate us to dissociate from ourselves, to perform critical self-evaluation, which is to say to provide a *logos* of our actions. Such pathologies also more precisely show the difficulty that we face in attempting to transform our affective dispositions. Insofar as one's adult character is the product of a lifetime of action, it becomes increasingly challenging to change one's behavior. Our discussion here is, it should be noted, not concerned with vicious people who have become effectively incapable of transforming their bad habits. Rather, we are concerned with those people who have accomplished a state of character generally virtuous, but with some bad habits that they wish to break. The difficulty of calming one's anger, resisting one's unhealthy desires, or being more resilient in the face of one's fears occurs here for the kind of person *willing* to subject herself to scrutiny with the aim of changing. To make use of this power to dissociate from one's habits to account for them already suggests a state of character that is good. It is, nonetheless, not the case that one can simply give a rational account of one's bad behavioral tendencies and expect them to be changed, because one's dispositions incline one toward those kinds of behavior and those dispositions set the terms within which one can reason in the immediacy of the situation. Put simply, one can only reason *within* the state of character one is trying to change.

Let us consider the immediate deployment of a rational account or *logos*—what I will call the first stage of dissociation. Doing so will show the insufficiency of reason on its own to accomplish virtue, insofar as reason itself can be made the enabler of one's bad habits. This is demonstrated through the practical syllogism, the tacit reasoning operative in action, that provides a merely formal account of action, an account whose content—whatever its value—accounts for any action, whether good or bad.[22]

What is immediately lacking during this first stage of dissociation is the ability to control one's inclinations toward undesirable affections. Regardless of such a person's assessment of their pathological feelings, they will continue to feel how they are habituated to feel. They will therefore still incline toward being affected pathologically while criticizing themselves for being so affected. Such a person possesses, in some sense, the knowledge necessary to act well—otherwise, they would not have identified the problem to begin with—but is not exercising that knowledge effectively.[23] What is the nature of this knowledge, and what does it lack?

Aristotle addresses this issue of how a person can in a certain sense know that they ought to behave differently without putting that knowledge into action. He attempts to answer the question "In what sense can we say that a person lacking in self-control behaves knowingly?" Many people certainly experience pathological affections that they recognize to be bad. Such people know that their excessive affection is harmful, and yet, in the moment, find themselves unable to resist it. However, the sense in which they "know" this rests upon an equivocation. According to Aristotle, when a person is unable to resist her inclinations and is compelled to act against the rational principle, she has come, through reflection, to know her own behavior and how it ought to be changed, but only in a sense akin to an actor reciting lines on a stage (VII.3 1147a19-24). This notion of being capable merely of reciting what one ought to do, rather than living within the practice articulated through the rational principle, underscores the point made earlier that control of passions is not automatic, but, rather, requires a history of practice through which one cultivates affective dispositions that incline one toward the action that is good. When one merely "knows" how one ought to behave in general but fails to act on that "knowledge," one has yet to understand how the good can be applied to this particular situation. One has not yet transformed that articulated knowledge into a habit, which is to say that one has yet to transform the use of one's critical reflection into a practice.[24]

It is a mistake to imagine that one's pathological affections are merely irrational. Merely "knowing" how one ought to act, without doing the difficult work of putting into practice this "knowledge" in a way that changes one's habitual disposition in the desired way, illustrates this. Indeed, those angry, fearful, or licentious responses can be articulated by an implicit practical syllogism. That is, even pathological actions display the activity of reason but reason in the service of the bad affection or behavior. The syllogism articulates the habituated rationality that has shaped, and that is reflected in, the action. One might, for example, have an excessive tendency to desire food that is unhealthy. In such instances, one's compulsion by the desire to eat is rationally articulated by the implicit practical syllogism, "everything sweet ought to be tasted," "this is sweet" therefore "I will taste it" (VIII.2 1146a25-30).[25] In such circumstances, the rational principle *not* to indulge one's harmful desires is undermined by a form of reasoning serving only the dictates of one's desires. A person who concludes, from reflection on past experiences, that she ought not to overindulge in eating delicious food that is unhealthy for her has not yet necessarily cultivated the capacity to take control of her criticized desires. Reason, in such instances, is capable of operating at the behest of any particular desire and does so counter to the self-critical rational principle at which she has arrived through reflection on past experience. In contrast to such a condition of lack of self-control, people who have, over time, habitually made the rational principle a "part of themselves" are not only capable of being articulate about the most desirable patterns of behavior but also capable of acting in a manner that implies a practical syllogism that corresponds to the explicitly desired state of character.

Note that the person whose actions are inclined against the rational principle—the person lacking self-control—remains unable to grasp *what* is called for by the situation that she is in.[26] Whereas the person consumed by her affections was unable to grasp the situation in which she acted from *within* the affection, here, the person lacking in self-control fails to grasp the situation due to her preoccupation with the object of her affections *only* at the register of explicit rationality. The excessively angry person identifies slights to be *in principle* worthy of anger, but the practical syllogism that justifies anger is so general that it indicates nothing about the degree to which she will in fact—perhaps excessively and harmfully—express that anger. The excessively self-indulgent person recognizes food she currently desires to eat to be worthy of consumption *in principle*, but the practical syllogism that justifies consumption indicates nothing about the excessive indulgence of the desire to eat those foods. By being simultaneously consumed by particular affections, and reasoning only at the level of (highly selective and desire-serving) universality, the person acting in such a situation can "know" that her inclinations are misleading her but can be persuaded by a kind of abuse of *logos* into acting against the principles she has begun to develop through reflection.

This discussion of undesirable habitual dispositions, and the fact that they make the transformation of one's behavior something that can only be done over time, demonstrates that *logos* is capable of operating at various levels of awareness that are at times at odds with one another. Consequently, *logos* ought not to function merely as a means for us to criticize our particular actions and inclinations if we hope to change ourselves for the better. *Logos* must serve us in calculating how those inclinations are shaped, taking into account the whole life of the person, and must do so without a permanently clear sense of what results those calculations will yield. *Logos* must function as the part of the person that examines the changeable manifestations of the person's state of character, anticipating future states of character.

III. *Logos* as Calculation Concerning One's Future Self

Aristotle claims that "it is no easy task to be good" (II.9 1109a24). Anyone can get angry, he says, just as anyone can desire pleasures and experience fears—but "to do this to the right person, to the right extent, at the right time, with the right motive, and in the right way, *that* is not for everyone, nor is it easy" (II.9 1109a26-29). We can see clearly now what the difficulty is. As we discussed in Section I, when our affections determine how we act, we are not in fact directed, in our actions, to the situation in which we act, but rather to the affections themselves. As we discussed in Section II, when we merely adopt a stance of critical dissociation from our affections, the brute rational principles we adopt fail to attend to our accumulated habitual dispositions, which are themselves supported by implicit and conveniently narrowly circumscribed rational principles. We must thus attend to a second register of dissociation from our absorption in immediate experience. Let us briefly account for this second register.

We are capable of treating our own characters as objects to be shaped. Aristotle discusses this orientation to ourselves, claiming that "we must consider the things towards which we ourselves also are easily carried away" suggesting further that "we must drag ourselves away to the contrary extreme; for we shall get into the intermediate state by drawing well away from error, as people do in straightening sticks that are bent" (II.9 1109b1-7). What Aristotle is characterizing through the analogy to straightening a stick is acting *now* in a fashion that will make our *future* selves better able to act in similar situations.[27] We can self-consciously shape our future selves by acting against the affective dispositions which we wish to change. Most generally, the task with which we are faced by our nature as animals with *logos* is to take on our own character as a project for the purpose of generating practices that cultivate virtue. We will now reflect on this task which, if Aristotle is right, all of us ought to perform.

The first order of dissociation involved examining the situation in which one acted and identifying the tension between one's affections and one's rational judgment concerning how to act as well as recognizing the way in which one's affections undermined one's ability to discern how best to act. The second order of dissociation requires us to turn against our inclinations and do so in a fashion that is directed at the future determinations of ourselves which we hope to be produced through shaping new habits. Though we undoubtedly remain partially absorbed in our immediate circumstances, we must, simultaneously, concern ourselves with the anticipated determinations resulting from how we act in our current situation. We abstain from *this* particular pleasurable action, not because it would be bad in principle for us to indulge this particular desire but rather because doing so now will make us—in unanticipated future situations—less beholden to the desires which we are now struggling to control. We resist our impulse to flee *this* particular social event that intimidates us, not because this particular social event is necessarily very important to us but because we hope to shape our future selves to be inclined more toward facility in social situations at unanticipated future times. We work as hard as we can not to express the rage we feel in our bodies at this particular slight against us, not because the slight does not merit an angry response, but because only in this way can we prevent ourselves from being overcome by the very same anger we are now struggling to contain. To make choices about how to act such that we will improve our characters by the transformation of bad habits is to take our own actions to be the material with which we attempt to create future selves we want to be. The choices that we make to break out of patterns of behavior that we hope to change are directed *not* merely at the immediate conditions with which we are faced but at hoped-for future states of character. The situations in which we act thus consist not merely of immediate concern but also of the determination of our future selves.

Conclusion: Perceiving Situations as They Are

I began by mentioning Aristotle's claim in Book VI of the *Nicomachean Ethics* that practical wisdom is concerned with perception and with particulars. What I take Aristotle to mean is that, insofar as practical wisdom is about deliberating concerning which actions will produce the good, it also concerns one's ability to identify the good to be accomplished. Moral virtue, too, is directed to particulars, insofar as it concerns how we are disposed to respond to the immediate situations in which we act. Our emotional dispositions can be such that they inhibit our ability to "read" the situations as they are in and instead respond to those situations prompted entirely by our affections. In contrast to this, well-cultivated states of character produce affective responses to situations that facilitate choice, and thus, good action. The affections themselves are not the problem. They are a necessary element to our proper discernment of how to act. If we experience no anger in the face of slights against us, we might fail to act in our own defense or in the defense of deserving others. If we do not experience fear sufficiently, we will not recognize when it is appropriate for us to exercise caution. If we do not experience intense erotic desire, we will fail to cultivate important kinds of meaningful relationships with others. The emotions, in other words, essentially frame the situations in which we act. We therefore have important reasons to desire that our emotional dispositions or states of character shape situations for us *well*. Are we angry when we should be? Are we afraid when we should be? Do the right people awaken our erotic desires? Are we capable of enjoying sophisticated forms of physical pleasure? These are the questions that we ought to be asking ourselves. The task of making ourselves disposed to anger, fear, and desire in the best way is one to which we can never *directly* attend, because our attention to our own character can only ever operate through the medium of habituation and over time. This amounts to distancing ourselves from our immediate experiences and taking ourselves—our states of character—as a means by which such questions are answered. Beyond being critics of ourselves, we have within us the ability to project future states of character and to attend to current states of progress toward those desired future conditions. Being capable of asking oneself these questions constitutes an essential part of the burden of responsibility of being the animal with *logos*.

Notes

1. Francis Sparshott, *Taking Life Seriously: A Study of the Argument of the Nicomachean Ethics* (Toronto: University of Toronto Press, 1996), 11, makes this point in reflecting on the project of the *Nicomachean Ethics* itself.
2. Aristotle discusses the distinctive character of choice (*proairesis*) in III.1-5 of *EN*. He distinguishes between choice (*proairesis*) and the voluntary (*to hekousion*) (III.2 1111b6-17). The voluntary concerns a wider range of actions, including those performed by young children and animals, as well as spontaneous actions. By contrast, choice is "involved with reason and thinking things through" (*meta logou kai dianoias*) (III.2 1112a16), which is to say that choice generates action from *logos*. He goes on to claim that "the thing chosen is decided out of deliberation" (III.3 1113a2-4). See also VI.2 1139a21-b11.
3. Though one can call one's life a project in this loose sense, one ought to be careful not to confuse this "project" with productive action. Aristotle distinguishes between making (*poiēsis*) and action (*praxis*) on the grounds that the former has as its end something other than itself, while the latter has itself as its end (VI.5 1140b7).
4. Deborah Achtenberg, *Cognition of Value in Aristotle's Ethics: Promise of Enrichment, Threat of Destruction* (Albany, NY: SUNY Press, 2002), 22, characterizes deliberation as "the activity of discerning which activities, of those that are in our power, are conducive to our aims."
5. On the theme of the interconnections between moral virtue and practical wisdom, see Chapter 9 of this volume, Eve Rabinoff, "Aristotle on the Rationality of Virtue."
6. Reeve, *Aristotle on Practical Wisdom: Nicomachean Ethics VI* (Cambridge, MA: Harvard University Press, 2013), 103, presents this distinction between rational and nonrational parts sharply: "The desiring part of the soul . . . lacks reason, because, unlike the reason-possessing part, it cannot give reasons or construct explanatory demonstrations or syllogisms. Yet it can listen to such reasons and obey them." For a contrasting position that presents the distinction between emotions and reason as an abstraction of elements necessarily coexisting in human nature, see Rabinoff, "Aristotle on the Rationality of Virtue."
7. Sparshott, *Taking Life Seriously*, 74, claims that this analogy does not quite fit. This being so, the central importance of Aristotle's analogy is to distinguish between the visibility of paralysis and the invisibility of what "moves" the soul.
8. See *Movement of Animals* 7, 701a2-32. In the context of presenting what later became known as the "practical syllogism" that is operative in non-deliberative action, Aristotle compares the movements of animals resulting from stimulations to changes in "automatic puppets." See also Sparshott, *Taking Life Seriously*, 246–7.

9 See *Nicomachean Ethics* VI.5 1140b11-13, where temperance is said to preserve practical wisdom (*sozousan ten phronesin*). Sparshott, *Taking Life Seriously*, 238, characterizes this relationship as one in which the ideal of virtue is "a coincidence of true judgment and correct desire in a mutually reinforcing circle." See also Achtenberg, *Cognition of Value*, 126, and Reeve, *Aristotle on Practical Wisdom*, 159–61.

10 Burnyeat, "Aristotle on Learning to Be Good," in *Essays on Aristotle's Ethics*, ed. Rorty (Berkeley, CA: University of California Press, 1980), 74, claims practical wisdom is required for one to cultivate virtuous habits. Though this is undoubtedly true, it is also true that practical wisdom is the culmination of moral virtues, in the sense that one is only properly oriented to what is actually good as a result of having one's passions and one's sense of what is pleasurable adequately shaped. Moral virtues and practical wisdom are mutually supportive; it is a reflection of the reality that we begin cultivating habits before we are capable of reason and that we begin making decisions about our goals before we have completed the project of moral virtue. See also Kosman, "Being Properly Affected: Virtues and Feelings in Aristotle's Ethics," in *Essays on Aristotle's Ethics*, ed. Rorty (Berkeley, CA: University of California Press, 1980), 109–10. Julia Annas, "Aristotle on Pleasure and Goodness," in *Essays on Aristotle's Ethics*, ed. Rorty (Berkeley, CA: University of California Press, 1980), 294, suggests that Aristotle paid insufficient attention to the unevenness of moral development. Against this, it seems to me that the distinction between moral virtues and practical wisdom draws attention to why such development would be uneven.

11 Burnyeat, "Aristotle on Learning to be Good," 79, presents the account of anger here in connection to the discussion in Plato's *Republic* of Leontius (439e6-440a3).

12 Compare Socrates' account of the emotions in *Phaedo* 83c-d.

13 See *Rhetoric* II.2 1378b2-3. Aristotle characterizes the state of anger as entailing within it a kind of pleasure at the thought of revenge. See also II.2 1378a31-33, where anger is said to be a "desire accompanied by pain, for a conspicuous revenge for a conspicuous slight at the hands of men who have no call to slight oneself or one's friends."

14 See *Nicomachean Ethics* IV.5 1126a8-30.

15 See *Rhetoric* III.5 1382a27-32.

16 See *EN* VII.3 1147a25-1147b6 for a discussion of appetites distorting one's grasp of universal principles.

17 Regarding this issue of identifying an object, not as what it is, but rather with respect to its relevant relation to oneself, see *EN* III.10 1118a17-25, where Aristotle talks about the lion seeing the wild goat as what it is only incidentally, seeing the goat rather primarily as its potential meal. Aristotle presents this example to emphasize the primacy of touch and taste and the secondary character of the other senses in desire for pleasure. It nonetheless exemplifies perceiving the object in terms of the subject's own interests and only incidentally for what it is.

18 For a rich engagement with Aristotle's account of habits and the formation of character, see Chapter 6 of this volume, John Russon, "'Actuality in the First Sense' and the Question of Human Nature in Aristotle."

19 See *Rhetoric* II.5 1383a25-1382b11.

20 See John Russon, "The Virtues of Agency: A Phenomenology of Confidence, Courage and Creativity," in *Phenomenology and Virtue Ethics*, ed. Hermberg and Gyllenhammer, (Bloomsbury Press, 2013), 165–79, for a discussion of the importance of caregivers in regulating the child's exposure to the challenges one must face in cultivating virtues necessary for possessing agency.

21 Though Aristotle's discussion of fear occurs primarily in the context of courage and not temperance, it is nonetheless related to lack of self-control at least with respect to what Aristotle calls softness (*malakias*) and endurance (*karterias*) with respect to pain (VII.7 1150a31-b4), since fear is a relation to pain (III.9 1117a28-24).
22 On the practical syllogism, see MA 6.700b4-7 and 7.701b32. C. F., Martha Nussbaum, Chapter Four, "Practical Syllogisms and Practical Science," in *Aristotle's De Motu Animalium*, (Princeton, NJ: Princeton University Press, 1978), 165–220, and Brad Inwood, Chapter One "The Aristotelian Background," in *Ethics and Human Action in Early Stoicism* (Clarendon Press, 1995), 9–17.
23 Jonathan Lear, *Aristotle: The Desire to Understand* (Cambridge: Cambridge University Press, 1988), 181, points out that Aristotle's distinction between possession and exercise of knowledge is a useful way to account for the insufficiency of *knowledge* of how to act in acting rightly.
24 David Charles, "Nicomachean Ethics VII.3: Varieties of *akrasia*," in *Aristotle: Nicomachean Ethics, Book VII. Symposium Aristotelicum*, ed. Carlo Natali (Oxford: Oxford University Press, 2009), 51, interprets the analogy to the person reciting lines on a stage as demonstrating that the person lacks knowledge in the sense of lacking "evidential support required for them to have rational confidence in their judgements." I take Aristotle to be claiming that the person's relationship to her knowledge of the best way to act is akin to recitation of lines, not because she does not have evidential support but rather because the person has not sufficiently connected the right principle to particular practices. Achtenberg, *Cognition of Value*, 16, helpfully presents the kind of knowledge of the good that does not result in good action as knowledge "by analogy" in which "we can know the analogy, which is universal, without knowing how good will show up in different cases."
25 Sparshott, *Taking Life Seriously*, 247, calls it an "in-built or acquired preference." Burnyeat, "Aristotle on Learning to be Good," 84–5, presents a version of a basic practical syllogism in the context of a discussion of anger—one which justifies the pursuit of revenge—and compares it to the more sober syllogism that begins with a universal premise that frames the situation as one cautioning against rashness. He points out that the latter is one that is a newer, less well-established development of the person's conscious experience, one that takes time to be set firmly into one's immediate responses to situations.
26 Bobonich, "Nicomachean Ethics VII.7: *Akrasia* and Self-Control," in *Aristotle: Nicomachean Ethics, Book VII. Symposium Aristotelicum*, ed. Natali (Oxford: Oxford University Press, 2009), 155–6, draws upon Aristotle's distinction between impetuosity (*propeteia*) and weakness (*astheneia*) as two types of *akrasia* (VII.7 1150b19-28), suggesting that the impetuous person, who has deliberated but cannot resist her affections, has the potential to apply strategies to avoid being overcome, such as anticipating when the affection will arise (VII.7 1150b-23-35). By contrast, the weak person, who hasn't deliberated and is led by her passions (presumably only later regretting the action), can adopt no such strategies.
27 Kosman, "Being Properly Affected," 113–4, claims that Aristotle's concern is with the widest register of action and that this means recognizing the sense in which feelings are—at this widest level—deliberate and chosen. Since we are the kinds of beings with emotions, which is to say, with affections resulting from contact with objects acting upon us, we must take *how* we are affected by those objects as part of our deliberations.

9

Aristotle on the Rationality of Virtue

Eve Rabinoff

Introduction

The human being is the animal that has *logos* (reason), uniquely so (*Pol.* I.2 1253a9-10). This conception of human nature both founds Aristotle's understanding of human virtue or excellence (*aretē*) and structures the inquiry into virtue in the *Nicomachean Ethics*. Because rationality—having *logos*—is the defining feature of a human being, to be an excellent human being is to live an excellent rational life, and the person who lives such a life is virtuous. The virtue of the animal with *logos* lies in the excellent use of that distinctively human feature, reason.

But the human being does not fully coincide with her rational nature: she is an *animal* that has *logos*, after all, and animal nature lacks reason. Aristotle expresses this by identifying a nonrational (*alogon*) and a rational (*logon echon*) part of the human soul. The nonrational part admits a further distinction between a part responsible for nutrition and growth, on the one hand, and a part responsible for desires, emotions, and appetites, on the other. This emotional part[1] of the nonrational part of the soul, we learn, is not *simply* nonrational. Rather, it "shares somehow in reason inasmuch as it heeds it and is apt to share its commands" (*EN* I.13 1102b30-31).[2] As a result, Aristotle concludes, there are two kinds of rational excellence: intellectual virtue, which is the excellence of the rational part of the soul, and virtue of character, which is the excellence of the nonrational, emotional part of the soul. Both kinds of virtue are necessary for living an excellent human life and for being a virtuous human being.

This division into a rational and a nonrational part of the soul, however, raises problems for understanding the excellent rational life as a whole, and in particular, the relationship between the virtues of the two parts of the soul. There is a long-standing debate among interpreters of Aristotle's *Nicomachean Ethics* concerning the respective roles of virtue of character and *phronēsis*, practical wisdom, in the pursuit of the good life and in pursuit of virtuous activity.[3] In several passages, Aristotle straightforwardly says that virtue of character is responsible for the goal or end of virtuous action, and practical wisdom is responsible for "the things toward" that end (*ta pros to telos*).[4] This claim is troublesome, for it appears to *subordinate* the rational activity to that of the nonrational, leaving the excellent activity of the rational part of the soul, practical wisdom, merely an instrumental value in achieving the ends set by the nonrational soul's excellent activity. As I see it, this is a problem because it would mean that the distinctly human capacity that is supposed to serve as the basis for virtue—our intellect and our ability to reason—is put in the service of our common, animal nature—our desires and appetites.[5] Human virtue, in other words, would consist in being an excellent *animal* of a certain kind. But, on the other hand, to deny that nonrational virtue sets our aim flies in the face of Aristotle's straightforward claims to the contrary.

This problem arises on the supposition that the activity of the two parts of the soul are independent of one another: the emotional part of the soul does one thing—it sets the aim of action—and the rational part of the soul does something else—it determines how to achieve that aim. But what if the parts of the soul and their activities are not so separate? What if, in other words, the distinction between rational and nonrational applies not to parts of the soul but to two inseparably intertwined aspects of the soul's single activity? Suspicion about the separation of rational and nonrational activities of soul is raised by the explicit imprecision of the division, a division which Aristotle introduces only for its usefulness (*EN* I.13 1102a23-32). Indeed, Aristotle does not even decide on which side of the division the emotional part of the soul falls (I.13 1102b25-a3).[6] If the division of soul into rational and nonrational parts ceases to be useful to us, perhaps it ought to be reconsidered. Aristotle sets aside as unimportant the question of whether the rational and the nonrational parts are "divided like the parts of the body and every divisible thing, or whether they are two in account (*logos*) but naturally inseparable, like the convex and the concave in the circumference of a circle" (I.13 1102a28-31). But, perhaps, if they are inseparable in this way, it would change our understanding of the work of the two "parts" and their relationship to one another.

This chapter explores the possibility that the parts of the virtuous soul do not act independently of one another. I aim to show two things: first, the virtuous person's desires and emotions are rational in the sense that they are implicitly mediated by reason.[7] Because of this, I suggest that excellent rationality belongs to the virtuous soul as a whole, rather than being the possession of one part to the exclusion of the other. Thus, even if virtue of character determines the aim of virtuous action, it does not subordinate the rational to the nonrational. Second, I aim to show that in the virtuous soul, emotion and thought work cooperatively and inseparably in producing virtuous action, such that the virtuous person's thinking is emotional and her emotions are thoughtful. Emotion and thought—virtue and practical wisdom—name two distinct but united aspects of the virtuous person's psyche. More specifically, the former makes what is truly good appear to the virtuous person, the latter makes the *truth* or the *goodness* of what is good appear.[8] Thus, what practical wisdom contributes to virtuous action is full awareness of the virtue of the action and of the actor. This is essential for the virtuous person's excellence to be distinctly *human* excellence.[9]

I. The Rational and the Nonrational

Aristotle draws the distinction between a rational and a nonrational part of the soul from popular writings, declaring it to be sufficient for the purposes of ethical inquiry.

In what does this distinction consist? By what criterion is the nonrational identified? And why is it suitable to ethical inquiry?[10]

Although Aristotle does not (and is not concerned to) speak precisely about these matters, his discussion of the nonrational parts of the soul suggests that he identifies the nonrational in virtue of its independence from reason. That is, if the principle upon which the soul acts is not derived from reason, its activity is the activity of a nonrational part.[11] This is the nature of the strictly nonrational part of the soul, its vegetative part. Digestion, blood circulation, and so forth occur in creatures that lack reason and also while the rational part is inactive in sleep (I.13 1102a32-b12), which shows that the principle of nutritive activity is not reason and is not derived from reason. The emotional part of the soul is shown to be nonrational on the basis of a similar sort of independence: it, too, is common to creatures that lack reason, and, furthermore, it may act in a way that *opposes* reason (I.13 1102b16-18). Independence from reason is the basic feature of a nonrational power of the soul.[12]

However, it is immediately apparent that these two nonrational parts are independent of reason in different ways. The vegetative part is independent but also indifferent to reason—reason has no bearing on and no concern with this part of the soul, and vice versa. It has a neutral sort of independence. By contrast, the independence of the emotional part of the soul is charged: far from being indifferent to reason, it is concerned to *oppose* it. The former is independent and unrelated to reason, the latter is independent but related to reason. It is for this reason that Aristotle identifies this nonrational part of the soul as sharing in reason in a way—it bears a relation to reason (initially, it bears a relation of opposition to reason).[13]

This is a rough criterion, not least because it yields a part of the soul that is not simply nonrational, rendering the very distinction between emotion and thought on the basis of rationality unstable.[14] This does not trouble Aristotle, though, for he deems it suitable for the purposes of ethical inquiry. Why, then, is this a suitable distinction to draw for the purposes of ethical inquiry? It seems to me that what makes this a suitable distinction to employ is that it serves a protreptic function: the distinction between the rational and the nonrational—between reason and what is in some way independent from reason—is one that we are all familiar with in our own experience. But *our* experience is not the experience of the virtuous person, and the instability of the distinction propels us to see beyond our own experience and to envision a different relationship between reason and emotion in the life and soul of the virtuous person.[15]

Aristotle's aim in the *Nicomachean Ethics* is a practical one. Aristotle is speaking to well habituated but not virtuous folk (I.4 1095b3-13), and he is undertaking an inquiry into ethics with them, not for the sake of knowledge alone but so that they might become good (II.2 1103b28). It is plausible to presume that in order to accomplish this, Aristotle speaks in a way that resonates with the experience of his students while also providing the resources to see how their experience is insufficient, propelling them to see past their own experience and to imagine the condition and experience of the virtuous.[16] In other words, *we* live with a divided soul and this division informs our experience, but the project of developing virtue is precisely to improve our souls and our experience; it is *not* to take our ordinary experience as fully disclosive of virtue.[17]

II. The Nonrational in Ordinary Experience

The *Nicomachean Ethics* starts with a discussion of the appropriate audience for the study of ethics (I.3 1094b27-1095a13; I.4 1095b3-13). It starts, in other words, with us: people who are generally well habituated so as to be able to hear a discourse on ethics profitably but who are not yet virtuous (I.4 1095b3-13). In this context the distinction between the rational and the nonrational parts of the soul is a powerful one, for it codifies and reflects our ordinary experience of ourselves.[18] Our emotions, desires, and appetites emerge without our consent and often in direct conflict with what we *think* we desire or think we ought to desire. Examples abound: one may wish one did not have such a strong desire for sweet foods or that one did not get angry at inconsequential things; one finds oneself falling in love with the wrong person. It is because of this that we call emotions and desires nonrational: they are independent of reason in the sense that they are neither subject to nor responsive to reasons.

Aristotle distinguishes the rational and the nonrational parts of the soul on the basis of just such an experience:

> in the case of the self-restrained person and of the one lacking self-restraint,[19] we praise their reason and that part of their soul possessing reason, since it correctly exhorts them toward the best things. But there appears to be something else in them that is by nature contrary to reason, which does battle with and strains against reason. (I.13 1102b14-18)[20]

Psychic opposition to reason illustrates that there is a significant experiential distinction to be drawn between one part of us that reasons and another part that opposes what we think. What is the character of this other part? The passage continues:

> For just as when we choose to move paralyzed parts of the body to the right and they are, to the contrary, borne off to the left, so also with the soul: the impulses of those lacking self-restraint are toward things contrary [to their reason]. Yet whereas in the case of bodies, we see the thing being borne off, in the case of the soul we do not see it. But perhaps one must hold there to be, no less in the case of the soul too, something contrary to reason that opposes it and blocks it. (I.13 1102b18-25)

What the analogy between the desires and the motion of the paralyzed limb suggests is that we *are* our thinking part and we experience our desiring part as something *other* to us. The limb is moved not by the person whose body moves but by an independent and audacious force. This is what it means to be nonrational: to operate independently of the guidance of reason. So in the case of the soul, too, some independent force moves the desires. This is also reflected in ordinary experience: in a rage, it is not *me* who acts violently; I do not condone my actions, I am overtaken and moved by my rage. Correlatively, *I* am most of all the part of me that is being *opposed* by emotion: I am my thinking part most of all. Aristotle will later confirm this saying, in different contexts, that "it would seem that it is the thinking part that each person is or is most of all" (IX.4 1166a22-23), but that, by contrast, "he who acts from spiritedness (*thumos*) is not the origin (*archē*) of the act" (V.8 1135b26-27).[21] It seems, then, that it is insofar as the emotional part is other to what we take ourselves to be that it is nonrational: insofar as our desires act on their own initiative, without listening to or responding to us—to our reason—they are nonrational.

This, then, is where we begin, both as readers and as subjects of the *Nicomachean Ethics*: with a soul composed of a rational part and a nonrational part, where the rational part has the character of a thinking I—explicit, deliberative choosing—and the nonrational part has the character of a desiring other—opaque, obstructive, and out of the control of reason. This division represents a split way of being in the world, manifest in experiences of conflict between reason and desire, and ordinary life is characterized by the conflict between these two sides of human nature. If this were the definitive picture of the human soul, excellent rationality—human virtue—would be confined to the excellent use of the thinking part of the soul; the emotional part of the soul is so devoid of reason that it is out of the reach of rationality, just as the paralyzed limb is impervious to reason's intention to move it.

This is, however, only where we *begin*: this picture of the human soul is immediately modified. At the conclusion of the analogy with the paralyzed limb, Aristotle remarks: "In the case of the self-restrained person, at any rate, it [the emotional part] is obedient to the commands of reason—and perhaps it heeds those commands still more readily in the case of the moderate or courageous person, since then it is in all respects in harmony with reason" (I.13 1102b26-28). The nonrational part of the soul of some people is not devoid of reason, as it is in the case of the person who lacks self-restraint. In the case of the self-restrained person, it may obey the commands of reason (however reluctantly), and in the case of the virtuous person, the emotional part of the soul is in harmony with reason: the emotional part of this soul shares in reason to such a degree that the virtuous person's life is not at all characterized by a contest of wills between the two parts of the soul, as the self-restrained person's life is. To the contrary, the virtuous person "is of like mind (*homognōmein*) with himself and desires the same things with his whole soul" (IX.4 1166a13-14). Indeed, virtue of the nonrational part and practical virtue of the rational part are mutually dependent: Aristotle is quite explicit about this mutual dependency in VI.13, concluding, "It is clear, then, on the basis of what has been said, that it is not possible to be good in the authoritative sense in the absence of practical wisdom, nor is it possible to be practically wise in the absence of virtue of character" (1144b30-32).

Where we begin, then, is very different from where we end up: we begin with a divided and oppositional soul and we end up with a harmonious soul. This is to be expected, if indeed Aristotle is appealing to our experience in order to propel us beyond that experience. In what follows, I aim to show that the virtuous person's soul is not divided into two independently operating parts but is instead a single rational whole by exploring the notion of obedience to reason. I will argue that a nonrational part of the soul is obedient to reason in the sense that it "recognizes" the authority of reason and therefore assumes its appropriately subordinate place in the hierarchy of the soul. This suggests that rationality is a property of the soul as a whole, rather than the possession of one part to the exclusion of the other: the excellently rational soul is one that is well ordered.

III. Obedience to Reason

The nonrational part of the human soul shares in reason insofar as it is able to obey reason,[22] "in the sense of being apt to listen as one does to one's father" (I.13 1103a3). What kind of rationality is this? As he will make explicit in a later illustration of obedience to reason,[23] Aristotle is drawing an analogy between the rationality of the desiring part of the soul and the rationality of a child: neither has reason in the full sense, but neither is fully devoid of rationality.

As Aristotle sees it, the child lacks reason in two respects. In the first place, she lacks reason because she does not produce her own reasons for behaving in one way or another. Rather, "children live according to appetite, and the desire for pleasure is present in them especially" (III.12 1119b5-7). In the second place, the child lacks the ability to understand fully the reason behind the father's command. Aristotle distinguishes the one who is obedient to the commands of the father from the one who learns mathematics (I.13 1102b31-33).[24] To know mathematics involves having learned and being able to produce mathematical demonstrations[25]—it is to comprehend and have full command of the reasons behind the conclusion. But the one who is obedient does not have reason in this manner; instead, she understands only the "conclusion," that is, the command. Even if she is able to recite the reasons behind the command, this shows only that she understands the words, not the argument (cf. VII.3 1147a18-22). Imagine a child who is being scolded for hitting her brother. A parent might ask her if she understands why she is being punished and why hitting is wrong, and she may be able to answer these questions, but she does not fully understand what she says. A child may not even recognize reason as the basis for this command: no doubt some rational commands, although obeyed, appear arbitrary to the child precisely because she does not understand the reason behind it. Thus, the rationality of the child consists neither in producing nor in comprehending reason.

In what way, then, does the child share in reason? She shares in reason insofar as she is able to recognize authority and her proper place with respect to that authority. Early in the *Nicomachean Ethics*, Aristotle approvingly quotes Hesiod saying, "This one is altogether best who himself understands all things. . . . But good in his turn too is he who obeys one who speaks well. But he who neither himself understands nor, in listening to another, takes this to heart, he is a useless man" (I.4 1095b10-13). A child does not "understand all things" herself, but she is good if she listens to and obeys the one who does. This recognition is deeply felt—the good child does not merely pay lip service to authority; she changes her behavior so as to accord with it. The child is rational insofar as she allows her behavior to be determined by authority, no longer acting solely on her own independent initiative.

In this way, too, does the emotional part of the soul share in reason. Its rationality lies in its "recognition" of the authority of another, and its recognition takes the form of rescinding its independent initiative in favor of reason. The emotional part of the soul shares in reason to the degree that it ceases to be other to the thinking "I" and instead shares in its initiative. The excellent rational life, then, requires not only the excellent activity of the rational *part* of the soul but also the excellent relation among the parts of the soul. A soul in which the emotional part is not obedient to reason is less excellently rational, as a whole, than a well-ordered soul, for in this soul the emotional part does not manifest its capacity for rationality.

Obedience to reason, however, has more than one form. On the one hand, as in the case of a mischievous or a forgetful child, obedience may require the constant guidance and present supervision of authority. In this case, the child is obedient only to the explicit and direct guidance of reason. On the other hand, as in the case of a well-behaved child, obedience does not require such constant supervision, for the rules of the authority have been internalized and the child's initiative has changed accordingly. In this case, a child is obedient to the indirect guidance of reason. Analogously, the rationality of the emotional part of the soul—its "recognition" of the authority of reason—may be exhibited only when the rational part of the soul is fully active or it may also be exhibited when the rational part of the soul is inactive.[26]

Among the many characters that Aristotle describes in the course of the *Nicomachean Ethics*, the former kind of obedience describes the rationality of the desires of the self-restrained person, who feels pleasure in a manner contrary to reason but is not led by this and instead acts according to reason (VII.9 1151b34-1152a3). The emotional part of the soul of the self-restrained person is obedient to reason only when it is overpowered (*kratein*) by reason (VI.7 1150a33-36); it recognizes the authority of reason only in the presence of reason, when it actually withdraws its motive force. Were reason to be absent, as, for example, it is when a person is intoxicated, the self-restrained person would misbehave, like the mischievous child, guided only by passion.[27] This person's emotional soul is, we might say, only superficially and intermittently rational. Underlying the recognition of authority, the emotional part of this soul maintains its otherness to reason, its independent and obstructive nonrational nature.

In the latter form of obedience, however, the relationship between the emotional part and the rational part is much more intimate. Reason is never absent from the emotional part, even when the rational part of the soul is not fully active: the emotions are implicitly rational in the sense that the way they operate is internally mediated by reason. This is how Aristotle describes the condition of the soul of the virtuous person. The moderate person's appetites, for example, "ought to be measured, and few, and in no way opposed to reason—we say that a thing of this sort is 'obedient' and 'chastised'—and just as a child ought to live in accord with the commands of his tutor, so too the appetitive ought to live in accord with reason (*kata logon*)" (III.12 1119b11-15). In this kind of obedience to reason, the emotions are no longer foreign to reason but wholly shaped by it. The otherness and independence of the emotions—their nonrational nature—are overcome.[28]

In both of these cases, the nonrational part of the soul is developed so as to become rational, to varying degrees. This is not to say that the nonrational part of the soul has the capacity to become a thinker or to make explicit the reason behind its behavior, but that reason has come to mediate its activity. In the case of the self-restrained person, this mediation is explicit. This person thinks "I should not eat this because it is bad for my health" and her desire backs down (although it does not alter or disappear) and lets the thought guide the action. In the case of the virtuous person, the active thought is not required to guide the action: reason implicitly mediates the activity of desire.[29]

Two points may be drawn from this: first, the activity of the virtuous soul is guided by reason, whether we mean the activity of the thinking part, the emotional part, or both together. Because of this, the virtuous person's *actions* are rational, whether they are guided by thought, by emotion, or by both. The second point is that in the case of the virtuous soul, dividing the soul into parts according to having or not having *logos* is no longer very useful. The relevant distinction is rather in the *modes* of having reason, namely, implicitly or explicitly. Experientially, this is the distinction between thinking and feeling.[30]

IV. Acting with Awareness

In the virtuous soul, the emotional part is obedient to the reasoning part in the sense that it acts as reason would command, if the emotions needed such command: it is implicitly rational. What does this say about the relationship between the virtues of these two parts of the soul, virtue of character and practical wisdom? How does this affect the interpretation of Aristotle's troublesome claim that "virtue makes the target correct, practical wisdom the things toward the target" (VI.12 1144a7-9)?

For one thing, it seems to me that if virtuous desire is implicitly rational Aristotle's claim is less troublesome. Virtuous desire is guided by reason, albeit implicitly, and so to assign the correctness of the aim of action to desire is not, in the case of the virtuous soul, to assign it to a nonrational power. Everything the virtuous person does is rational, to the extent that even her dreams are better than that of a non-virtuous person (I.13 1102b9-11). Furthermore, she can reliably act well and swiftly, following only her immediate desire, when she does not have the time to stop and think about her action (III.8 1117a17-22).

However, even if the claim is *less* troublesome if virtuous desire is implicitly rational, it still may rankle. Aristotle raises the problem that if desire is so thoroughly infused with reason so as always to produce the right action, if virtue of character is so informed by reason that it both "discovers and chooses the middle term" in action and passion (II.6 1107a3-6), there is nothing left for practical thinking to contribute:

> If in fact it [practical wisdom] is concerned with the things just, noble, and good for a human being, and these are the things it belongs to a good man to do, we are no more skilled in the relevant action by dint of knowing them, if in fact the virtues are characteristics, just as in the case of things healthful or distinctive of good conditioning—all such things are said to exist, not simply as a result of one's doing something, but as a result of one's possessing the relevant characteristic. For we are not more skilled in the actions that correspond to health by possessing the arts of medicine and gymnastic training. (VI.12 1143b21-28)

The charge is that knowledge is superfluous. If, for example, one's appetites are good, such that they lead one to eat only as much as and what one ought, *knowing* in what health consists and how it is produced would not influence one's behavior.[31] It is in this context that Aristotle claims, "virtue makes the target correct, practical wisdom the things toward that target" (VI.12 1144a7-9). Even if desire is implicitly rational, if it is *desire* that sets the aims of our action, practical thinking is restricted to the technical and amoral role of figuring out the best way to achieve these aims. For example, one has an appetite for vegetables, and practical wisdom determines how best to acquire and prepare vegetables.

It may be that practical wisdom does indeed contribute to virtuous activity in this restricted sense, but I would like to entertain the possibility that there is a deeper sense in which practical wisdom is necessary for virtuous action: it is the power by which a virtuous person is *aware* of her goal and her action *as* good and of herself *as* virtuous.[32]

Consider the first answer Aristotle gives to the problem of the superfluity of practical wisdom. Practical wisdom cannot simply be superfluous, for it is "choiceworthy in itself" just because it is a virtue of a part of the soul, independently of any practical effect it may have (VI.12 1144a1-3). Even if one were perfectly virtuous in one's actions and character without practical wisdom, practical wisdom would still be desirable. Why? In the first place, it is desirable because part of what it is to be a human being is to be a *thinking* being. To fail to exercise excellence in thought is to fail to realize fully one's human nature.

But this alone does not secure the desirability of *practical* thinking—theoretical pursuits would serve to realize the thinking part of human nature. The reason that practical wisdom is desirable is because one's human nature is not fully realized in one's actions—one's actions are not fully *human* actions—unless they are undertaken *thoughtfully*.[33] Imagine the opposite case: a person is fully virtuous in her actions without thinking about them, either about what makes them virtuous or about how to go about them. Her virtue is automatic, natural, unthinking. Nothing distinguishes this kind of virtue from that of an excellent nonhuman animal, which similarly responds as it should to each situation it faces, although unthinkingly. For excellent action to be excellent *human* action, it must be thoughtfully undertaken, even if thinking does not contribute anything practical to one's behavior, neither by determining nor by changing one's action.[34] What kind of thinking would this be, this ineffective yet desirable practical thinking? It could only be an awareness of oneself as acting virtuously.

In his discussion of virtue of character, Aristotle makes the claim that the virtuous person "is distinguished perhaps most of all by his seeing what is true in each case, just as if he were a rule and measure of them." By contrast, "in the case of the many, a deception appears to occur on account of the pleasure involved, for what is not good appears to them as good" (III.4 1113a32-b1). It is, however, markedly the work of the intellectual virtues to "attain the truth" (*alētheuein*) (VI.2 1139b12-13). This suggests that, in the case of practical life, virtue of character makes it so that *what is true* appears, and practical wisdom makes it so that *the truth* of those appearances is evident.[35] What is implicit in virtue of character is explicit in practical wisdom; virtue of character causes one to be aware of what virtue requires and practical wisdom causes one to be aware of the *virtue* of what is required.[36] This is to be expected, if virtuous emotions are implicitly mediated by reason: practical thinking makes the reason implicit in virtue of character explicit.

In this context it is significant that Aristotle defines practical wisdom *not* as a *hexis meta logou alēthous*, as he defines the other virtue of practical intellect, art (*technē*) (VI.4 1140a9-10), but as a *hexis alēthē meta logou* (VI.5 1140b4-7, 1140b20-21): practical wisdom is not a characteristic with true reason but a *true characteristic* with reason. Aristotle explains the difference between practical wisdom and art at the conclusion of VI.5:

> And although there is a virtue of an art, there is not of practical wisdom; in the case of an art, it is more choiceworthy for one to err voluntarily, less choiceworthy in the case of practical wisdom (as also in the virtues). It is clear, then, that practical wisdom is a certain virtue and not an art. . . . Yet practical wisdom is not solely a characteristic with reason, a sign of which is that it is possible to forget such a characteristic, but not to forget practical wisdom. (1140b21-30)

The difference between art and practical wisdom lies in the respective relations between the *hexis* and the *logos* of each. In the case of art, the characteristic *just is* having a true account, true reason. Aristotle defines *lack* of art (*atechnia*) as *hexis meta logou pseudous*, a characteristic with a *false* account (VI.4 1140a21-23).[37] For this reason, it is better to err willingly in the case of art: a doctor who willingly causes harm to a patient is still a doctor for she is using, albeit misusing, her art of medicine, but if a doctor mistakenly causes harm, presumably due to ignorance, this shows an imperfection in or lack of her art.[38] In the case of practical wisdom, however, the characteristic exceeds the *logos*. With or without a particular *logos*, the characteristic remains, and remains true: "practical wisdom is not solely a characteristic with reason, a sign of which is that it is possible to forget such a characteristic, but not to forget practical wisdom." I take this to be the same point as above: practical wisdom is a condition of soul that enables the virtuous person to be *aware* of the truth of what appears to her to be truly good. This condition of soul is prior to the deliberation that determines how best to act with respect to this goal.[39]

In *De Anima*, Aristotle argues that perceiving and being aware that one perceives are accomplished in one and the same act of perception (III.2 425b12-25).[40] I suggest that the same is true of the appearance of the good and the awareness of the goodness of that appearance: just as in the case of perception and being aware of one's perception, desiring the right thing and being aware of the rightness of that desire are inseparable. In this sense the virtuous person's thinking and desiring are not "divided like the parts of the body and every divisible thing," but rather "they are two in account (*logos*) but naturally inseparable, like the convex and the concave in the circumference of a circle" (I.13 1102a28-31).[41]

Conclusion

Aristotle's initial division of the soul into a rational and a nonrational part is, I take it, merely a provisional division. It is provisional both in a methodological sense—it is a division that gets the inquiry into virtue off the ground but is transformed in the progression of the inquiry—and in an experiential sense—it describes the experience of the ordinary person, like you or me, who is on the path of virtue and whose experience will change once virtue is developed. We are, after all, both subjects and readers of Aristotle's *Nicomachean Ethics*, which we read so that we may become good (II.2 1103b28). In becoming good we surpass the condition of being a thinking "I" over against an emoting other, becoming, we might say, fully ourselves. Being fully oneself requires not only habituating one's emotions so that they act *kata logon* but also having reason in a certain way, so that one's emotions and one's thinking act cooperatively and as one.

Notes

1. I refer to this as the emotional part, even though Aristotle introduces it as the desiring and appetitive part (*epithumetikon kai orektikon*) (I.13 1102b30), because *pathos* (emotion) appears to be the broader category. In *Nicomachean Ethics* II.5 Aristotle determines that virtue is a *hexis*, which is that "in reference to which we are in a good or bad state with relation to the *pathē*" (1105b25-26). *Pathē*, in turn, include "appetite, anger, fear, confidence, envy, joy, friendship, hatred, longing, emulation, pity—in general, those things that pleasure or pain accompany" (1105b21-23). Virtue of character involves feeling well in all respects, both in desiring the right things and in feeling the right emotions in the right way. Moreover, it is experientially true to say that desire and emotion are often interwoven: to feel sympathy, for example, is to feel drawn to help or comfort another; to feel anger is to feel drawn to punish or injure. I will, however, use "emotion" and "desire" interchangeably: I will use "desire" when I want to emphasize aiming at some end, "emotion" when I want to emphasize responsiveness to one's circumstances more generally. See Leighton, "Aristotle and the Emotions," *Phronesis* 27, no. 2 (1982): 144–74, for discussion of the relationship between emotion and desire.
2. Translations of the *Nicomachean Ethics* are taken from Bartlett and Collins, *Aristotle's Nicomachean Ethics*, modified.
3. See, e.g., Moss, "'Virtue Makes the Goal Right': Virtue and *Phronēsis* in Aristotle's Ethics," *Phronesis* 56 (2011): 204–61, and "Was Aristotle a Humean?" *Cambridge Companion to Aristotle's Ethics*, ed. Polansky (Cambridge: Cambridge University Press, 2014), 221–41; Irwin "Reason, Desire, and Virtue," *The Journal of Philosophy* 72, no. 17 (1975): 567–78; Smith, "Character and Intellect in Aristotle's Ethics," *Phronesis* 41, no. 1 (1996): 56–74; Fortenbaugh, "Aristotle's Distinction between Moral Virtue and Practical Wisdom," *Transactions and Proceedings of the American Philological Association* 95 (1964): 77–87; Fortenbaugh, "Aristotle's Conception of Moral Virtue and Its Perceptive Role," *Transactions and Proceedings of the American Philological Association* 95 (1964): 77–87; Sorabji, "Aristotle on the Role of Intellect in Virtue," in *Essays on Aristotle's Ethics*, ed. Rorty (Berkeley, 1980), 201–20; Lorenz, "Virtue of Character in Aristotle's *Nicomachean Ethics*," *Oxford Studies in Ancient Philosophy* 37 (2009): 177–212; McDowell, "Some Issues in Aristotle's Moral Psychology," *Mind, Value, and Reality* (Cambridge: Harvard University Press, 1998), 23–40.
4. *Nicomachean Ethics* VI.12 1144a7-9: "For virtue makes the target (*skopos*) correct, practical wisdom the things toward (*ta pros*) that target"; VI.12 1144a20-22: "As for the choice (*prohairesis*), virtue makes it correct; but as for doing all that is naturally done for the sake of that choice, this belongs not to virtue but to another capacity (*dunamis*)"; VI.13 1145a4-6: "It is clear too that there will be no correct choice in the

absence of practical wisdom, nor in the absence of virtue; for the latter makes one do (*prattein*) the end, the former the things toward the end (*ta pros to telos*)."

5   See *Eudemian Ethics* II.1 1219b39-1220a3: "For if virtues belong to a human being qua human, reasoning must inhere, as a starting point, and action must inhere too; but reasoning is a starting point not of reasoning but of desire and the affections, so a human must have these parts" (translated by Brad Inwood and Raphael Woolf). Moss, "Was Aristotle a Humean?" 222, and Smith, "Character and Intellect in Aristotle's Ethics," *Phronesis* 41, no. 1 (1996): 65 similarly identify this as a problem. Cf. Irwin ("Aristotle on Reason, Desire, and Virtue"): "Wisdom and practical reason are, as we would expect, strictly subordinated to the desires formed nondeliberatively by habituation and virtues of character" (569). All animals feel pleasure and pain, and therefore have desires (cf. *De Anima* 431a11-12); by its own nature, desire is independent of reason. If human desire is to share in reason, reason cannot simply be in service of desire but must somehow also govern desire.

6   This imprecision will not surprise the reader of Aristotle's *De Anima*, for Aristotle himself flags it there. In *De Anima* III.9, Aristotle complains of problems with the way some distinguish parts of the soul, saying: "For in one way there seem to be an indefinite number and not only those which some mention in distinguishing them—the parts concerned with reasoning, passion, and desiring, or according to others the rational (*logon echon*) and the non-rational (*alogon*) parts; for in virtue of the distinguishing characteristics by which they distinguish these parts, there will clearly be other parts too with a greater disparity between them than these" (432a24-28) (translation is from Hamlyn, *Aristotle's De Anima Books II and III*, modified).

7   This is not to say, as other scholars have argued, that virtue of character is a partly intellectual characteristic, if that means that virtue of character *itself* has a deliberative component (see, e.g., Sorabji ["Aristotle on the Role of Intellect in Virtue"], Irwin ["Aristotle on Reason, Desire, and Virtue"], and Lorenz ["Virtue of Character in Aristotle's *Nicomachean Ethics*"]). See Moss, "Virtue Makes the Goal Right," for a detailed refutation of this position. It is, rather, to say that the emotional part of the soul acts as reason *would* command. What I take issue with is not the distinction between the two kinds of virtues but with the characterization of them as rational and nonrational. I specify further what I take "rational" and "nonrational" to mean.

8   I take truth and goodness to be the same, in the context of Aristotle's ethics. His discussion in III.4 supports this: to see what is true is to see what is truly good. See Olfert, "Aristotle's Conception of Practical Truth," *Journal of the History of Philosophy* 52, no. 2 (2014): 205-31, for a discussion of the relationship between the good and the true.

9   Eli Diamond, "For There Are Gods Here Too," 50-3, in this volume, offers an intriguing discussion of "the animal with *logos*" in relation to the upright posture of the human body to show that human form (in this case, thinking) imbues every part of the human (including its animality). In the end, I find a similar structure in the relationship between the rational and the nonrational parts of the human soul in the virtuous person. This position, loosely speaking, combines the main insight of Diamond's chapter—that the capacity for rationality (thinking) defines every part of the human, including its (nonrational) body—and the main insight of Russon "Actuality in the First Sense," in this volume—that what defines the human is its ability to self-transform—insofar as the position I take holds that the (self)-development of virtue results in the integration of rationality in the otherwise nonrational parts.

10 R. Kamtekar, "Speaking with the Same Voice as Reason," *Oxford Studies in Ancient Philosophy* 31 (2006): 167–202, raises a similar question, 170, but turns to Plato to answer it.
11 This is a rougher version of the way that Aristotle distinguishes the parts of the soul when he *is* being precise, in *De Anima*. See Corcilius and Gregoric, "Separability v. Difference," *Oxford Studies in Ancient Philosophy* 39 (2010): 81–120, for discussion of the strict criterion that Aristotle employs to distinguish parts of the soul.
12 See *Metaphysics* IX.5 for a more precise discussion of the difference between rational and nonrational powers (of both soul and otherwise).
13 Following Aristotle, I now set aside the vegetative nonrational part (1102b11-12). In what follows, nonrational refers to the emotional part.
14 Kamtekar, "Speaking with the Same Voice as Reason," similarly wonders "whether, in attributing rationality to the non-rational, Aristotle has not undermined the explanatory value of analyzing our mental attitudes into rational and appetitive and emotional components" (169).
15 Russon, "Actuality in the First Sense," interprets the human's possession of language, *logos*, as a power that "lets me live in other realities—realities that are not my own" (133), and argues that this demonstrates the essential characteristic of being human: being defined by self-transformation or the ability to develop abilities (131–2). Russon argues that this feature of humanity is evident in the open-endedness of Aristotle's introduction of ethics as the pursuit of happiness (133–5); it may also be evident in the educational aim of the *Nicomachean Ethics*.
16 Kamtekar, "Speaking with the Same Voice as Reason," interprets Plato's practice of personifying the "parts" of the soul as similarly protreptic. She takes Plato to differ from Aristotle on this point: "While Aristotle affirms the lack of precision as appropriate to practical matters in general (*EN* 1094b12, 1098b28, 1137b19), Plato seems only to countenance it for the protreptic purposes" (187 n. 35). It seems to me that for Aristotle the study of practical matters is not separate from the protreptic aim, at least in the *Nicomachean Ethics*.
17 What I am suggesting is that Aristotle's division of the soul into a rational and a nonrational part is merely a provisional division employed to get the inquiry started, but that such a division does not apply to the virtuous soul and the virtuous life. This may seem an odd thesis, for Aristotle sustains the distinction between virtue of character and virtue of intellect, which is predicated on the distinction between the rational and the nonrational parts throughout the *Nicomachean Ethics*. Despite the interdependence of virtue of character and practical wisdom (1144b30-32), Aristotle reiterates the distinction between the two kinds of virtue at the opening of VI, prefacing his discussion of the intellectual virtues. However, the distinction between virtue of character and intellectual virtue is predicated on the distinction between the thinking and the emotional parts of the soul, rather than strictly on the distinction between the rational and the nonrational. Aristotle identifies the two kinds of virtue after he has expressed the instability of the distinction between the rational and the non-rational parts of the soul.
18 I take Aristotle's adoption of a popular division of the soul as a useful heuristic for inquiring into ethics (1102a23-32) as an indication that Aristotle's discourse is operating at the level of experience. The reason that it is a useful distinction, at least to begin with, is that it is one we can all agree with based on our own experience.
19 Aristotle here is not describing the audience of ethical discourses but the akratic and enkratic characters (that *akrasia* and *enkrateia* are not conditions ordinary people

suffer from, see VII.7 1150a9-15). These characters represent the most extreme and therefore clearest examples of the commonly experienced opposition between reason and desire.

20 Plato uses similar reasoning in distinguishing the parts of the soul in *Republic* IV 436a-441d. There is a difference in argumentative strategy: where Plato appeals explicitly to (what comes to be called) the principle of noncontradiction, Aristotle appeals only to ordinary experience. This reflects both the imprecision with which Aristotle is drawing the distinction and the experiential level of discourse on which he is operating.

21 I am including *thumos* in the emotional part of the soul. For what other part would be responsible for it? *Thumos* is common to animals and children, who lack reason (III.2 1111b8-13).

22 I.7 1098a3-4; I.13 1102b26-1103a3; III.12 1119b7-15: in these passages Aristotle explicitly refers to the emotions or the emotional part of the soul as obedient to reason, but the idea that they can and ought to be governed by reason is mentioned throughout.

23 At the conclusion of the discussion of moderation, Aristotle says, "whatever longs for shameful things and can undergo much growth ought to be chastised, and appetite and a child are especially of this description: children too live according to appetite, and the desire for pleasure is present in them especially" (III.12 1119b3-7).

24 This sentence is sparse, but the contrast seems clear enough. The relationship that a person has to the *logos* of her father and friends is different than the relationship that attains with regard to the *logoi* in mathematics.

25 So in VI.3, Aristotle defines scientific knowledge (*epistēmē*) as "a characteristic bound up with demonstration (*hexis apodeiktikē*). . . . For whenever someone trusts in something in a certain way, and the principles are known to him, he has scientific knowledge; for if [he does not know those principles] to a greater degree than the conclusion, he will be in possession of the scientific knowledge [only] accidentally" (1139b31-35).

26 So, for example, Aristotle comments that even the *dreams* of the good person are better than that of a random person (I.13 1102b9-11): even when *all* that is active is the nonrational part of the soul, rationality is exhibited.

27 It is noteworthy that Aristotle compares the akratic, one whose emotional part is out of reach of reason, to a person who is drunk (VII.3 1147a10-18).

28 Although see Kamtekar, "Speaking with the Same Voice as Reason," 184-6, for a discussion of the ways that considering some of one's emotions and reactions to be "other" is a useful tactic in the project of self-betterment.

29 This throws into doubt the usefulness of practical thinking: if one's emotions and desires are implicitly rational, why does one need to think about what one is doing? Aristotle raises this problem in VI.12, and I discuss it further.

30 Smith, "Character and Intellect in Aristotle's Ethics," argues that emotions cannot be perfectly *kata logon* without practical wisdom (i.e., they cannot be perfectly implicitly rational), on the basis that Aristotle compares virtue without practical wisdom to a stumbling person without sight (63). I address this later.

31 Even if, as is the case with humans, one's desires need to be trained and training requires practical wisdom, "it will make no difference whether they themselves have practical wisdom or obey other who have it . . . just as it is also in what concerns health: although we wish to be healthy, nonetheless we do not learn the art of medicine" (VI.12 1143b30-33).

32 Moss, "Was Aristotle a Humean?" and Smith, "Character and Intellect," offer similar positions, through different arguments.
33 Cf. Smith, "Character and Intellect in Aristotle's Ethics," who arrives at a similar point by a different path (69).
34 Cf. Gottlieb, "Aristotle on Uniting the Soul and Dividing the Virtues," *Phronesis* 39, no. 3 (1994): 275–90, who, in discussing the necessity of acting with choice, remarks, "To be ethically virtuous, it is not enough to have some non-rational impulse that happens to line up with the demands of reason" (282).
35 See Fortenbaugh, "Aristotle's Conception of Moral Virtue," who persuasively shows that virtue of character is responsible for the true appearance of the good. However, he restricts *phronēsis* to excellence in explicit processes of practical reasoning, analogous to cleverness.
36 Moss, "Was Aristotle a Humean?," makes a similar point. She argues that it is practical wisdom that grasps the end *as* good and that virtue of character only *implicitly* grasps it (232–3).
37 Similarly, in *Metaphysics* I.1, Aristotle admits that art (*technē*), unlike experience (*empeiria*), need not be practical in the sense of enabling the artisan to perform the work. *Technē* is achieved when one gains the appropriate knowledge alone.
38 Cf. Plato's *Republic* I (340c-341a), wherein Thrasymachus asserts that it is only when performing *well* that one is truly said to be, for example, a doctor.
39 I take this to be similar to Coope, "Why Does Aristotle Think that Ethical Virtue Requires Practical Wisdom?" *Phronesis* 57 (2012): 142–63, who argues that the self-restrained person lacks practical wisdom because she lacks full understanding of the goodness of her action due to her inability to take pleasure in such goodness.
40 See Kosman's essays, "Perceiving that We Perceive," *Philosophical Review* 84 (1975): 499–519 and "Aristotle on the Power of Perception," *Presocratics and Plato: Festschrift at Delphi in Honor of Charles Kahn*, ed. Patterson, Karasmanis, and Hermann (Las Vegas: Parmenides Publishing, 2012), 459–89, for discussions of the unity of perception and awareness of the perception. For an opposing position, see Johansen, "In Defense of the Inner Sense," *Proceedings of the Boston Area Colloquium in Ancient Philosophy* 21 (2005): 235–76.
41 The unity and cooperation of the emotional and the rational parts of the soul describe the soul of the virtuous person alone. Non-virtuous characters suffer from the two being out of sync, to varying degrees. Gottlieb, "Aristotle on Dividing the Soul and Uniting the Virtues," makes a similar suggestion (286).

10

Learning How to Be at Leisure through Musical Education

Jacob Singer

Introduction

Although our copy of Aristotle's *Politics* is incomplete, the treatise, as far as we know, ends with an inquiry into the purpose of education (*paideia*) in the best *polis* and, in light of this inquiry, a determination of the forms of education that fulfill this purpose. Provocatively, Aristotle claims that the goal of education in the perfect *polis* is to teach young people not only necessary and useful skills but also how to engage in the practices of leisure (*scholē*) (*Pol.* VIII.3 1337b30-33; 1338a11-20).[1] Perhaps even stranger, he argues that individuals can learn how to engage in leisure by performing and listening to music (*mousikḗ*).[2] Thus, in the best state, the legislator not only directs "his attention above all to the education of youth" but, more specifically, ensures that the youth learn how to engage in leisure by discovering how to play and listen to music (VIII.1 1337a1).

But what is the nature of leisure such that it requires an education? And how exactly does music teach us how to be at leisure? This chapter will address both questions. The first section shows that three predominant ends around which people tend to organize their lives are reflected in different ways in which they engage in leisure. These forms of leisure reveal that only the life spent in contemplation (*theoria*) meets the demand that leisure be self-sufficient (*autarkēs*) and autotelic (*autoteleis*) or intrinsically valuable. The second part of the chapter argues that music teaches young people how to be at leisure because, through musical modes (*harmoníā*) and rhythm (*rhuthmós*), it cultivates a moral character and practical judgment (*phronēsis*), both of which are indispensable to contemplation. By learning how to play and listen to music, young people learn how to exercise and listen to language and reason (*logos*), actualizing themselves as animals with *logos* and opening the possibility to fully realize *logos* in the leisurely activity of contemplation.[3]

I. The Hierarchy of Leisure: Play, Relaxation, and Contemplation

Aristotle generally characterizes leisure as a self-sufficient condition in which activities can be pursued for their own sake. As he notes, "many necessities have to be present before we can have leisure" (*Pol.* VII.15 1134a20-24).[4] Biological, economic, and political conditions need to be met to achieve a state in which nothing else is required for maintaining and securing mere life. Once we are free from the heteronomous demands of survival, the situation of leisure emerges wherein we are free to pursue the good life by engaging in activities for their own sake. Hence, leisure is at once the accomplishment of activities that are necessary and sufficient to attain and protect the requirements of life, and at the same time the necessary condition for activities that appear sufficient for attaining and maintaining the good life. In short, leisure is the achievement of instrumental activities and the condition of intrinsic activities—a threshold between two modes of engaging with the world.

In addition, leisure manifests itself in different forms depending upon the end associated with the good life.[5] In Book X of the *Nicomachean Ethics*, Aristotle examines contemplation, as well as other ends identified with happiness, in the context of leisure. He observes that some people spend their leisure in "the pleasures (*hēdeiai*) that come from playing (*paidia*)" (*EN* X.6 1176b10);[6] some spend their leisure in relaxation (*anapaysis*), using it as a means "for the sake of activity (*energeia*)" virtuously in practical affairs (X.6 1176b33 and X.7 1177b8-17); and some spend their leisure in contemplation (X.6 1177a30-1177b6).[7] Play, relaxation, and contemplation are thus forms of leisure that express the desire for a life of pleasure, practical virtue, and contemplation respectively. Leisure, then, is not only a threshold between instrumental and intrinsic activities; it appears in different forms corresponding to the end identified with the good life. Moreover, just as contemplation is identified with the good life, so too, does it exemplify leisurely activity. So, how does Aristotle establish this hierarchy of ends and their corresponding forms of leisure? And why does contemplation exemplify the nature of leisure?

First, consider those who identify the good life with the experience of pleasure and leisure spent in play. For Aristotle, such people are typified by the child and the tyrant, for whom pleasure takes the form of immediate gratification (*EN* VII.14 1154b10-15). Their experience appears to constitute the good life because, first, it seems self-sufficient. The pleasure of immediate gratification, like the joy of play, satisfies desire instantaneously. The immediate pleasure of play makes no explicit reference to what comes before or after, instead appearing sufficient to grant happiness all at once, all by itself. Second, the pleasures of immediate gratification in play are pursued entirely for their own sake, fulfilling neither a necessary end, like satisfying hunger, nor an advantageous end, like securing wealth. If play does satisfy one of these ends, then it appears merely incidental to the pleasure that is the purpose of playing. In colloquial terms, we play because "we just want to have fun." The child and the tyrant thus appear as a source of envy because they are the freest from practical responsibilities, able to "escape into play (*paidia*)" (X.6 1176b11-15). Instead of engaging in the toil of instrumental activities, they passively reap the benefits of the world around them, receiving the pleasure of consumption without the grief of production.

However, although the immediate pleasure of play appears self-sufficient and intrinsically valuable, it is in fact determined by what precedes the activity. As Aristotle notes, pleasure is immediate insofar as it alleviates and replaces pain (*EN* VII.14 1154a23-30). The satisfaction of a meal is preceded by hunger, while the relief of a cigarette reduces stress. Likewise, leisure spent in play is pleasurable "because of things that have already happened, such as exertions and pains" (*Pol.* VIII.5 1339b39). The immediacy of pleasure thus only appears self-sufficient and intrinsically valuable; in fact, it is not immediate at all, but rather pleasurable because it is distinct from the grief of the past. The pleasures of play are thus determined relative to the strife of the practical activities that precedes them and makes them possible.

The implicit dependence that immediate pleasures have upon past pain and toil is not without its consequences. Aristotle observes that some people who, for example, enjoy the pleasure of quenching their thirst "even provide themselves with thirst in certain ways" (*EN* VII.14 1154b5). The commitment to immediate pleasure thus manifests itself in a simultaneous commitment to pain. Similarly, those who commit to being free from engaging in practical affairs depend upon the practical means for satisfying and maintaining their life of leisure in play. Consequently, they either neglect the labor of practical affairs that provides the conditions for their leisurely play, in which their life of play eventually becomes impossible (X.6 1176b20-21).[8] Or, inasmuch as their indulgences necessitate the excessive accumulation of wealth and property, they seek to acquire despotic power in order to secure the conditions for their pastimes (*Pol.* I.9 1258a3-10; VII.2 1324b1-10). In the latter case, the supposed passive, leisurely life of play will in fact require the perpetual labor of extending power and thus no real satisfaction at all. Therefore, although one explicitly seeks pleasure by spending leisure in play, one implicitly commits to the past and future labor that makes such pleasure possible.

The commitment to past and future labor is made explicit when play becomes a matter of relaxation for the sake of serious (*spoudaios*) and beautiful (*to kalon*) activity in practical affairs (*EN* X.6 1176b30-1177a1). In this case, the person oriented toward consumption recognizes the significance and value of production and seeks to perform their practical activities well. Unlike those motivated by pleasure, "it belongs to a man of serious stature" neither to eschew their practical affairs nor simply to address their affairs, but rather "to do ... things well and beautifully" (I.7 1098a15-16). For example, the serious harp player does not simply play the harp, whether it is for the sake of money or according to their whims and fancy, but instead for the sake of playing the harp beautifully, that is, in a way "that it is not possible either to take anything away from or to add anything to [it]" (II.6 1106b11). Aiming at the beautiful, those of serious stature must accordingly pay attention to the particular aspects of their practical affairs in light of an ideal end. Relaxation thus serves as a means for performing a beautiful, practical activity that embodies that ideal.

Such earnest and well-performed deeds are not without pleasure. The pleasure of the activity is pleasurable not because it implicitly relieves and replaces pain but rather because it is performed well and without inhibitions (*EN* VII.12 1152b33-1153a15).[9] Pleasure is thus not only momentary, appearing as the relief at the end of a process; it can be experienced in the activity itself—in the uninhibited expression of one's capacities. For example, there is a difference between the pleasure of eating food that satisfies one's hunger and the pleasure of cooking an excellent meal without obstacles. The former pleasure is momentary and implicitly relative to the relief of, or escape from, the pain of hunger, while the latter pleasure occurs over the course of the activity of cooking. The activity of cooking virtuously is not simply about a single moment experienced at the end of the process but rather about harmonizing a series of moments into a process beautifully. For this reason, those who are primarily motivated by beautiful work do not find the immediate pleasure of play during relaxation, but rather experience the enduring pleasure of their virtuous practical activity while they work.

However, while those who are principally motivated to do serious and beautiful practical activities do not experience these activities as instrumental, they do experience leisure as instrumental. Aristotle observes that for such people, "relaxation is not the end, since it comes about for the sake of activity" (*EN* X.6 1177a1). If those motivated by serious work could work continuously, undoubtedly they would, since serious and beautiful work appears to constitute the good life. Yet, "since people are incapable of laboring continuously, they need relaxation" (X.6 1177b34). Leisure, therefore, is not considered intrinsically meaningful and thus not desired for its own sake. Rather, it appears simply as an instrument for the sake of working better. In contemporary parlance, those motivated primarily by virtuous practical activities are "workaholics" for whom leisure, as relaxation, appears to be a burden of the body.

The devaluation of leisure means that serious and virtuous activities performed in leisure, such as contemplative activities, have little to no worth (*Pol.* VII.3 1325a21-25). Instead, only the virtues manifest in practical activities appear meaningful. Accordingly, in extended periods of leisure, the workaholic finds no happiness, just as certain states, "like unused iron... lose their edge in times of peace" (VII.14 1134a20). It is thus likely that external means will be sought and conditions of duress will be manufactured for the sake of exercising virtuous action. It is also likely that inasmuch as these artisanal, economic, militaristic, and political activities rely upon the complex acquisition and use of external goods, these goods can come to be regarded as the primary motivation of the activity (I.9 1258a10-15). In either case, those who reduce leisure to relaxation risk valuing the conditions necessary for the performance of practical activities rather than the activities themselves.

By devaluing leisure, and thereby contemplative activities, the reduction of leisure to relaxation eliminates the possibility of experiencing leisure as a condition for reflecting upon the *archē* and *telos* of the activity as well as the activities of the cosmos in general. In practical activities, each moment only ever appears as a particular means for the sake of achieving an end that is relative to human concerns (*EN* 1140a20-24; 1140b1-3). Hence, each moment appears in light of a determinate beginning—the work at hand—and a determinate end—the ideal execution of said work. In practical activities, the particular possibilities given by the past and belonging to the future are thus privileged and fixed, for they determine the very possibilities of the activities themselves. The problem is that if leisure is reduced to relaxation, then no moment exists in which to reflect upon the principles and ends that determine practical engagements; that is, there is no time, or reason, to question the grounds and goals according to which one is acting in the world.

In fact, once leisure is reduced to relaxation, there is no time to question the principles within the cosmos in general. Inquiries concerning physics, mathematics, or theology, for example, are disparaged, as the good life only appears in the virtuous exercise of practical affairs. Therefore, just as those who reduce leisure to play contradict themselves, explicitly privileging the immediate moment while implicitly relying upon past and future practical activities, so too those who reduce leisure to relaxation contradict themselves: they explicitly privilege the past and the future, namely, the work at hand and its ideal completion, but they implicitly reduce it to their present interests.

In the first chapter of the *Metaphysics*, the experience of leisure makes possible not only the emergence and development of mathematics but the very capacity for contemplation itself (*Metaph.* I.1 981b15-25).[10] Free from necessary and advantageous activities, leisure is the condition for contemplating what is universal and incapable of being otherwise. Contemplation thus makes explicit the universals and necessary truths presupposed whenever and wherever practical virtues are beautifully performed (*EN* VI.7 1141b14-21). The past does not appear in terms of its possible use for accomplishing an ideal end, but rather precisely as that which is invariable, regardless of our actions (VI.2 1139b7-10). Similarly, the future does not appear in terms of a particular beautiful end to be accomplished, but rather is capable of appearing in terms of *the* beautiful. In contemplative leisure, being is thus capable of appearing *qua* number, nature, and being itself—all of which are subjects of Aristotle's lectures. Spending leisure in contemplation thus enables us to move beyond anthropocentric concerns and reflect upon the whole of the cosmos. In the activity of contemplation, we experience the pleasure of freely exercising our *logos* without seeking to accomplish a present, practical goal.

Significantly, inasmuch as these theoretical pursuits depend upon leisure, if they are performed seriously and beautifully, they cannot neglect the biological, economic, and political activities that make them possible (*EN* X.7 1179a1-10). Leisure is thus not only an opportunity to reflect upon the cosmos but also what it means to be human, as seen in the *Nicomachean Ethics*, *Politics*, and the *Poetics*.[11] Spending leisure in contemplation, therefore, is not self-sufficient because it ignores worldly, material affairs, needing nothing other than itself. Rather, contemplation is self-sufficient because it acknowledges the necessity of practical affairs as well as the precariousness of its own possibility.[12] Similarly, contemplation is intrinsically valuable because it acknowledges the value and importance of the other activities that make it possible. After all, while we choose what we want in leisure, only the gods can choose to be in leisure (X.7 1177b25-1177a10). Those who spend their leisure in serious contemplative activities are thus committed to taking seriously the conditions that make such activities possible.

II. Learning to be at Leisure through Music: Modes and Rhythm

We have seen that leisure is a threshold between instrumental and intrinsic activities, which appears in various forms, and is ultimately exemplified through the exercise of *logos* in contemplation. However, humans are not born with the capacity to freely exercise *logos*, let alone to spend their leisure time in contemplation; we develop the capacity as we grow older (*Pol.* VII.15 1134b21-24). This means that we must learn how to reason and, accordingly, how to spend our leisure time appropriately. One of the questions in Book VIII of the *Politics* is thus, how should young people learn to be at leisure in the right way?

The difficulty of teaching young people how to fully exercise *logos* is that it cannot be done through *logos* alone. If children could learn how to reason solely through rational discourse, they would already have the capacity that they are supposed to acquire. However, rather than living according to reason, children "live by feelings," pursuing what is immediately pleasurable and avoiding what is immediately painful (*EN* X.9 1179b13).[13] Since the feeling of pleasure and pain "has grown up with us all from infancy" and "is ingrained in our life," "it is difficult to scrub away this feeling" (II.3 1105a1-3). As Aristotle writes: "it is not possible, or not easy, to change by words things that have been bound up in people's characters since long ago" (X.9 1179b18-19).[14] Rational discourse, therefore, is not sufficient for teaching children how to be at leisure properly because it is unable to appeal to and sway the strength of their feelings. Instead, young people must develop a virtuous moral character (*ēthos*) capable of listening to and obeying *logos* (I.13 1102b30-1103a10).

At the end of the *Politics*, Aristotle argues that music fulfills this educational need. Music is neither necessary nor useful for preserving and securing the necessities of life (*Pol.* VIII.3 1338a14-15). It is customarily included as a branch of education not because it teaches us how to fulfill or maintain our basic needs, but rather for the sake of "the leisure in the course of one's life" (VIII.3 1338a15). Musical education thereby reveals a kind of education whose purpose is "suited to freedom and is beautiful" (VIII.3 1338a30-32). It is "for the part of life that one spends in leisure," in which one is capable of pursuing ends for their own sake, exercising freedom, and acting beautifully (VIII.3 1338a20). But how exactly does musical education teach young people how to be at leisure?

First, Aristotle observes that music is a source of pleasure that appeals to the desire of young people regardless of their character:[15] "the teaching of music is well fitted to their nature at such an age, for at their age, the young do not willingly submit to anything unsweetened, and music is a natural sweetener" (*Pol.* VIII.5 1340b16-17). Besides appealing to the sensual feelings of the youth, the pleasure of music does not depend upon the consumption of an external good and, accordingly, the strife of its endless acquisition or production. Rather, music is a "harmless" pleasure, conducive to relaxation, and, accordingly, engaging in practical affairs more seriously and beautifully (VIII.5 1339b25-26).[16] As a pleasure that appeals to all young people, music addresses their immediate desires without harm and in a way that helps them relax and thereby better engage in their practical affairs.

More importantly, musical modes (*harmonía*) "*are* images of states of character" (*Pol.* VIII.5 1340a39; 1340b9-10). When we hear music we "are affected sympathetically [*sungeneia*] [. . .] and we experience a change in the soul" (VIII.5 1340b1-2; 1340b17). Other arts, like painting or sculpture, may be "indications of states of character," but only music bears "a *likenesses* of states of character" (VIII.5 1340a30-32). To hear a sad song *as sad* is to feel mournful and grave, while to hear an angry song *as angry* is to feel passionate and aggressive. Different styles of music arouse different emotional dispositions (*diathesis*).[17] On the one hand, music can thus have a cathartic affect, releasing us from subjugation to a particular emotion and leaving a new disposition in its wake (VIII.7 1342a1-11). On the other hand, music can be educational, teaching young people, through habitual exposure, to take pleasure in certain characters as opposed to others. For example, Aristotle approves of the Dorian style of music because it presents a courageous and serious moral character instead of the excitement exhibited by the Phrygian style. While the Phrygian mode has an important cathartic role to play, in musical education it instills the desire for play and immediate gratification by exhibiting exciting sounds. The Dorian mode, in contrast, instills a character that is more temperate, capable of enjoying a pleasure that is subdued and mediated by its context. Repeated listening to and practice of the Dorian style thus produce the habits necessary "to delight in decent kinds of character and beautiful actions," enabling young people to follow reason (VIII.5 1340a18-19).

The modes of music, then, appeal to and affect the irrational part of the soul, shaping our emotional disposition and even our habits. Each note receives its musical texture in relation to the community of sounds in its company, exhibiting a character that is irreducible to the mere sum of its parts. Similarly, music brings the soul immediately and pre-reflectively into a certain kind of harmony, determining its emotional disposition and character, which is irreducible to a collection of desires (*Pol.* VIII.5 1340b18-19). Finally, music reflects the *polis* in general, which "is not a mere aggregate of persons, but, as we say, a union sufficing for the purposes of life" (VII.8 1328b15).[18] Given the power of music to determine the character of citizens without rational discourse, it is no surprise that educating the young in a certain mode of music is a matter of utmost legislative concern (VIII.1 1337a1-5). After all, the soul, the state, and the form of leisure all reflect the harmony exhibited in a different mode of music.

Besides instilling the character necessary for contemplative leisure, musical education teaches the timing essential for the virtue of practical judgment. To express feelings at the right time involves a sense of time itself. One needs to have an awareness of the temporal context to know the appropriate moment to express one's character. Present emotions are thereby checked and balanced against a sense of what has gone before and what will come after. As Aristotle states in *De Anima*, "for while thought bids us to hold back because of what is in the future, desire is influenced by what is just at hand" (*DA* III.10 433b6-7).[19] The problem is that the young "are apt to follow their impulses" and immediate desires, concerning themselves with the present rather than the past or the future (*EN* I.3 1095a5-10). They have not developed the *logos* by which to mark out, enumerate, and count the time, determining the temporal circumstances that would condition an appropriate expression of character. Without a sense of time, young people appear unable to recognize the opportune moment and thereby act in accordance with moral virtue.

However, Aristotle suggests that young people develop a sense of time by learning musical rhythm.[20] In the *Politics*, he observes that besides modes, rhythms also imitate character, as some appear steady, while others appear much livelier (*Pol.* VIII.5 1340b10-11). In the *Rhetoric*, he elaborates: "it is number that limits all things; and it is the numerical limitation of the forms of a composition that constitutes rhythm, of which metres are definite sections" (*Rhet.* III.8 1408b28-29). Rhythm thus appears to be constituted by numerically parsing out a composition and enumerating it into limited segments in different ways that are capable of imitating different characters. The character expressed by the mode of the music is thus meted out over the course of the piece, and, depending upon the way it is measured, it imitates different characters. Accordingly, we do not hear the character imitated by a mode of music all at once in a single note, but rather over the course of the piece in accordance with its rhythm. By learning to count the rhythm of music, young people thus learn to recognize the right moment by hearing each moment in relation to the others as well as the song as a whole.

By cultivating moral character and practical judgment in a context that is free from practical concerns, music paves the way toward contemplation, which likewise occurs in a condition free from practical affairs. Rather than replacing purely theoretical concerns, musical education thus mediates the ascent toward contemplation.[21] It lifts the desires of the youth above immediate gratification, brings them into harmony with one another, and teaches them how to judge the right moment by counting out the lifetime of a song. As a result, young people acquire the moral character and practical judgment that make it possible to hear reason, be at leisure, and contemplate both the whole of the cosmos and the cosmos as a whole.

Notes

1 Aristotle, *Politics*, trans. Sachs (Focus Pub., 2012).
2 The Greek word "*mousike*" is broad, covering "the art of the Muses" in its entirety. Besides including the art musical modes and rhythms, it also includes dance as well as "discourses" (*logoi*). The current chapter will focus on music in the narrow sense as the art of modes and rhythms.
3 Cf. John Russon, "'Actuality in the First Sense' and the Question of Human Nature in Aristotle," in the current volume. Russon rightly notes that the human being is not born with the developed power of *logos* in the sense of language, but rather must learn how to participate in the capacity for language. *Logos*, he observes, is thus natural in the sense that it is the power to develop the power of language. As a compliment, I contend that musical education is indispensable to such a development.
4 Cf., *Metaphysics* I.1.981a114-23.
5 Cf., Solmsen, "Leisure and Play in Aristotle's Ideal State," *Rheinisches Museum Für Philologie* 107, no. 3 (1964): 193–220, who notes these two senses of leisure.
6 Aristotle, *Nicomachean Ethics*, trans. Sachs (Focus Pub., 2002) modified.
7 Play and contemplation are forms of activity. However, both are ways of being active *in* leisure, while leisure spent in relaxation is a means for the sake of activity in artisanal, economic, militaristic, or political activities.
8 Cf., *Politics* VIII.5.1339b30-35.
9 Cf., VII.14.1154b15-20.
10 Aristotle, *Metaphysics*, trans. Sachs (Green Lion Press, 2002).

11 For an excellent account of the personal and political significance of tragedy in the *Poetics*, see Patricia Fagan's chapter "*Logos* and the *Polis* in the *Poetics*" in the current volume.
12 For a complimentary account of the relation between contemplation and embodied activities, which shows how the latter must express former, see the conclusion of Eli Diamond's chapter, "'For There Are Gods Here Too': Embodied Essence, Two-Footedness, and the Animal with *Logos*," in the current volume. See also David J. Depew, "Politics, Music, and Contemplation in Aristotle's Ideal State," in *A Companion to Aristotle's Politics*, ed. Miller and Keyt (Oxford: B. Blackwell, 1991), 346–80, 358–9.
13 Cf., I.2.1095a5-11; *Politics* VII.15.1334b21-23; *Rhetoric* II.12.1389a33-34.
14 Cf., X.9.1179b26-28.
15 *Pol.* VIII.5.1340a5-6: "for music does have a certain natural pleasure, which is why the use of it is beloved by all ages and all types of character."
16 Cf., *Politics* VIII.5.1339b16-21:
17 See Juan Pablo Mira, *Aristotle on Music and Emotions* (University of Edinburgh, PhD Dissertation, 2016), 140–55. Mira convincingly shows that instrumental music does not produce a *pathos* but rather *diathesis*.
18 Cf., III.3 1276b7-9.
19 Aristotle, "On the Soul," in *The Complete Works of Aristotle: The Revised Oxford Translation*, ed. and trans. Barnes (Princeton, NJ: Princeton University Press, 1984).
20 I am indebted to an unpublished paper by Doug Halls for drawing my attention to the relation between rhythm, timing, and practical judgment.
21 For a more detailed treatment of music as that which mediates practical judgment and contemplation, see David J. Depew, "Politics, Music, and Contemplation in Aristotle's Ideal State," 367–74. As Depew notes, one way this occurs is through musically attended forms like tragedies, which, in exhibiting to the audience the human condition, reveal that human beings are not the highest beings in the cosmos. For alternative views, see Pierre Destrée, "Education, Leisure, and Politics," in *The Cambridge Companion to Aristotle's Politics*, ed. Deslauriers and Destrée (New York: Cambridge University Press, 2013), 318; Solmsen, "Leisure and Play in Aristotle's Ideal State," 24–6; and Richard Kraut, *Aristotle: Political Philosophy* (Oxford: Oxford University Press, 2002), 200.

Part IV

The *Logos* of the *Polis*

11

The Vicissitudes of *Logos*

On Nature, Character, and Time-of-Life

Robert Metcalf

Aristotle's definition of human beings as the *zōion logon echon*—the animal "having" *logos*—is so familiar a formulation that it can escape our attention for what is truly provocative about it. In fact, upon examination we find that Aristotle's formulation has many shades of meaning, precisely because *logos* itself holds together many disparate meanings for Aristotle's thinking. In this chapter, I shall focus on Aristotle's approach to *logos* in his *Rhetoric*, for there "having *logos*" is understood not in terms of the more typical illustrations of human reason—such as rational deliberation or contemplation—but as being open to discourse most fundamentally or, as Heidegger captures it in his 1924 lecture course, "*letting something be said by others* . . . in the sense of having a directive for concrete practical concern."[1] Indeed, it is precisely because Aristotle's *Rhetoric* approaches the human capacity for *logos* in this most fundamental way that Heidegger wrote: "Aristotle's *Rhetoric* must be understood as the first systematic hermeneutic of the everydayness of being-with-one-another."[2] But to appreciate what is distinctive about this text's perspective on the *zōion logon echon*, let us begin our examination with the more familiar account of "having *logos*" found in the *Nicomachean Ethics*.

To be sure, the *Nicomachean Ethics* traces out the implications of understanding human beings as the *zōion logon echon* in a systematic and comprehensive way: after all, the "function" or "characteristic work [*ergon*]" of human beings is theorized here as "an activity of soul in accord with *logos* or at least not without *logos* [*estin ergon anthrōpou psychēs energeia kata logon ē mē aneu logou*]" (I.7 1098a7-8), and for this reason human happiness is located in "an active life of the element that has *logos* [*praktikē tis tou logon echontos*]" (I.7 1098a3-4).[3] But already we find a fecund ambiguity in Aristotle's conception of "having *logos*" in the *Nicomachean Ethics*: on the one hand, human beings cannot fail to "have *logos*" in some important sense, since "having *logos*" just is to be a human animal; on the other hand, by "having *logos*" in this minimal but essential way, human beings are open to the possibility of "having *logos*" in a perfected sense, such that the irrational parts of the soul would themselves no longer oppose *logos* but harmonize with it, living in accord with it, in the way that Aristotle likens to the child's heeding his tutor.[4] For example, in his discussion of moderation (III.12), Aristotle remarks that the desire for pleasure is insatiable (*aplēstos*)—so much so, in fact, that "if the appetites are strong and violent they even expel reasoning [*ton logismon ekkrouousin*]" (1119b10-11). For this reason, Aristotle continues, the appetites should be few and measured, and should "in no way oppose reason [*tōi logōi mēthen enantiousthai*]" but rather be "obedient and disciplined [*eupeithes . . . kai kekolasmenon*]" (1119b11-12)—at which point he offers the following analogy to capture it: "and as the child should live according to the direction of his tutor, so the appetitive element should live according to reason [*houtō kai to epithumētikon kata ton logon*]" (1119b13-15).[5] The argument then concludes as follows: "Hence the appetitive element in the *sōphrōn* should harmonize [*symphōnein*] with *logos*; for what is noble is the target for both, and the *sōphrōn* craves for the things he ought, as he ought, and when he ought; and this is what *logos* enjoins" (1119b15-19). This sets the stage for Aristotle's subsequent illustrations of the *zōion logon echon* exhibited in various activities of soul that spell out human happiness, such as rational deliberation (*bouleuesthai*) (III.3 1112a30-32ff.) and contemplation (*theōria*) (IX.9 1170a2-5, X.7 1177a18, ff.).[6]

Nonetheless, despite this rich tapestry of the *zōion logon echon* as displayed in the *Nicomachean Ethics*, Aristotle pauses, in the last chapter of Book X, to reject the idea that arguments or rational discourses are sufficient by themselves to make men good (*hoi logoi autarkeis pros to poiēsai epieikeis*), except those men who are true lovers of what is noble (*hōs alēthōs philokalon*) (X.9 1179b4-9).[7] What *logoi*, Aristotle asks, would persuade those who have not a sense of shame to obey but only fear?—who,

> living by *pathos*, pursue their own pleasures and the means to them, and avoid the opposite pains, and have not even a conception of what is noble and truly pleasant, since they have never tasted it. . . . It is difficult, if not impossible, to remove by *logos* the traits that have long since been incorporated into character [*ou rhadion ta ek palaiou tois ēthesi kateilēmmena logōi metastēsai*]." (X.9 1179b11-18)

Aristotle explains as follows:

> [A]rgument and teaching . . . are not powerful with all men, but the soul of the listener must first have been cultivated by means of habits for noble enjoyment and noble antipathy [*alla dei prodieirgasthai tois ethesi tēn tou akroatou psychē pros to kalōs chairein kai misein*], like earth which is to nourish the seed. For he who lives according to *pathos* will not hear argument that dissuades him, nor understand it if he does; and how can we persuade one in such a state to change his ways?—for, in general, *pathos* seems to yield not to *logos* but to force [*alla biai*]. The character, then, must somehow be there already with a kinship to virtue [*dei dē to ēthos prouparchein pōs oikeion tēs aretēs*], loving what is noble and hating what is shameful [*stergon to kalon kai dyscherainon to aischron*]." (X.9 1179b23-31)[8]

This passage is fascinating for a number of reasons—but for our purposes its interest lies in what it says about the preconditions for *logos* persuading someone: the soul of the listener must already have been cultivated by way of habits (*dei prodiergasthai tois ethesi* . . .), the character's kinship to virtue must somehow already exist (*dei . . . to ēthos prouparchein pōs*). These preconditions of persuasive *logos* are even called the "heart of Aristotle's ethics" by Hans-Georg Gadamer: "[T]he fact that reward and punishment, praise and blame, exemplar and imitation, along with the ground of solidarity, sympathy, and love upon which their effect depends, that all these still form the 'ethos' of humankind prior to all appeals to reason and thus makes such appeals possible in the first place."[9] For us the question must be how these preconditions of persuasive *logos* bear upon what it means for human beings to be the *zōion logon echon*.

On the one hand, Aristotle's claim that someone who lives according to *pathos* will not have the "frame of mind" (*pōs echonta*) to be receptive to *logos* echoes the doubts raised in Book I, Chapter 3, of the *Nicomachean Ethics*, as to whether young people or those adults who remain "immature in character [*to ēthos nearos*]" will be, in Aristotle's words, "proper hearers of lectures on political science," since the lectures will profit only those who desire and act in accord with *logos*, not the hearer who follows his *pathē* (*tois pathesin akolouthētikos ōn*) (I.3 1095a2-12). On the other hand, the sharp distinction suggested by *Nicomachean Ethics* X.9 between living in accord with *logos* and living according to *pathos* is complicated considerably by the *Rhetoric*, where *logoi* are treated very broadly in terms of discourses persuasive-to-the-audience, whether they are well-founded, manipulative, pandering, or what have you. Situated within the discursive terrain of the *Rhetoric*, being the *zōion logon echon* signifies not so much the exercise of rationality over irrational parts of the soul, but rather being immersed in the full range of public discourse and thus being exposed to various possibilities of persuasion.[10] Consider, to take just one example from the *Rhetoric*, Aristotle's observations on the effectiveness of "appealing to maxims [*to gnōmologein*]" if one's audience is rather unsophisticated:

> The maxim, as has already been stated, is a general statement, and people love to hear stated in general terms what they already believe in some particular connection: e.g., if a man happens to have bad neighbors or bad children, he will agree with anyone who tells him, "Nothing is more annoying than having bad neighbors," or "Nothing is more foolish than to be the parent of children." The orator has therefore to guess [*stochazesthai*] the subjects on which his hearers already happen to hold views, and what those views are, and then must express these views as general truths [*hōste dei poia tunchanousi proupolambanontes, eith' houtōs peri toutōn katholou legein*]. (II.21 1395b5-12)[11]

Aside from the comedic value of this passage, we should not overlook its significance for Aristotle's project in the *Rhetoric*: for example, the claim that "people love to hear stated in general terms what they already believe in some particular connection" mirrors the claim made earlier in the text, that people always think well of "speeches adapted to and reflecting their own character [*tous tōi spheterōi ēthei legomenous logous kai tous homoious*]" (II.13 1390a25-26)—and, indeed, much of the most important work in the *Rhetoric* involves the profiling of different audience-types so as to assist the speaker in persuading them.

At the same time, it can scarcely be denied that the *logoi* analyzed in the passage above fall short of any logically normative model of reasoning. Indeed, we seem to find here an illustration of the "babble [*Geschwätz*]" remarked on by Heidegger in a famous passage from his 1924 lecture course, which is worth quoting at length:

> It is not accidental that, in their natural self-interpretation, the Greeks defined the existence of human beings as *zōion logon echon*. We do not have a corresponding definition. At best, an approximately corresponding definition would be: the human being is a living thing that reads the newspaper. . . . When the Greeks say that the human being is a living thing that speaks, they do not mean, in a physiological sense, that he utters sounds. Rather, the human being is a living thing that has its genuine existence in conversation and discourse. The Greeks existed in discourse. The orator is the one who has genuine power over Dasein. . . . [T]he ability-to-discourse is that possibility in which I have genuine dominion over the persuasion of human beings in the way that they are with one another. In this basic Greek claim, the ground for the definition of the human being is to be sought. . . . One must take fully into account that the Greeks lived in discourse, and one must note that if discourse is the genuine possibility of existence, in which it plays itself out, that is, concretely and for the most part, then precisely this speaking is also the possibility in which Dasein is *ensnared*. It is the possibility that Dasein allow itself to be taken in a peculiar direction and become absorbed in the immediate, in fashions, in babble. For the Greeks themselves, this process of living in the world, to be absorbed in what is ordinary, to fall into the world in which it lives, became, through language, the basic danger of its existence. The proof of this fact is the existence of sophistry. (§13.107-109, 74-75)[12]

Nonetheless, even if the *logoi* analyzed in the *Rhetoric* strike us as that from which Plato and Aristotle had to "extricate themselves," as Heidegger puts it, studying such *logoi* does belong properly to rhetoric—which Aristotle defines as "the ability to see/ consider in each case what allows for persuasion [*hē rhētorikē dynamis peri hekaston tou theōrēsai to endechomenon pithanon*]" (I.2 1355b26-27).[13]

However, the most important point is that, in taking the *Rhetoric* as our focal context for understanding human beings as the *zōion logon echon*, the *logos* that we have in mind will be the altogether engaged kind that Heidegger, in his treatment of Aristotle's *Rhetoric*, unpacks as "being-as-speaking-with-one-another through communication, refutation, confrontation" (§8.47, 33).[14] Implicit in Aristotle's definition, Heidegger writes, "is an entirely peculiar, fundamental mode of the being of human beings characterized as 'being-with-one-another,' *koinōnia*. These beings who speak with the world are, as such, through *being-with-others*" (§8.45, 33).[15] Heidegger explains:

> [h]uman beings are with one another in the mode of encouraging, persuading, exhorting. Insofar as the human being lets something be said, he is *logon echon* in a new respect. He lets something be said insofar as he hears . . . in the sense of having a directive for concrete practical concern. (§13.111, 76)

Accordingly, "having" *logos* also involves listening to others, letting something be said, or, to say it most broadly, being open to discourse, being open to persuasion by others, which is exactly what Heidegger aimed at with his own formulation: "*letting something be said by others* [Sich-etwas-sagen-Lassens-von-anderen]." As with Aristotle's account of "having *logos*" in the *Nicomachean Ethics*, "having *logos*" in the manner of "letting something be said by others" allows for both a minimal sense—in which case it signifies the most basic being open to discourse in "having a directive for concrete practical concern"—and a perfected sense of "having *logos*," wherein one cultivates those intellectual virtues of persuading and being persuaded *for the right reasons*.[16] But in either of these senses, we find that "having *logos*" here in the *Rhetoric* carries a texture of meaning far beyond how that defining characteristic of human beings is typically understood.

Perhaps what is most interesting for our purposes—and certainly what Heidegger found most illuminating—is the central place of the *pathē* in Aristotle's account of persuasion-by-*logos* in the *Rhetoric*. This is evident already near the beginning of the text, in Aristotle's account of the three *pisteis entechnoi*, that is, the three types of "speaking-for-something imparted through discourse itself," in *Rhetoric* I.3. We find persuasive force (1) in the character of the speaker (*en tōi ēthei tou legontos*); (2) in how the hearer is disposed toward the *logos* (*en tōi ton akroatēn diatheinai pōs*); and (3) in the *logos* itself (*en autōi tōi logōi*).[17] It is the second of these *pisteis entechnoi* that leads us into an examination of the various *pathē*, for, as Aristotle explains, persuasion is effected "through the hearers [*dia de tōn akroatōn*], when the *logos* stirs their *pathē* [*hotan eis pathos hupo tou logou proachthōsin*]" (I.2 1356a14)—the *pathē* being defined here as "all those feelings that so change men as to affect their judgments, and that are also attended by pain or pleasure" (II.1 1378a20-21).[18] Accordingly, Aristotle points out that rhetoric is an "outgrowth of sorts from dialectic and from ethical studies [*paraphues ti tēs dialektikēs einai kai tēs peri ta ēthē pragmateias*]" (I.2 1356a25-26), for it involves studying three essential factors: first, the ability to reason logically (*syllogisasthai*); second, an understanding of human character-types and moral excellences (*tou theōrēsai peri ta ēthē kai peri tas aretas*); and finally, an understanding of the *pathē*—"what each one is and of what sort it is, as well as from what causes it comes to be and in what manner (*tou peri ta pathē, ti te hekaston estin tōn pathōn kai poion ti, kai ek tinōn enginetai kai pōs*)" (I.2 1356a23-25). It follows, then, that rather than treating the *pathē* as separate from the persuasive character of *logoi*—as if the *pathē* were accidents of the human psyche blurring the clarity of *logos*, if you will— Aristotle treats them as co-constitutive of *legein* in the broad sense. What results from this line of inquiry is an account of *logos* rooted in human character-types and the *pathē*: since a given *logos* "is persuasive," Aristotle explains, "because there is somebody whom it persuades [*epei gar to pithanon tini pithanon esti*]" (1356b28), in the same way, "the theory of rhetoric is concerned not with what seems probable to a given individual [*oude hē rhētorikē to kath' hekaston endoxon theōrēsei*] like Socrates or Hippias, but with what seems probable to men of a given type [*alla to toioisdi*]" (I.2 1356b33-34).

It should therefore be clear why Heidegger saw in Aristotle's *Rhetoric* a penetrating look into what he calls "being-in-the-world," as he writes: "The *pathē*, in an entirely general way, are characteristic of a disposition of human beings [*eine Befindlichkeit des Menschen*], a how of being-in-the-world [*ein Wie des Seins-in-der-Welt*]" (120, §17.177-78).[19] Heidegger expands on this thought in a memorable passage from the 1924 lecture course:

> Insofar as the *pathē* are not merely an annex of psychical processes, but are rather *the ground out of which speaking arises, and which what is expressed grows back into* [der Boden, aus dem das Sprechen erwächst und in den hinein das Ausgesprochene wieder wächst], the *pathē*, for their part, are *the basic possibilities in which Dasein is primarily oriented toward itself*, finds itself. The primary being-oriented, the illumination of its being-in-the-world is not a *knowing*, but rather a *finding-oneself*. (§22.262, 176)

A phenomenologically adequate account of the *pathē* requires that we appreciate them as the ground out of which *logos* arises, which also (when *logos* is efficacious) is transformed by *logos* in ways that are the proper aim of rhetoric and philosophy. William McNeill captures this point as follows: "the primary disclosure of the presencing of a world is thus, on [Heidegger's] account, accomplished not by intellectual or philosophical knowledge, but by a fundamental *pathos* or attunement (*Befindlichkeit*)."[20] It is precisely this hermeneutic approach to being-in-the-world through the *pathē* that we find highlighted in Heidegger's gloss on Aristotle's text: "In relation to every *pathos* the question arises: *pōs diakeimenoi eisi*: How do we find ourselves genuinely, of what sort is our being-in-the-world, when we are in a rage, when we are in fear, when we feel pity?.... In the basic structure of the *pathē*, we find, once again, the orientation to the being-with-one-another of being-there as being-in-the-world" (§17.179, 121).[21]

At the same time, it must be said that Aristotle's focus in *Rhetoric*, Book II, is, strictly speaking, not the *pathē* as such; rather, it is the complex of factors within a situation that allows for a hearer to be induced to experience a specific *pathos*. For example, in his discussion of anger (*orgē*)—the first *pathos* analyzed in Book II—Aristotle's aim is to make plain "in what frame-of-mind [*pōs echontes*], with what people [*tisi*], and on what grounds [*dia poia*] people grow angry" (1379a8-10). After listing such factors as being afflicted by sickness or poverty or love or thirst, or being slighted, and so on, Aristotle writes that "each man is predisposed [*proōdopoiētai*] to his own particular anger by the emotion now prevailing upon him [*pros tēn hekastou orgēn hupo tou huparchontos pathous*]" (1379a21-22). Two remarks are in order here: one is that the *pathos* at issue here is both the anger that is to be elicited by the orator's speech and the specific *pathos* that is constitutive for the "frame-of-mind" (*pōs echontes*) of the hearers—in this case, being-in-love or being-thirsty, and so on.[22] The second is that there is thus a complex of factors at play in the *pōs echontes* of the hearers, and it is this complex of factors that "pave the way" or "set the course" (*proodopoiein*) for the *pathos* targeted by the orator. Consider, for example, the complex of factors that allow for calm (*praotēs*) on the part of the audience, as Aristotle describes it: "As to the frame of mind that makes people calm, it is plainly the opposite of that which makes them angry, as, for example, in recreation, in laughing, in feasting, in prosperity, in success, in satiety, and in general, in freedom-from-pain or pleasures not involving insolence, and in good hope" (1380b2-5). Being free from pain and being pleased—where this is morally unobjectionable—provide the context within which one is apt to feel calm. But notice that the "frame-of-mind [*pōs echontes*]" paving the way for calmness lies in their hope as to the future, their sense of how their lives are going—whether they are prospering, are successful, and so on—as well as in their relation to others in communal activities such as feasting. Inquiring into the "frame-of-mind" (*pōs echontes*) of the hearers quickly involves us in the rich terrain of what Heidegger calls being-in-the-world.[23]

One of the most interesting places in Aristotle's *Rhetoric* where this terrain of being-in-the-world is mapped in some detail is the discussion of "times-of-life" (*hēlikia*) in Chapters 12–14 of *Rhetoric*, Book II.[24] There Aristotle addresses the interconnections between characters (*ēthē*), *pathē*, "states of character" (*hexeis*), as well as times-of-life (*tas hēlikias*) and fortunes (*tas tuchas*) (1388b31-33). For the *pathē*, Aristotle offers as examples *orgē*, *epithumia*, and the like; for *hexeis* he mentions only *aretē* and *kakia*; for times-of-life he specifies the three very broad spans of youth (*neotēs*), prime of life (*akmē*), and old age (*gēras*) (1388b33-36). What follows, then, is a sketch of these three times of life that makes for some of the funniest writing in Aristotle's works. On this portrait, the *ēthos* of the young is such that they have strong desires—particularly *peri ta aphrodisia*—but also they are fickle in their desires, hot-tempered, indignant, ambitious, uncomplicated, trusting, full of good hope, both courageous and susceptible to shame, great-in-soul. Aristotle explains that "since they have not yet been humbled by life nor have they been brought up short by its constraints," all their errors—loving, hating, and all the rest—are due to excess: "And they think they know everything, and confidently affirm it, and this is the cause of their excess in everything; and if they do wrong, it is on account of *hybris*, not malice [*kakourgia*]; and they feel pity toward others because they suppose that everyone is decent and better than they are ... estimating their neighbors by their own lack of vice" (1389b7-13). By contrast, those who are past their prime are the opposite of all of this in their character:

> For, on account of having lived many years and having been more often deceived by others or made more mistakes themselves, and since most things turn out badly [*ta pleiō phaula einai tōn pragmatōn*], they are certain of nothing and in everything they show an excessive lack of energy. And so they think, but do not know anything—and, being of two-minds, they always insert "perhaps" or "maybe," and everything they say is like this, nothing without qualification. And they are ill-disposed [*kakoētheis*], for being ill-disposed is a matter of seeing the worst in everything [*kakoētheia to epi to cheiron hupolambanein panta*]. Further, they are always suspicious on account of being mistrustful, and they are mistrustful on account of experience. And they neither love nor hate intensely, but, in accord with the precept of Bias, they love as if they will one day hate, and hate as if they will one day love. And they are small-souled [*mikropsychoi*] on account of having been humbled by life, for they desire nothing great or uncommon.... And they do not have much hope on account of their experience [*kai duselpides dia tēn empeirian*], for most things turn out badly, and at all events generally turn out for the worse [*ta gar pleiō tōn gignomenōn phaula estin· apobainei goun ta polla epi to cheiron*]—and also on account of their cowardice.... Their passions [*hoi thumoi*] are violent but

weak, and as to their desires, some desires have been snuffed out and others are weak, so that they are neither desirous nor do they act in line with their desires, but only for the sake of gain [*kata to kerdos*]. Consequently, men at this time of life appear to be *sōphronikoi*, since their desires have slackened and they have become slaves to gain. (II.13, 1389b18-1390a17)

As amusing as this portrait of the old is, it is also a caricature bordering on the absurd. Indeed, the one-sidedness of this portrait is clear from earlier sections of the *Rhetoric*, where he discusses the possibility of reaching old age much more favorably: "Happiness in old age [*eugēria*] is the coming of old age slowly and painlessly; for a man has not this happiness if he grows old either quickly, or tardily but painfully. It arises both from the excellences of the body and from good luck [*estin de kai ek tōn tou sōmatos aretōn kai ek tuchēs*]" (1361b27-29).[25] Should the one-sidedness of Aristotle's portrait of the old in *Rhetoric* II.13 matter to us, philosophically?

Admittedly, the overriding consideration for Aristotle is whether such a profiling of the old (along with the young, etc.) serves the effort to see what will be persuasive in a specific setting, in the face of a specific audience, and so on. His concluding words as he wraps up discussion of the young and old are telling along these lines:

> Such are the character-types [*ta ēthē*] of young men and elderly men. People always think well of speeches adapted to, and reflecting, their own character [*tous tōi spheterōi ēthei legomenous logous kai tous homoious*]—and we can now see how to compose our speeches so as to adapt both them and ourselves to our audiences. (1390a24-27)

Still we might wonder whether a caricature of these different times-of-life adequately serves his purposes.[26] Furthermore, we should notice that, in its broad outlines, Aristotle's portraits of young and old in the *Rhetoric* are echoed by what he says about them elsewhere in his writings. Consider his remark in *Nicomachean Ethics* that friendship for the sake of utility, not for the sake of the other's character, "seems to exist chiefly among old people, for at that age people pursue not the pleasant but the useful [*ou gar to hēdu hoi tēlikoutoi diōkousin alla to ōphelimon*]" (VIII.3 1156a25-26). Later in the same book, Aristotle likens old people to those whose temperament is "sour," since both types of people make friends only with difficulty (1158a1-9). Claims like these would seem to call for corrections such as Cicero's rejoinder, that "old men are fretful, fidgety, ill-tempered and disagreeable . . . also avaricious. But these are faults of character, not of the time of life. . . . The fact is that, just as it is not every wine, so it is not every life, that turns sour from keeping" (§18, 70).[27] Yet Aristotle offers no such corrections of his account's one-sidedness.

And how are we to gauge the implications of this account of times-of-life in the *Rhetoric* for Aristotle's ethical theory? About the young, Aristotle writes:

> They would always rather do noble deeds than useful ones [*kai mallon hairountai prattein ta kala tōn sumpherontōn*]: their lives are regulated more by character than by calculation [*tōi gar ēthei zōsi mallon ē tōi logismōi*]; and whereas calculation

leads us to choose what is useful [*esti d' ho men logismos tou sumpherontos*], moral excellence leads us to choose what is noble [*hē de aretē tou kalou*]. (1389a32-36)

By contrast, Aristotle portrays the old as follows:

They are too fond of themselves, for this, too, is *mikropsychia*. Because of this, they guide their lives too much by considerations of what is useful and too little by what is noble—for the useful is what is good for oneself [*to men gar sumpheron autōi agathon esti*], and the noble what is good without qualification [*to de kalon haplōs*].... They guide their lives by calculation more than by character [*kai mallon zōsi kata logismon ē kata to ēthos*], calculation being directed to utility and character to virtue." (1389b35-1390a18)

The rhetorical implications of this portrait are straightforward enough: namely, we can expect that an audience composed of the young will be much more receptive to appeals to *to kalon* than an audience of the old; conversely, we can expect an old audience to be more responsive to appeals to *to sumpheron*.[28] But the ethical implications of this portrait are unsettling: with age comes an atrophying of character as a determining factor for how we live our lives, so that the old will come to live more by calculation (*logismos*) than by character (*ēthos*).[29] Aristotle uses the language of becoming "weak," becoming "chilled," and becoming "small-souled"—so that growing old appears to him to be not just an atrophying but also a cooling and shrinking. This would appear to be "being-in-the-world," said with a sigh of world-weariness.

Again, it is strange that Aristotle does not include in his portrait anything like what Cicero highlights as contributing to happiness in old age: above all, "the consciousness of a well-spent life and the recollection of many virtuous actions are exceedingly delightful" (§3, 48), but also the acquiring of the right perspective from which to enjoy pleasure—such as the idea of *convivium*, where the pleasure of company and conversation is primary, physical pleasure secondary (§13, 62). Less ambitious than Cicero, perhaps, Garver focuses on the question whether *phronesis* can be proof against aging, and he argues on recognizably Aristotelian grounds that "the *phronimos* who is able to integrate the just and the useful in his deliberations is less likely to abandon considerations of justice as he ages."[30] If we can agree with Garver that "the virtuous desire for the noble can make the old more ethical and less calculating than they would otherwise be,"[31] then we can at least hope for the sort of good luck requisite for *phronēsis* to resist the atrophying of character in old age.

Perhaps it was with an eye to the unsettling implications of this account of times-of-life for ethical theory that Aristotle expressed some ambivalence in the *Rhetoric* about the role played by time-of-life in determining one's actions. He writes:

Every action must be due to one or other of seven causes: chance, nature, compulsion, habit, reasoning, anger, or appetite. It is superfluous [*periergon*] further to distinguish actions according to the doers' times-of-life [*kath hēlikian*], moral states [*hexeis*], or the like. It is of course true that, for instance, young men do have hot tempers and strong appetites; still, it is not through youth that they act accordingly, but through anger or appetite. . . . Still we must consider what kinds of actions and what kinds of people usually go together; for while there are no definite kinds of action associated with the fact that a man is fair or dark, tall or short, it does make a difference if he is young or old, just or unjust. And in general, all those accessory qualities that cause distinctions of human character are important—e.g., wealth or poverty, being lucky or unlucky. (1369a5-29)

So, to restate Aristotle's reasoning here: time-of-life (*hēlikia*) is not "responsible," or an *aition*, for action in the way that chance, nature, compulsion, habit, reasoning, anger, or appetite are *aitia*, but still time-of-life is an important determinant of character, whereas skin color, for example, is not—since hot-headedness and appetitiveness and so on belong to youth, just as other character traits belong to other times-of-life. But if time-of-life conditions the possibility or likelihood of the specific *pathē* in relation to which we act virtuously or viciously, does it not follow that time-of-life signifies a kind of *pathos* for human beings, perhaps even a *pathos* that is deeper than the individual *pathē*? Heidegger himself suggests this understanding of time-of-life as *pathos*, in the context of commenting on a kind of *paschein* that has the character of the *sterētikon*. He writes: "Something happens to me, by which I lose the *hexis*, for example, becoming-old. *Pathos* is, therefore, that which deprives me of a matter [was mich einer Sache verlustig macht...]" (§18.196, 132).

Here, in Heidegger's thinking alongside Aristotle's *Rhetoric*, the *hēlikia* of old age is understood as a most fundamental *pathos* for one's being-in-the-world, since it paves the way—*proodopoiei*—for what *pathē* are likely, perhaps even possible, in a given rhetorico-political setting. To be sure, time-of-life is *pathos* in a different sense than the various *pathē*, and Heidegger's analysis of the different operative senses of *pathos* in Aristotle points us in the right direction: whereas each of the various *pathē* amounts to something along the lines of "the occurring-to-one [das Mit-einem-Geschehen] that has the character of the unpleasant (for example) . . .," or "a becoming-relevant of something, which aims at my attunement, a becoming-otherwise in the sense of becoming-depressed (for example)" (§18.195, 131), time-of-life signifies *pathos* of a different order. The latter is captured in the more fundamental sense of *pathos* as Dasein's 'being-taken [Mitgenommenwerden]' from without. The *pathē*, Heidegger explains, "are not 'psychic experiences,' are not 'in consciousness,' but are a being-taken of human beings in their full being-in-the-world. That is expressed by the fact that the whole, the full occurrence-context, which is found in this happening, in being-taken, belongs to the *pathē*" (§18.197, 132-33). If *pathos* in its fundamental sense as "being-taken" applies to the various *pathē*, then it belongs even more profoundly to each time-of-life paving the way for the various *pathē*. Thus, when Heidegger writes later in the lecture course, and with his own italicizing, that "*pathē are modes of being-taken with respect to being-in-the-world*; through the *pathē*, the possibilities of orienting oneself in the world are determined essentially" (§20.242, 162), it stands to reason that times-of-life ground our being-taken with respect to being-in-the-world, that is to say, they are basic conditions for the possibility of orienting oneself in the world.

Aristotle's focus on the *pathē* to understand human beings as "having *logos*" in the most fundamental sense of being open to discourse has the effect of bringing to the forefront what we might call the "vicissitudes of *logos*"—those changing circumstances in the *zōion logon echon* that allow for, but also compromise or preclude, the possibility of rational persuasion. These vicissitudes bear upon "having *logos*" in its range of meanings, and most importantly for ethical theory, they are conditions for the possibility of "having *logos*" in the perfected sense of achieving *aretē*, as articulated in the *Nicomachean Ethics*. Being the *zōion logon echon* in the perfected sense designated as *aretē* is difficult to achieve because, as we've seen, we "have *logos*" through the *pathē*, not only the various *pathē* such as fear or shame but above all, the times-of-life that constitute our deepest *pathos*. To be an animal "having" *logos* brings these vicissitudes in tow—at least for us, creatures of a day, who always already find ourselves in a given time-of-life, from the hot-bloodedness of youth to sober, calculating old age. In this way, Aristotle's *Rhetoric* complicates the meaning that attaches to the definition of human beings as the *zōion logon echon* and thus allows for an appreciation of the complexities of human temporality.[32]

Notes

1 Heidegger 2009, §13.111, 76. Quotations from Heidegger's *Basic Concepts of Aristotelian Philosophy* will first cite the German text (*Grundbegriffe der aristotelischen Philosophie*, GA 18, Frankfurt am Main: Vittorio Klostermann, 2002) and then the English translation by Robert Metcalf and Mark Tanzer (Bloomington, IN: Indiana University Press, 2009).

2 Martin Heidegger, *Being and Time*, trans. John Macquarrie and Edward Robinson (New York: Harper and Row, 1962), 139. In *Being and Time*, Heidegger credits Aristotle's investigation of the *pathē* in *Rhetoric*, Book II, as a precursor to his own phenomenological account of attunement (*Befindlichkeit*) as that "disclosive submission to world out of which things that matter to us can be encountered." In his 1924 lecture course, *Basic Concepts of Aristotelian Philosophy*, Heidegger writes that "*rhetoric is nothing other than the interpretation of concrete being-there, the hermeneutic of being-there itself*. That is the intended sense of Aristotle's rhetoric" (§13.110, 75). On the connections between *Being and Time* and the 1924 lecture course, see Brogan, *Heidegger and Aristotle: The Twofoldness of Being* (Albany, NY: Stat University of New York Press, 2005), Chapter 5; McNeill, *The Time of Life: Heidegger and Ethos* (Albany, NY: SUNY Press, 2006), Chapter 3; and Metcalf, "Aristoteles und Sein und Zeit," *Heidegger Jahrbuch*, 2007.

3 Quotations of Aristotle in English translation are those of W. D. Ross, *The Basic Works of Aristotle*, ed. Richard McKeon (New York: Modern Library, 2001), or J. H. Reese, in Aristotle, *The Art of Rhetoric* (Loeb Classical Library, 1926), or my own translations.

4 Heidegger himself gestures toward this difference between the minimal and perfected senses of "having *logos*" in the 1924 lecture course when he writes: "[T]he human being is in the mode of being-with-one-another . . . . This being-with-one-another has its basic possibility in speaking, that is, in speaking-with-one-another, speaking as expressing-oneself in speaking-about-something. *Logos* comes into play not only with this fundamental determination, but also precisely where Aristotle poses the question concerning the possible *aretai*" (§13.104, 71–2).

5   See Rabinoff, "Aristotle on the Rationality of Virtue" in this volume, for an incisive account of Aristotle's example of the obedient child and its significance for thinking about the meaning of "having *logos*."
6   For an illuminating account of *logos* as theorized by Aristotle in *Nicomachean Ethics*, see Ömer Aygun, *The Middle Included: Logos in Aristotle's Philosophy* (Evanston, IL: Northwestern University Press, 2017), Chapter 5.
7   For discussion of Aristotle on this point, see Burnyeat 1981, "Aristotle on Learning to Be Good," in *Essays on Aristotle's Ethics*, ed. Rorty (Berkeley/Los Angeles: University of California Press, McDowell, 1978); McDowell "Are Moral Requirements Hypothetical Imperatives?" *Proceedings of the Aristotelian Society*, Supplementary Volume 52, 13–29, reprinted in *Mind, Value and Reality* (Cambridge, MA: Harvard University Press, 2002); "Might There Be External Reasons?" in *World, Mind and Ethics: Essays on the Ethical Philosophy of Bernard Williams*, ed. Altham and Harrison (Cambridge: Cambridge University Press, 1996); "Deliberation and Moral Development in Aristotle's Ethics," in *Aristotle, Kant, and the Stoics: Rethinking Happiness and Duty*, ed. Engstrom and Whiting (Cambridge: Cambridge University Press, 1996); "Two Sorts of Naturalism," in *Virtues and Reasons: Philippa Foot and Moral Theory*, ed. Hursthouse, Lawrence, Quinn (Oxford: Clarendon Press, 1996), and Metcalf, "Capturing the Power of Logos: Gadamer, McDowell, and Moral Argument," *Philosophy Today* (SPEP Supplemental Volume), 2005.
8   As to the difficulty involved in being trained for virtue, Aristotle writes that the upbringing and practices (*tēn trophēn kai ta epitēdeumata*) of the young should be fixed by *nomoi*, "for they will not be painful when they have become customary [*sunēthē*]. Yet it is surely not enough that when they are young they should get the right upbringing and attention; since they must, even when they are grown up, practice and be habituated to them [*dei epitēdeuein auta kai ethizesthai*], we shall need *nomoi* for this as well, and generally speaking to cover the whole of life; for most people obey necessity rather than *logos* [*anankē mallon ē logōi peitharchousi*], and punishments rather than what is noble [*kai zēmiais ē tōi kalōi*]" (X.9 1179b30-1180a4).
9   Gadamer, *Hermeneutics, Religion and Ethics* (New Haven/London: Yale University Press, 1999), 34. Aristotle's reflection on such preconditions finds expression elsewhere in his writings—for example, in Book I of the *Topics*, where he writes that on some matters of controversy what is needed is not *argument* so much as punishment or perception: "For those who puzzle about whether one must honor the gods and care for one's parents or not need punishment, while those who puzzle about whether snow is white need perception" (105a2-6).
10 See Russon, "'Actuality in the First Sense' and the Question of Human Nature in Aristotle," in this volume, for its discussion of how both history and habit are constitutive for *logos* in Aristotle's sense of the *zōion logon echon*–a point underscored by Aristotle's treatment of *logos* in the *Rhetoric*.
11 Aristotle's rhetorical use of "guessing [*stochazesthai*]" is perhaps an echo of Plato's *Gorgias* 464c-d. Fortenbaugh, *Aristotle's Practical Side: On His Psychology, Ethics, Politics, and Rhetoric* (Leiden/Boston: Brill, 2006), notes the parallel between *Rhetoric* 2.13, "All men are receptive of speeches spoken in their own character and like themselves" (II.13 1390a25-26), and *Gorgias* 513b-c: "each group is delighted with speeches spoken in its own character," 410.
12 Heidegger concludes the passage as follows: "The Greeks were completely absorbed in the outward. At the time of Plato and Aristotle, Dasein was so burdened with babble

that it required the total efforts of them both to be serious about the possibility of science."
13 Fortenbaugh, *Aristotle's Practical Side*, relates this definition to what we find in Plato's *Gorgias*: whereas Gorgias called rhetoric the "artificer of persuasion [*peithous dēmiourgos*]" (*Gorgias* 453a), Aristotle defines rhetoric as "a faculty of considering in each case the possible means of persuasion" (*Rhetoric* I.2 1355b25-26; cf. *Topics* 101b5-10), 15.
14 Heidegger identifies "speaking-with-one-another [*Miteinandersprechen*]" as the clue to uncover the "discoveredness of being-there as being-in-a-world [*der Entdecktheit des Daseins als Sein-in-einer-Welt*]" (*Being and Time*, §15.139, 95), having in view *legein* in its "everydayness," the *legein* operative in rhetorico-political contexts, where *êthos*, *pathos*, and *hexis* are centrally important.
15 See McNeill, *The Time of Life*, on this point: "in humans, the common world is disclosed and constituted primarily through the *logos*, on the basis of a *legein*: the having of a common world and a common good is a speaking 'with' the world as a speaking with one another (GA 18: 50)," 80.
16 See Diamond, "'For There Are Gods Here Too': Embodied Essence, Two-Footedness, and the Animal with *Logos*" in this volume, for its discussion of the ambiguity of *logos*-as-reason and *logos*-as-language, in relation to Aristotle's formulation of the *zōion logon echon*.
17 Heidegger translates the first of the *pisteis entechnoi* as "in the comportment [*Haltung*] of the speaker," the second as "in the manner by which the hearer is brought into a disposition," and the last as "in *logos* itself." See the discussion in Heidegger, *Basic Concepts*, 2009, §14.120, 82.
18 The "disposition [*diathesis*]" of the hearer in rhetorico-political discourse can be explicated in terms of one or more of the *pathē*. Heidegger explains: "The *Rhetoric's* analysis of the *pathē* has this intention: to analyze the various possibilities of the hearer's finding himself [*die verschiedenen Möglichkeiten des Sichbefindens beim Hörer zu analysieren*], in order to provide guides as to what must be cultivated on the part of the hearer himself" (§16.170, 115).
19 One of Heidegger's principal aims in appropriating Aristotle's *Rhetoric* is to argue against traditional accounts of the *pathē* as "affects"—which thereby entail a partitioning of the *pathē* as phenomenon into "states of the soul" on one side and bodily symptoms on the other. See his rough sketch of the influence of the Stoic theory of the affects at §17.177-78, 120.
20 McNeill, *Time of Life*, 78.
21 This is not to say that Heidegger's glossing of Aristotle's test is not without issues of his own. Consider, for example, Heidegger's understanding of *pathos* as "losing-composure, being-brought-out-of-composure [*Aus-der-Fassung-Kommen, Aus-der-Fassung-gebracht-Werden*] . . . such that it is able to be composed once again [*daß sie wieder gefaßt werden kann*]. . . . Thus, *pathos already has within itself the relation to hexis*" (§17.171, 116). That perhaps makes sense for *phobos*, which, after all, is a *pathos* connected to one's expectation of something destructive: *ti phthartikon pathos* Aristotle calls it (1382b29-30). But while *pathē* such as anger, fear, hate, shame, and indignation are plausibly examples of losing-composure, what sense can it make to think of calmness (*praotēs*) as a case of losing-composure? Or friendly-love (*philia*)?, or charitableness (*charis*), or the nearly untranslatable *zēlos*, "emulation," or "aspiration"?
22 Indeed, Aristotle goes on to write: "It is clear that [the orator] must, through his *logos*, put the hearers into the frame-of-mind of those who are disposed to be angry" [*dēlon*

d' hoti deoi an auton kataskeuazein tōi logōi toioutous hoioi ontes orgilōs echousin] (1380a2-3).

23 Aristotle uses the expression *pōs* or *hōs diakeimenoi* at 1377b27-28, 1378a24, and 1382b29; he uses the expressions *pōs echontes*, *houtōs echontes*, and *hōs echontes* at 1379a9, 1379a28, 1379b39, 1380a6, 1382a20, 1383a14, 1383a25, 1383b14, 1385a17, 1385b13, 1386a4, 1387a7, 1387b22, 1388a24, 1388a30, 1388b24.

24 Heidegger discusses these chapters of *Rhetoric* II at GA18.194, 130–1.

25 Nonetheless, Aristotle continues his remarks here, underscoring the luck that is involved in reaching old age happily: "If a man is not free from disease, or if he is not strong, he will not be free from suffering; nor can he continue to live a long and painless life unless he has good luck" (1361b27-30).

26 Eugene Garver, "Growing Older and Wiser with Aristotle: Rhetoric II.12-14 and Moral Development," *Proceedings of the Boston Area Colloquium in Ancient Philosophy*, Volume X, (2004) remarks on this issue: "The rhetorician operates on people's beliefs, but what Aristotle says about youth and age has to be true, not just what people believe, for the rhetorician to succeed," 172.

27 See also his argument (at §3, 48) that one's *character* is to blame, not time-of-life. When reminded of his wealth, Cato says: "the philosopher himself could not find old age easy to bear in the depths of poverty, nor the fool feel it anything but a burden though he were a millionaire." Cf. Plato's *Republic* 329e-330a.

28 Of course, the inclination to choose the useful over the noble is a choice that most people make, regardless of their time-of-life. On this point, Garver, "Growing Older and Wise," quotes *Nicomachean Ethics* VIII.8 1162b34-1163a1: "All or most men wish what is noble but choose what is profitable," 185.

29 We should note that "calculation [*logismos*]" is not to be confused with "intelligence/mind [*dianoia*]." In *Politics*, Book VII, Aristotle approximates the *akmē* of *dianoia* at around age fifty (1335b30-34). Since, in the same work, he estimates seventy years of age to be the "dissolution time-of-life [*katalelumenēs tēs hēlikias*]" (1335a34), it follows that he conceives of old age as a gradual loss of *dianoia* along with other powers.

30 Garver, "Growing Older and Wise," 192.

31 Ibid., 196.

32 Earlier versions of this essay were presented at the University of San Francisco and Northern Arizona University. For insightful comments on these earlier versions, I am indebted to the following scholars: Joe Arel, Walter Brogan, Eli Diamond, Ryan Drake, Patricia Fagan, Jill Gordon, Shannon Hoff, Whitney Howell, Gregory Kirk, Marjolein Oele, and John Russon.

12

Practical *Logos* in Aristotle's Ethics, Rhetoric, and Politics

Fred Guerin

Introduction

In Aristotle's *Rhetoric*, *logos* is given a very specific, though central, role as *one* of three key constituents in the art of persuasion (*Rhet*. I.2 1356a 1-20).[1] To persuade others requires that speakers not only possess excellent reasoning skills (*logos*) but also be of good character (*ethos*) and be able to move, inspire, or evoke in us feelings of compassion, righteous anger or indignation, sorrow or solidarity (*pathos*).[2] There is a very good reason why Aristotle decided to enlarge the art of persuasive speech to include both ethical and emotional dimensions. In the practical public realm of ethical-political decision-making and persuasive speech, opinions proliferate and circumstances change, but things nevertheless *need to get done*. To get things done, the complex, obscure, and abstract must be rendered straightforward, accessible, and concrete. Long chains of intricate argument will not be very helpful here. To be sure, reasoned speech (*logos*) is central to rhetoric. But civic audiences must also "feel" that what is being proposed is "the right thing" to do. In political rhetoric, *ethos* and pathos are guided by *logos* but have a role that is at least as important as *logos* since the end or *telos* of rhetoric is judgment (*krisis*) and the latter is wholly oriented not by the strict logic of argument but also by ethical evaluation and emotion. Speakers persuade audiences when the latter are able to acknowledge the reasonableness of a given course of action (*logos*), in light of shared ethical-political ends (*ethos*) in a way that "feels" right (*pathos*). The best speakers are those who over time have gained practical wisdom (*phronēsis*) and insight (*nous*) into the workings of the *polis* and the human *peri psyches* or soul. Thus if "*logos*" is the word for the animal that reasons, "*phronēsis*" is the word that captures how *logos* takes shape in the world of ethical, rhetorical, and political affairs, where ethical deliberation and persuasion are vital to realizing the good. Here we speak of the rhetorician as *phronimos* or the *rhētōr* as a person who embodies (*logos*) practical wisdom in all that they do. It is the intellectual virtue of *phronēsis* that orients *logos* as "right *logos*" in the practical and speaking realms of ethics, politics, and rhetoric. Thus, *logos* as *phronesis* situates ethical and political judgment within the realm of praxis and embodied human learning and experience—"back to the rough ground" of lived experience, as Joseph Dunne has aptly described it.[3]

In bringing the cognitive, evaluative, and affective dimensions together in rhetoric, Aristotle is telling us not just that there are emotional and reasoning elements in deliberation and persuasion but also that a robust concept of human rationality must not exclude the emotions. In both the excellent rhetor and the virtuous individual, emotion and reason work together. In this sense, as Eve Rabinoff persuasively argues, "desires and emotions are rational in the sense that they are implicitly mediated by reason."[4] More importantly, Aristotle's rhetoric presupposes a radical reimagining of the human psyche such that the emotions are seen as fundamentally suffused with reason, and *logos* as reasoned speech is complemented rather than undermined by *pathos*. Indeed, it could be claimed that Aristotle's effort to bring together the thinking, feeling, and normative judgment under the roof of a more philosophically oriented rhetoric was his way of preventing the latter from too easily devolving into sophistry. To be sure, in ethics, politics, and rhetoric complete certainty is never possible. We can misperceive the world, make erroneous or bad judgments, allow our emotions to get the better of us. But it is precisely because of these epistemic limits, normative failings, and affective excesses that rhetoric must assiduously guard against the specious arguments of the sophist. The *rhētōr* as *phronimos* is able to do this because he has a solid moral character—that is, he acts, feels, and speaks as the "right *logos*" commands and has gathered through long experience the capacity to deftly mediate excesses and deficiencies, discovering the appropriate "mean" in any particular circumstance. Moreover, if he is to *move* an audience, or put it in a proper emotional frame of mind, the speaker with good character must know the "means by which the several emotions may be produced or dissipated, and upon which depend the persuasive arguments connected with the emotions" (*Rhet.* II.11 1388b29-31). He must also be seen as someone who entertains "the right feelings toward his listeners and also that his hearers themselves should be in just the right frame of mind" (*Rhet.* II.1 1377b25-27).

All of this is to say that the *logos* of rhetoric is for Aristotle a situated, civic, participative, and practical *logos* oriented toward action that is realized through the virtue of *phronēsis*. In this sense rhetoric can be considered to be the bridge between ethics and politics. To put this in another way, *logos* as reasoned speech is not only complemented by *ethos* and *pathos*, but each of these elements of rhetoric subtly orients the others. They belong *together* in a human world where decisions need to be made and things need to get done for the good of each and all. *Logos* would be merely procedural and devoid of content without *ethos*; it would be indifferent without *pathos*. *Ethos* would be erratic without *logos* and unfeeling without *pathos*. *Pathos* would be aimless without *ethos* and potentially warp judgment without *logos*. It is these uniquely practical limits as well as ethical and political concerns that persuaded Aristotle of the need to broaden the meaning and application of rhetoric beyond mere ornamental speech. This is achieved through the subtle interplay of *logos*, *pathos*, and *ethos* in persuasive speech. But importantly it is an interplay that is carried through by way of *phronēsis* and *nous*.

In the following, I will argue two related theses. First, I will claim that precisely because we inhabit a practical world of words and deeds, of emotions, evaluations, and reasoning, of probability, particularity, and human finitude, *logos* will be *enacted* with and through others, but it will be practically realized through the intellectual virtue of *phronēsis* and what Aristotle describes as "insight" or *nous*. *Phronēsis*, or "practical wisdom," is not something that unfolds in a private or "subjective" realm. Rather, it is a kind of wisdom that involves acute discernment and can only be acquired over time in the activity of doing and being with others. *Phronēsis* and *nous* are the means through which *logos* becomes *practical logos*, inextricably tied to ethical choice and insight regarding individual and collective goods. Second, I will claim that by extending the application of *phronēsis* elaborated by Aristotle in the *Nicomachean Ethics* beyond this latter work to his discussion of rhetoric and politics, we can begin to grasp how it is that *logos*, *ethos*, and *pathos* work together in a world where situated and participative reasoning, speaking, and listening are paramount. In ethical discernment, rhetorical persuasion, and political deliberation, practical *logos* does not emerge as abstract reasoning that yields certain truth. Rather, it inhabits a world where reasoning and insight occur at the level of the concrete and the particular, yielding probabilities rather than certain truths. As such practical *logos* is implicated in the everyday doing of things—where *logoi kai erga* (words and deeds) "work" together and where the evaluative, cognitive, and affective dimensions of rhetoric, ethics, and politics are inseparable. It is precisely because we inhabit this practical world of words and deeds, of emotions, evaluations, and reasoning, of probability, particularity, and human finitude that practical *logos* is *enacted* with and through others but practically realized through *phronēsis* and *nous*.

I. *Phronēsis* and *Nous* in Aristotelian Virtue Ethics

Both rhetorical and ethical deliberation concern particulars. Thus, the intellectual virtue of *phronēsis* is perfectly suited to the latter since it is both reasoning with regard to particulars or situated contexts and a developing capacity to properly determine what the good is for the individual and the polis. As a reasoning capacity it is widened and deepened through human experience. More importantly, it is not merely our reasoning faculty that is engaged here but our entire psyche or "soul"—including our memories, emotions, and insights. What this means is that in the exercise of *phronēsis* we are not merely cultivating our reasoning capacity but schooling the desires and emotions that will help us realize the ends which we determine as good. Neither reason nor desire alone will be able to realize the genuine good. Accordingly, when Aristotle tells us that the "intellect itself moves nothing" (*EN* VI.2 1139a35) but instead that appetite "originates movement" (*DA* III.10 433a32-433b1) and that it is in virtue of "imagination that appetite is capable of self-movement" (*DA* III.10 433b27-30), he is not just saying that practical reasoning (*orthos logos*) and right desire (*orthē orexis*) must work together to achieve the good but that at a fundamental embodied level, human choices presuppose that desires can be understood as thoughtful, and reasoned thinking can be animated by emotions—or to use Aristotelian terms, choice involves desiderative reason and ratiocinative desire (*EN* VI.2 1139b4).

Ethical reasoning involves both choice and sound deliberation. Thus, desiderative reason and ratiocinative desire presuppose that our reasoning can help us choose "that which is intermediate, not the excess nor the defect" (*EN* VI.1 1138b15). Our reasoning must be true and our desire right in each particular occasion where deliberation is called for. How do we know when we have hit the mark? When Aristotle tells us that virtue is "a state of character concerned with choice, lying in a mean, i.e. relative to us, this being determined by a rational principle, and by that principle by which the man of practical wisdom would determine it" (II.6 1106b36-1107a3), we may still wonder what precisely is the rational principle or standard of judgment that helps our reasoning move toward the truth in practical affairs that is also in accord with right desire. It will not be an abstract or a priori principle. Nor will it be one that can be taught in any conventional formulaic way. What Aristotle has in mind is not theoretical knowledge but practical wisdom. Here we are brought to one of key sections of the *Nicomachean Ethics*: Book VI.

In Book VI of the *Nicomachean Ethics*, Aristotle tells us that we arrive at the theoretical, philosophical, or practical truth of things in five distinct ways that realize different levels of certainty: *epistēmē* knowledge that seeks the necessary and invariable truth of things (*EN* VI.2 1139b15-35); *sophia* or philosophical wisdom (VI.7 1141a10-20); *nous* or intuitive knowledge or insight, which takes two distinct forms depending upon whether it is paired with scientific or with practical knowing. *Nous* is situated in the realm of "that which *cannot be* otherwise," that is, in the eternal, divine, or unchanging world presupposed by science and philosophy, and in the realm of "that which *can be* otherwise," the practical world of ethics. *Nous* plays an epistemological role in the acquisition of theoretical and practical wisdom, but it is not a "reasoning" or calculative mode of knowing; *technē* or making that includes, but is not limited to, craftsmanship or skill in fine art. Like *phronēsis*, *technē* involves reasoning in the context of the variable (VI.4 1140a5-20); *phronēsis*, or "a reasoned and true state of capacity to act with regard to human goods" (VI.5 1140a25-1140b30). *Phronēsis* is practical reasoning in the context of the changing or variable, dealing with reasoned "doing" rather than reasoned "making."

In rhetoric, in ethics, and in politics it is not *technē*, *sophia*, or *epistēmē* that is central but *phronēsis* and practical insight (*nous*). It is *phronēsis* that reorients and disciplines rhetoric as a civic, ethical, deliberative undertaking as distinct from a *technē*. We can begin by taking note of four key aspects of *phronēsis* and elaborating these latter within the context of Aristotle's *Nicomachean Ethics*. The first thing to notice about *phronēsis* is that it is an intellectual virtue that helps us determine the best *means* to achieve a given end. Second, because it is reasoning that is ongoing and related to everyday practice, *phronēsis* is the intellectual means through which we may cultivate a virtuous character by instructing us in how to deliberate and choose well in situ. Choosing well presupposes both that our reasoning is true *and* that our desire is right (*EN* VI.2 1139a20-25). Third, *phronēsis* is an intellectual virtue that belongs to us as individual thinking-desiring beings, but also as beings whose self-understanding is intimately tied to practical relations with others. In other words, it is not the sort of *theoretical* reasoning that helps us determine universal or unchanging moral commands, or subsume particulars under universals, but reasoning about how best to realize character virtues of justice, courage, moderation in this or that particular situation or context, so that we might live well with others in a shared community or polity. We become accomplished at this sort of reasoning in situ not by abstracting *from* but by closely attending *to* the particular situation and also to each other. Indeed, according to Aristotle, we only become capable of embodying the intellectual virtue of *phronēsis* by observing others who do it well—by attending closely to those who embody practical wisdom in all their determinations (VI.5 1140a24-25). Not only do we grasp what *phronēsis* is by observing it in others, we realize the *arête* or excellence of *phronēsis* in the political and ethical realm only in concert with others who, alongside us, deliberate regarding "the good life in general" (VI.5 1140b25-30). Fourth, we do not excel at *phronēsis* by rote memorization of formulae or by slavishly or literally adhering to laws or commandments. Rather, we excel at *phronēsis* when we demonstrate that we can, at once, insightfully and reasonably grasp what the particular situation is calling upon us to do or say in light of *past* determinations and perspectives, the particularities of the *present* contingent situation, and *future* considerations of how best to realize well-being (*eudaimonia*) in ourselves and in our polity. We can sum these four aspects of *phronēsis* up by saying that the latter is practical reasoning about the best means to secure given ends that, at the same time, solidifies good character and virtuous relations with others within a past, present, and future self-understanding. However, we cannot fail to also remember the pivotal relation that *phronēsis* or practical reasoning has to desire or what Aristotle describes in the *Rhetoric* as *pathos* or emotions.

What *phronēsis* entails is that we are not merely *thinking* or rational beings but also feeling, expressing, acting, embodied beings, and that all of these latter elements can be understood together as exemplifying our distinctive *logos*-comportment. Thus, we do not cultivate merely the reasoning capacity that helps us realize practical truth; we also cultivate the accompanying *right desire* to follow in the path of such a course of truth. This relation of codetermination between desiring and reasoning gives us a clue to why Aristotle believes that unlike other sorts of reasoning states (e.g., *technê*) *phronēsis* is reasoned knowing that cannot be forgotten. To forget *phronēsis* would be, in a crucial way, to forget or lose oneself. This is because *phronēsis* is the embodied bringing together of our individual experience of "being," "acting," "reasoning," and "desiring": that is, it implicitly recognizes that "who we are" is related to what we do and how we reason and deliberate, and conversely, "what we do" establishes "who we have been," "who we are," and "who we want to be." To put this in more familiar modern terms, to cultivate the virtue of *phronēsis* is to embody a certain temporalizing self-understanding—a way of being, or, if you will, a way of seeing our experiences, desires, and actions as part of a distinctive and intelligible temporal whole.

Aristotle argues that moral virtues such as temperance, civility, justice, courage, and sincerity are not anything we have innately "by nature," even though "nature" in some sense (i.e., our reasoning and linguistic capacity) makes it possible for us to receive them. However, when he states that "it is by doing just acts that the just man is produced, and by doing temperate acts the temperate man; without doing these no one would have even a prospect of becoming good" (*EN* II.4 1105b9-12), he is not assuming that becoming virtuous is a question of unthinking repetition. In each new situation we are called upon to thoughtfully deliberate and adjust our emotional judgment, heighten or relax our activity according to the mean relative to us in this or that particular case. Aristotle's intuition here is that the sort of in situ reasoning that *phronēsis* embodies allows us to meet the challenge of contingency and particularity by occasionally interrupting routine or habitual thinking. *Phronēsis* is activated when we are confronted by the unique situation before us, and it helps us get things *right* because we cannot always rely on conventional habits of thinking and doing. Sometimes we must innovate. But, importantly, our innovations presuppose a certain background of commonly held general rules, conventions, or assumptions that were themselves arrived at through the particularity of many experiences over time. *Phronēsis* is thus a kind of practical reasoning that enables us to take these background assumptions, traditions, or rules and test their intelligibility and applicability against the in situ contexts that arise in a variety of different experiences. Thus, Aristotle relates that "wisdom is concerned not only with universals but with particulars, which become familiar from experience" (VI.8 1142a13-15). Each new experience broadens and deepens our perspective and our capacity to meet the new and unforeseen with equanimity.

Over the course of time we become capable of responding in the right way at the right time according to the right desire. We are thus continuously refining our ability to reason well while at the same time forming and cultivating those desires or emotions that will stand us in good stead each time we are confronted by a new situation. We are not only thinking about doing the right thing, at the right time, in the right way; in so doing, we are implicitly reinforcing a desire to follow this reasoning course, thereby deepening our capacity to resist the desire to act in a thoughtless or unreflective manner.

Again, it is important to remember that this reflective and reflexive capacity does not unfold at the theoretical or philosophical-contemplative level. Rather it is activity-oriented thinking, that is, the *logos* of *phronēsis* is its embodiment as *praxis*. Aristotle reminds us that the goal of his inquiry into ethics is not to "know" definitively what virtue is but "to become good" (*EN* II.2 1103b28-30). The problem then (and, arguably, still today) is that instead of grasping the centrality of *praxis*, philosophers typically

> take refuge in theory and think they are being philosophers and will become good in this way, behaving somewhat like patients who listen attentively to their doctors, but do none of the things they are ordered to do. As the latter will not be made well in body by such a course of treatment, the former will not be made well in soul by such a course of philosophy. (II.4 1105b13-19)

Thus, it is not established theory that guides us in ethics but rather the activity of reflection and emotional judgment here and now in this situation. We become adept at such thinking and judging when we attend closely to how others who have practical wisdom—who have achieved a certain excellence of practical *logos* in *phronēsis*—consistently "do the right thing." Bearing witness to the wisdom of others can take a number of forms: observing or interacting with them while in the activity of doing something, listening to elders or teachers, grappling with authoritative texts, and so on. Aristotle's insight here is simple. When we are young we do not really understand the full spectrum of reasons regarding why we should do certain things or why we must "choose" a certain course of action.[5] The pedagogical notion presupposed in *phronēsis* is simply that as we mature and experience a world with and among those who have already in some measure embodied practical wisdom, and as we ourselves thoughtfully respond to different situations, our practical *logos* is enriched and deepened.[6] Two things are happening here: we are becoming better at reasonably grasping what is at stake in any particular context and we are schooling our desires in such a way that they tend us toward and not away from the good. How does *phronēsis* relate to the virtues of character?

With respect to virtue, Aristotle tells us that in every particular situation there is a "mark" that those who embody the *arête* of the *logos* of *phronēsis* will unfailingly aim for—a mark that instructs them when to "heighten or relax" their response accordingly (*EN* VI.1 1138b20-25). This mark is a "mean" between excess and deficiency relative to the given situation we find ourselves in, which could be anything from a battlefield, an occupational context, a law court, or a political assembly. To say that we enact *phronēsis* in any of these situations is to say that the "mean" we discern is a mean determined by a *logos* (a reasoning expressed in words) that not only "hits the mark" but hits it in a way that would be immediately and obviously "right" to any practically wise and insightful person (II.6 1106b36-1107a5).

It is crucial to see here that determining an intermediate point between a vice of deficiency and a vice of excess is not a calculative exercise. It is not as if we were mathematically plotting a definitive course on a coordinate graph. Nor does it involve "splitting the difference" between two extremes or vices in order to determine a "middle ground." Rather, *phronēsis* is activated by each particular and concrete situation. Each situation calls upon us to exercise *phronetic* reasoning in order to determine a mean that is *relative to us*—it must be *relative* to us not in the sense that we are some "abstract individual" but relative to the *situation* we find ourselves in. The mean is not, therefore, something arithmetically equidistant between two points that is unchanging. It must be an intermediate that is characterized by fluidity or elasticity since human experience is marked by difference, alteration, and diversification. Ethical decision-making is decision-making that must take account of the fact that things *could be otherwise* and that we might often find ourselves in differing situations and contexts that presuppose distinct possibilities and limits. If we have properly informed our practical *logos* through the exercise of the intellectual virtue of *phronēsis*, we will be able to locate where the intermediate is in each different situation, and thereby grasp how to respond with equanimity, or how to determine the best means of persuasion, or how to realize the overall well-being of the *polis*. However, discovering the mean relative to the situation we find ourselves in is not something we accomplish in a vacuum. Rather, it is something that occurs to us in the midst of a situation and in relation to others. It is in these situations with others that we are called upon to reflect, interpret, modify, and judge what we deem as the best course of action—or again as a rhetor, what needs to be said at this particular moment in time

Put another way, to determine the mean "relative to us" could never be to say that we, as autonomous agents, are the sole measure of truth or good. It is true that each of us has a slightly different capacity for practical reasoning because each of us will have experienced life differently through a broad range of activities. For example, if I am an experienced parent, teacher, speech-writer, or janitor, the determination of a mean—

not going too far one way or falling too short in another—will be less difficult for me to determine than it would be if I were very new at parenting or speech-writing. Indeed, as a novice, I will precisely *lack phronēsis*. I will be much more susceptible to being rash, incontinent, inarticulate, fearful, or indecisive. On this interpretation "relative to us" does not mean relative to me in the sense of "subject to my whim" but relative to me in the sense of being defined in reference to the particularities of the situation itself and my own depth of experience. It does not mean that "I can do whatever I want" but *exactly the opposite*—that I am enjoined to do what is appropriate and correct in the situation that calls for me to decide. What is appropriate and correct in the situation will be discovered through virtues that are oriented by *eudaimonia* (well-being or flourishing) not merely as individual but, finally, as a member of the *polis* or community. We do not, therefore, reflect and act as if we were wholly egocentric or autonomous individuals, detached from the world. Rather, we act "as if" we embodied the *practical logos* of the *phronimos*—a practical *logos* that presupposes that evaluative (*ethos*), affective (*pathos*), and cognitive elements (*logos*) work together in each particular situation and a practical *logos* that is shaped, cultivated, and deepened only with, through, and among others.

Not only is *phronēsis* enabled through our *being-with* others, it is complemented by insight or *nous*. If *phronēsis* helps the *phronimos* reasonably determine the best means to realize a given end, it is insight that suggests which ends might better enable us to realize our individual and collective well-being (*eudaimonia*). In a manner of speaking *nous* is the active intuitive and intellective capacity—the "light" —that makes ends visible to us. In Book VI of the *Nicomachean Ethics*, Aristotle tells us that *nous* or intuitive reason is what "grasps first principles" (*EN* VI.6 1141a7). In the *Posterior Analytics* he relates that "we suppose ourselves to possess unqualified scientific knowledge of a thing, as opposed to knowing it in the accidental way ... when we think that we know the cause on which the fact depends, as the cause of that fact and of no other, and, further, that the fact could not be other than it is" (*An Post* I.2 71b8-12). Therefore, in the *theoretical* realm *nous* is indispensable insofar as it apprehends fundamental truths or principles—an apprehension that occurs not by way of demonstrative reasoning or inference but through *insight*. Insight is a grasping power that operates *independently* of sense perception, though it is connected to the latter. Aristotle tells us that "it is clear that we must get to know the primary premises by induction" (*An. Post.* II.19 100b3-5), but "it will be intuition (*nous*) that *apprehends* the primary premises" (II.19 100b13) (emphasis added). Apprehension here is not arrived at through deduction or even sense perception. Rather it is a sudden "intelligent grasp of things."[7] To put this in more modern phenomenological terms, induction is the content-oriented *noematic* "gathering together" of many instances, and *nous* is the intelligent or *noetic* "grasping together" of these latter. Interestingly, Aristotle thinks that our capacity to suddenly apprehend first principles is the defining mark of our particularly "human" *logos*—a *logos* understood as not just "theoretically" but also *practically* oriented (*EN* VI.11 1143a35-1143b5). The question is then how *nous* is configured within the realm of practical concerns—how does it work with *phronēsis*?

As mentioned earlier, on a conventional interpretation it would seem that *phronēsis* is really only concerned with reasoning about *means*, not *ends*—ends which presuppose that the *telos* (purpose) of ethical, political, and rhetorical thinking is, in fact, to aim toward living well overall—that is, *with and among others*. However, it is clear that *phronēsis* is not meant to operate entirely in isolation from other modes of practical reasoning. A more nuanced approach would grasp *phronēsis* as reasoning toward ends in conjunction with *nous* or insight. *Nous* is distinct from, yet a necessary counterpart to, *phronēsis* (*EN* VI.11 1143a-1143b). The power of moral insight or *nous* is not occult or paranormal but unfolds within the medium of our experiences. Thus, as we are exposed to the different situations and possibilities which living among each other provides, *nous* is that sort of noetic act of perception that can help us immediately and intuitively grasp what the most basic "first practical principles" must be in order for us to realize the virtues of character and the good of the polity. Just as *nous* and *epistēmē* yield theoretical wisdom, *nous* and *phronēsis* give us practical wisdom. *Nous* is the immediate grasp of that which is individually and collectively of *ultimate concern* to us. It is the grasp *of*, and the desire *for*, the particular end as well as a concomitant desire to integrate that end into our character in order to realize *eudaimonia* or well-being as a whole. Therefore, *nous* operates in two directions: it gives us insight into the general or ultimate good and insight into how the specific situation we are confronted by relates to that general good. Aristotle affirms that

> not only must the man of practical wisdom know particular facts, but understanding and judgment are also concerned with things to be done, and these are ultimates. And intuitive reason (*nous*) is concerned with the ultimates in both directions ... intuitive reason which is presupposed by demonstrations grasps the unchangeable and first terms, while the intuitive reason involved in practical reasons grasps the last and variable fact, i.e. the minor premises. For the variable facts are the starting points for the apprehension of the end, since the universals are reached from particulars; of these, therefore, we must have perception, and this perception is intuitive reason. (*EN* VI.11 1143a33-1143b7)

Why is all of this important in the context of *phronēsis*? The limitation of *phronēsis* would appear to be that it must be confined to deliberation about means.[8] *Phronēsis* does not contemplate ends because the activity of *phronēsis* is its own end. In other words, the "end" of *phronēsis* is realized in the very doing of it—not the imagining of a good as something outside of it. *Phronēsis* does not give us the reasons *why* we should be virtuous or why we should work toward realizing one sort of state rather than another. The question then is: "How do "ends" make themselves known to us" if not through reasoned determinations? The fact is that they do make themselves known both before and after *nous* or insight has unveiled what the good is.

First, we know that the ends we arrive at must be grounded in our experience of the world. What *nous* provides for us is precisely this grasping power or insight that issues from such experience and is thereafter articulated through the *arēte* of practical *logos* as *phronēsis*—that is, our many engagements and experiences with and among others are intuitively grasped under principles and ends; through individual and collective deliberation we determine how these principles and ends can be realized in the practical contexts of action. If, as Aristotle claims, what uniquely defines us as "human" is a capacity to reason in various ways with regard to various ends, then our ultimate *telos*, from an ethical perspective, is to strive through our practical thinking activity to continuously extend and elaborate such a reasoning capacity in as many different spheres as possible.

Beyond the determination of ends, there is another important reason to pair *nous* with *phronēsis*. It is evident that practical wisdom as a whole would be rather limited if it were to reside only in the *rational* determination of where an intermediate is located relative to the situation we find ourselves in. In other words, it is often the case that the wisest among us are wise *precisely* because they have *that sort of insight which is not an exclusive matter of rational calculation or cleverness*. Indeed, their wisdom often lies *outside* of conventional logical thinking. The wise person often surprises us because her thinking abruptly interrupts our reasoned opinions, inductions, and conventional perspectives. Her insights can, in fact, turn our truisms upside down, forcing us to suddenly see the world, or the matter at hand, very differently. Anyone who has observed this kind of practical insight in someone will know precisely how arresting it can be. It is not that the practically wise person is irrational or injudicious, but that she perceives a truth that we can easily miss, often because we fail to attend carefully to all of the particularities of a situation or fail to grasp the good toward which we must strive toward.

What enables *nous*, what allows it to get to the heart of the matter and suddenly "see" things, is clearly a certain range and depth of *experience*. However, *nous* is enabled also by an acute quality of mind and depth of *character* that has been instructed through *phronēsis*. It is evident here that once we grasp the wisdom that *nous* suddenly arrives at, we can then immediately step back and grasp *why* this must be so at a more conventional, rational level. In this sense the *arête* of *logos* actualized in *phronēsis* both precedes (through experience) and follows (by way of reason) our insightful grasp of things. In a parallel way, to follow Aristotle's original thinking, *nous* or insight grasps both the general or ultimate good *and* the good that a specific situation points to or must be grasped within.

What is interesting and rather paradoxical is that the *phronimos* (i.e., the person that quintessentially embodies *phronēsis*) is considered wise not just because her *logos* is an achievement of excellence through *practical reasoning* but also because her reasoning acumen has uniquely combined with her years of experience in a way that yields perceptive insights that often run *against the grain* of rationally arrived at rules and conventions. The wisdom of the *phronimos* relies upon the day-to-day experience of reasoned deliberations and determinations where a relative "mean" might be discovered in each particular situation. The contingency and particularity of these experiences are, if you will, the *conditions of its possibility*. However, because her exemplary *orthos logos* realizes *phronēsis* and *nous together* in a way that allows thinking to reach beyond the limitations implied by reason alone, she can think new possibilities of meaning and understanding—she can, to use a modern expression, creatively think "outside of the box." This is why it is a mistake to believe that *nous* and *phronēsis* operate independently of each other, or that the *arête* of our practical *logos* lies exclusively with reasoning instructed by *phronēsis* in the absence of *nous*.

Described in a modern idiom, *phronēsis* assumes that the world of ethical and political decision-making is characterized both by tradition, or what has been, and by otherness or by "that which could be other than it is." It is precisely this effort continuously to mediate difference and sameness, familiarity and strangeness, particularity and generality, that characterizes the hermeneutic depth of activity that *phronetic* reasoning encompasses. Thus, as practical wisdom is gradually embodied over time, we find ourselves occasionally running slightly *against* the grain of a formerly learned habit of thinking or saying. We encounter difference or ambiguity, and we experience various insights about the present and future ramifications of our decisions and deliberations. It is not then merely the linear accumulation or aggregation of decisions that defines *phronēsis* but an ever-widening and deepening capacity to grasp different possibilities and situations by thinking laterally or sometimes against a convention or rule. It is the sort of built-in elasticity or flexibility which inheres in practical reasoning as *phronēsis* and noetic *nous* that make the latter indispensable for understanding how we can adopt and cultivate a critically oriented awareness that is not confined merely to ethical discernment but also informs the rhetorical and political fields of human practical activity.

II. *Phronēsis* and *Nous* in Rhetoric and Politics

I have described how practical *logos* realizes excellence by way of the intellectual virtue of *phronēsis* along with *nous* or insight in our ethical orientations. In Aristotelian ethics the character virtues such as courage, temperance, and justice are brought together with the intellectual virtue of *phronēsis* and insight or *nous*. We have now reached a point where it is possible to see how *phronēsis* and *nous* are indispensable in the practical activities of speaking, listening, and legislating—or simply put, in both rhetoric and politics. This is important not only for understanding how these three subjects form a unified practical perspective in Aristotle, but it also can shed light on our present-day understanding of the relation between rhetoric, ethics, and politics.

It is clear that Aristotle is most interested in deliberative or politically oriented rhetoric because it is here where much is at stake for individuals and the *polis*. It is also at the political level where rhetoric either becomes associated with truth or devolves into the sort of sophistry that condemned Socrates to death (and later threatened Aristotle with a similar fate). Political discourse and public reasoning would have been just as essential for democracy in Athens as they are in the modern state. This is not merely because rhetoric enables debate about the common good but because in doing so it provides a public space for the proliferation of different opinions as well as the articulation of something true. It is the *rhētōr* as *phronimos* who knows this. She not only includes and invites listeners into a kind of conversation, she also asks them to participate in acknowledging the truth of what is being said.

To make such a truth claim it is not only necessary that a *rhētōr* reason well, but that he have practical insight into what is important for the future of the polis. This assumes that deliberative rhetoric should not be merely a matter of *technē* but fundamentally oriented by the virtues of character and *phronēsis*.[9] To be sure, when the *rhētōr* puts forward a persuasive argument she is in an important sense "making" or "producing" something, as any craftsman would. This qualifies rhetoric as, in some measure, a question of what was earlier described as *technē*. However, it is also clear that rhetoric is "making" as an "art," which means that it is "making" that follows a true course of reasoning (*Rhet.* I.2 1355b26-27). Insofar as this is the case, rhetoric will always involve making wise determinations about where the intermediate between excess and defect should be located. This presupposes that rhetoric will involve *phronēsis*—an intellectual virtue associated with character virtue. However, it will also involve *nous*. Since the *rhētōr* is publicly situated she must be adept at determining not only the best *means* (*phronēsis*) but the best *ends*: ends that realize the flourishing of the polity as a whole (*eudaimonia*) and ends that are intuitively arrived at through *nous* or insight. She must observe and draw upon "the available means of persuasion" to produce good arguments, and she must also determine within a particular situated context what will count as good reasons that support her conclusions. In so doing, the *rhētōr* as *phronimos* expresses, creatively, through argument not only appropriate logical reasoning but practical reasoning in the form of deliberation. Moreover, she also says something about *who she is*—what her character (*ethos*) is—as well as demonstrating a practical knowledge of the varieties of human experience and desire. It is this combination of practical reasoning acuity (*logos*), sympathetic understanding (*pathos*), and good character (*ethos*) which, for Aristotle, allows an audience to differentiate the *rhētōr* as *phronimos* from the *rhētōr* as sophist.

It is the relation that rhetoric has to *phronēsis* and *nous* that should then signal to us that "observing the available means of persuasion" is an invitation to look at the many-sidedness of persuasive speech, not a casuistic conclusion that "anything goes." Rhetoric is not sophistry. As a practical desire to persuade along ethically oriented truthful lines Aristotle unhesitatingly declares that "what makes a man a sophist is not his faculty but his moral purpose" (*Rhet.* I.1 1355b17-18). He reminds us not only repeatedly that rhetoric is useful but crucially that using it *rightly* or speaking well confers "the greatest benefits whereas wrongful use inflicts the greatest of injuries" (I.1 1355b6-8). Aristotle, student of Plato, would have recognized more than anyone that rhetoric has the power not only to persuade persons of the good but also to destroy those who embody virtues of character and intellect. The *rhētōr* does not only go wrong when he makes logical errors; he goes wrong when he hubristically turns rhetoric into a tool of power over others. For Aristotle, it is clear that such a debasement of rhetoric obstructs our most basic natural desire to realize human flourishing (*eudaimonia*) by upholding what is true and just (I.1 1355a20-23). One cannot read the latter passage without hearing echoes of the voices of Socrates and his accuser Meletus in Plato's *Apology*.[10] Indeed, it is precisely the lack of good character that shows through in Meletus' rhetoric. It is this lack of good character that insures Meletus will not be able to speak the truth either persuasively or wisely.

What does good character (*ethos*) amount to with respect to rhetoric? For Aristotle, as we have already noted, the development of good character through virtue is a way of saying that we become what we do—our actions make possible a certain sort of character and a certain quality of thinking and feeling. Good character is not something we develop wholly on our own—it is also cultivated through the right polity that has a just "constitution." Hence, it is no surprise that Aristotle would assert that "legislators can make citizens good by forming habits in them" (*EN* II.1 1103b3-5).[11] But we can also emphasize that for Aristotle *speaking* is a human activity enacted with and among others. It is speech that contributes to the formation of character over time. Not only must the *rhētōr* exhibit virtuous character and wisdom in her speech (and thereby prove an exemplar of good judgment and deliberative excellence), she must also, in the course of interchange with citizens of the polis, fortify the goodness of her and *their* characters.

We can conclude that the cognitive, emotional, and deliberative capacities that Aristotelian rhetoric presupposes under the definition of rhetoric as a "faculty of observing in any given case the available means of persuasion" point to *phronēsis* as central. Rhetorical speech is well-reasoned speech when speakers embody the virtue of *phronēsis* and *eudaimonia* or concern for human flourishing. *Phronēsis* enables the individual moral agent to deliberate well; it enjoins the rhetorician to balance reason and passion, intellect and desire, in his search for the best possible means of persuasion. It gives a space of possibility for the citizen and legislator to enjoy the "greatest degree of happiness, and acquire fullest measure of virtue." When rhetoric is seen through the lens of *phronēsis* and the constituents of practical wisdom, it becomes less obviously reducible to merely a technique or *technē* and becomes, instead, a practical-reflective, ethically and politically oriented enterprise.

What of politics? Politics, like rhetoric, was considered by Aristotle to be both a practical "activity" and a kind of "making." The activity of rhetoric within politics is persuasion, and persuasion, in part, involves producing convincing argument. Similarly, politics involves the practical activity and creative making of laws and constitutions that will help us to live a good life. The end or goal of both disciplines is not a matter of securing self-aggrandizing power but one of advancing the good of the individual and the good of the state. The opening words of Aristotle's treatise on *Politics* make this quite clear:

> Every state is a community of some kind, and every community is established with a view to some good; for mankind always act in order to obtain that which they think good. But, if all communities aim at some good, the state or political community, which is the highest of all, and which embraces all the rest, aims at good in a greater degree than any other, and at the highest good. (*Pol.* I.1 1252a1-5)

Aristotle's *Politics* should not then be considered as merely a description of different sorts of government. It is, in fact, a normative account of what Aristotle believes would comprise the best sort of city-state—a state that is a *community* of free persons (*Pol.* III.6 1279a22) that comes into being not merely to meet the exigencies of bare existence but for the sake of "a good life" (I.2 1252b27-30). In other words, a good political state is a state that is concerned with *arête*—with the virtues:

> If what was said in the Ethics is true, that the happy life is the life according to virtue lived without impediment, and that virtue is a mean, then the life which is in a mean, and in a mean attainable by everyone, must be the best. And the same

principles of virtue and vice are characteristic of cities and of constitutions; for the constitution is in a figure the life of the city. (*Pol.* IV.11 1295a35-40)

Thus, in the best political state, more important than the accumulation of external goods is the solidity of excellence of character (*ethos*). In the *Nicomachean Ethics* we saw that excellence in character presupposes the kind of practical wisdom (*phronēsis*) that enables us to determine the appropriate mean between excess and deficiency in any given circumstance. In the politics, likewise, the best kind of government will be one that discovers the mean between the excess of wealth and deficiency of poverty, the excesses of exclusive rule by the rich and the deficiencies of exclusive rule by the poor. Even though politics is considered by Aristotle to be the master art that includes rhetoric and ethics (*EN* I.2 1094a28-1094b10), it is clear that he believes the best sort of politics is one that is grounded in an ethics of right reason and right desire. In this sense it is both the case that ethics needs politics and politics presupposes ethics. What mediates between the ethical and political, what enables the possibility of an ethically oriented politics, is the rhetorician who embodies in persuasive speech the right admixture of argumentative acumen (*logos*), good character (*ethos*), and a perspicacious grasp of human emotion (*pathos*). If the *phronimos* as political *rhētōr* possesses these qualities she will have the power to appeal to reason in order to change attitudes and put audiences in the right frame of mind by heightening the right emotions or censuring the wrong emotions. In so doing, she will be determining the "mean" relative to the particular situation at hand in a way that furthers the good of individuals and the polity.

We may wonder at this point what rhetoric or politics might look like without *phronēsis* and the context of the virtues. Clearly, Aristotle thinks it is quite possible for a speaker or politician of bad character, if he is clever, to persuade an audience to draw conclusions about some state of affairs that he himself does not believe or perhaps actually knows are untrue or fantastical. This is certainly the case when persuasion is reduced to *technē*—mere cleverness as persuasion is in this sense mere sophistry. This does not mean that the *phronimos* as *rhētōr* cannot be clever, but only that he cannot be *merely* clever, since his cleverness will always be associated with virtue. *Phronēsis*, Aristotle reminds us, must be realized as presupposing virtue: "Practical wisdom . . . this eye of the soul acquires its formed state not without the aid of virtue . . . therefore it is evident that it is impossible to be practically wise without being good" (*EN* VI.12 1144a26-32). Given this, the wise rhetorician will employ *enthymemes* cleverly (persuasively), but also in such a way that the conclusions reached articulate what is good or best for human flourishing. What is "good" or "best" is what aims at human flourishing, or the good "with and among others" in a just polity. This is the realization of the excellence of rhetoric through *phronēsis* in the context of realizing *eudaimonia* as an ongoing activity that attempts to encourage, realize, and sustain the flourishing of the individual and the state.[12] What I have proposed in the foregoing analysis is that the relation between Aristotle's ethics, rhetoric, and politics is governed by practical *logos*. It is practical *logos* that makes our status as "political animal" unavoidable and our need for rhetoric inescapable. More than that, Aristotle reminds us that the *aretē* of practical *logos* is not arrived at through theory but by way of practical wisdom or *phronēsis*—an intellectual virtue that can only occur in us with, through, and among others

Notes

1. I deal in the main here with deliberative or political rhetoric since the ends of the latter deal with concerns of goodness or harm for the *polis* as a whole (*Rhet*. I.2 1358b5-25)—even if they are addressed to particular audiences that are making determinations about a specific matter at hand.
2. In more modern terms we might translate these three components as the cognitive, evaluative, and affective dimensions required for speech to be persuasive speech.
3. Joseph Dunne, *Back to the Rough Ground: "Phronesis" and "Techne" in Modern Philosophy and in Aristotle* (University of Notre Dame Press, 1993). E. Diamond draws a very interesting analogy between our hands and our capacity to use language: "What I am suggesting is that the way our hand and its power to make any number of tools is the physical manifestation of our productive thinking, that our mouths and their ability to address through articulate language our fellow citizens and family members through education, debate, and political deliberation are the physical embodiment of *nous praktikos*." See Diamond, "'For There Are Gods Here Too': Embodied Essences, Two-Footedness, and the Animal with *Logos*" in the present volume.
4. See Eve Rabinoff, "Aristotle on the Rationality of Virtue" in the present volume. Rabinoff argues that "excellent rationality belongs to the virtuous soul as a whole, rather than being the possession of one part to the exclusion of the other" and that "in the virtuous soul emotion and thought work cooperatively and inseparably in producing virtuous action, such that the virtuous person's thinking is emotional and her emotions are thoughtful. Emotion and thought—virtue and practical wisdom—name two distinct but united aspects of the virtuous person's psyche. More specifically, the former makes what is truly good appear to the virtuous person, the latter makes the *truth* or the *goodness* of what is good appear. Thus, what practical wisdom contributes to virtuous action is full awareness of the virtue of the action and of the actor. This is essential for the virtuous person's excellence to be distinctly *human* excellence," 185. In an important sense, *logos* not only mediates emotion and desire in the virtuous person but in so doing enables excellence in speech and deliberative political affairs.
5. Worldly experience is for Aristotle crucial for "while young men become geometricians and mathematicians and wise in matters like these, it is thought that a young man of practical wisdom cannot be found. The cause is that such wisdom is concerned not only with universals but with particulars, which become familiar with experience; but a young man has no experience, for it is length of time that gives experience" (*EN* VI.8 1142a12-16).
6. It may appear odd to speak of *phronēsis* as a *paideia* when it is clear that for Aristotle it cannot be "taught." However, it is crucial to grasp that *phronēsis* involves not just right reasoning but the deepening of a dispositional self-understanding through doing. In other words, *phronēsis* involves a praxis that forms us as a certain kind of knowing-being: a being who has achieved practical wisdom. This is quite different from making which involves a "knowing how" or knowing that." This latter distinction between *phronēsis* (acting) and *technē* (making) has profound implications

for pedagogy. A pedagogy based on *technē* would be one the sophists might easily embrace—as well as their modern counterparts who extol the virtue of a method-driven, instrumentally oriented, "behavioral objectives model of teaching to the test. Both would relegate teaching to an instrumental approach to students guided by 'efficiency' and 'success-orientations.'" This approach intentionally and systematically removes contingency and particularity, flattens differences, and minimizes anything resembling independent thought and reflection or the cultivation of "qualities of mind and character, a habit of truthfulness, a sense of justice, a care for clarity and expressiveness in speech and writing." Joseph Dunne, *Back to the Rough Ground*, 6.

7 In his article "Aristotle's Animative Epistemology," *Idealistic Studies* 25, no. 3 (1995): 246–9, John Russon does a very nice job of illustrating how this kind of "sudden grasp of things" might work in the context of the classroom where after many repetitions and continuous engagement with the text and lectures on the text students suddenly put together or synthesize a number of disparate elements into a coherent whole.

8 It is noteworthy that when Aristotle discusses the ethical aspects of *rhetoric* he speaks of *aretē* or virtue not as a state or "*hexis*" but as a capacity (i.e., as *dunamis*): "Virtue is, according to the usual view, a faculty of providing and preserving good things; or a faculty of conferring many great benefits, and benefits of all kinds on all occasions" (*Rhetoric* I.9 1366a36-1366b1).

9 The idea of linking rhetoric to virtue and *phronēsis* is not new. Cf. Susan K. Allard-Nelson, *Philosophy & Rhetoric* 34, no. 3 (2001): 245–9. See also Lois S. Self, *Philosophy & Rhetoric* 12, no. 2 (Spring 1979): 130.

10 Plato, *Apology* 24d-26a.

11 From Aristotle's perspective, even if legislators, educators, and rhetoricians cannot "teach" virtue in any direct sense, there is no reason to believe that they cannot play a crucial role in educating citizens by showing in exemplary fashion how the character virtues and the intellectual virtue of practical reasoning or *phronēsis* can be realized through right rhetoric and just laws that realize the good of the state for all citizens. This is precisely what the *rhētōr* or statesman as *phronimos* embodies. We cannot be taught virtue, but we can learn from the example of others in their speech and action how we might be able to perceive, in a more complete way, what the good is. Through the example of others who have a measure of wisdom we might also discover how we are often blind to our own prejudices and, therefore, to the good itself.

12 The realization of eudaimonia (and I would add politics and rhetoric) as ongoing and open-ended is thoughtfully summed up by John Russon, "Actuality in the First Sense," in his discussion of two senses of *entelecheia* (actuality): "the idea that we can take a perspective on our lives as a whole and ask the question of meaning, the question of happiness, means that *we experience ourselves as beings of possibility*. It is precisely because we know our own actualization has not lived up to our first actuality that we can have our future path as a question, that we can have choice. But this also means that nothing we do will ever settle the question. We will always experience ourselves as more (and less) than what we are. We will always be able to see how our potentiality is not fully captured or expressed in any choice we make, in any situation to which we commit ourselves," 135.

13

The Movement of Political Animals

Joseph Arel

Introduction

In the *Phaedo*, Socrates takes issue with how people have tried to talk about movement. He was interested in Anaxagoras' claim that mind directs all and is the cause of everything. This claim captured the true force behind what appears to us instead of superficially taking what is most immediate to be what is most original (97c). Although provocative, he found that in the end Anaxagoras did not follow through with this idea. Instead, he attributed causal force to things like air and water. Socrates found this unsatisfying because it does not put any responsibility on "mind." In response, Socrates says,

> That seemed to me it was very much as if one should say that Socrates does with intelligence whatever he does, and then, in trying to give the causes of the particular thing I do, should say first that I am now sitting here because my body is composed of bones and sinews, and the bones are hard and have joints which divide them and the sinews can be contracted and relaxed and, with the flesh and the skin which contains them all, are laid about the bones; and so, as the bones are hung loose in their ligaments, the sinews, by relaxing and contracting, make me able to bend my limbs now, and that is the cause of my sitting here with my legs bent. (98c)

They fail, Socrates says, "to mention the real causes, which are, that the Athenians decided that it was best to condemn me, and therefore I have decided that it was best for me to sit here and that it is right for me to stay and undergo whatever penalty they order" (98e). He continues,

> If someone said that without bones and sinews and all such things, I should not be able to do what I decided, he would be right, but surely to say that they are the cause of what I do, and not that I have chosen the best course, even though I act with my mind, is to speak very lazily and carelessly. (99b)

Socrates summarizes the difference: "Imagine not being able to distinguish the real cause from that without which the cause would not be able to act as a cause" (99b).

This kind of reductive thinking is familiar. We often allow a simple material explanation to satisfy the need to account for something. In this case, we might be satisfied, acting as though we have understood something, by noting the material required for movement, like the bodily functions or processes that would be required to move one's legs. We do in fact need this material and the material processes for movement to occur. However, they do not explain why Socrates is sitting in jail and would not answer the question that we would intend if we asked why Socrates was in jail.

In *On the Soul*, Aristotle searches for "what it is in the soul which originates movement" (*DA* III.7 432a15). There are many parts of us that play a role in movement, just as bones and sinews play a role in the movement of Socrates. Aristotle gives an account of the parts of us that are involved in movement but with the aim, like Socrates, of finding the ultimate cause of how our movement originates. Primarily, Aristotle argues that it is the object of our appetites that is the initial cause of our movement. However, by looking at the broader picture of Aristotle's conception of our movement, that is, the movement of the animals with *logos*, we will see that Aristotle offers an account that resembles that of Socrates. Following Aristotle, we will see that this involves going beyond the individual mover, and I will argue that Aristotle finds that the origin of our movement resides in an important sense in the *polis*.

I. The Practical Syllogism

Aristotle argues that, while thought and appetite are involved in movement, neither can be considered the origin of movement alone. Experience tells us that our movement can originate in thought. In thought, we often arrive at some conclusion and then set about to plan a way to achieve our aim. But, while we can imagine thinking of some action and having this spur us to action, we also know that our thinking can be overruled by desire. If I am morally weak, although my mind may take one object to be the good, desire may move me toward another (*DA* III.9 433a2). This means that my cognitive apprehension of something is insufficient to explain my movement: "the knowledge alone is not the cause" (III.9 433a6). Something besides thought is therefore required to talk about movement being originated, and, indeed, our experience also tells us that our movement can originate in desire. We have the experience, for example, of being drawn toward something and moving without any noticeable prior planning. Yet desire too is insufficient as an explanation for the origin of movement because it can be overruled by thought. Though we may desire something, we have the experience of choosing not to follow our desire because we think it would not be the best course of action. Consequently, though both thought and desire can be involved in movement, neither can simply be identified with the origin of movement.

To explain "the common cause of any sort of animal movement whatsoever," Aristotle presents what is referred to as the "practical syllogism" (*MA* 1 698a5). If I think two propositions, that "dogs are animals" and that "this is a dog," I immediately infer the conclusion, that "this is an animal." Here the purpose (*telos*) of the syllogism is to see the speculative truth (*theōrēma*). In a practical syllogism, instead of seeing the truth (*theōrein*), the conclusion becomes an action (*gignetai hē praxis*) (*MA* 7, 701a11). For example, if I imagine that it would be good to drink water and I see water capable of being drunk by me, I drink the water. The action of drinking is thus the conclusion of this "practical syllogism."[1]

In analyzing movement, Aristotle is careful to distinguish between appetite itself and the object of appetite. It is the object of appetite that can be seen as the beginning of movement. Appetite itself is for the sake of the object of appetite (*to orekton*). This is the primary stimulant or beginning (*archē*) of practical thought (*dianoia praktikē*) (*DA* III.10, 433a18). As Aristotle says, "that which is last in the process of practical thinking is the beginning of the action" (III.10 433a18). In other words, when we think about reaching some goal in terms of our movement, we will reason backward, from the end to be achieved to where we are, though in terms of action, we will proceed in the opposite order. But the movement only begins when some imagined objects are "present." Consequently, it is first the object of appetite that originates movement.

According to Aristotle, it is thus the *object* of action or the object of appetite, the water, which is the starting point or origin of the action. The object—the *telos*—is thus the primary cause of action. This object of appetite is the origin of movement only in a restricted sense, though, and a fuller analysis of the kind of animals that we are will show us that there is a more fundamental source from which the object of appetite is able to appear. In short, in order to function as the cause of motion, the object must be seen *as* good and *as* a possibility. In this sense, the ability of the object to function as cause of our action is dependent upon the powers of interpretation and imagination—*phantasia*. Exploring these themes will allow to understand the distinctive actions of "animals having *logos*."

II. The Object of Action

The premises of the "practical syllogism" are of two kinds, the good (*agathos*) and the possible (*dunatos*). The major premise is "the good" and the minor premise is the "possible." What we can see by distinguishing between these "premises" is that objects do not simply appear as possibilities for our appetite; instead, these possibilities are generated. The "what" from which movement originates (*ta kinoun*) is the object of appetite, but it is only by first grasping an object *as* good and *as* capable of being otherwise that we begin the process of moving toward it. For this reason, we cannot simply identify the object of appetite as the beginning of movement. As Nussbaum notes, it is first the animal's *phantasia* of its goal that begins movement.[2] As Nussbaum explains, "If they see the meat as meat, they will go towards it; if they mistakenly believe it to be some harmful substance, they will run away."[3] The object of appetite is not necessarily the good but rather must be something "seen as" good (in *phantasia*).[4] Again, when we think about doing something, we are thinking about something as a possibility. If we are unable to recognize something *as* possible, we will not be able to recognize it as a possible action of ours.⁵ In both cases, then, it is our ability to see the object *as* something rather than simply our recognition *that* it is (*hoti*) that allows the object to originate motion. The object of our appetite—what we will see *as* good—will thus vary according to our appetites.

Aristotle says that the conclusion of the practical syllogism—the action—will occur unless there is something to hinder the action (*MA* 7 702a18). One explanation for how something could hinder action in the practical syllogism is given in *On the Soul*. As we noted earlier, appetite and thought can both interrupt what would lead to action. Here, Aristotle notes that we may have multiple appetites running counter to each other when *logos* and desire (*epithumia*) are opposed to each other (*DA* III.10 433b5). This kind of conflict, he argues, is a temporal conflict relevant to temporal beings, because it is not one and the same desire that is attracted and opposed at the same time; rather, desire moves toward an object in the present, while *logos* holds us back from it with a sense for the future. For example, I may desire to continue eating, but reason, by sensing that the future will not be pleasant if I do, holds me back. Aristotle concludes that "that which causes movement" must be specifically, or in form (*eidei*), one, but "the things which cause movement are numerically many" (III.10 433b12). In this way, we see that the nature of the major premise differs for animals with *logos* from what it is in animals that act more immediately by nature (*phusei*). Finding the origin of movement in this case is thus more complex.

As we saw, the last step of the practical mind is the beginning of action (*DA* III.10 433a17). But when Aristotle speaks of humans, we see that the scope of practical mind is wider. In the *Nicomachean Ethics*, Aristotle remarks that humans who act well use practical wisdom (*phronēsis*). We here see a similar story with practical wisdom that we saw with practical mind (*nous praktikē*). The object being acted upon must be capable of being otherwise (*EN* VI.5 1140a33).⁶ Practical wisdom is also directed toward the "last step" (*eschaton*), the object of action (*to prakton*) (VI.8 1142a24). The specific characteristic of practical reason is that it is concerned not only with how best to achieve an end and whether an object is good but also with what sorts of things are good in general (VI.5 1140a27). This, for Aristotle, is characteristic of the animal with *logos*, the one who is capable of indicating (*deloō*, able to "make manifest") the good and the beneficial as such.

As Aristotle argues in the beginning chapters of *Nicomachean Ethics*, our aims are structured in reference to our *idea* of what is good. When I look around and perceive the world, I do much more than process light waves with my eye. Things appear to me in terms of how the world has already been organized by that for the sake of which I act. Although the object of appetite is what starts the process going because I must first see a good before I begin to act, this is already organized by the major premise of the syllogism. It is only in the light of this broader way in which the world is organized by a sense of the good—the broadest "major premise"—that this concrete situation (seeing a drink of water as a good thing, for example) will present itself to me as an occasion for action. In other words, although the object of appetite, the water, is the beginning of this particular action of drinking, it could only be the beginning because the major premise, something that I already take to be good, made it possible for it to appear as good.⁷

III. The Political Concern for the Good

We have seen that the animal with *logos* has a character of movement that is distinct because the major premise orienting its movement, what is seen as good, can change. We see this in the *Nicomachean Ethics* and the *Politics*. These texts rely on the basic idea that what appears as good to us, as well as our ability to pursue it, is the subject of deliberation and can be shaped and changed.

Aristotle states that the *polis* comes into existence for the sake of bare needs but continues in existence for the sake of the good life (*Pol.* I.2 1252b28). Though our pursuit of the good life is natural in the sense that it is our ultimate aim,[8] the good life is still something that must be decided upon and enacted in the *polis*. This good must be embodied in its material (the citizens), its form (the constitution), and its "moving cause" (the ruler), all of which must aim at the good life (the final cause). Politics is the science of forming and shaping all aspects of the *polis* so that it will enable its citizens to achieve the good life. Aristotle describes the *polis* as the "most architectonic science" or the master-craft (*EN* I.2 1094a26). He says this because it is in the political realm that what should be studied, by whom, and for how long is decided. As Dorothea Frede writes, "its prime task is the care for the citizen's acquisition of knowledge and their moral conditioning."[9] Thus, what we see is that politics involves the structural implementation of the conditions under which certain goods will be seen *as* good. In the terms we established earlier, the statesman is concerned with, among other things, the "major premise" of its individual citizens.

Aristotle gives the *polis* a crucial role in the establishment of what is seen as good. A person is not sufficient without the *polis*, not merely because they have material needs that must be satisfied but also because they need the *polis* in order to understand the good. We see this when Aristotle writes, "For man, when perfected, is the best of animals, but, when separated from law and justice, he is the worst of all . . . and he is equipped at birth with arms, meant to be used by intelligence and virtue" (*Pol.* I.2 1253a31). Intelligence and virtue, it seems for Aristotle, are not likely available to one who is outside of a political world. Even those already disposed toward virtue will need to be raised in a political world that will encourage good habits and a view to what is good. Aristotle says that it is difficult to be raised correctly without laws of a certain kind (*EN* X.9 1179b31-5) and also that "It makes no small difference, then, whether we form habits of one kind or of another from our very youth; it makes a very great difference, or rather *all* the difference" (II.2 1103b23-35).[10] The goal of habituation is "enjoying and hating well" (X.9 1179b25). In order to do this, we need to be able to view what is to be enjoyed as enjoyable and what is to be hated *as* hateful.[11] What I will focus on now is how the establishment of laws and the care over public education aim to shape how we see something as good.

The law, says Aristotle, ordains what is good (*EN* X.9 1180a23). It declares for people what is to be pursued and avoided. In the *Eudemian Ethics*, in a discussion of the possible dissonance between the good itself and what merely appears as good, Aristotle says that they must be "harmonized" and that "the political art exists to make them agree for those to whom as yet they do not" (*EE* VII.2 1236b36-1237a4).[12]

Law aims to "harmonize" us with the *polis* by shaping our view of what is good both by incentives to right action and by powers that impose discipline (*EN* 1179b31-1180a4).[13] These forces, if the *polis* is a good one, aim to habituate citizens into virtuous behavior. As Aristotle writes, "the law has no power to command obedience except that of habit" (*Pol.* II.8 1269a20). That is, they aim to encourage certain things to be viewed as good and others to be viewed as shameful. Myles Burnyeat argues that it is by performing actions repeatedly that we come to view them as intrinsically good.[14] For example, by requiring public service, military service, or participation in civic engagements, the law can aim to habituate us into this practice with the aim that we become properly disposed toward these activities.

In addition to law itself, Aristotle also sees a public care over education as essential to affect what its citizens view as good. Book VIII of the *Politics* begins with the assertion that "No one will doubt that the legislator should direct his attention above all to the education of youth; for the neglect of education does harm to the constitution" (*Pol.* VIII.1 1337a10-11). There is a kind of symmetry or inseparability between the citizens and the *polis*.[15] The character of the citizens needs to reflect the type of regime one is a part of: "The character of democracy creates democracy, and the character of oligarchy creates oligarchy" (VIII.1 1337a15). In other words, all parts of the *polis* must aim in the same direction, and for this reason it is best that education be a public concern and will be a matter of interest to the legislator. Thus in a democracy, one will want to instill "democratic values" into one's citizens, that is, with a view of democracy and the democratic as goods. "The whole city has one end" (VIII.1 1337a21) and each of its parts must have this end for the whole to truly embody this end.

IV. The Internal Stability Required for Movement

Though the *polis* has a concern for what we view as good, and takes part in deciding and shaping this, it does not have a necessary hold on what we view as good in any given moment. For example, the *polis* may fail to educate us into embodying the character of the regime. Even in a successful *polis*, where the aim is to educate citizens with a view toward virtue, its goal is not to create mechanical beings[16] but those actively disposed toward choosing what is good. That is to say, the aim of the *polis* is to ensure that the good is in fact actively chosen in each case. As opposed to a mechanical account, the animals with *logos* can change their views and orient themselves toward different goals or conceptions of the good. Though it is characteristic of the animal with *logos* to be capable of and to deliberate about the good, movement requires that one has already decided upon the good. In this final section, I will argue that, though we may deliberate and be unsure of what we take to be good, the very fact of our movements indicates that we must have already decided what we take to be good in each case.

Aristotle's method is to proceed from what is more clear to what is less clear.[17] Consequently, he begins the investigation into movement from the world of sense, focusing on the simple movement involved in moving one's arm.[18] In this movement, we notice that either the whole arm moves and pivots from the shoulder joint or the forearm will pivot from the elbow joint. The arm moves, but its origin, where the movement arises, remains at rest. "Accordingly," writes Aristotle, "it is plain that each animal as a whole must have within itself a point at rest, whence will be the origin of that which is moved, and supporting itself upon which it will be moved both as a complete whole and in its members" (*MA* 1 698b2).[19] Now, what does Aristotle mean by "each animal as a whole"?

We may try to locate this point in a physical point like the elbow joint. Some of our movements involve moving one part of our bodies while leaving the remainder of our body at rest. This could mean that "local" joints must relate to a more substantial nonmoving point, like our feet or hips while standing or our buttocks while sitting. We could also read "each animal as a whole" to mean that there must be one stable point when the entire body is moving. Are we to see the nonmoving character of the joint as support by another nonmoving part of the body? If so, what would this be? The spine? The abdomen? In *The Movement of Animals*, Aristotle's discussion eventually includes the soul, moving from an understanding of the center as a magnitude, as in bodily joints, to the center as a point, analogous to the joint. In Chapter 9, he returns to the discussion of the center, considering what unites left and right. He mentions the spine as well as "the middle section of the body" (*MA* 9 702b25). Finally, he finds that this center must not be a magnitude but is the soul. He writes, "There must be some one thing that moves them both, and this is the soul, which is distinct from a spatial magnitude of this kind, though it is in it" (703a). At the same time, Aristotle discusses the "connate pneuma" because there must be something material in the body which is moved. This material, however, is ultimately moved by the soul, which is not reducible to some material part of the body. Aristotle explains that the "connate pneuma," which must both move and be moved, "appears to stand to the soul-center or original in a relation analogous to that between the point in a joint which moves being moved and the unmoved" (703a10). As the mover of the material origin of movement in the body, the soul is the unmoved mover of the material body. If we return to the "practical syllogism," we can find yet another, more fundamental nonmoving origin of movement. In *On the Soul*, Aristotle writes that the universal (major) premise does not originate *movement* per se but "does so while it remains in a state more like rest, while the other [the particular premise] partakes in movement" (*DA* III.12 434b20). For this reason, Aristotle takes the universal premise to be a nonmoving origin of the animal as a whole.

In addition to the joint, the center of the material body, or the soul as such, the major premise more precisely aims to distinguish the nonmoving mover to our account of motion in Aristotle. In her second essay in *Aristotle's De Motu Animalium*, Nussbaum, whose focus lies on "teleological explanation," compares the nonmoving origin of movement in animals with the nonmoving mover of "heavenly motions." We have shifted to the teleological explanation, but, having argued for the *polis* as the origin of the teleological aim, we are focusing on the major premise at the level of the individual as another way of using Aristotle's analogy of the joint.

Aristotle notes the importance of understanding the final cause as the primary explanation for human behavior in the beginning of the *Nicomachean Ethics*. Here, Aristotle identifies many different objects of appetite but continues in his understanding of human action because he takes the objects of appetite to give an insufficient explanation for our action. He continues asking why we pursue these objects of appetite until he finds a final cause—happiness. In terms of Aristotle's more immediate discussion of movement, it is the universal premise that represents our conception of the good. This initiates movement as a final cause. The universal premise guides our actions first by determining what will show up as good in the first place. Thus, it is the most fundamental origin of movement. Like the joint, the universal premise functions as a stable point out of which movement originates.

However, unlike the joint, Aristotle believes our conception of the good can change. We can debate about the good politically and being raised within different political communities shapes our character and how we embody the good. We may change our minds, be uncertain, or feel lost with respect to what we value; nevertheless, Aristotle also clearly believes that we must have such a stable point within us in order to move. Consequently, though we may debate about what kinds of things are good, in order for the kind of movement particular to animals with *logos* to take place, we must determine this as a point from which movement can originate. This is simply a formal requirement for movement, according to Aristotle. His argument in the *Movement of Animals* and *On the Soul* is that we must have both a major and minor premise in place for movement to occur. Consequently, movement cannot occur until we have decided upon a general conception of the good.

The creation of joints in octopi can provide an analogy for how the animals with *logos* can, on the one hand, change their views and aims, yet must, on the other hand, take some stance (at least implicitly) in order to move their bodies. The octopus does not have fixed joints like the human arm; however, when performing precise movements like putting food into its mouth, it shapes its arm into an appendage with three bends which function like our joints do.[20] Thus, though the octopus does not have fixed joints, such joints must be created to account for certain movements that it makes. In a similar way, though we can debate about the good and certain kinds of good, and we may take ourselves to be uncertain about having a conception of the good, the very fact of our movement indicates that we have determined what we take to be good in concrete situations. It is in this way that we can view the animal with *logos* as the embodiment of ideas. The mechanics of our movement is such that our movements point to certain goods that we have determined in advance. This can remind us of Socrates' initial concern. If we are to account for the movement of Socrates, or of what accounts for him sitting there, we must understand what is stable within him.[21] An explanation of the immediate realities of the body's capacities is insufficient to explain why he is sitting where he is because these movements are understood abstractly unless they are given the more fundamental explanation of having a belief in a certain type of life as the good life.

Notes

1 For rich discussions of the Aristotelian notion of the practical syllogism, see Essay 4 in Martha Nussbaum's edition of *De Motu Animalium* (Princeton, NJ: Princeton

University Press, 1978) and Chapter 1 of Brad Inwood, *Ethics and Human Action in Early Stoicism* (Oxford: Oxford University Press, 1985).
2. "Aristotle on Teleological Explanation," 86. See *DA* III.10 433a27: mind (*nous*) is always right, while appetite (*orexis*) and *phantasia* can be right or wrong.
3. Nussbaum, *Aristotle's De Motu Animum*, 87.
4. This point is echoed in the *Nicomachean Ethics* in Aristotle's discussion of wish (*boulēsis* in Book III, Chapter 4). Here, Aristotle says in general that we can say the object we wish for is the apparent good (*to phainomenon agathon*) (*NE* III.4 1113 a 25). See also *Nicomachean Ethics* VII on the idea that the lion sees food, not goat.
5. Aristotle distinguishes between theoretical mind (*theoretikos*) and practical mind (*praktikos*) with respect to this issue, noting that they have a different end (*telos*). The concerns of practical mind must be things that we can see otherwise (*DA* III.10 433a30). For example, I cannot think practically about being in two places at once because this cannot be done. Instead, this capacity must involve the apprehension of something in which I could cause a change. The object of practical mind must be something that can be changed because if it could not be changed there would be nothing to think about. Compare *EN* 1139a12: we do not deliberate about the invariable.
6. We saw this in *On the Soul* as well, where the practical good was found to be something that must be "capable of being otherwise" (III.10 433a32).
7. As Aristotle writes, "desire is the last cause of movement, and desire arises through perception or through imagination and thought" (*MA* 701b1).
8. As "the nature of a thing is its end" (*Pol.* 1252b32).
9. Dorothea Frede, "The Political Character of Aristotle's Ethics," in *The Cambridge Companion to Aristotle's Politics* (Cambridge: Cambridge University Press, 2013), 15.
10. Peter Simpson, *A Philosophical Commentary on the Politics of Aristotle* (University of North Carolina Press, 2002), 3, has a helpful summary and analysis of this argument.
11. This is not to say that the law is always, or even generally, successful. Aristotle finds that most cities do not accomplish this. See Thomas L. Pangle's chapter "The Deficiency of Actual Legislation," in *Aristotle's Teaching in the "Politics"* (Chicago, IL: University of Chicago Press, 2013). Looking beyond the law, see Patricia Fagan's chapter in this volume for a discussion of tragedy and how we come to better see how we may come to connect others through tragedy.
12. "Political knowledge is what harmonizes the real good with the apparent good; the means of doing this, Aristotle says, is through pleasure." Zena Hitz, "Aristotle on Law and Moral Education," in *Oxford Studies in Ancient Philosophy,* ed. Inwood. Vol. XLII, Summer 2012, 267.
13. This is important for Aristotle since most people do not respond to argument alone (*EN* 1179b4-15).
14. Miles Burnyeat, "Aristotle on Learning to Be Good," in *Essays on Aristotle's Ethics*, ed. Rorty (California: University of California Press, 1980), 69–92, 73.
15. For an examination of this symmetry, see Randall R. Curren's discussion, beginning on page 144 of *Aristotle on the Necessity of Public Education* (Rowman and Littlefield, 2000).
16. When discussing children learning useful things, Aristotle says, "to young children should be imparted only such kinds of knowledge as will be useful to them without making mechanics of them. And any occupation, art, or science, which makes the body or soul or mind of the freeman less fit for the practice or exercise of excellence, is mechanical" (*Pol.*1137b5-11).

17 See *Phys.* I, 184a17-20.
18 See *MA* III, 11 698a15.
19 Comparing animal motion to the necessary immovability of the prime mover, he writes: "in the world of sense too it is plainly impossible for movement to be initiated if there is nothing at rest, and before all else in our present subject—animal life" (698a15). Most immediately, these stable points are joints.
20 For an empirical study of this, see phenomenon of octopi Sumbre, Germán, Fiorito, Graziano, Flash, Tamar, and Hochner, Binyamin, "Octopuses Use a Human-Like Strategy to Control Precise Point-to-Point Arm Movements," *Current Biology* 16 (2006): 767–72.
21 We can also note that for Aristotle, "the point of rest in the animal is still quite ineffectual unless there is something outside it which is absolutely at rest and immovable" (698b7). He explains that this ground must be solid and not "give way." If the ground is constantly shifting and moving, like a person walking on sand, movement would either be hindered or made impossible. This is also relevant to Socrates' initial concern. If we are to account for the movement of Socrates, or of what accounts for him sitting [there], we must understand what is stable within him, but we must also understand the kind of political reality in which he is living. These together allow us to understand why he is sitting where he is.

14

Aristotle

The Politics of Life and the Life of Politics

Walter Brogan

Introduction

Aristotle's *Politics* might be called a politics of life, a treatise about how the *polis* stands with regard to forms of life that do or do not fully belong to the human community. In this chapter, I will examine passages where Aristotle describes political life per se, a life made possible, as we will see, by a series of exclusionary gestures that serve to differentiate the beautiful life of the *polis* from lives that are, in his view, incapable of the same degree of self-rule and freedom—animal lives, for example, and the lives of slaves. To fully appreciate Aristotle's *Politics*, it is necessary to consider not just the politics of life but the life of the political, namely human life, the life that Aristotle demarcates when he defines the human being as a political *zōon*, a living being whose very way of living is political. This will entail a discussion of *logos* as life, as the living *logos*, the *logos* of life. We will see that in a certain way for Aristotle *logos* is life, that is, the *telos* of life and thus the source of life. We will see that this kind of life arises after the most fundamental caesura of all is marked, namely the line that divides human life from all other forms of life. This will also require us to discuss the space of political community and how and why political associations are constituted. It would not be wrong at all to say that dichotomous thinking frames Aristotle's understanding of the relationship between ordinary life and the life of politics, between life and *eu zēn*, living well. How is this life that we live, which in Aristotle's terms is opened up in the space of the political, namely the life of *logos*, how is this life related to life itself? Ultimately, I will argue, the very meaning of life in general for Aristotle is determined by the superior term in this dichotomy in the conjunction of the human and other than human life.

Aristotle traces the origin of the *polis* from the household to the village to the city, establishing in this way that the city has a natural basis or content. When the city first emerges, this natural content, contained in a privative and even defective way in prior associations, finally reaches its form and end toward which it is directed. Thus the city emerges from or out of prior kinds of natural associations. The movement toward the city is governed by two principles, the principle of need and appetitive desire on the one hand, and, on the other hand, the sovereign, governing force of the *telos*, which encompasses all prior associations based on need and lack and leads them in the direction of the genuine fulfillment and completion and self-sufficiency (*autarkeia*) which Aristotle calls the most sovereign good of all (*Pol.* 1252 a5). What characterizes the village is that there is a movement from operating for the sake of basic needs to operating for the sake of non-daily needs, to something more than need. But this still remains primarily a quantitative, numerical extension. Aristotle makes altogether clear that these partnerships pursue merely intermediate goods that are physical and material and are not the ultimate for sake of which of life. It is as if the mere sustaining of life is not the same as the living of life.

In contrast, the *polis* is a community that is different in kind. There is an irruption involved in the birth of the city, a sudden emergence at a kairological moment that is not at all a continuity with what came before. Human history and political life begin after the event that gives birth to the *polis*. The difference is ontological; the being of the city is constituted in a way other than these previous associations. Aristotle says: "The partnership arising from the union of several villages that is complete is the city. It reaches the limit of full self-sufficiency and, while coming into being for the sake of living, it is for the sake of living well (*eu zēn*)" (1252b27-30). The city is no longer governed by its coming into being; it holds itself in its limit and end and dwells therein. The *telos* is the limit or border (*peras*) that separates coming to being and being. This staying with itself is the very meaning of completion and self-sufficiency and is why Aristotle characterizes the human being in the *polis* as a sovereign, autonomous being and, at least on a human level, the ultimate and sovereign good.

According to Aristotle, the city is self-sufficient, no longer constituted by a lack and no longer needing to take from outside itself what it needs to exist.[1] It is no longer just living that matters, that is, being-occupied and determined by appropriating what one needs to preserve life. Another way of formulating this important distinction is to say that for Aristotle it is not *that* one lives but how that is important. It is the question "how" that one must raise in order to distinguish the *polis* from other ways that humans are governed. Living in the *polis* is not just living and sustaining life; it is a way of life, a way of taking up one's life and directing it on one's own in such a way that life returns to life and holds itself in the end. The fulfillment of need is the final end of a need-based regime, but the final end of a human *polis* is a liberty from need.[2]

I. *Logos* and the Failure of Speech

One of the passages in Book I where it is most clear that Aristotle is drawing a firm line of demarcation that separates the political community from all others is in his discussion of the transformation of voice to speech, the relationship of *logos* and *phōnē*. He acknowledges that animals too form community and communicate with one another, bees and herd animals, for example. But only those who are political have speech. Animals indicate to each other pain and pleasure; their voice is the voice of the body and in more advanced species they are able to announce themselves physically to each other. But this is not speech; though using this vocal ability, *logos* transcends the merely responsive and physical dimension of sounds. Aristotle says: "*logos* is for revealing what is advantageous and what is harmful, and hence also the just and unjust . . . and good and bad" (1253a15-20). For Aristotle, this is what makes the political community possible and what it is about. Speech transcends mere voice because it is infused with foresight that does not respond immediately to its environment and thus stands freely in relationship to its surroundings and does not simply respond to it.[3] The *polis* is the site where the ability to carry out this kind of communication and debate can flourish.

Aristotle also declares that the *polis* is prior to the individual (1256a20). Here he is addressing the citizens and why the gift of *logos* that makes them human gains its proper expression only within the city. Cut off from the city, the individual is an individual in name only, as when we speak of a hand made of stone.[4] Like Plato, Aristotle views this severance as the greatest evil for humans, a state appropriate to beasts that are incapable of community and gods who have no need of it. Such an individual is deficient. The incapacity for community results in a lack of self-sufficiency and savagery in the human individual, Aristotle says. In fact, such separation unleashes a powerful destructive force when not properly checked. At 1253a32, he says: "human beings are born naturally possessing weapons for *phronēsis* and *aretē*, which are very susceptible for being used for their opposites." One supposes Aristotle to mean the close relationship of opposites such as tyranny and philosophy. He thereby focuses on the fragility of the human community, an experiment that situates humans between beasts and gods and risks that what makes us the best of animals may make us the worst. Aristotle considers such an individual cut off from community and *logos* to be a war-like person (1253a10). War is a lack of *koinōnia*; it is the failure of speech. War is the deprivation of our natural fulfillment. Desire for war is an unnatural condition. According to Aristotle, we are by nature political and that means nonviolent, not governed by force. The focus on the just (advantageous) and unjust (harmful) rather than pleasure and pain opens up the opportunity for noncoercive choice.

II. Slavery

An example of the failure of *logos* that results in a coercive relationship is slavery. For Aristotle, the lack of individuality and the concomitant incapability of participating fully in the community as a whole are the defining characteristics of the slave. The slave is one who does not own his being by nature. The slave belongs wholly to the master, *is* through the master. Aristotle is employing the whole-parts model here. The part depends for its being on the whole but not vice versa. The slave is for the master an instrument of action that is separable from the owner (like an accidental property).[5] But like an accidental property, it has its being only by virtue of being-attached. The slave belongs to the master as an extension of the master but one that is separable. The slave in that sense is the externalization of the body of the master. The slave allows the master to be outside himself and to leave the life-sustaining business of preservation and survival to his being-outside-himself, while he engages in other sorts of leisurely activity that are more conducive to the circle of life that dwells in the end and stays with itself. In the slave, the self banishes from itself its life of need and excludes it by virtue of including it within itself as outside itself. Aristotle says the slave is a separable *organon*, a separable instrument of life involved in the carrying out and externalization of life in action. He even suggests the use of an overseer to represent the master in guiding the slaves in the performance of those duties necessary for life (at 1255b35) in order to further free the master from his involvement with the neediness of life. However, Aristotle is very careful to differentiate the life of mastery from free political expression. The master has the knowledge and foresight necessary for political rule, but he is turned in the wrong direction and remains in that regard connected to the natural deficiency of the physical. In that sense, Aristotle would agree with Marx about the dialectical dependency of master and slave, but he would disagree in allowing that the master does have the capacity to turn away in another direction and be otherwise than a master. Not so lucky of course is the slave. The *polis* is the completion and end of all prior associations and from the end one can look down toward these other associations and encompass them, but this very threshold that brings us to an end is also a beginning, the beginning of free and sovereign political life. It is by virtue of standing at a threshold that belongs to the master, as the one who has knowledge, that the master can free himself from his mastery and differentiate himself from the slave. Aristotle says that the master is as different from the slave as the soul is from the body (1254b16). As usual, this demarcation of difference is problematic as Aristotle acknowledges. He says:

> He is a slave by nature who is capable of belonging to another—and this is also *why* he belongs to another [in addition to the fact that his work is the use of the body]. The slave participates in reason only to the extent of perceiving it, but does not have it. The other animals, not perceiving reason, obey their passions. Moreover the need for them differs only slightly: bodily assistance in the necessary things is forthcoming from both, from slaves and from tame animals alike. (1254b20-26)

One wonders about the vast network of differences that Aristotle draws, now associating yet differentiating slaves and animals, but also one wonders about how the slave can perceive reason but not have it.

One may also be puzzled about how slavery, even when allowed only if it is natural, could actually be practiced in a *polis* wherein human beings aim toward sovereignty and toward flourishing as autonomous living beings. Aristotle attempts to resolve this dilemma by carving out a distinction between two kinds of power, the power of force and the power of virtue (1255a13ff.). Aristotle argues that the power of virtue and excellence is not that of force but advantage and that such relationships of master and slave, if justified in a virtuous *polis*, must be beneficial for both parties. The ruler-ruled relationship must be appropriate to the being of those involved and therefore good; it must be a relationship based on what is proper. Affection or benevolence is operative in the master-slave relationship, according to Aristotle. After all, the slave is a physical part of the master. Force would be self-abuse. The use of force to constitute the relationship would indicate a lack of self-sufficiency on the part of the ruler, a bondage to necessity. Moreover, virtuous rule, rule that is appropriate for the *polis*, involves rule for the sake of the other. Force implies, in contrast, taking what is not naturally one's own; its true character is compulsory, whereas virtue is the power to act freely and beyond compulsion. Slavery, inasmuch as it is based on force, is not politically justified. However, it is justified as a fact of nature that is rooted in the kind of being of the slave.

III. On Human Appropriation: The Banning of Commerce as an Activity of Free Citizens

Besides natural slaves, there is yet another group of people that Aristotle bans from full participation in the political community, namely those who engage in commercial exchange. This no doubt strikes us as particularly odd since this activity has by some accounts become the central focus of political life in our times. I want to focus mainly on one thing: how Aristotle's structural principles—the frameworks of his thinking—govern his treatment of this issue and other related issues in the *Politics*. In Chapter 8 of Book I, Aristotle distinguishes between the acquisition of goods and the appropriation of goods. The model for understanding appropriation is really biological; that is, appropriation has to do with matter, with the consumption of what must be incorporated into oneself in order to survive and grow. Behind this analysis of consumerism lies, of course, the distinction of matter and form, and the possibility of taking things as mere matter and separating them from their own being as appropriate for conversion into something other than what it is in itself. One example of such natural appropriation is food for sustenance (*trophē*). Aristotle gives the example of the yoke of an egg that requires the white for protein. Nature naturally provides this nourishment for the sake of the development of the yoke into a living being. All natural beings require possessions in this sense in order to survive. As we saw earlier in our discussion of slavery, the slave is such a possession. Possessions (*ktēsis*) are instruments of life that without which life would be impossible. Possessions belong to the being of the one who owns them—food, for example, and clothing that we use for our bodies and that is necessary for surviving the elements.

Aristotle argues that possessions (*ktēma*) of this sort need to be distinguished from the supplies and instruments that are needed to provide the goods that are used in the process of appropriation. Expertise in the use and appropriation of things is household management (*oikonomia*). Expertise in supplying acquisitions and crafting instruments is business expertise (*chrēmatistikē*). This second kind of expertise is, according to Aristotle, unnatural. The structural point is important. What is necessary for growth and sustenance belongs to the city but, as we saw earlier, is excluded in varying degrees from full participation in political life. Those who are defined by their relationship to necessity are incorporated into political life but only by virtue of becoming part of something they themselves do not fully share in. The slave, for example, has no say of his own and can belong to the polity only by virtue of providing sustenance for the one who rules over him. So in this case at least, the slave belongs by virtue of not belonging. In one sense he is part of the city, but in another sense he is not part of the whole in the sense of sharing and participating in the self-sufficiency and self-rule that characterizes genuine participants in the city or citizens. What emerges here are two senses of the relationship of whole to parts. In the case of the slave, she is part of the *polis* but she does not share in its end or participate in it as belonging equally to the community as a whole. She participates in the substantial being of the *polis* only accidentally by virtue of being-attached to the master. In contrast, in the case of those who are free, the relationship of whole and part is more complex. Citizens are free and equal participants of the whole. In the first case, in the case of slaves, the whole is above and apart from the parts and governs over them. In the second case, the case of political participation, the individuals, the citizens in the *polis*, are themselves each the whole that governs. Aristotle's task will be to show how such an arrangement might be possible such that the human being who is defined as standing in the whole and as the *telos* who has achieved self-sufficiency and independence can and must nevertheless belong together in political community.

There is yet a different sort of exclusion than that of slavery that applies to tradespeople and craftspeople who craft the means of production. These people are not allowed to belong to the city and would seriously undermine the stability and territorial security of the city were they to become citizens. Yet they are not slaves and in fact do have knowledge and expertise. These vulgar artisans (*banausos technitēs*) are not permitted the status of citizenship in the *polis*. Being apart from the natural and not directly pursuing activities that sustain their own life but providing goods for others, they are also excluded from the city. Their skill is without any natural limit or end because it has been detached from the fulfillment of need. Yet they are necessary for the city. Thus the second form of exclusion sets up a relationship of the free city and free citizens with what is alien to it and foreign, thus creating another irresolvable tension between the self-sufficiency and self-enclosure of the city and its outside.

Aristotle justifies, on the basis of a view of nature, a vast network of appropriation, culminating in the anthropocentric statement that nature made all things for the sake of the human being. Aristotle's passage on this is pivotal to his understanding of political life:

> It is clear that for grown things as well one must suppose both that plants exist for the sake of animals and that the other animals exist for the sake of human beings—the tame animals both for use and sustenance, and most if not all of the wild animals, for sustenance and other assistance, in order that clothing and other instruments may be got from them. If then nature makes nothing that is incomplete or purposeless, nature must necessarily have made all of these for the sake of human beings. (1256b15-22)

This is one of the decisions that often leads to a reading of Aristotle that sees him as setting up a priority of *logos* (in the sense of *technē*) over *phusis*. Natural beings can be viewed not as ends in themselves but as matter or raw materials for the ends we have in mind, albeit that this end of serving the human is said to be what these other beings were all along striving for. In other words, a natural basis for human appropriation of nature would seem to be asserted by Aristotle. As we saw earlier, Aristotle gives an example of such an appropriative relationship in nature, namely how the yoke of an egg that is surrounded by white protein whose purpose and end is to feed the yoke (1256b10). Then he asserts that, in the same way, all nature is given over to human appropriation in the form of consumption of sustenance and use of clothing, and so on, for the sake of preserving human life. Here we have an interesting understanding of the connection between coming to be and growing on the one hand and sustaining and preserving life on the other. Yet another line is drawn. Here coming to be is for the sake of and ultimately subservient to the preserving of human life.

In making the distinction between household management and commercial expertise, Aristotle is quite harsh in his criticism of the latter. He says:

> Possessions serve the same use (as commercially gained wealth), though not in the same respect, but in one case the end is increase, in the other something else (self-sufficiency). So some hold that this is the work of expertise in household management and they proceed on the assumption that they should either preserve or increase without limit their property in money. The cause of this is that they are serious about living but not about living well; and since that desire of theirs is without limit, they also desire what is productive of unlimited things. (1257 b37-1258a2)

What is at issue is the pursuit of unlimited desires—in other words, desires that have been divorced from need and are no longer tethered to the proportionate measure of *logos* which otherwise rules in the *polis*. The limitless pursuit of wealth is unnatural. It arises due to the double character of acquisition as an art in itself (the art of exchange) and as a part of possession (use). The structural problem Aristotle is here addressing, then, is the distinction of means and end, which for Aristotle are codetermining when the city is just. When desire is detached from need, it runs rampant and is akin to the pursuit of means without end. Aristotle worries about the possibility of a perversion of a proper teleological governance of the city, whereby the end, the good of the whole, determines the means. He therefore exiles the vulgar artisans and tradesman from the city. The banning of commercialism and the unbridled pursuit of wealth is also necessary to keep the political community intact. It is clear that Aristotle is not into globalization, empire-building, and expansionism. In Aristotle's detailed analysis of what causes the deterioration of a flourishing political community, he most often points to a failure to limit production and accumulation of goods to the household realm where the governing principle is that appetite and desire must be connected to need and necessity. In his discussion of commercialism, it is clear that Aristotle is having a hard time keeping the principle of self-sufficiency that founds the *polis* intact. In order to sustain the *polis*, one needs goods but the acquisition of what is useful is not the end of the city. Thus, Aristotle says in Book VII: "Living happily ... is available to those who have in excess the adornments of character and intellect (*dianoia*) but behave moderately in respect to the external acquisition of good things" (1323b3-6).

IV. The Place of Women in Aristotle's *Polis*

Aristotle acknowledges that free people include men, women, and children. But there are differences in kind among free citizens and not all participate in the *polis* in the same way. Aristotle insists that both women and children, having achieved the capacity for *logos* and being capable of self-sufficiency, should be educated and participate thereby in a flourishing, virtuous life. He points out that, after all, women are half the population so that if the regime is to be good, one cannot create a situation where half the population are prevented from achieving excellence. But human excellence is not one-dimensional and the rule of *logos* can occur in many ways. Each of these groups, men, women, and children, not only belong to the whole of the *polis*—they are also part of it. So the whole-parts structure is again operative here. It is with a view to the whole that each of the parts has its proper role and place in the *polis*. Aristotle suggests benevolent kingship is the appropriate model of rule for parents in relationship to children. But between husband and wife, the model of rule is "political," that is, rule between equals. One would assume that this implies that as equals each of these gender-based groups of citizens would rule and be ruled by turns, and both men and women would be capable of holding both positions. And this is true, for, he says, "it is not possible to rule well without having been ruled" (1277b13), and the capacity for ruling and for being ruled are very different things. While granting that a free citizen needs both kinds of excellence, since self-rule means that one rules oneself and is thus both ruler and ruled, still, nonetheless, some of us are more inclined toward being ruled and others toward ruling, though both belong to the alternating circle of sovereignty. Aristotle arbitrates these distinctions on the basis of his earlier division of the parts of the soul. The man is more closely associated with the deliberative part of the soul, the ruling part. The woman has the power of deliberation, but it lacks authority, and she is more properly ruled than ruler—though both male and female, in principle, are capable of both ruling and being ruled. This allows Aristotle to again affirm one of the mainstays of his treatise, namely that even among free persons our souls and dispositions are not the same and in fact it is precisely this divergence that needs to be honored in the coming together of political regimes for the sake of the good of the whole. He argues on this basis that what counts as virtue is in each case situational and dependent on the person and the appropriate role of this person in the *polis*. He says:

> For it is clear that a virtue—the virtue of justice for example—would not be a single thing for a ruler and a ruled but free person who is good, but has different kinds in accordance with which one will rule and the other be ruled, just as moderation and courage differ in a man and a woman. For a man would be held a coward if he were as courageous as a courageous woman, and a woman talkative if she were as modest as a good man; and household management differs for a man and a woman as well, for it is the work of the man to acquire and of the woman to guard. But *phronēsis* is the only virtue peculiar to the ruler. The others it would seem must necessarily be common to both ruler and ruled, but practical wisdom is not a virtue of one ruled, but rather true opinion. (1277b16ff.)

Aristotle compares the city to a ship in which there are many sailors performing different roles and manifesting different virtues, though all nevertheless exemplifying in their peculiar way the virtue of the whole (1276b20-25). This is a difficult position for Aristotle to maintain, in my view, but it is crucial to his overall understanding of the *polis*. Belonging to the *polis* as a whole, which is how he repeatedly characterizes the political animal who has *logos* and holds herself self-sufficiently in the end, does not preclude locating oneself particularly in terms of one's particular contribution to the whole according to what is suitable to one's nature. Obeying the ruler, or in the case of the *polis* the law, does not, for example, necessarily make one subservient, unless it is by force or necessity that one is ruled. Being ruled can be a free expression of that part of the circle of sovereignty and self-rule that requires both ruling and being ruled together. While ruling oneself holds together both ruling and being ruled in one person, who takes charge of herself, in the city, many people come together and the activity of ruling and being ruled is distributed among different people, who are at least capable of taking turns, even if some, in Aristotle's view, are more disposed to ruling and others to being ruled. Just as the soul needs both, the intellect as ruling and the passions as being ruled, so also does the *polis*. In the model that Aristotle is proposing, there is a friendship and affection in the *polis* that puts these otherwise opposite roles in touch with each other so that activity and passivity, leading and receptivity, are reciprocal and codetermined as equal, just as there is no speaking without listening even though these are opposite roles. Aristotle argues that women are better suited for receptivity but a receptivity that freely yields the power that she has. In the end, Aristotle, however, agrees with a statement in Sophocles' *Ajax*: "To a woman, though not to a man, silence is an ornament" (1260a30). The woman who best fits among the citizens of the *polis* represses or is encouraged to repress the sovereign and authoritative aspect of her *logos*, part of the very trait that makes her human rather than a mere living being. And, Aristotle appears not to have realized that silence is the origin of speech.

V. Citizens in the Beautiful City

There is a passage from Book II that will help frame a discussion of the relationship between free citizens and about the politics of friendship, which I think is a somewhat hidden but major theme in the *Politics*. The passage is at 1261a15-25:

> It is evident that as the city becomes increasingly one it will no longer be a city. For the city is in its nature a sort of multitude, and as it becomes more of a unity it will be a household instead of a city, and a human being instead of a household. So even if one were able to do this, one ought not to do it, as it would destroy the city. Now the city is made up not only of a number of human beings, but also of human beings differing in kind: a city does not arise from persons who are similar. . . . It is thus reciprocal equality which preserves cities. . . . This is necessarily the case even among persons who are free and equal, for all cannot rule at the same time . . . some rule and some are ruled in turn, as if becoming other persons.

This notion of alternating between ruling and being ruled is probably one of the most famous resolutions of the dilemma in constituting a regime based on political equality.

I will return to this, but first wanted to address Aristotle's insistence in this passage that the genuine *polis* is a multiplicity and further that this multiplicity is not just numerical quantity but also one of quality, a multiplicity of kinds. In Chapter 3 of Book Two, Aristotle argues from another perspective that Plato fails to understand the difference between the whole and the parts. The "one" is not the same as the "whole." The whole does not destroy multiplicity; it permits multiplicity and makes multiplicity possible. Socrates commits the fallacy of the collective, according to Aristotle. He fails to recognize that the notion of "all" that is operative in the political *koinōnia* means each individually. This false notion of the collective "all" supposedly leads him to support common property rather than ownership. Aristotle argues that if everyone is my son, then no one is.

Aristotle asks what is the for sake of which for which the city is established in Chapter 6 of Book III. His answer is that the city is a partnership and community in life. That he means human life, and therefore *logos*, is obvious from what he says next: "Humans are by nature political animals. Hence they strive to live together even when they have no need of assistance from one another, though it is also the case that the common advantage brings them together, to the extent that it falls to each to live beautifully" (1278b20ff.).

This whole passage is incredible, but let me just pause here to note two points. The members of the political community do not need assistance from one another. This is not a coming together based on use or on exchange of goods. We are not together because I have bread you need and you have shoes that I need. And yet there is common advantage (*sumpherōn*). We have already seen that this word "advantage" is contrasted with its opposite, namely what is harmful. So why is it advantageous, in a way that is not useful, for us to be together? What benefit can there be for one who has achieved sovereign self-sufficiency to be with others? This question is a serious one for Aristotle, as we know from his *Ethics*. Aristotle says the genuine *polis* is a space for friendship. He speaks of the bonds that are formed and recognized by the *polis* and says:

> These bonds are the work of *philia*; for friendship is the *proairesis*, the intentional choice, of living together (*suzēn*). Living well is the end of the city, and these things are for the sake of this end. . . . The political partnership must be regarded, therefore, as being for the sake of beautiful actions, and not just for the sake of being alongside each other in a location. (1280 b38-1281 b4)

Aristotle indicates that it is not only mutual benefit as distinguished from use that brings us together but we also come together to live beautifully. Friendship offers us the beautiful life (1278 b22). Finally, in this same passage, he says:

> But we also come together for the sake of living itself. For there is perhaps something beautiful in living just by itself, provided there is no great excess of hardships. It is clear that most men will endure much hard treatment in their longing for life, the assumption being that there is a kind of joy inherent in it and a natural sweetness. (1278 b24ff.)[6]

So *logos* and the forethought and openness to choice between contraries that were the conditions for freedom from necessity and self-rule now are seen to open out toward others because they make it possible to live well, and to participate in beautiful actions that can be made manifest and allowed to shine forth in their beauty for others to see, and because we can better appreciate and experience the natural sweetness of life in this way. Because they are steadfast and sovereign, friends, Aristotle's citizens, love each other for their own sake rather than for a desire to gain from the relationship. The point is that the truly self-sufficient, happy person acts for the sake of the other, as Aristotle emphasizes throughout the *Politics*, since he or she has no need to gain from the action.[7]

Once Aristotle has resolved the question of why living together as free and equal persons is the proper expression of our autonomy and freedom, Aristotle begins the project of determining what kind of community or regime is best for the fulfillment of the happiness and self-expression of those who are members or citizens of the community. The fundamental decision that Aristotle makes is based on his model of self-rule. There is already in self-rule a double relationship to the self of ruling and being ruled. The identity of the self is already from the beginning a split identity in such a way that the sovereign self already experiences itself as relational. The self is absolutely sovereign only by virtue of drawing itself up into itself and apart from prior dependent relationships.[8] The structure is parallel to the one we saw earlier when we discussed how the human being who has *logos* is not merely life but a being that lives its life. When this sovereign self becomes a citizen and is living together with others in the shared space of the political, then ruling and being ruled, both of which belong together in the person, now needs to find its expression in the shared space of the political. Friendship is the way free people externalize themselves and experience themselves as outside and othered. Aristotle says the double character of *logos*, as both commanding and obeying and giving and receiving, is resolved by an arrangement in which the citizens are ruling and being ruled in turn. He says: "A citizen in the common sense is one who shares in ruling and being ruled; but he differs in accord with each regime. In the case of the best regime, he is one who is capable of and intentionally chooses being ruled and ruling with a view to a life according to virtue" (1283b44ff.). This taking turns is possible because of the double sense of self, a double sense that in time[9] can each in turn now gain expression. Already we can see how for Aristotle the friendship of those who are free citizens allows best of all for the possibility of a certain externalization of the experience of the self whereby we can recognize in the other who is now ruling ourselves as free rulers and vice versa. It is only when this arrangement of taking turns collapses and someone claims the permanent right to rule that the city as such is destroyed and tyranny takes its place.

The question with which I would like to close is: Does Aristotle's view of political friendship and vision of living well, as the space in which all the divisions and demarcations of inside and outside and belonging and not belonging are resolved by taking turns, adequately compensate for the vast structural network of inclusion and exclusion that we have seen he sets up on the way to this description of the natural sweetness of life that is experienced by free citizens?

Notes

1. For an alternative view of Aristotle's claim to the self-sufficiency of human beings in the *polis*, a reading of Aristotle based on the *Poetics* that emphasizes the tragic vulnerability of human beings in community, see "*Logos* and the *Polis* in the *Poetics*," by Patricia Fagan in this volume.
2. For a discussion of the importance of habit in the formation of human nature and its capacity to transcend natural necessity, see Russon, "'Actuality in the First Sense' and the Question of Human Nature in Aristotle," in this volume.
3. For an excellent discussion of the distinction between the animal voice and human speech (the orality of the human mouth) in the context of a broader discussion of Aristotle's *Parts of Animals*, see Diamond, "'For There Are Gods Here Too': Embodied Essence, Two-Footedness, and the Animal with Logos," in this volume.
4. Diamond, "For There Are Gods Here Too," makes clear the way in which Aristotle's notion of the living hand as an instrument of production plays a significant role in his understanding of the relationship of soul to body.
5. For an important discussion of Aristotle's treatment of slavery in relationship to his understanding of life, see Giorgi Agamben, *The Use of Bodies*, trans. Kotsko (Stanford, CA: Stanford University Press, 2014), 3–30.
6. See the commentary on this passage by Giorgio Agamben in *Homo Sacer: Sovereign Power and Bare Life,* trans. Heller-Roazen (Stanford, CA: Stanford University Press, 1998), 1–12.
7. This point is especially emphasized by Patricia Fagan, who develops a notion of care-based community out of Aristotle's treatment of tragedy and the role of *logos* in the *polis*. See "*Logos* and the *Polis* in the *Poetics*," in this volume.
8. See Jacque Derrida's *Rogues: Two Essays on Reason*, trans. Brault and Nass (Stanford, CA: Stanford University Press, 2005), for a discussion of ruling and being ruled by turns in Aristotle's *Politics*.
9. For an important discussion of Aristotle's understanding of temporal consciousness and its relationship to self-awareness and the incompleteness of the finite human being whose being is an issue for it, see Russon "Actuality in the First Sense," in this volume.

15

Logos and the *Polis* in the *Poetics*

Patricia Fagan

Introduction

For Aristotle, what marks human beings off from other animals most profoundly is our possession of *logos*. That word, *logos*, covers a great deal of ground: it is language and rationality; it is proportion and accounting for; it is story and word. To turn to the *Poetics*, then, when one thinks about Aristotle's discussions of *logos* makes good sense. Poetry is manifestly an activity and product of *logos* at its richest. What remains of the *Poetics* for the most part addresses itself to tragedy, a genre of performance poetry that flourished in Athens during the fifth century BC, produced for presentation to the Athenians at the annual festivals in honor of Dionysos. When we now think about Greek tragedy, we are more accurately (especially given what remains to us of tragedy) thinking about Athenian tragedy and, as we shall see, about Athenian *democratic* tragedy. Tragedy was a behavior and a product of language (of *logos*) and a behavior of the city-state, of the *polis*. We see in tragedy, then, a manifestation of another of Aristotle's distinguishing features of human beings, that we are by nature political. In what follows I attempt to unpack from the *Poetics* some implications of the fact that in tragedy we find something that is both of language and of the city.

Discussion of Aristotle's *Poetics* tends to focus on what that text tells us about a kind of literary interpretation of drama, drama essentially divorced from performance and, consequently, divorced from the life of the world that first produced tragedy.[1] That world is the world of democratic Athens during the fifth and fourth centuries, where tragedy functioned as a crucial and regular part of the life of the *polis*, Athens; the experience of drama for the Athenians was not, as it is for us now, elective or primarily for pleasure but a responsibility of the citizen *qua* citizen and part of *polis*-based religion. The watching of the plays was a *political activity*. Looking to Aristotle's definition of tragedy as a *mimēsis* (reenactment) of a *spoudaia praxis* (serious action) that accomplishes through pity and fear a *katharsis* (cleaning out) of those emotions, I want to explore how tragedy is political and how the goal of tragedy as Aristotle states it can be seen to be a political goal and a good for the *polis*.

I begin by providing some information about the context in which tragedy was performed in order to provide a fuller sense of what Aristotle is pointing at when he says *tragōidia* (tragedy) and of how, for the Athenians, tragedy was an activity of the *polis*. Tragedy was performed at two of the city festivals for Dionysos, most splendidly at the Great Dionysia. I will discuss some of the activities that surrounded the performance of the plays at this festival. This discussion will show how seamless the interconnection of the political, religious, and artistic was at the festival. I shall argue that when we bring these data about drama to bear on the *Poetics* that text becomes richer and its arguments about tragedy become farther-ranging in their implications. Having provided this information about tragedy, I shall look at two passages in the *Poetics* with some care. Those passages are Chapter 6, 1449 b20 ff., the definition of tragedy as *mimēsis* of a *praxis* (action with intention) that accomplishes through pity and fear (*di' eleos kai phobou*) the *katharsis* (cleaning out) of such emotions; and 14, 1453b10-15, where Aristotle says that the poet should produce through *mimēsis* (reenactment) the pleasure (*hēdonē*) that comes from pity and fear, which is the proper (*oikeia*) pleasure of tragedy. In each case, I shall explore how *mimēsis*, pity and fear, and the experience of the pleasure of pity and fear are activities and experiences that can be seen to serve the interests and well-being of the *polis*. We shall see that Aristotle's account of tragedy helps make clear the political function of tragedy in a humane and compelling way.

I. Drama and the *Polis* in Ancient Athens

The performance of drama (tragedy, comedy, and satyr play) in democratic Athens took place exclusively at the annual festivals in honor of Dionysos. The largest of these festivals was the Great Dionysia, created by the tyrant Peisistratos sometime between 540 and 535 BC. Peisistratos took a small rural festival of Dionysos and transplanted it to the city. He gave control over the new festival to the people (the *dēmos*) of Athens, that is, to the *polis*. This move was contrary to the usual practice in Greek city-states, in which priesthoods and the management of religious festivals were the exclusive privilege of the elite. Peisistratos' new Dionysos festival, then, undermined the traditional control that elite families had over the religious life of Athens. Peisistratos poured money into the new festival to ensure that it would succeed and take its place as a prestigious Athenian *polis*-based festival.[2] This new festival was one example of the many ways that Peisistratos, to secure his own position, undermined the position of the elite families and enhanced the prestige and influence of the *dēmos*: for example, an enormous building program on the acropolis to provide work for ordinary citizens and major reforms of Athens' judicial system to allow ordinary citizens more access to the protections of law. This new festival of Dionysos, then, began as a festival that celebrated the *polis* Athens (not elite families) and belonged to the people as the people of Athens.

The dramatic festival began as a way to enhance the *polis* as an institution and to undermine the role of kin-ties in the functioning of the city. This basic impetus took greater hold within Athens over the following decades until the institution of the first democratic constitution by Kleisthenes in 508/7 BC; the unifying feature of his reforms was similar to the unifying feature of Peisistratos' reforms: to enhance the *polis* at the expense of the family, especially the elite family. For example, Kleisthenes abolished the previous division of citizens into four tribes (*phulai*) based on kin-ties and installed a new organization of citizens into ten tribes based on location of residence; these new tribes reduced the influence of elite families in the workings of the *polis* as a whole.[3] In Athens, the tragic festival and democracy arose out of the same situation and the same concerns.[4]

As the festival grew and as its practices crystallized, the interconnection of the political, religious, and artistic emerged in a variety of ways. The plays were performed in a competition judged by the ten generals of Athens.[5] The production of the plays was funded by wealthy citizens as a *leitourgia*, a service to the people, which was a legal responsibility undertaken by the rich on behalf of the *polis*. Prior to the performance of the plays boys whose fathers had been killed in battle and who had reached the age of majority were brought into the theater and displayed with a full hoplite panoply. The message of these behaviors was, be impressed by the resources of Athens and by how the city will expend these resources for the benefit of the citizenry and notice that when the family fails (as in the case of the war orphans) the *polis* steps in to nourish and protect citizens who respond by serving the city in their turn.[6]

When we turn to the dramatic productions themselves we see similar messages. The plots of extant tragedies regularly tell the same story: problems within a royal household threaten the destruction of the entire *polis* and are effectively addressed only by *polis*-based institutions, especially religious rituals. We see this pattern in the *Oresteia*, the *Bacchae*, the *Antigone*, the *Ajax*, and in the *Medea*, for example; in *Medea* we see Medea's murder of her children atoned for and commemorated through the creation of an annual sacrifice to Hera.[7] The experience of watching a tragedy and the basic structure of the performance space participate in encouraging the audience to take up this message. Tragic plots are overwhelmingly drawn from heroic myth. The aristocratic figures from myth appear onstage, performed by masked actors, who were professionals; each character is distinguished from the others by mask and costume. The actors are elevated above the performance space of the chorus, the orchestra. The chorus members were amateurs, citizens performing in the chorus as part of the regular round of citizen activities. The chorus performers had no named individual identities but were identified as a group, such as citizens of Thebes or Asian slave women. Within the play, the social and political status of the chorus in the orchestra is lower than that of the major characters onstage.

Anthropologists have argued that this performance situation encouraged the audience to admire at but feel alienated from the hero/actor, while feeling identified with the chorus/citizens.[8] The audience also sees itself in the theater, where the seats were arranged in a semicircle. These elements of the performance context of tragedy indicate that, among many other things, the performance of tragedy was aimed at encouraging the citizens of Athens to feel their bond with each other as *citizens of Athens* and not as members of kin groups or families. The identification of citizen with citizen arose in part from the recognition of the goodwill and efficacy of the *polis* itself in nourishing and protecting citizens.[9]

II. Tragedy Is *Mimēsis* of a *Praxis*

This discussion of the performance context of tragedy helps us to see what it is that Aristotle is pointing at when he says "*tragōidia*." He is pointing at not just a body of texts but an Athenian religious and political institution.[10] In light of this larger sense of tragedy it is possible to see in the *Poetics* implications relevant to political thought. These implications, I shall argue, derive from a similar notion of the *identification* of audience and performer and audience and *polis*. Having laid out this more expansive notion of tragedy, I shall now come at Aristotle's basic statement, that tragedy is a *mimēsis* of a *praxis*, from a number of different angles to draw out the different senses in which we can see political implications in Aristotle's account of tragedy.

For Aristotle, *mimēsis* is the activity through which tragedy achieves its goal of producing *katharsis* of pity and fear in the audience (1449 b20 ff.). There are two particularly relevant parties here, the poet who crafts the text that is or will be the basis of the *mimēsis* and the audience that watches the *mimēsis*.[11] If we think about tragedy as aimed at an audience that is to be affected, we are, in an ancient Athenian context, thinking about tragedy as a behavior of the *polis*. Tragic performance is, apart from its role as art, a political and religious activity; it is primarily a political activity, given its place in a *polis*-based and *polis*-serving festival for Dionysos.[12] This political activity aims to make people in the audience feel joined with each other as *politai*, as fellow citizens, not as members of particular households, kin groups, and discrete networks of social allies; tragedy in performance seeks to foster ties between citizens.

Given the goals of tragic performance, one might expect that the content of the plays would aim at similar things. When we look at extant tragedy we discover that this is the case,[13] which implies that the *katharsis* of pity and fear from the audience members can also be seen to be a political goal that encourages us to identify with each other as fellow citizens. The word "*katharsis*" has two dominant uses in ancient Greek: a medical sense, as in purging from the body through emetics, and a ritual sense, as in purifying a place or person of a stain, usually a stain associated with a death; the medical sense of *katharsis* appears to be at play in the *Poetics*.[14] What occurs in tragic *katharsis* is the cleaning out or away of two emotions, pity and fear, from audience members and the rendering of audience members clear and ready for normal human interactions.

Tragedy is, Aristotle says, a *mimēsis* of a *praxis*, an action with intention. *Mimēsis* most basically means something like "reenactment"; it is a word that pertains especially to ritual.[15] As Aristotle notes, *mimēsis* is the reenactment of an *action*. Within ancient Greek ritual what we do most regularly is reenact the primordial crime for which the ritual we now annually perform atones.[16] This reenactment is now safe because it is performed within the controlled environment of ritual, because it is performed in the same way every time and because it has the same result every time: within ritual, nothing can happen that is unexpected, no human desires can erupt into unrestrained violence. Further, ritual activity and space take us out of our everyday selves and into the timeless time of ritual; the moment of the original crime is with us once again, as is each previous and subsequent performance of the ritual. Ritual, then, makes present to us our identity as a group with our past, with the past of our group; it marks our group as one and continuous over time. Finally, ritual makes present to us our individual dissolution into the timeless being that is our group. Tragic performance, taking place as part of a religious festival and religious rituals, participates in this transportation of its audience out of the everyday and into the timeless and enhanced world of ritual.[17]

The plots of tragedy came overwhelmingly from myth. Myth, like ritual, works through patterns of action.[18] Consequently, these mythic plots stress the regular, repeated, shared structures of human experience while at the same time they portray the unpredictable results that can occur when we act intentionally in *praxis*. For example, Orestes is sent away from home as an infant, returns home to kill his mother and claim his throne, but is driven away again before he can claim the throne. Oedipus is sent away as an infant, returns home to kill his father and marry his mother, and successfully claims his throne. Each of these stories follows the basic pattern of withdrawal and return of a youth who becomes an adult upon his return: the pattern of boy's initiation into adulthood. The reenactment of a *praxis* based on myth puts before us the sameness that is the traditional tale (every telling of an Oedipus story is a telling of an *Oedipus* story and is thus the same as the other tellings);[19] it puts before us the sameness of the patterns of action (we all recognize an initiatory withdrawal and return when we see it). It also puts before us the difference of one myth of initiation from another and, more significantly, the gap, the difference between the intention of and within an action and what can happen when particular human beings act with intention. We see at the least that our intentions can fail to be realized. In tragedy we see repeatedly how, in a world that is not subject to the dictates of our wills, what we intend can produce results beyond our expectations and contrary to our expectations. Oedipus, intending only to protect the city he rules, Thebes, by finding out the source of the pollution that causes the plague in his city, discovers that he himself is the source of the pollution because, not even knowing that he did it, let alone intending it, he killed his father and then married his mother. The mythic plot reveals to us the stable structures of our lives and the ways in which, despite that stability, we are always vulnerable to what we do not know and understand.[20] In tragedy, the mythic plot, whose resolution so often comes through the creation of *polis*-based institutions that address the dilemmas within the plot,[21] reveals to us that we are to some extent protected from this uncontrollable reality by our unity and corporate identity.

Tragedy, Aristotle says, is a *mimēsis* of a *praxis* that arouses pity and fear and achieves a *katharsis* of pity and fear that produces pleasure (*hēdonē*). It is the gap between what is intended in action and what actually happens that is critical for the arousing of pity and fear.[22] In the *Rhetoric* (II.8 1385b13 ff.) Aristotle says that pity (*eleos*) derives from our witnessing a disaster that befalls someone who does not deserve it and our feeling that we, too, or someone we care for, can, like the afflicted one we see, have the same experience; pity, then, is rooted in our identifying with its object. Fear (*phobos*) (*Rhet.* II.4 1382a15 ff.) is also a pain or disturbance that arises from witnessing something; in the case of fear we witness the image of some immediately impending disaster. The disaster, Aristotle says, is the kind of thing that makes a person feel *pity*. In each case pity or fear derives from *our ability to see ourselves in the afflicted other*. That is, we come to see the afflicted other as, in Greek terms, *philos* to us: as friend, dear, important, as one of our own.

Tragedy, Aristotle says, arouses pity and fear in the audience members. That is, they are made to feel pain through their seeing the characters on the stage as themselves; they see themselves implicated in the events enacted onstage. The sensation of pain aroused through watching the tragic action can itself be pleasurable in that, as spectators, we are basically safe from these events, which are themselves not *actual* deaths, betrayals, or wars, but reenactments in the tightly controlled context of the art and ritual of the drama. We can watch, feel pain, and learn from this experience something about what can happen when human beings act (*prattein*). This learning is itself a source of pleasure. The pain, though, is not primary: what is primary is seeing others as myself. If the tragedy does not achieve that sense of identification in its audience, then the audience will feel no pity, no fear, no pain. Tragic action, properly done, succeeds in achieving its ends by alerting us to the fact that we can see others as ourselves, that others matter to us.

What tragedy does, Aristotle says, is achieve a *katharsis* (a cleaning out) of pity and fear. It empties us of the pain, I suggest, by revealing to us the thing we know but are always forgetting in our lives outside of the festival theater: that we all matter to each other, that we all affect each other, that we all share something, and that we rely on each other. Having watched a tragedy as members of an audience leaves us immersed in a clear, emptied, recognition that we are all together, all vulnerable to the problems enacted in the play, all supported by our institutions and traditions. It leaves us with the profound pleasure that is experiencing ourselves as, knowing ourselves to be, with and for others.

I suggest that Aristotle's discussion of the goal of tragedy, of the *katharsis* of pity and fear, is at play at the level of the *polis* as a whole and not just at the level of intimate life between *philoi* (friends, dear ones). At the festival of Dionysos we share this experience with our fellow citizens. The pity and fear are aroused by the actions, usually, of characters who are *not* like us—by aristocrats in the distant past who are not our fellow citizens. In feeling pity and fear for these others we feel our ability to be attached to others outside of our immediate group of friends and family; we experience the fact that care extends beyond the kin group. In the moment that we feel this care for the outsider, we can recognize that we are enhanced by the fact that we are others; we are "taken out of ourselves" when we are in the moment of being others. This experience of being taken out of ourselves and of being others is the core of the madness, the *mania*, of Dionysos; it is the experience of the audience through pity and fear.[23]

Aristotle says, finally, that tragedy aims to arouse the pleasure (*hēdonē*) that is proper (*oikeia*) to it, which is the kind of pleasure that comes through pity and fear (1453b10-15). I have argued that the content of the pleasure that comes through pity and fear is our experience of a cleansed sense of identity with others, our experience of being taken out of our everyday selves into the timeless world of unity with our group and its institutions. The last thing that I want to note is that Aristotle marks what we get from watching tragedy as *pleasure*. According to *Nicomachean Ethics* 1153a, pleasures are activities that emerge from exercising our capacities. When these capacities are functioning at their best, pleasure is the completion of that functioning. In light of this notion of pleasure, what Aristotle is saying in the *Poetics* seems quite powerful. The proper pleasure of tragedy comes about when we recognize and experience our connection to other human beings; what this point reveals is that one of our capacities as human beings is this kind of identification with each other. In tragedy we see quite concretely one of the essential things that *logos* gives us, a path into the lives and experiences of others. Consequently, I suggest, one of the things that Aristotle is getting at in the *Poetics* is that as human beings we are, by nature, oriented toward each other.[24] This point is of course quite similar to Aristotle's claim in the *Politics* that human beings are by nature political animals (*Pol.* I.2 1253a1-8). The fundamental goal of tragedy is to compel us to experience that truth about ourselves in a context in which we are all in fact safe from the particularities of the everyday that cloud our recognition of ourselves in others. Tragedy reveals a truth of our human nature to us and forces us to feel the power and pleasure of our being human beings together.[25]

Conclusion

Aristotle's account of tragedy as the reenactment of an action that accomplishes a cleaning out of pity and fear and causes pleasure has allowed us to see the intimate connection between the human orientations toward language and storytelling and toward the organized group formation of the *polis*. In particular, as I have shown, we have seen that the historical realities of tragic performance at the Great Dionysia proclaimed tragedy as an activity of the *polis*, Athens; one of the fundamental goals of this political activity was to remind citizens in the audience of tragedy of bonds, beyond those of the family, that tied citizen to citizen and citizen to *polis*. I have shown that Aristotle's analysis of tragedy in the *Poetics* is consistent with and enhances our understanding of the political activity of tragedy in performance. Beginning with Aristotle's account of tragedy as the *mimēsis* of a *praxis* (as the reenactment of an action with intention), I have shown that in tragedy we see the reenactment of mythic patterns of action that remind an audience of shared aspects of human life and experience as well as of human vulnerability to what is beyond our control. Aristotle notes of tragedy that it reminds us of what we share by causing us to feel pity and fear at what is onstage; these emotions, for Aristotle, proceed from our human ability to identify with and feel implicated in other human beings; witnessing the reenactment of failure of intention we come to feel that identification. In Aristotle's account of tragedy, as I have shown, we can see a political implication to the catharsis of pity and fear in that the eliciting and cleaning out of these emotions reveal to audience members their ability to care for people who are, as is the case with the actors on the tragic stage, radically other (as foreigners, as royalty, as members of the race of heroes), reminding the audience of its care for those who are its own. Successful tragedy, Aristotle says, arouses its own proper pleasure; I have shown, finally, that this pleasure proceeds from the fact of a natural human orientation toward other human beings and toward care for others. What the *Poetics* helps us to see, then, is the ground out of which the claim of the *Politics* that the human being is by nature a political animal works: we are political because we care about and rely upon each other and because this care and reliance are enacted through creation of and participation in institutions of *logos* like the tragic festivals.

Notes

1 See, for example, John Jones, *On Aristotle and Greek Tragedy* (Stanford University Press, 1980); Leon Golden, *Aristotle on Tragic and Comic Mimesis* (Scholars Press, 1992); Amélie Oksenberg Rorty, ed., *Essays on Aristotle's Poetics* (Princeton University Press, 1992); Malcolm Heath, "Cognition in Aristotle's *Poetics*," *Mnemosyne* 62 (2009): 51–75. Recent exceptions are Gregory Michael Sifakis's, *Aristotle on the Function of Tragic Poetry* (Crete University Press, 2001), and Marina Berzina McCoy's discussion of the *Poetics* in *Wounded Heroes: Vulnerability as a Virtue in Ancient Greek Literature and Philosophy* (Oxford University Press, 2013).
2 For the most thorough discussion of all aspects of the performance and production of ancient Greek drama, see Eric Csapo and William Slater, *The Context of Ancient Drama* (University of Michigan Press, 1995).
3 See Victor Ehrenberg, *From Solon to Socrates: Greek History and Civilization during the Sixth and Fifth Centuries BC* (Routledge, 1989).
4 See, for example, Josiah Ober, *Mass and Elite in Democratic Athens: Rhetoric, Ideology, and the Power of the People* (Princeton University Press, 1991).
5 The office of *stratēgos* (general) was the most politically powerful office in democratic Athens and one of the very few chosen by election rather than sortition. The Athenians elected one general from each of the ten tribes annually; the Kleisthenic system mitigated even here the amalgamation of power by self-interested groups.
6 For a thorough and enlightening discussion of these and other activities at the Great Dionysia, see Simon Goldhill, "The Great Dionysia and Civic Ideology," *Journal of Hellenic Studies* 107 (1987): 58–76. See also Nicole Loraux, *The Invention of Athens: The Funeral Oration in the Classical City*, trans. Alan Sheridan (Zone Books, 2006), for an examination of tragedy's insistence on democratic freedom in opposition to tyrannic or oligarchic rule.
7 Richard Seaford, *Reciprocity and Ritual: Homer and Tragedy in the Developing City-State* (Oxford University Press, 1994), provides a full account of tragedy and democracy.
8 See, for example, Jean-Pierre Vernant and Pierre Vidal-Naquet, *Mythe et tragédie en Grèce ancienne* (Éditions La Découverte, 1972).
9 For a helpful discussion of the role of tragedy in the religious life of ancient Athens, see Robert Parker, *Polytheism and Society at Athens* (Oxford University Press, 2005).
10 Aristotle does argue, in his discussion of the parts of tragedy and their functions (*Poetics* 1449b-1450b), that the performance aspects (song and spectacle) contribute the least to the creation of a good tragedy. I am not arguing here that the *Poetics* addresses itself to the performance aspects and to the performance context within the Dionysos festivals. Rather, I am suggesting that Aristotle's analysis of tragedy allows us to think about these other matters in an enhanced way. Further, while it is the case that Aristotle's analysis focuses on those aspects of tragedy that reside solely in the texts of tragedy (plot, character, diction, and thought), the texts of extant tragedy do demonstrably locate themselves somewhere within democratic ideology and were

composed in order to be performed at festivals run by and for the *polis*. See Simon Goldhill, "Civic Ideology and the Problem of Difference: The Politics of Aeschylean Tragedy, Once Again," *Journal of Hellenic Studies* 120 (2000): 34–56.
11 In the *Poetics* Aristotle talks more about texts and poets than he does about production.
12 Indeed, in Greek religion generally, the relationship served by religious activity was that between the city-state and its gods. See Walter Burkert, *Greek Religion* (Harvard University Press, 1985), and *Homo Necans: The Anthropology of Ancient Greek Sacrificial Ritual and Myth*, trans. Peter Bing (University of California Press, 1983).
13 Keeping in mind here the basic structure of tragic plots: problems caused by royal households threaten everyone within a group and are addressed only by *polis*-based institutions.
14 I would like to suggest that some element of the religious sense is resonant with Aristotle's use of the word "*katharsis*" at *Poetics* 1450b. In ritual *katharsis* is a cleaning out of pollution or *miasma*; in general, it is the cleansing out of the pollution of murder or death. In each of these cases the *katharsis* takes a house or a person that has been rendered untouchable and makes that house or person capable of proper and normal interaction with other houses and people. The polluted, until purified, must be isolated from other members of its group. *Katharsis*, in some sense, then, takes what has been removed from the community of the *polis* and makes it political again. See Robert Garland, *The Greek Way of Death* (Cornell University Press, 2001).
15 See the classic analysis of Erich Auerbach in *Mimesis: The Representation of Reality in Western Literature*, trans. Willard R. Trask (Princeton University Press, 2003). See also René Girard, *Violence and the Sacred*, trans. Patrick Gregory (Johns Hopkins University Press, 1977); Gregory Nagy, *Poetry as Performance: Homer and Beyond* (Cambridge University Press, 1996). In his article in this volume, Eli Diamond discusses how the basic form of human embodiment, as two-footed, is what, for Aristotle, gives rise to our *logos*. Tragic performance is in part a telling of the story through bodily movement and sound; the effect of tragedy on its audience in large part derives from that immediate sensory experience (sounds, sights, perhaps even the smells within the theater) of the traditional story.
16 See Walter Burkert, "Greek Tragedy and Sacrificial Ritual," *Greek, Roman and Byzantine Studies* 7 (1966): 87–121.
17 Compare here Russon, "Actuality in the First Sense," in this volume. Russon notes that, for Aristotle, human nature reaches its fulfillment in the *polis* through the development of a history of practices. The *polis* is the context for and the result of people, as individuals and as the group that forms the *polis*, living through structures and commitments that grow and persist over time. The dramatic festivals are an example of one such *shared* history of practices.
18 See Walter Burkert, *Structure and History in Greek Mythology and Ritual* (University of California Press, 1982).
19 See A. B. Lord, *The Singer of Tales* (Harvard University Press, 1981), for the classic account of the traditional and experienced sameness of all told versions of a myth.
20 See Diamond, "For There Are Gods Here Too," in this volume. Diamond discusses Aristotle's accounts of three distinct kinds of human thinking: theoretical, practical, and productive (*nous poiētikos*). It seems possible to me that, in *Poetics*, we see a fourth kind of thinking emerge: storytelling thinking, which is distinctly human and distinctly of humans within groups.

21 For example, the problems of kin-killing in Aeschylus' *Oresteia* are addressed by the creation of jury-courts in Athens; the anger of Oedipus is made productive for the *polis* by his adoption into cult in Athens in Sophocles' *Oedipus at Colonus*; the royal family's refusal to accept new gods is atoned by the institution of *polis*-based worship of Dionysos in Euripides' *Bacchae*.
22 I am indebted to the insights of Dennis J. Schmidt in *On Germans and Other Greeks: Tragedy and Ethical Life* (Indiana University Press, 2001), for clarifying my thinking on this question.
23 See the entry-song of the chorus in Euripides' *Bacchae* (64–169) for an articulation of the nature of Dionysiac *mania*. Sensitive analyses of Dionysiac *mania* appear in Marcel Detienne, *Dionysos at Large*, trans. Arthur Goldhammer (Harvard University Press, 1989), and Albert Henrichs, "'He Has a God in Him': Human and Divine in Modern Perceptions of Dionysos," in *Masks of Dionysus*, ed. Thomas H. Carpenter and Christopher Faraone (Cornell University Press, 1993).
24 Compare here Russon, "Actuality in the First Sense." Russon argues that humans, in our ability to think about and ask questions about our lives and about meaning within our lives, "experience ourselves as beings of possibility." Tragic performance, I am arguing, serves to put in front of us some of the possibilities that confront us; it does this work through compelling us to witness these possibilities in the experiences of the characters onstage and through sharing our witnessing with our fellow citizens in the audience.
25 In her article in this volume, "Aristotle on the Rationality of Virtue," Rabinoff argues that, for Aristotle, the virtuous person exercises *logos* and experiences emotions that are ordered by and somehow obedient to the dictates of *logos*. *Logos* and emotions are not simply distinct; instead the emotions of the virtuous, since they are the emotion of a human being, of an animal with *logos*, have learned, essentially, to cooperate with *logos*. Part of what I am getting at here is that the tragic festivals work in the interests of the *polis* to try to cultivate and teach the emotions of the individual citizens within the audience to orient themselves toward the *logos* of the city.

Bibliography

Achtenberg, Deborah. *Cognition of Value in Aristotle's Ethics: Promise of Enrichment, Threat of Destruction*. Albany, NY: State University of New York Press, 2002.

Ackrill, J. L. "Aristotle's Definitions of psuchē." *Proceedings of the Aristotelian Society* 73 (1973): 119–33. Reprinted in *Articles on Aristotle Vol 4: Psychology and Aesthetics*. Edited by Jonathan Barnes, Malcolm Schofield, and Richard Sorabji, 65–75. Bristol Classical Press, 1979.

Aeschylus. *Seven Against Thebes*. Translated by Alan H. Sommerstein. Cambridge, MA: Harvard University Press, 2009.

Agamben, Giorgio. *Homo Sacer: Sovereign Power and Bare Life*. Translated by Daniel Heller-Roazen. Stanford, CA: Stanford University Press, 1998.

Agamben, Giorgio. *The Use of Bodies*. Translated by Adam Kotsko. Stanford, CA: Stanford University Press, 2014.

Al Farabi. *Commentary and Short Treatise on Aristotle's De Interpretatione*. Translated by F. W. Zimmermann. Oxford: Oxford University Press, 1988.

Allard-Nelson, Susan K. "Virtue in Aristotle's Rhetoric: A Metaphysical and Ethical Capacity." *Philosophy & Rhetoric* 34, no. 3 (2001): 245–59.

Annas, Julia. "Aristotle on Pleasure and Goodness." In *Essays on Aristotle's Ethics*, edited by Amélie Oksenberg Rorty, 285–300. Berkeley, CA: University of California Press, 1980.

Aquinas, Thomas. *Summa Contra Gentiles*. Translated by Anton C. Pegis as *On the Truth of the Catholic Faith*. Garden City, NY: Doubleday, 1955.

Aristotle. *Analytica Priora et Posteriora*. Edited by Sir David Ross and L. Minio-Paluello. Oxford: Oxford University Press, 1981.

Aristotle. *Ars Rhetorica*. Edited by Sir David Ross. Oxford: Oxford University Press, 1959. Translated as *The Art of Rhetoric* by J. H. Reese. Loeb Classical Library, 1926; as "Rhetoric." In *The Complete Works of Aristotle: The Revised Oxford Translation*, Vol 2, edited by Jonathan Barnes, translated by W. Rhys Roberts, 2152–269. Princeton, NJ: Princeton University Press, 1984; and as "Rhetorica." In *The Basic Works of Aristotle*, edited by Richard McKeon, translated by W. Rhys Roberts, 1325–451. New York: Random House, 1941.

Aristotle. *Categoriae et Liber de Interpretatione*. Edited by L. Minio-Paluello. Oxford: Oxford University Press, 1936. Translated as "Categories." In *The Complete Works of Aristotle: The Revised Oxford Translation*, Vol. 1, edited by Jonathan Barnes, translated by J. L. Ackrill, 3–24. Princeton, NJ: Princeton Universtiy Press, 1984.

Aristotle. *De Anima*. Edited by Sir David Ross. Oxford: Oxford University Press, 1956. Translated as *De Anima*, edited with an introduction and commentary by Sir David Ross. Oxford: Oxford University Press, 1961; as "De Anima." In *The Basic Works of Aristotle*, edited by Richard McKeon, translated by J. A. Smith, 535–603. New York: Random House, 1941; as "On the Soul." In *The Complete Works of Aristotle: The Revised Oxford Translation*, Vol. 1, edited by Jonathan Barnes, translated by J. A. Smith, 641–92. Princeton, NJ: Princeton University Press, 1984; as *On the Soul*, translated by Joe Sachs. New York: Green Lion Press, 2004.

Aristotle. *De Arte Poetica Liber*. Edited by Rudolph Kassel. Oxford: Oxford University Press, 1922.
Aristotle. "De Interpretatione." In *The Complete Works of Aristotle: The Revised Oxford Translation*, Vol. 1, edited by Jonathan Barnes, translated by J. L. Ackrill, 25–38. Princeton, NJ: Princeton University Press, 1984.
Aristotle. *De Partibus Animalium I and De Generatione Animalium*. Translated with Notes by D. M. Balme. Oxford: Clarendon Press, 1972. Translated as "Parts of Animals." In *The Complete Works of Aristotle: The Revised Oxford Translation*, Vol. 1, edited by Jonathan Barnes, translated by W. Ogle, 994–1086. Princeton, NJ: Princeton University Press, 1984.
Aristotle. *Ethica Eudemia*. Edited by R. R. Walzer and J. M. Mingay. Oxford: Oxford University Press, 1991. Translated as "Eudemian Ethics." In *The Complete Works of Aristotle: The Revised Oxford Translation*, Vol. 2, edited by Jonathan Barnes, translated by J. Solomon, 1922–1981. Princeton, NJ: Princeton University Press, 1984; as *Eudemian Ethics*, edited and translated by Brad Inwood and Raphael Woolf. Cambridge: Cambridge University Press, 2013.
Aristotle. *Ethica Nicomachea*. Edited by I. Bywater. Oxford: Oxford University Press, 1920. Translated as "Ethica Nicomachea." In *The Basic Works of Aristotle*, edited by Richard McKeon, translated by W. D. Ross, 935–1112. New York: Random House, 1941; as "Nicomachean Ethics." In *The Complete Works of Aristotle: The Revised Oxford Translation*, Vol. 2, edited by Jonathan Barnes, translated by W. D. Ross, 1729–867. Princeton, NJ: Princeton University Press, 1984; as *Nicomachean Ethics*, translated by Joe Sachs. Newbury, MA: Focus Publishing, 2002; as *Nicomachean Ethics*, edited and Translated by R. C. Bartlett and S. D. Collins. Chicago, IL: University of Chicago Press, 2011.
Aristotle. "History of Animals." In *The Complete Works of Aristotle: The Revised Oxford Translation*, Vol. 1, edited by Jonathan Barnes, translated by d'A. W. Thompson, 774–993. Princeton, NJ: Princeton University Press, 1984.
Aristotle. *Metaphysica*. Edited by Werner Jaeger. Oxford: Oxford University Press, 1957. Translated as "Metaphysics." In *The Complete Works of Aristotle: The Revised Oxford Translation*, Vol. 2, edited by Jonathan Barnes, translated by W. D. Ross, 1522–728. Princeton, NJ: Princeton University Press, 1984; as *Metaphysics*. Translated by Joe Sachs. Santa Fe, NM: Green Lion Press, 2002.
Aristotle. "Meteorology." In *The Complete Works of Aristotle: The Revised Oxford Translation*, Vol. 1, edited by Jonathan Barnes, translated by E. W. Webster, 555–625. Princeton, NJ: Princeton University Press, 1984.
Aristotle. "Movement of Animals." In *The Complete Works of Aristotle: The Revised Oxford Translation*, Vol 1, edited by Jonathan Barnes, translated by W. D. Ross, 1087–96. Princeton, NJ: Princeton University Press, 1984.
Aristotle. "On Generation and Corruption." In *The Complete Works of Aristotle: The Revised Oxford Translation*, Vol. 1, edited by Jonathan Barnes, translated by H. H. Joachim, 512–54. Princeton, NJ: Princeton University Press, 1984.
Aristotle. "On the Heavens." In *The Complete Works of Aristotle: The Revised Oxford Translation*, Vol. 1, edited by Jonathan Barnes, translated by J. L. Stocks, 447–511. Princeton, NJ: Princeton University Press, 1984.
Aristotle. "On Youth, Old Age, Life and Death, and Respiration." In *The Complete Works of Aristotle: The Revised Oxford Translation*, Vol. 1, edited by Jonathan Barnes, translated by G. R. T. Ross, 745–63. Princeton, NJ: Princeton University Press, 1984.
Aristotle. *Physica*. Edited by Sir David Ross. Oxford: Oxford University Press, 1951. Translated as "Physics." In *The Complete Works of Aristotle: The Revised Oxford*

Translation, Vol. 1, edited by Jonathan Barnes, translated by R. P. Hardie and R. K. Gaye, 315–446. Princeton, NJ: Princeton University Press, 1984.

Aristotle. *Politica*, edited by Sir David Ross. Oxford: Oxford University Press, 1957. Translated as "Politica." In *The Basic Works of Aristotle*, edited by Richard McKeon, translated by Benjamin Jowett, 1113–316. New York: Random House, 1941; as "Politics." In *Aristotle: The Politics and the Constitution of Athens*, edited by Stephen Everson, translated by Benjamin Jowett. Cambridge: Cambridge University Press, 1996; as *Politics*. Translated by Joe Sachs. Focus Publishing, 2012.

Aristotle. "Sense and Sensibilia." In *The Complete Works of Aristotle: The Revised Oxford Translation*, Vol. 1, edited by Jonathan Barnes, translated by J. I. Beare, 693–713. Princeton, NJ: Princeton University Press, 1984.

Aristotle. "Topics." In *The Complete Works of Aristotle: The Revised Oxford Translation*, Vol. 1, edited by Jonathan Barnes, translated by W. A. Pickard-Cambridge, 167–277. Princeton, NJ: Princeton University Press, 1984.

Auerbach, Erich. *Mimesis: The Representation of Reality in Western Literature*. Translated by Willard R. Trask. Princeton, NJ: Princeton University Press, 2003.

Aygün, Ömer. "L'être humain, animal précaire. *Eukhē* chez Aristote." In *Aristote, l'animal politique*, edited by Refik Güremen and Annick Jaulin, 121–37. Publications de la Sorbonne, 2017.

Aygün, Ömer. "On Bees and Humans." *Epoche* 17, no. 2 (2013): 337–50.

Aygün, Ömer. *The Middle Included: Logos in Aristotle's Philosophy*. Evanston, IL: Northwestern University Press, 2017.

Bailly, Anatole. *Dictionnaire Grec-Français*. Paris: Hachette, 2000.

Balme, D. M. "Aristotle's Use of Differentiae in Zoology." In *Articles on Aristotle I. Science*, edited by edited by Jonathan Barnes, Malcolm Schofield, and Richard Sorabji, 183–93. London: Duckworth, 1975.

Berti, Enrico. "Multiplicity and Unity of Being in Aristotle." *Proceedings of the Aristotelian Society, New Series* 101 (2001): 185–207.

Block, Irving. "Truth and Error in Aristotle's Theory of Sense Perception." *The Philosophical Quarterly* 11, no. 42 (1961): 1–9.

Bobonich, Chris. "Nicomachean Ethics VII.7: *Akrasia* and Self-Control." In *Aristotle: Nicomachean Ethics, Book VII. Symposium Aristotelicum*, edited by Carlo Natali, 130–56. Oxford: Oxford University Press, 2009.

Bolton, Robert. "Scepticisme et véracité dans le *De Anima* et *La Métaphysique* d'Aristote." In *Corps et âme: Sur le De Anima d'Aristote*, edited by G. Romeyer-Dherbey and C. Viano, 295–330. VRIN, 1996.

Bouchard, Frédéric and Philippe Huneman (eds). *From Groups to Individuals: Evolution and Emerging Individuality*. Cambridge, MA: MIT Press, 2013.

Bradshaw, David. "Aristotle on Perception: The Dual-Logos Theory." *Apeiron* 30, no. 2 (1997): 143–61.

Brague, Rémi. *Aristote et la question du monde: essai sur le contexte cosmologique et anthropologique de l'ontologie*. Paris: Presses Universitaires de France, 1988.

Brogan, Walter. *Heidegger and Aristotle: The Twofoldness of Being*. Albany, NY: State University of New York Press, 2005.

Buck, Carl. *Comparative Grammar of Greek and Latin*. Chicago, IL: University of Chicago Press, 1933.

Burkert, Walter. *Greek Religion*. Cambridge, MA: Harvard University Press, 1985.

Burkert, Walter. "Greek Tragedy and Sacrificial Ritual." *Greek, Roman and Byzantine Studies* 7 (1966): 87–121.

Burkert, Walter. *Homo Necans: The Anthropology of Ancient Greek Sacrificial Ritual and Myth*. Translated by Peter Bing. Berkeley, CA: University of California Press, 1983.

Burkert, Walter. *Structure and History in Greek Mythology and Ritual*. Berkeley, CA: University of California Press, 1982.

Burnyeat, Myles. "Aristotle on Learning to Be Good." In *Essays on Aristotle's Ethics*, edited by Amélie Oksenberg Rorty, 69–92. Berkeley, CA: University of California Press, 1980.

Burnyeat, Myles. "Aristotle on Understanding Knowledge." In *Aristotle on Science: "The Posterior Analytics,"* edited by E. Berti, 97–139. Cambridge, MA: Harvard University Press, 1981.

Burnyeat, Myles. "Is an Aristotelian Philosophy of Mind Still Credible?" In *Essays on Aristotle's De Anima*, edited by Martha Nussbaum and Amélie Oksenberg Rorty, 15–26. New York: Clarendon Press, 1995.

Cassin, Barbara. "*Logos* et Politique: Politique, rhétorique et sophistique chez Aristote." In *Aristote politique, études sur la Politique d'Aristote*, edited by Pierre Aubenque, 367–98. Paris: Presses Universitaires de France, 1993.

Charles, David. "Nicomachean Ethics VII.3: Varieties of *Akrasia*." In *Aristotle: Nicomachean Ethics, Book VII. Symposium Aristotelicum*, edited by Carlo Natali, 41–71. Oxford: Oxford University Press, 2009.

Coles, Andrew. "Biomedical Models of Reproduction in the Fifth Century BC and Aristotle's *Generation of Animals*." *Phronesis* 40, no. 1 (1995): 48–88.

Coope, Ursula. "Why Does Aristotle Think that Ethical Virtue Is Necessary for Practical Wisdom?" *Phronesis* 57 (2012): 142–63.

Corcilius, Klaus and Pavel Gregoric. "Separability vs. Difference: Parts and Capacities of the Soul in Aristotle." *Oxford Studies in Ancient Philosophy* 39 (2010): 81–120.

Csapo, Eric and William Slater. *The Context of Ancient Drama*. Ann Arbor, MI: University of Michigan Press, 1995.

Curren, Randall R. *Aristotle on the Necessity of Public Education*. Lanham, MD: Rowman and Littlefield, 2000.

Darwin, Charles. *The Expression of the Emotions in Man and Animals*. Oxford/New York: Oxford University Press, 1998.

Depew, David J. "Politics, Music, and Contemplation in Aristotle's Ideal State." In *A Companion to Aristotle's Politics*, edited by Fred Dycus Miller and David Keyt, 346–80. Oxford: B. Blackwell, 1991.

Derrida, Jacques. *Rogues: Two Essays on Reason*. Translated by Pascale-Anne Brault and Michael Naas. Stanford, CA: Stanford University Press, 2005.

Derrida, Jacques. *The Animal that Therefore I Am*. Translated by David Wills. New York: Fordham University Press, 2008.

Destrée, Pierre. "Education, Leisure, and Politics." In *The Cambridge Companion to Aristotle's Politics*, edited by Marguerite Deslauriers and Pierre Destrée, 301–23. New York: Cambridge University Press, 2013.

Detienne, Marcel. *Dionysos at Large*. Translated by Arthur Goldhammer. Cambridge, MA: Harvard University Press, 1989.

Dewey, John. *Democracy and Education: An Introduction to the Philosophy of Education*. Los Angeles, CA: Hardpress Publishing, 2016.

Diamond, Eli. *Mortal Imitations of Divine Life: The Nature of Soul in Aristotle's De Anima*. Evanston, IL: Northwestern University Press, 2015.

Dunne, Joseph. *Back to the Rough Ground: Phronesis and Techne in Modern Philosophy and in Aristotle*. London: University of Notre Dame Press, 1993.

Düring, Ingemar. *Aristotle in the Ancient Biographical Tradition*. Stockholm: Almqvist & Wiksell, 1957.

Dyscolus, Apollonius. *Syntax*. Translated by F. W. Householder. Amsterdam: John Benjamins Publishing Company, 1981.

Ehrenberg, Victor. *From Solon to Socrates: Greek History and Civilization During the Sixth and Fifth Centuries BC*. London and New York: Routledge, 1989.

Everson, Stephen. *Aristotle on Perception*. Oxford: Clarendon Press, 1997.

Euripides. *Phoenician Women*. Translated by David Kovacs. Cambridge, MA: Harvard University Press, 2002.

Fortenbaugh, Williams W. "Aristotle's Distinction between Moral Virtue and Practical Wisdom." In *Essays in Ancient Greek Philosophy IV: Aristotle's Ethics*, edited by John P. Anton and Anthony Preus, 97–106. Albany, NY: State University of New York Press, 1991.

Fortenbaugh, Williams W. "Aristotle's Conception of Moral Virtue and Its Perceptive Role." *Transactions and Proceedings of the American Philological Association* 95 (1964): 77–87.

Fortenbaugh, Williams W. *Aristotle's Practical Side: On His Psychology, Ethics, Politics and Rhetoric*. Leiden/Boston: Brill, 2006.

Frede, Dorothea. "The Political Character of Aristotle's Ethics." In *The Cambridge Companion to Aristotle's Politics*, edited by Marguerite Deslauriers and Pierre Destrée, 14–37. Cambridge: Cambridge University Press, 2013.

Frede, Michael. "Aristotle's Rationalism." In *Rationality in Greek Thought*, edited by Michael Frede and Gisela Striker, 157–73. Oxford: Oxford University Press, 1996.

Freudenthal, Gad. *Aristotle's Theory of Material Substance: Heat and Pneuma, Form and Soul*. Oxford: Oxford University Press, 1995.

Furth, Montgomery *Substance, Form and Psyche: An Aristotelean Metaphysics*. Cambridge: Cambridge University Press, 1988.

Gadamer, Hans-Georg. *Hermeneutics, Religion and Ethics*. Translated by Joel Weinsheimer. New Haven/London: Yale University Press, 1999.

Gadamer, Hans-Georg. "Man and Language." In *Philosophical Hermeneutics*, translated by David E. Linge, 59–68. Berkeley, CA: University of California Press, 1976.

Garland, Robert. *The Greek Way of Death*. Ithaca: Cornell University Press, 2001.

Garver, Eugene. "Growing Older and Wiser with Aristotle: *Rhetoric* II.12-14 and Moral Development." In *Proceedings of the Boston Area Colloquium in Ancient Philosophy*, Vol. X, edited by John J. Cleary and William Wians, 171–200. 2004.

Girard, René. *Violence and the Sacred*. Translated by Patrick Gregory. Johns Hopkins University Press, 1977.

Golden, Leon. *Aristotle on Tragic and Comic Mimesis*. Atlanta: Scholars Press, 1992.

Goldhill, Simon. "Civic Ideology and the Problem of Difference: The Politics of Aeschylean Tragedy, Once Again." *Journal of Hellenic Studies* 120 (2000): 34–56.

Goldhill, Simon. "The Great Dionysia and Civic Ideology." *Journal of Hellenic Studies* 107 (1987): 58–76.

Gottlieb, Paula. "Aristotle on Dividing the Soul and Uniting the Virtues." *Phronesis* 39, no 3 (1994): 275–90.

Gregorić, Pavel. "Plato and Aristotle's Explanation of Human Posture." *Rhizai: Journal for Ancient Philosophy and Science* 2, no. 1–2 (2005): 183–96.

Halls, Doug. *Aristotle on Music*. 2012. [Unpublished Manuscript].

Hamlyn, D. W. *De Anima Books II and III*. Translation and commentary. Oxford: Oxford University Press, 1968.

Heath, Malcolm. "Cognition in Aristotle's *Poetics*." *Mnemosyne* 62 (2009): 51–75.
Heidegger, Martin. *Being and Time*. Translated by John Macquarrie and Edward Robinson. New York: Harper and Row, 1962.
Heidegger, Martin. *Grundbegriffe der aristotelischen Philosophie*. GA 18. Frankfurt am Main: Vittorio Klostermann, 2002. Translated as *Basic Concepts of Aristotelian Philosophy*, by Robert Metcalf and Mark Tanzer. Bloomington/Indianapolis: Indiana University Press, 2009.
Henrichs, Albert. "'He Has a God in Him': Human and Divine in Modern Perceptions of Dionysos." In *Masks of Dionysus*, edited by Thomas H. Carpenter and Christopher Faraone. Cornell University Press, 1993.
Hicks, R. D. *Aristotle: De Anima*. Cambridge: Cambridge University Press, 1907.
Hitz, Zena. "Aristotle on Law and Moral Education." In *Oxford Studies in Ancient Philosophy XLII*, edited by Brad Inwood, 263–306. Oxford: Oxford University Press, 2012.
House, D. K. "Did Aristotle Understand Plato?" *Dionysius* 17 (1999): 7–25.
Inwood, Brad. *Ethics and Human Action in Early Stoicism*. Oxford: Clarendon Press, 1995.
Irwin, T. H. "Aristotle on Reason, Desire, and Emotion." *The Journal of Philosophy* 72, no. 17 (1975): 567–78.
Johansen, T. K. *Aristotle on the Sense-Organs*. Cambridge: Cambridge Classical Studies, 1998.
Johansen, T. K. "In Defense of Inner Sense: Aristotle on Perceiving that One Perceives." *Proceedings of the Boston Area Colloquium in Ancient Philosophy* 21 (2005): 235–76.
Jonas, Hans. "The Nobility of Sight." *Philosophy and Phenomenological Research* 14, no. 4 (1954): 507–19.
Jones, John. *On Aristotle and Greek Tragedy*. Stanford, CA: Stanford University Press, 1980.
Kahn, Charles H. "Aristotle on Thinking." In *Essays on Aristotle's De Anima*, edited by Martha Nussbaum and Amélie Oksenberg Rorty, 359–79. New York: Clarendon, 1995.
Kamtekar, Rachana. "Speaking with the Same Voice as Reason: Personification in Plato's Psychology." *Oxford Studies in Ancient Philosophy* 31 (2006): 167–202.
Kietzmann, Christian. "Aristotle on the Definition of What It Is to Be Human." In *Aristotle's Anthropology*, edited by Geert Keil and Nora Kreft, 25–43. Cambridge: Cambridge University Press, 2019.
Kosman, Aryeh. *The Activity of Being: An Essay on Aristotle's Ontology*. Cambridge, MA: Harvard University Press, 2013.
Kosman, Aryeh. "Saving the Phenomena: Realism and Instrumentalism in Aristotle's Theory of Science." In *Virtues of Thought: Essays on Plato and Aristotle*, 138–56. Cambridge: Oxford University Press, 2014.
Kosman, L. A. "Animals and Other Beings in Aristotle." In *Philosophical Issues in Aristotle's Biology*, edited by A. Gotthelf and J. Lennox, 360–91. Cambridge: Cambridge University Press, 1987.
Kosman, L. A. "Aristotle on the Power of Perception: Awareness, Self-Awareness, and the Awareness of Others." In *Presocratics and Plato: Festschrift at Delphi in Honor of Charles Kahn*, edited by Richard Patterson, Vassilis Karasmanis, and Arnold Hermann, 459–89. Las Vegas: Parmenides Publishing, 2012.
Kosman, L. A. "Being Properly Affected: Virtues and Feelings in Aristotle's Ethics." In *Essays on Aristotle's Ethics*, edited by Amélie Oksenberg Rorty, 103–16. Berkeley, CA: University of California Press, 1980.

Kosman, L. A. "Perceiving that We Perceive: *On the Soul* III.2." *Philosophical Review* 84 (1975): 499–519.
Koyré, Alexandre. "Galilée et Platon." In *Études d'histoire de la pensée scientifique*, 166–95. Gallimard, 1985.
Kraut, Richard. *Aristotle: Political Philosophy*. Oxford: Oxford University Press 2002.
Kupreeva, Inna. "Aristotle on Growth: A Study of the Argument of *On Generation and Corruption* I 5." *Apeiron* 38, no. 3 (2005): 103–59.
Labarrière, Jean-Louis. *Langage, vie politique et mouvements des animaux*. Librarie Philosophique J. Vrin, 2004.
Lear, Jonathan. *Aristotle: The Desire to Understand*. Cambridge: Cambridge University Press, 1988.
Leighton, Stephen R. "Aristotle on the Emotions." *Phronesis* 27, no. 2 (1982): 144–74.
Lennox, James G. "Aristotle's Biology and Aristotle's Philosophy." In *A Companion to Ancient Philosophy*, edited by Mary Louise Gill and Pierre Pellegrin, 292–315. Blackwell Publishing, 2006.
Liddell, Scott & Jones. *Greek-English Lexicon*. Oxford: Oxford University Press, 1843.
Loraux, Nicole. *The Invention of Athens: The Funeral Oration in the Classical City*. Translated by Alan Sheridan. Zone Books, 2006.
Lord, A. B. *The Singer of Tales*. Cambridge, MA: Harvard University Press, 1981.
Lorenz, Hendrick. "Virtue of Character in Aristotle's *Nicomachean Ethics*." *Oxford Studies in Ancient Philosophy* 37 (2009): 177–212.
McCoy, Marina Berzina. *Poetics in Wounded Heroes: Vulnerability as a Virtue in Ancient Greek Literature and Philosophy*. Oxford: Oxford University Press, 2013.
McDowell, John. "Some Issues in Aristotle's Moral Psychology." In McDowell, *Mind, Value, and Reality*, 23–40. Cambridge, MA: Harvard University Press, 1998.
McDowell, John. "Are Moral Requirements Hypothetical Imperatives?" *Proceedings of the Aristotelian Society*, Supplementary Volume 52 (1978):13–29. Reprinted in *Mind, Value and Reality*, 77–94. Cambridge, MA: Harvard University Press, 2002.
McDowell, John. "Deliberation and Moral Development in Aristotle's Ethics." In *Aristotle, Kant, and the Stoics: Rethinking Happiness and Duty*, edited by Stephen Engstrom and Jennifer Whiting, 19–35. Cambridge: Cambridge University Press, 1996.
McDowell, John. "Might There Be External Reasons?." In *World, Mind and Ethics: Essays on the Ethical Philosophy of Bernard Williams*, edited by J. E. J. Altham and Ross Harrison, 95–111. Cambridge: Cambridge University Press, 1995. Reprinted in McDowell, 2002.
McDowell, John. "Two Sorts of Naturalism." In *Virtues and Reasons: Philippa Foot and Moral Theory*, edited by Rosalind Hursthouse, Gavin Lawrence, and Warren Quinn. Oxford: Clarendon Press, 1996. Reprinted in McDowell 2002, 167–97.
McGinn, Marie. "Real Things and the Mind Body Problem." *Proceedings of the Aristotelian Society* 100 (2000): 303–17.
McNeill, William. *The Time of Life: Heidegger and Ethos*. Albany, NY: State University of New York Press, 1992.
Merleau-Ponty, Maurice. *Phenomenology of Perception*. Translated by Donald A. Landes. New York: Routledge, 2012.
Merleau-Ponty, Maurice. "The Intertwining—The Chiasm." In *The Merleau-Ponty Reader*, edited by Ted Toadvine and Leonard Lawlor, 393–413. Northwestern University Press Studies in Phenomenology and Existential Philosophy, 2007.
Metcalf, Robert. "Aristoteles und Sein und Zeit." In *Heidegger Jahrbuch*. Freiburg & München, 2007.

Metcalf, Robert. "Capturing the Power of *Logos*: Gadamer, McDowell and Moral Argument." In *Philosophy Today*, SPEP Supplemental Volume (2005): 48–60.
Mira, Juan Pablo. *Aristotle on Music and Emotions*. University of Edinburgh, PhD Dissertation.
Modrak, Deborah K. W. *Aristotle: The Power of Perception*. Chicago, IL: University of Chicago Press, 1987.
Modrak, Deborah K. W. "The Nous-Body Problem in Aristotle." *The Review of Metaphysics* 44, no. 4 (1991): 755–74.
Moore, Ralph Westwood. *Comparative Greek and Latin Syntax*. Bristol: Bristol Classical Press, 1934.
Morel, Pierre-Marie. *Aristote: une philosophie de l'activité*. Flammarion, 2003.
Moss, Jessica. "'Virtue Makes the Goal Right': Virtue and *Phronēsis* in Aristotle's Ethics." *Phronesis* 56 (2011): 204–61.
Moss, Jessica. "Was Aristotle a Humean?" In *Cambridge Companion to Aristotle's Ethics*, edited by Ronald Polansky, 221–41. Cambridge: Cambridge University Press, 2014.
Nagy, Gregory. *Poetry as Performance: Homer and Beyond*. Cambridge: Cambridge University Press, 1996.
Noë, Alva. *Action in Perception*. Cambridge, MA: MIT Press, 2004.
Nussbaum, Martha. *Aristotle's De Motu Animalium*. Princeton, NJ: Princeton University Press, 1978.
Nussbaum, Martha. *The Therapy of Desire*. Princeton, NJ: Princeton University Press, 1994.
Ober, Josiah. *Mass and Elite in Democratic Athens: Rhetoric, Ideology, and the Power of the People*. Princeton, NJ: Princeton University Press, 1991.
Olfert, C. M. M. "Aristotle's Conception of Practical Truth." *Journal of the History of Philosophy* 52, no. 2 (2014): 205–31.
Owens, Joseph. *The Doctrine of Being in the Aristotelian Metaphysics: A Study in the Greek Background of Mediaeval Thought*. Toronto: PIMS, 1978.
Pangle, Thomas. *Aristotle's Teaching in the "Politics."* Chicago, IL: University of Chicago Press, 2013.
Parker, Robert. *Polytheism and Society at Athens*. Oxford: Oxford University Press 2005.
Pépin, Jean. "Aristote: De la Prière." *Revue Philosophique de la France et de l'Étranger* 157 (1967): 59–70.
Plato. "Apology." In *Plato: Complete Works*, translated by G. M. A Grube, edited by John M. Cooper, 17–36. Indianapolis, IN: Hackett Publishing Company, 1997.
Plato. *Opera*. Vols. I–IV. Edited by J. Burnet. Oxford: Oxford University Press, 1922.
Plato. "Parmenides." In *Plato: Complete Works*, translated by Mary Louise Gill and Paul Ryan, edited by John M. Cooper, 359–97. Indianapolis, IN: Hackett Publishing Company, 1997.
Plato. *Phaedo*. Translated by Eva Brann, Peter Kalkavage and Peter Salem. Focus Publishing, 1998.
Plato. *The Republic of Plato*. 2nd ed. Translated by Allan Bloom. New York: Basic Books, 1968.
Polansky, Roland. *Aristotle's De Anima: A Critical Commentary*. Cambridge: Cambridge University Press, 2010.
Rashed, Marwan. "Les *Définitions* d'Aquilius." In *Ancient Philosophy in Memory of R. W. Sharples*, edited by Peter Adamson, 131–72. Oxford: Oxford University Press, 2012.
Rabinoff, Eve. "Aristotle on the Intelligibility of Perception." *The Review of Metaphysics* 68, no. 4 (2015): 719–40.

Reeve, C. D. C. *Aristotle on Practical Wisdom: Nicomachean Ethics VI*. Cambridge, MA: Harvard University Press, 2013.
Rist, John M. "The End of Aristotle's on Prayer." *The American Journal of Philology* 106, no. 1 (1985): 110–13.
Rorty, Amélie Oksenberg, ed., *Essays on Aristotle's Poetics*. Princeton, NJ: Princeton University Press, 1992.
Ross, D. *Aristotle: De Anima*. Edited with introduction and commentary. Oxford: Oxford University Press, 1961.
Ross, David. *Aristotle*. 6th ed. London: Routledge, 1995.
Russon, John. "Aristotle's Animative Epistemology." *Idealistic Studies* 25, no. 3 (1995): 241–54.
Russon, John. "Self-Consciousness and the Tradition in Aristotle's Psychology." *Laval Théologique et Philosophique* 52, no. 5 (1996): 777–803.
Russon, John. "The Elements of Everyday Life: Three Lessons from Ancient Greece." *Philosophy in the Contemporary World* 13, no. 2 (2006): 84–90.
Russon, John. "The Virtues of Agency: A Phenomenology of Confidence, Courage and Creativity." In *Phenomenology and Virtue Ethics*, edited by Keven Hermberg and Paul Gyllenhammer, 165–79. Bloomsbury Press, 2013.
Russon, John. "To Account for Appearances: Phenomenology and Existential Change in Aristotle and Plato." *Journal of the British Society for Phenomenology* 52 (2021): 155–68.
Schmidt, Dennis J. *On Germans and Other Greeks: Tragedy and Ethical Life*. Indianapolis, IN: Indiana University Press, 2001.
Seaford, Richard. *Reciprocity and Ritual: Homer and Tragedy in the Developing City-State*. Oxford: Oxford University Press, 1994.
Self, Lois S. "Rhetoric and Phronesis: The Aristotelian Ideal." *Philosophy & Rhetoric* 12, no. 2 (1979): 130–45.
Simpson, Peter L. Phillips. *A Philosophical Commentary on the Politics of Aristotle*. Chapel Hill, NC: University of North Carolina Press, 2002.
Sifakis, Michael Gregory. *Aristotle on the Function of Tragic Poetry*. Herakleion: Crete University Press, 2001.
Smith, A. D. "Character and Intellect in Aristotle's Ethics." *Phronesis* 41, no. 1 (1996): 56–74.
Smyth, Herbert Weir. *Greek Grammar*. Cambridge, MA: Harvard University Press, 1920.
Solmsen, Friedrich. "Leisure and Play in Aristotle's Ideal State." *Rheinisches Museum Für Philologie* 107, no. 3 (1964): 193–220.
Solmsen, Friedrich. "The Vital Heat, the Inborn Pneuma and the Aether." *Journal of Hellenic Studies* 77, no. 1 (1957): 119–23.
Solmsen, Friedrich. "Tissues and the Soul: Philosophical Contributions to Physiology." *Philosophical Review* 59, no. 4 (1950): 435–68.
Sorabji, Richard. "Aristotle on the Role of Intellect in Virtue." In *Essays on Aristotle's Ethics*, edited by Amélie Oksenberg Rorty, 201–20. Berkeley, CA, 1980.
Sorabji, Richard. "Intentionality and Physiological Processes: Aristotle's Theory of Sense-Perception." In *Essays on Aristotle's De Anima*, edited by Martha Nussbaum and Amélie Oksenberg Rorty, 195–225. New York: Clarendon Press, 1995.
Sparshott, Francis. *Talking Life Seriously: A Study of the Argument of the Nicomachean Ethics*. Toronto: University of Toronto Press, 1996.
Sumbre, Germán, Graziano Fiorito, Tamar Flash and Binyamin Hochner. "Octopuses Use a Human-Like Strategy to Control Precise Point-to-Point Arm Movements." *Current Biology* 16 (2006): 767–72.

Thompson, Evan. *Mind in Life: Biology, Phenomenology, and the Sciences of Mind.* Cambridge, MA: Harvard University Press, 2007.
Thrax, Dionysios. *Ars Grammatica.* Leipzig: Teubner, 1883.
Vernant, Jean-Pierre and Pierre Vidal-Naquet. *Mythe et tragédie en Grèce ancienne.* Éditions La Découverte, 1972.
Ward, Julie K. "Perception and *Logos* in *De Anima* ii 12." *Ancient Philosophy* 8 (1988): 217–33.

Contributors

Joseph Arel teaches philosophy at the University of Southern Maine. His primary work is on Hegel, but he has interests in the broader phenomenological tradition and critical theory. He is the founder and editor of localphilosophy.org.

Ömer Aygün is Assistant Professor of Philosophy at Galatasaray University and Lecturer at Leiden University. He specializes in ancient Greek philosophy, especially Plato and Aristotle. His book *The Middle Included: Logos in Aristotle* was published by Northwestern University Press in 2017. He is currently working on a new Turkish translation of Plato's *Republic*.

Walter Brogan is Emeritus Professor of Philosophy at Villanova University. He is on the board of directors of the Collegium Phaenomenologicum and a past member of the executive committee of the APA (Eastern) and SPEP. He is the cofounder of the Ancient Philosophy Society and a past editor of *Epoché*. His publications include a book on Heidegger and Aristotle, several edited volumes, and an array of articles on ancient philosophy and contemporary continental philosophy.

Eli Diamond is Associate Professor of Ancient Philosophy in the Department of Classics at Dalhousie University (Nova Scotia, Canada) and the author of *Mortal Imitations of Divine Life: The Nature of Soul in Aristotle's De Anima*.

Patricia Fagan is Associate Professor of Greek and Roman Studies at the University of Windsor. She is the author of *Plato and Tradition: The Poetic and Cultural Context of Philosophy* (2013).

Rebecca Steiner Goldner is on the faculty at St. John's College, Annapolis. In this role, she has had the opportunity to expand her thinking of Aristotle and sensation not only through reading and discussing his work but through laboratory work, including observation and dissection of plants and animals (she prefers to dissect only plants), and carefully seeing, drawing, and documenting the generation, growth movements, and parts of living beings. She has published on both Aristotle and sensation in Greek tragedy.

Fred Guerin, now retired, lives in Powell River BC and has taught philosophy at Vancouver Island University. He also moderates a bimonthly Philosopher's Café, which is open to the general public. His philosophical interests include political philosophy, rhetoric, ethics, and particularly environmental ethics.

Whitney Howell is Associate Professor of Philosophy at La Salle University, in Philadelphia. While her orientation as a researcher is rooted in the phenomenological tradition, she is broadly interested in philosophical accounts of the role of environments in facilitating or hindering the development of bodily and moral capacities.

Gregory Kirk is Associate Teaching Professor of Philosophy at Northern Arizona University. His book *The Pedagogy of Wisdom: An Interpretation of Plato's Theaetetus* was published by Northwestern University Press in 2015. His other published work focuses on both Plato and Aristotle, with particular emphasis on moral, epistemological, and political implications of their respective accounts of the education of the soul.

Robert Metcalf is Professor of Philosophy at the University of Colorado Denver. He is the author of *Philosophy as Agôn: A Study of Plato's Gorgias and Related Texts* (2018) and co-translator, with Mark Tanzer, of Martin Heidegger's *Basic Concepts of Aristotelian Philosophy* (2009). He has published numerous articles in philosophy journals, such as *Ancient Philosophy, Epoché, Internationales Jahrbuch für Hermeneutik, Philosophy and Rhetoric*, and *Research in Phenomenology*.

Eve Rabinoff's work has focused on Aristotle's moral psychology, in particular the role that perception plays in ethical decision-making, action, and the development of virtue. More broadly, she is interested in the mutually informing relationship between self and world, particularly self and others. Her book *Perception in Aristotle's Ethics* was published by Northwestern University Press.

Greg Recco teaches at St. John's College, Annapolis, and holds a Ph.D. in philosophy from the Pennsylvania State University. He is the author of *Athens Victorious: Democracy in Plato's Republic* and editor (with Eric Sanday) of *Plato's Laws: Force and Truth in Politics*. In addition to ancient Greek philosophy, he writes on aesthetics, existentialism, and phenomenology.

John Russon is Professor of Philosophy at the University of Guelph in Canada and Director of the Toronto Summer Seminar in Philosophy; he is also the editor of the *Rereading Ancient Philosophy* series at Northwestern University Press. He has published extensively on ancient Greek philosophy and contemporary European philosophy. His most recent book is *Politics, Money, and Persuasion: Democracy and Opinion in Plato's Republic*; he has also edited two volumes of essays on Plato, *Retracing the Platonic Text* (with John Sallis) and *Reexamining Socrates in the Apology* (with Patricia Fagan). He has many lectures on philosophy available on YouTube (https://www.youtube.com/c/JohnRusson123).

Jacob Singer is a PhD candidate currently writing his dissertation on Hegel's account of the syllogism. He received a BA in European studies from Dalhousie University and an MA in philosophy from the University of Guelph. His research interests focus on German Idealism, ancient philosophy, and questions concerning the relation between logic and metaphysics.

Index

actuality (*entelecheia*) 82
   distinction between 'first' and 'second' 82–7
   and mind 71–2
   and perception 70
affections, *see* emotion
animals
   as distinct from plants 54, 62–3
   and the question of an animal's 'whatness' 84
Aristotle
   Categories 83–4
   De Anima 26, 31–2, 39–50, 54–64, 68–76, 81–3, 86–7, 95–6, 101, 131, 143, 165, 180–2, 185–6
   Generation of Animals 58
   Metaphysics 26–8, 141
   Movement of Animals 184–6
   Nicomachean Ethics 1, 32, 86, 88, 100, 109–19, 122–32, 138–44, 149–51, 156, 165–73, 175–7, 183–6, 206–7
   observational method 11–13
   On Generation and Corruption 57
   On Interpretation 98
   Parts of Animals 21–2, 24–5, 29–30, 33, 57–9
   Physics 39, 81–4, 96, 104
   Poetics 98–100, 103, 201–8
   Politics 1, 33–4, 86, 137–44, 175–6, 183–4, 189–99, 207
   Rhetoric 98–100, 143–4, 149–59, 163–5, 174–5

beautiful, the (*to kalon*)
   and political community 196–9
   in relation to leisure 139–40
   in relation to the young 157

character (*ethos*)
   and bodily affection 109–13
   of citizens 184–6
   as setting terms of action 113–17

childhood 127–8
   and leisure spent at play 138–9
choice 101
   as a product of moral virtue 113
Cicero 157
citizenship 184–6
   and tragic poetry 201
community 174–6
contemplation (*theoria*) 141–4

definition 11–13, 27
desire
   as implicitly rational in the virtuous person 129–31
   and motion 95–7
drama
   and democracy 201–8
   and the Great Dionysia festival 202–3
   and the political implications of tragedy 204–7
   and tragic poetry 201–8

emotion 110–17
   and anger 111, 114, 116–17, 154–5
   and living according to them 151
   and sharing in reason 127–9
Empedocles 43–4
essence (*ousia*) 22

final cause (*hou heneka* or *telos*) 24, 41, 183–6, 189–90
flesh 54–64
   as distinct from skin 58
   as medium of touch 56, 60–1
   as organ of touch 57–61
   as principle of generation and growth 59
   as threshold 60
form 24, 62–3
function (*ergon*) 14, 26, 49, 88, 149

habit (*hexis*)   84–7, 113–17, 150
happiness (*eudaimonia*)   87–8, 101
Heidegger, Martin   149, 152–5, 158–9
human nature
   as defined by self-transformation   86–8
   as distinct from animals/the rest of nature   11–13, 15–16, 26, 74
   in relation to 'first' and 'second' actuality   84–7

intellectual virtue
   practical wisdom (*phronēsis*)   111, 118–19, 129–31, 144, 166–73, 182
   productive knowledge (*technē*)   130–1
   theoretical wisdom (*sophia*)   3, 166

katharsis   204–7
Kleisthenes' reforms   202–3

law (*nomos*)
   and character   184–6
   and good legislators   174–5
   and practical wisdom   175–7
leisure   137–44
   and contemplation   141
   not reducible to relaxation   140–1
   and play   138–9
   and serious activity   139–40
logic   13–15
   as abstraction   14
   critique of treatment as discipline distinct from other areas of philosophy   17 n.8
logos
   as definition   11–13, 46
   as discourse   33–4
   and dissociation   2–3, 109–19
   diversity of meaning   1–8, 11, 201
   as giving an account   12–13
   as grounded in *pathē*   154
   as language   34–5, 86–7
   as logic   13–15
   and perception   69–71
   and the preconditions of its persuasiveness   151–2
   as rationality   122–32
   as rationality, critique of   17 n.10
   as ratio of the body   46
   in relation to *praxis*   163–77
   as rhetorically enacted among others   165–73
   as self-reflection   117–19
   as speech (*phōnē*)   13, 190–1

Marx, Karl   192
matter
   in relation to form   24, 27–9
Merleau-Ponty, Maurice   63, 67 n.25
mimēsis, see reenactment
mind (*nous*)   15–16, 31–3, 71–4, 166, 170–1
   as analogous to perceiving   68
   and error   74–6
   and its cultivation   73–4
   in relation to other powers of the soul   68, 73
moderation (*sōphrosunē*)   135 n.23, 150
moral virtue   3–4, 113–14, 169–70
   as permitting one to be guided by reason   129–31
   and proper perception of situations   112–13
   in relation to practical wisdom   118–19, 122–3, 130–1, 166–73, 180–2
motion (*kinesis*)
   as a display of values   184–6
   and how it originates in animals   180–1
   as implying desire   95–6
   as locomotion   29–30
music   142–4
   comparison of Dorian and Phrygian modes   143
   as images of states of character   142–3
   and reason   137

nature (*phusis*)   81–2
   as constant motion   95–6
   as growth   29, 45
   as process   12
nutrition   39–50
   and food   47–50
   in relation to reproduction   40–2

old age   155–6

passions, *see* emotion
Peisistratos' reforms   202–3
phronimos   171–3
Plato
   Apology   174
   Parmenides   22–5
   Phaedo   24–5, 179–80, 186
   Republic   104
   Timaeus   31–2, 50
political community (*polis*)
   and commercial activity   193–5
   as emergent from prior forms of association   189–90
   and friendship   198–9
   as multiplicity *vs.* unity   196–9
   and poetry   201–8
   as premised upon exclusions   189–99
   and slavery   191–3
   and women   195–7
potentiality
   and mind   71–2
practical syllogism   96–7, 116–17, 180–2

rational animal   122–3
   as misleading paraphrase   13
reenactment (mimesis)   204–7
rhetoric   152, 163–77
ruling and being ruled   196–9

self-control/lack of self-control (*enkrasia/akrasia*)   110–11, 115–16, 182
sensation (*aisthesis*)
   as the capacity to distinguish   96
   hearing   97–8
   as integration with one's world   71
   and passivity   69
   and ratio (*logos*)   70–1
   sight   56–7
   touch   54–64
simple bodies   44
slavery, *see* political community (*polis*)
soul (*psuches*)   42–7, 81–4
   animal soul   70–1
   and body   26–9, 42–7, 61–2
   human soul   123–6
   and movement   185–6
   and the relation between rational and non-rational parts   123–6
   vegetative soul   39–42, 124

thinking
   and its bodily expression   29–36
   as *nous poietikos*   29
   as *nous praktikos*   29, 33–4
   as structurally parallel to being   26–7
   of what can be otherwise   29
   of what is unchanging   29
time of life   155–9
tragic poetry, *see* drama

voice
   as invocation of another   97–8

wish (*eukhē*)   95–105
   as corresponding to the optative mood   100
   and ethics   103–5
   as non-kinetic desire   95

youth   155–7

www.ingramcontent.com/pod-product-compliance
Lightning Source LLC
Chambersburg PA
CBHW052106300426
44116CB00010B/1554